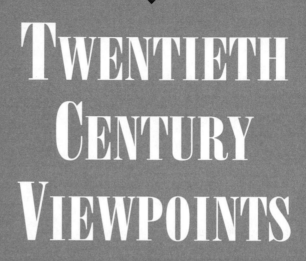

TWENTIETH CENTURY VIEWPOINTS

An Interpretive History

VICTOR ZELINSKI

GRAHAM DRAPER

DON QUINLAN

FRED McFADDEN

Toronto
Oxford University Press

Oxford University Press Canada, 70 Wynford Drive,
Don Mills, Ontario, Canada M3C 1J9

Oxford   New York
Athens   Auckland   Bangkok   Bombay
Calcutta   Cape Town   Dar es Salaam   Delhi
Florence   Hong Kong   Istanbul   Karachi
Kuala Lumpur   Madras   Madrid   Melbourne
Mexico City   Nairobi   Paris   Singapore
Taipei   Tokyo   Toronto

and associated companies in
Berlin   Ibadan

OXFORD is a trademark of Oxford University Press.

This book is printed on permanent (acid-free) paper. ∞

Canadian Cataloguing in Publication Data

Main entry under title:
Twentieth century viewpoints: an interpretive history

Rev. ed.
Includes bibliographical references and index.
ISBN 0-19-541213-3

1. History, Modern - 20th century. I. Zelinski, Victor A.

D421.T837 1996   909.82   C96-930181-2

Editor: Loralee Case
Editorial assistants: Micaela Gates, Mia London
Design: Brett Miller
Layout: Compeer Graphics
Cover Design: Brett Miller
Illustrations: VISU*TronX*
Photo research: Patricia Buckley Editorial Services
Printed in Canada by Friesens

Cover Photos: Ponopresse Internationale Inc./Alfred
(Inset): Canapress

3 4 5 99 98

DEDICATION

This book is dedicated to the late Fred
McFadden, one of Canada's finest teachers
and an inspiration to both students and
colleagues.

CONTENTS

❖ ABOUT THIS TEXTBOOK

Twentieth Century Viewpoints is divided into three units. Unit One: 1900-1945 begins with a look at the world at the turn of the century and follows through the extended world conflict that began in 1914 as the First World War and ended in 1945 after the Second World War. Unit Two: The Cold War focuses on relations between the two superpowers, the United States and the Soviet Union, from 1945 to the end of the Cold War and looks at the role of the United Nations in promoting peace and co-operation. Unit Three: The Global Village highlights world regions and examines issues related to imperialism, economic development, and current trends and issues. Two countries are used as case studies to provide a closer look at each region.

Each chapter begins with an Overview, followed by Focus Questions and includes special features that supplement the main text:

PROFILES

Profiles provide snapshots of key individuals who have helped to shape historical events in the twentieth century.

VOICES

Voices present opinions, comments, and expressions that will enrich your understanding of events.

VIEWPOINTS

Viewpoints offer conflicting readings in which authors argue for or against key issues or questions.

IN REVIEW

1. Review questions throughout each chapter reinforce understanding. At the end of each chapter, there are enrichment and extended research activities under the categories Making Connections, Developing Your Voice, and Researching the Issues.

INTRODUCTION

AN INTERPRETIVE APPROACH TO THE STUDY OF HISTORY

The study of history is more than a recollection of past events. The study of history should be an inquiry into the past. When we read history, we must deal with two kinds of knowledge—the historical record of events, names, dates, and places, often called the facts, and the interpretation of events from various points of view.

Historical facts can be proven by evidence. While it is important that we know the facts, there is much more to the study of history. Facts are used to help us understand the past. The interpretation of events is perhaps a more significant form of historical knowledge. Interpretations give us a sense of meaning. Historical interpretations are developed by people as they try to explain events. Unlike facts, these interpretations cannot be proven conclusively. Instead, the most that can be expected is that a consensus of opinion may be reached among most scholars and experts. Such a consensus then becomes the generally accepted understanding, or truth, about certain issues and events.

Interpretive knowledge is always subject to challenge and change. Historical accounts are written by people who have their own viewpoints and perspectives. They analyse and evaluate past events in the context of their own time and place. Thus historical interpretations, or **theses**, are always subject to review and change.

Twentieth Century Viewpoints encourages an interpretive approach to the study of history. This approach is intended to help you develop a greater understanding of the key events of the twentieth century.

Each chapter in this text introduces conflicting interpretations of key issues under the heading Viewpoints. The authors of these readings are generally regarded as authorities in their field

> "Any fool can make history, but it takes a genius to write it."
>
> *Oscar Wilde*

and so you will be reading informed opinions on both sides of an issue. Do not assume that one opinion is necessarily right while the other is wrong. Individuals who interpret evidence differently can arrive at different conclusions. This kind of debate leads to a more comprehensive understanding of past events.

> "History is a science, no more and no less."
>
> *J.B. Bury*

There are three parts to the interpretive approach used in this book:
- (1) *An understanding of the background to key events.* We need to know about events and issues before we can analyse and evaluate historical interpretations.
- (2) *The analysis and evaluation of different interpretations about an event or issue.* We need to separate fact from opinion and substance from rhetoric, to identify the reasoning of an argument, and to determine if the argument is logical. We must learn to identify oversimplified or exaggerated statements. As we analyse an interpretive reading we must also evaluate it—that is, we must make judgments about the position taken in the reading.
- (3) *Reaching a decision by developing our own position on the issue.* Reaching a conclusion is not simply a

matter of selecting one interpretation over another. We may decide to accept some aspects of an argument and reject others. Our conclusion might then be a composite based on certain aspects of different interpretations. It is also recognized that on occasion we are not ready to make a decision on an issue and must therefore decide to remain undecided. In any case, we must be prepared to defend our position. As you study key events of the twentieth century, you will critically analyse and evaluate the viewpoints you have

> "With the historian it is an article of faith that knowledge of the past is a key to understanding the present."
>
> *Kenneth Stamp*

read. In so doing, you will develop your knowledge of history and your abilities as a critical thinker. Developing an informed opinion is an essential skill for all citizens in a democratic society.

> "History cannot give us a program for the future, but it can give us a fuller understanding of ourselves, and of our common humanity, so that we can better face the future."
>
> *Rupert Warren*

ARGUMENT ANALYSIS AND EVALUATION GUIDE

The following Argument Analysis and Evaluation guide will help you to conduct a critical review of each of the readings in the Viewpoints section of this book. Refer to this as you complete the Argument Analysis and Evaluation Summary for each chapter.

A sample Argument Analysis and Evaluation Summary form is provided on the following page.

1: Identify the argument
• What is the central issue being addressed by the author?
• What is the author's main argument? What is the main point of the thesis?
• Does the author argue for or against other interpretations?

2: Identify the evidence that supports the argument
• What evidence and/or reasons does the author offer to support the argument? Is this evidence new information or a different interpretation of the same information?
• Is there a critical piece of evidence or a specific reason that is central to the argument?
• What key sources does the author use to support the argument?

3: Evaluate the argument
• Do you agree or disagree with the main argument?
• Are you convinced by the argument? Why or why not?
• Is this interpretation based on sound evidence and reasoning? Are the arguments logical? Are there contradictions in the argument?
• Which points of evidence and/or reasons are the strongest? Which are the weakest? Why?

ARGUMENT ANALYSIS AND EVALUATION SUMMARY SAMPLE FORM

Author of reading:_____

Issue or question: _____

_____

_____

1: Identify the key argument _____

_____

_____

_____

_____

_____

_____

_____

2: Identify the evidence that supports the argument _____

_____

_____

_____

_____

_____

_____

_____

3: Evaluate the argument_____

_____

_____

_____

_____

_____

Unit One:
1900–1945

❖ 1900 - 1909   1910 - 1919

POLITICS/MILITARY

1900 - 1909
- Russia occupies Manchuria (1900)
- Boxer Rebellion in China (1900)
- End of Boer War (1902)
- US acquires Panama Canal Zone (1903)
- Britain and France form Entente Cordiale (1904)
- Japanese victory in Russo-Japanese War (1905)
- Britain, Russia, France form Triple Entente (1907)
- Austria annexes Bosnia and Herzegovina (1908)

1910 - 1919
- Revolution in China (1911)
- Assassination of Archduke Ferdinand; WWI erupts (1914)
- British naval blockade of Germany (1915)
- German submarine blockade of Britain (1915)
- Italy joins war on Allied side (1915)
- Sinking of *Lusitania* (1915)
- Battle of the Somme (1916)
- Conscription in Canada (1917)
- US declares war on Germany (1917)
- Battle of Vimy Ridge (1917)
- Wilson outlines Fourteen Points (1918)
- Second Battle of the Marne (1918)
- Germany signs armistice to end WWI (1918)
- Treaty of Versailles (1919)
- Soviet Republic established in Russia (1919)
- League of Nations born (1919)

CULTURE/SOCIETY

1900 - 1909
- Freud, *Interpretation of Dreams* (1900)
- First Nobel Prizes (1901)
- First gramophone recordings (1902)
- Russell, *The Principles of Mathematics* (1903)
- Picasso, *Les Demoiselles d'Avignon* (1907)
- Exhibition of Cubist paintings in Paris (1907)
- D.W. Griffiths shoots first film (1908)
- Peary first to reach North Pole (1909)

1910 - 1919
- Amundsen reaches South Pole (1911)
- 5 million Americans visit cinemas daily (1912)
- *Rite of Spring* performance causes near riot in Paris (1913)
- Griffiths, *Birth of a Nation* (1915)
- Prohibition in US (1916)
- Birth of Dadaism (1916)
- Influenza epidemic (1918)
- Labour unrest in Europe and North America (1919)
- Bauhaus founded by Gropius (1919)

SCIENCE/TECHNOLOGY

1900 - 1909
- Planck's, Quantum Theory (1900)
- First transmission of human speech by radio waves (1900)
- Marconi sends wireless signal across Atlantic (1901)
- Wright Brothers make first airplane flight (1903)
- First radio transmission of music (1904)
- Einstein, Theory of Relativity (1905)
- First dreadnought (1906)
- Electric washing machine (1907)
- Ford introduces Model T (1908)

1910 - 1919
- Creation of tank (1911)
- First neon sign (1912)
- Sinking of *Titanic* (1912)
- Ford develops first assembly line (1913)
- Wireless messages between ships at sea (1914)
- Teletype machine invented (1914)
- Panama Canal opened (1914)
- Poison gas, flame-throwers on Western Front (1915)
- First fighter aircraft built (1915)
- First refrigeration of blood for transfusion (1916)
- First use of mustard gas (1917)
- Germans design bomber aircraft (1917)
- Plank wins Nobel Prize for Quantum Theory (1918)
- Rutherford splits atom (1919)
- Alcock/Brown fly non-stop across Atlantic (1919)

❖ 1920 - 1929   1930 - 1945

POLITICS/MILITARY

1920 - 1929
- Prohibition across US (18th Amendment) (1920)
- First meeting of League (1920)
- American women win vote (1920)
- Lenin creates NEP in Soviet Union (1921)
- Stalin becomes Secretary-General in USSR (1922)
- Mussolini rules Italy (1922)
- Hitler's Munich Putsch (1923)
- Death of Lenin (1924)
- Hitler, *Mein Kampf* (1925)
- Civil war in China (1926)
- Stalin launches first Five Year Plan (1928)

1930 - 1945
- Japan occupies Manchuria (1930)
- Hitler in power in Germany (1933)
- Roosevelt introduces New Deal (1933)
- Germany renounces Treaty of Versailles (1935)
- Japan invades China (1937)
- Munich Agreement (1938)
- Nazi-Soviet Pact (1939)
- German invasion of Poland (1939)
- WWII begins; Canada enters war (1939)
- German blitzkrieg overruns W. Europe (1940)
- Fall of France; Battle of Britain (1940)
- Germany invades USSR (1941)
- Japan bombs Pearl Harbor (1941)
- Germany and Italy declare war on US (1941)
- Battle of Midway (1942)
- Battle of El Alamein; Allied invasion of N. Africa (1942)
- Germans defeated at Stalingrad (1942)
- Allies invade Italy (1942); fall of Mussolini (1943)
- Soviets drive into Eastern Europe (1944)
- D-Day invasion of Nazi-held Europe (1944)
- Germany defeated (1945)
- Yalta Conference (1945)
- United Nations formed (1945)
- Potsdam Conference (1945)
- US drops A bomb on Japan (1945)

CULTURE/SOCIETY

1920 - 1929
- Joyce, *Ulysses* (1922)
- KKK conference in US draws 200 000 (1923)
- Gershwin, *Rhapsody in Blue* (1923)
- First Winter Olympics (1924)
- First woman cabinet minister in Western government (Nina Bang, Denmark) (1924)
- Charleston dance craze (1923)
- Unemployment insurance introduced in Germany (1926)
- Disney studios open in Hollywood (1926)
- Great Depression (1929)
- BBC launches experimental TV (1929)

1930 - 1945
- World unemployment reaches 30 million (1932)
- Huxley, *Brave New World* (1932)
- Prohibition repealed in US (1933)
- Famine in USSR (1933)
- Gershwin, *Porgy and Bess* (1935)
- Berlin Olympics (1936)
- Picasso, *Guernica* (1937)
- Hindenburg destroyed by fire (1937)
- Hemingway, *For Whom the Bell Tolls* (1940)
- Britain applies conscription to women (1941)
- Welles, *Citizen Kane*
- *Maltese Falcon* (1942)
- Orwell, *Animal Farm* (1945)

SCIENCE/TECHNOLOGY

1920 - 1929
- Banting/Best isolate insulin (1922)
- Hubble shows galaxies beyond Milky Way (1923)
- Tuberculosis vaccine developed
- Ford makes 10 millionth car (1924)
- Baird transmits human image on TV screen (1923)
- Kodak makes first 16 mm film (1926)
- Lindbergh makes first solo flight across Atlantic (1926)
- Discovery of penicillin (1928)
- Teleprinter invented (1928)
- Einstein, Unified Field Theory (1929)

1930 - 1945
- Discovery of planet Pluto (1930)
- Beebe descends 900 m under sea in bathysphere (1934)
- Nylon invented (1935)
- First Volkswagen (1936)
- Jet engine tested in UK (1937)
- First ship equipped with radar (1938)
- First helicopter (1939)
- Blood plasma used in transfusions (1940)
- Manhattan Project launched (1941)
- US builds nuclear reactor (1942)
- First automatic computer built in US (1942)
- V1, V2 German bombs launch Missile Age (1944)
- Atomic bomb unleashes Nuclear Age (1945)

The New World of the Twentieth Century

"Anyone desiring a quiet life has done badly to be born in the twentieth century."

Leon Trotsky (1879-1940),
Russian revolutionary and leader
in the Bolshevik Revolution of 1917

"Last century made the world a neighbourhood, this century must make it a brotherhood".

J.S. Woodsworth (1874-1942),
Canadian politician,
leader of the Co-operative Commonwealth Federation

Left: The Dust Fiend: Overtaking
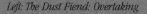

❖ OVERVIEW

In most of the world, life in 1900 was little different than it had been in 1800. The pace was slow and predictable. Most children grew up and followed in their parents' footsteps. The world scene was dominated by European nations—Britain, Germany, France, Russia, and Austria-Hungary. The economic and military powers of the United States and Japan were on the rise. But the principles of democracy were untested and distrusted in many countries. Women lacked many rights, including the right to vote. But as society moved into a new century, life began to change dramatically. The old ways were being challenged and our systems of government, our habitats, our occupations, our entertainment, and our lifestyles were embarking on a journey of remarkable transformation.

lights or refrigerators. Telephones were just coming into use. Movie theatres—or picture palaces, as they were called then—were beginning to show silent films, with captions to explain the dialogue and piano music as accompaniment.

Horses provided much of the transportation, pulling carts, wagons, carriages, and even fire engines. In a few cities, electric tramcars transported people from place to place. And there were bicycles, trains, and boats. But new inventions were being developed that would soon revolutionize travel. Henry Ford founded the Ford Motor Company in 1903; the classic Model T made its debut in 1908. The Wright brothers made the first successful airplane flight in 1903, remaining airborne for fifty-nine seconds! Their accomplishment heralded the new era of flight. Throughout the nineteenth century people had been migrating to the New World. By 1900, however, the wave of migration had reached unprecedented proportions. Immigrants flocked to North America, lured by the promise of prosperity. The west was opening up to settlement and cities and towns were growing rapidly. Opportunities abounded.

Despite the prosperity brought by industrialization, however, the inequality between rich and poor was dramatic. The working class had almost no protection under the law in terms of wages, working conditions, and unemployment. Demands for social reform were mounting, and it was women who were leading the way. In demanding equality and the right to vote, the women's suffrage movement

FOCUS QUESTIONS

1. What was Western society like at the turn of the century?

2. What issues fuelled the struggles of the women's suffrage movement?

3. What were some of the dominant political, cultural, and economic ideas of the time?

4. What were the relative strengths and weaknesses of the world's major powers?

5. What factors shaped Canada as it entered the twentieth century?

THE WORLD AT THE TURN OF THE CENTURY

To illustrate the extent of change from the beginning of the century until now, let's picture our society as it was in 1900. Most people lived on farms or in rural areas. Homes did not have electricity and so there were no electric

KING STREET, TORONTO, CANADA. 104.

challenged long-standing ideas of male supremacy. It was a campaign that would not achieve its goals without a long and hard struggle.

CHANGES IN POPULATION AND OCCUPATION

In 1900, the world population was 1.6 billion. Over the course of the twentieth century it has exploded to over 6 billion. But in spite of such a dramatic escalation, the distribution of people around the world then and now is similar. In 1900, out of every 1000 people, 570 lived in Asia, 260 lived in Europe and Russia, 75 lived in Africa, 50 lived in North America, 40 lived in Latin America, and 5 lived in Australia and New Zealand. Remarkably, these figures still reflect the world's population distribution today.

The turn of the century marked the beginning of important advances in controlling the spread of disease and improvements in medical care and san-

Electric tramcars rolled alongside horse-drawn carriages in downtown Toronto in 1910.

"People can have the Model T in any colour—so long as it's black."

Henry Ford, 1908

itation. These led to a reduction in mortality rates in the early part of the century. This in turn spawned a surge in population growth in Europe despite a decline in actual birth rates.

In 1900, about 70 per cent of the world's population earned a living from farming, although this figure was lower in industrialized nations. In the United States in 1830, for example, 70 per cent of the people were engaged

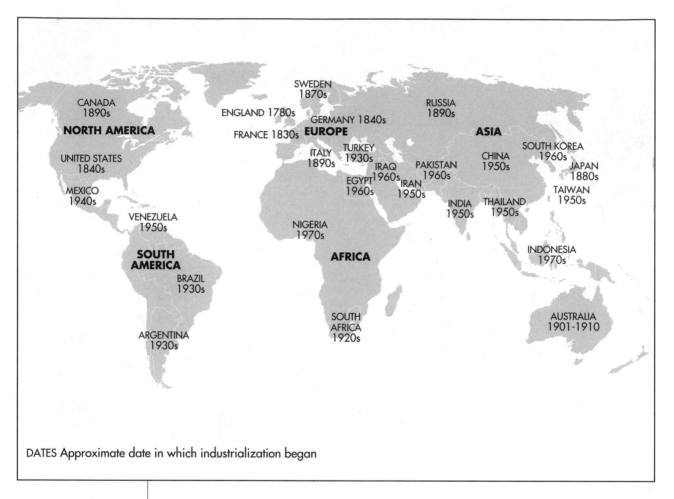

DATES Approximate date in which industrialization began

Figure 1.1:
*The Spread of
Industrialization,
Selected Countries.*

in farming; by 1900 this figure had dropped to 38 per cent, and by 1980 it was a mere 2.2 per cent. Farming was of greater importance in the Canadian

In 1900, the average life expectancy for a person living in the West was about fifty years. In Russia, it was only thirty years, and in India it was a mere twenty-three years. Today, in Canada the average life expectancy is seventy-eight. In Russia, it is seventy, while in India it is fifty-eight.

economy at the turn of the century as the pace of industrialization lagged behind that of the US. The rural population in 1900 was 62 per cent. But in the east, urbanization was spreading rapidly.

Western Europe and North America were the most industrialized and urbanized regions on earth. In 1900, there were only eleven cities with a population of over 1 million, and seven of these were in the West. Three of them—New York, Chicago, and Philadelphia—were in the United States, which was quickly becoming the world's major industrial power. By 1913, 36 per cent of all the world's manufactured goods were produced in the US. Germany followed a distant second at 16 per cent, while Britain accounted for 14 per cent. The industrialization of the Western economy was well under way.

IMMIGRATION

Increasing population, industrialization, urbanization, and unemployment combined to create conditions that inspired a huge wave of migration from Europe to the New World. Working class people crowded into steamships bound for North America, lured by offers of cheap passage and promises of new opportunities. The United States was a powerful magnet for immigrants hoping for a fresh start and a better future. Between 1861 and 1920, over 45 million Europeans emigrated, over half of them to the United States.

While Canada attracted far fewer immigrants than its southern neighbour, during the period 1900-14 immigration soared as an average of 200 000 immigrants arrived each year. In 1901, immigrants accounted for 13 per cent of the total population; ten years later this figure had jumped to 22 per cent. Half of these new arrivals headed west to the farmlands of the Prairies. In the first decade of the new century, the populations of Saskatchewan and Alberta more than quadrupled.

WOMEN'S SUFFRAGE

Inequality between the sexes at the beginning of the twentieth century was a long established way of life. Society was openly male-dominated. In most countries, women were treated as little more than the property of men. Men headed the household. Women were frequently treated more like children than responsible adults. The prevailing attitude was "a woman's place is in the home." The adherence to this adage severely hampered the efforts of women to affect change in society.

Educational and occupational choices for women were limited. Female roles were confined mainly to teaching and nursing. Few women managed to break into the world of business, except as typists and telephone operators. Working class women had no choice but to work, often as domestics or factory workers. But these jobs yielded very little in terms of money and less still in terms of power.

To make positive changes in society and to gain control over their own lives, women first needed to obtain the right to vote. The campaign for **enfranchisement** began in earnest in the mid-nineteenth century, but the ensuing struggle was to take decades. Women's suffrage became the key objective for women's movements in Western countries. In Britain, the

Emmeline Pankhurst and her daughter Sylvia (left and extreme left) were imprisoned for their participation in suffrage demonstrations. In one year, Sylvia engaged in numerous hunger strikes, which led prison authorities to feed her using a stomach tube.

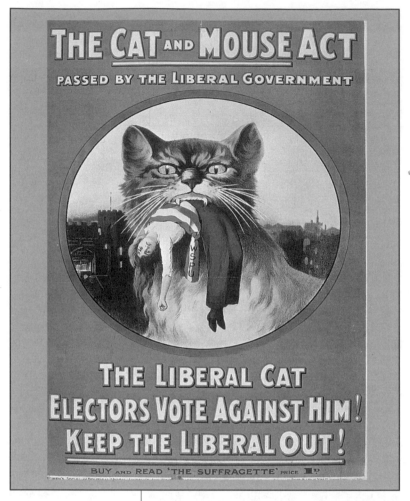

In response to the hunger strikes many suffragists staged while in prison, the British House of Commons passed a bill that allowed authorities to release women from prison when they went on hunger strikes and then rearrest them as soon as they regained their strength. The bill was dubbed the "Cat and Mouse Act."

women won the vote relatively peacefully. Not so in Britain, however, where resistance to giving women the vote was especially strong. The more extreme suffragists held public rallies, scuffled with police, chained themselves to fences, and threw objects through windows. Many were frequently arrested and jailed. In jail, the women went on hunger strikes. In 1918, the vote was finally granted to all women over thirty. (Men could vote at the age of twenty-one.) Ten years later, women's voting age was reduced to twenty-one.

In Canada, the Election Act stated that "No woman, idiot, lunatic, or criminal shall vote." Women across the country gathered to protest. In 1876, the Toronto Women's Literary Club met to discuss the status and rights of women and to organize the campaign for the right to vote. By 1883, the club was renamed the Canadian Woman Suffrage Association, and in 1886, the conservative yet powerful National Council of Women in Canada threw its support behind women's suffrage.

The Canadian suffrage movement was especially strong in the Prairies, where it received greater support from men than it did in the east. Perhaps the harsh life of the prairie homesteader made men more inclined to view women as equal partners. Most certainly, however, western farmers saw women's suffrage as a means of increasing the farm vote and strengthening their influence on provincial legislatures.

Nellie McClung led the movement in the west. Like other feminists of the day, McClung believed the only way to affect change throughout society was to enfranchise women. She fought for many social causes, among them prohibition, compulsory education, prison and factory reform, and the rights of women and children.

National Society for Women's Suffrage was founded in 1868; in the United States, the National American Women Suffrage Association was formed in 1890. Still, by 1910 only three countries—Australia, New Zealand, and Finland—had granted women the right to vote.

"We are not here to ask for a reform or a gift, or a favour, but a right—not mercy, but for justice."

Nellie McClung

Although the struggle took decades, in most Western countries

PROFILE

NELLIE McCLUNG (1873-1951)

Nellie McClung was one of Canada's great social reformers. She played an instrumental role in securing women's right to vote in the early part of the twentieth century. As you read this profile and McClung's own comments, reflect upon whether or not her words still apply in our society today.

"The world has never been partial to the thinking woman.... Long years ago, when women asked for an education, the world cried out that it would never do. If women learned to read there seemed to be a possibility that some day some good man might come home and find his wife reading and the dinner not ready—and nothing could be imagined more horrible than that! That seems to be the haunting fear of mankind—that the advancement of women will sometime, someway, someplace, interfere with some man's comfort!"

Nellie McClung,
In Times Like These, *1915*

"These tender-hearted gentlemen who tell you of their adoration for women cannot bear to think of women occupying public position. Their tender hearts shrink from the idea of women lawyers or women policemen, or even women preachers; these positions would 'rub the bloom off the peach' to use their own eloquent words. They cannot bear, they say, to see women leaving the sacred precincts of home—and yet their offices are scrubbed by women who do their work while other people sleep...is there any pity for them? Not that we have heard of. It is the thought of women getting into comfortable and well-paid positions which wrings their manly hearts."

Nellie McClung,
In Times Like These, *1915*

Born in Ontario and raised on a homestead in Manitoba, Nellie McClung began her career as a school teacher at the age of sixteen. After her marriage in 1896, she became an activist in the Woman's Christian Temperance Union.

In 1908, McClung received literary acclaim for her first novel, *Sowing Seeds in Danny*, a witty portrayal of life in a small prairie town. She became a successful writer, publishing sixteen books and several short stories and articles.

It was in Winnipeg in 1911 that McClung first emerged at the forefront of the women's rights and social reform movement. McClung was an effective speaker, winning audiences with her persuasive arguments wrapped in humour. She actively campaigned for the Liberal Party in Manitoba against the Conservative government, which had refused to enfranchise women. Moving to Alberta, McClung continued to campaign for female suffrage, prohibition, factory safety legislation, and other reforms. She gained increasing prominence through her speaking engagements across Canada, the United States, and Great Britain.

Nellie McClung was instrumental in gaining women the right to vote in Canada in 1918 and in focusing attention on the need for women to gain economic independence.

Emily Davison said on one occasion, "The Cause [women's suffrage] has need of a tragedy." In 1913 she threw herself in front of King George V's horse at the Epsom Derby in England. She died of her injuries. A leading British suffragist, Christabel Pankhurst, daughter of Emmeline Pankhurst who founded the Women's Social and Political Union in 1903, said of Davison: "So greatly did she care for freedom that she died for it. So dearly did she love women that she offered her life as their ransom." What is your opinion of the effectiveness of such actions in promoting the cause of the suffragettes?

Figure 1.2 The Enfranchisement of Women, Selected Countries*

1893	New Zealand
1902	Australia
1907	Finland
1915	Denmark
1917	Soviet Union; Netherlands
1918	Canada (federal enfranchisement); Britain (women over 30)
1920	United States
1922	Canada (provincial enfranchisement, except Quebec)
1928	Britain (women over 21)
1934	Turkey
1946	Brazil; France
1971	Switzerland
1986	Liechtenstein

*Women's right to vote is still not universal. In 1992, Kuwait held an election in which women were not allowed to vote.

Figure 1.3 The Enfranchisement of Women in Canada*

1916	Manitoba; Alberta; Saskatchewan
1917	Ontario; British Columbia
1918	Nova Scotia
1919	New Brunswick
1922	Prince Edward Island
1925	Newfoundland (joined Confederation 1949)
1940	Quebec

*Federal enfranchisement of women was granted in 1918. In 1919, women gained the right to be elected to the House of Commons.

VOICES

THE RIGHTS OF WOMEN

The struggle for women's suffrage began to polarize society at the end of the nineteenth and the beginning of the twentieth centuries. The idea that women were equal to men was simply not considered by most people at the time. For women to take part in acts of civil disobedience was totally unacceptable. In Britain, where the fight for equality was most fierce, outbursts of violence and hostility tore at the social and political fabric of the nation.

As you read the following quotations, consider whether any of these comments reflect current attitudes towards women.

Justice F.E. Barker
"The paramount destiny and mission of women are to fulfil the noble and benign offices of wife and mother. This is the law of the Creator."

Victorian proverb
"Stay home, stay pure, stay busy."

Frances Benyon, suffragist
"I consider it downright impertinence for a man on a farm to talk of supporting his wife. When she cooks his meals and sews and mends for him and his children from dawn to dark, what is she doing if not supporting herself?"

George Bernard Shaw, playwright
"Home is the girl's prison and the woman's workhouse." (*Man and Superman*, 1903)

Agnes Macphail, suffragist
"When I hear men talk about women being the angel of the home I always, mentally at least, shrug my shoulders in doubt. I do not want to be the angel of any home. I want for myself what I want for other women, absolute equality. After that is secured, then men and women can take turns at being angels."

THE EMERGENCE OF THE GLOBAL VILLAGE

Important changes were taking place at the turn of the century in transportation and communications. New technology was transforming not only the methods of travel and communication, but also the speed at which these could take place. The movement of people and products around the globe was becoming relatively easy. It seemed that the world was shrinking. As it did so, the pace of life was increasing.

Transportation

The refinement of steam power after 1870 revolutionized ocean transport. Huge ships could now sail the oceans without regard for wind or current. People could travel from one continent to another with relative ease and safety. Between 1901 and 1910, 11 million people boarded ships in Europe to find new lives in distant lands like Canada, the United States, and Australia. This massive flow of people resulted in a vibrant blending of languages, cultures, and ideas around the globe.

On land, steam power fuelled the great railways that spread across the Western landscape during the last half of the nineteenth century. No longer was it an economic necessity to build towns and cities along waterways; trains could now provide the vital link between communities. In 1869, work was completed on the first transcontinental railway in the United States when the Central Pacific and the Union Pacific lines met in Utah. The Canadian Pacific Railway completed its transcontinental line in 1885, linking Canada from sea to sea. In Russia, the Trans-Siberian railway was completed in 1905. These respective rail links enabled the settlement and economic development of the western provinces in Canada and of Siberia in Russia.

At the Paris Exposition in 1867, the world's first internal combustion engine made its debut. At first the combustion engine was used for simple industrial purposes such as sawing wood and pumping water. But its usefulness in transportation was quickly recognized. The engine was gradually improved and eventually adapted to run on gasoline, thereby marking the emergence of oil as a coveted resource. Soon the engine was ready for use in automobiles. By 1914, there were a million cars on American roads. American automobile manufacturers were producing more than 750 000 cars a year. The mass production of gasoline-powered vehicles was the single most important development in transportation and one that would dramatically shape the twentieth century.

Communications

New developments in communications were made possible by the long distance transmission of electric energy. The first invention to use electrical impulses to send messages was Samuel Morse's telegraph, patented in 1837. This invention was indispensable to the expansion of railways. Wireless telegraphs, developed in 1887, gained even greater importance because they could link ships at sea with stations on shore and with other ships.

In 1901, Guglielmo Marconi first established closer global links when he transmitted a signal on the wireless radio from St. John's, Newfoundland, across the Atlantic. Where a letter from Canada to England took several weeks, communication was now possible in a matter of seconds. The telephone, invented by Alexander Graham Bell in 1876, meant that verbal communication could be transmitted along a wire. Bell's first telephone call was made from his home near Brantford to Paris, Ontario, some 13 km away. By 1900 long distance telephone calls were common.

At the time few people were aware of these exciting new developments. As we look back on the twentieth century, however, we can see how important they were in changing our society and how they contributed to the globalization of the world.

IN REVIEW

1. Create a word collage of at least ten terms and phrases that describe life at the turn of the century in the Western world.

2. In your opinion, what was the most significant invention or development of the period? Why?

3. Who were the suffragists and what were their goals?

4. What were some of the most important developments in the creation of the global village?

Politics, Economics, and Culture

As industrialization spread, there was a general feeling of optimism and confidence about the century that lay ahead. At the same time, however, there was growing criticism of national political goals and the dark underside that lay beneath the new prosperity. These conflicting views and values were reflected in the politics and culture of the era.

The Political Atmosphere

Much of the world in 1900 was ruled by **authoritarian** regimes. In Russia, the Czar wielded absolute power. In Germany, the Kaiser ignored the weak **Reichstag** (parliament) at will. In Britain, while Queen Victoria had little political power, the royal family and the nobility maintained strong social influence. Most people in Asia and Africa were under the authoritarian rule of either local monarchs or European colonial powers. Ordinary citizens everywhere had few political or human rights. Obedience and respect for authority were paramount; individual liberty was rarely considered. Only in a few countries, such as Canada, Britain, France, Switzerland, and the United States, were political leaders elected by the people, and even in these countries they were elected by a select group.

Few people thought about the concepts of equality and individual rights. Most believed it was natural that rulers should rule and the rest should obey. The nation was seen as a family and the ruler as its head. A small group of intellectuals challenged this view, but support for them and their ideas was minimal. Most people simply wanted a peaceful and orderly existence. They were not interested in the

affairs of government. And those in power wanted to keep it that way. Most rulers opposed **universal suffrage.** They argued that uneducated farmers and labourers could not understand politics and so should not have the right to vote and influence governments. At the turn of the century, voting rights in most Western countries were restricted to men of property.

At the turn of the century it was not uncommon for children to work in the factories.

Economics

Change and progress emerged as important values in the first part of the twentieth century. These were expressed through the development and acceptance of new technology and the emergence of a new attitude affirming the importance of the individual. The American Revolution in 1776 and the French Revolution in 1789 had given birth to the ideals of democracy and

VOICES

THE CLASH OF IDEAS

As the new century dawned there was concern for the future of the human race. Three popular views caused great controversy. In time, these conflicting philosophies provided the basis for armed aggression.

Like many intellectuals of the nineteenth century, Herbert Spencer, an English philosopher, believed that science was the foundation of knowledge. He based an entire philosophy on Charles Darwin's theory of evolution, applying it not only to living things, but to government, economics, and society.

Brilliant but mentally unstable, Friedrich Nietzsche, a German philosopher, was one of the most controversial thinkers of his day. Unimpressed with nineteenth-century society, particularly democracy and Christianity, Nietzsche proclaimed that a superior individual, a noble genius with a "master morality," must rise to lead and dominate the masses with their "slave morality." He believed that the Christian ideals of meekness and humility were weakening and crippling society. Instead, he envisioned a society in which the strong would lead, and the qualities of courage, strength, and beauty of character would be prized.

One of the most powerful voices in the struggle for international socialism was Rosa Luxemburg's. In 1892, Luxemburg helped found the Polish Socialist Party, and in 1898 she became leader of the German Social Democratic Party. Alone among socialists in Germany, she spoke out against German workers fighting in the First World War. War, she felt, benefited the owners of factories—the capitalist class—not the people who fought.

As you read these philosophical views, try to identify a specific situation in history in which each was applied.

Herbert Spencer

"We have unmistakable proof that throughout all past time there has been a ceaseless devouring of the weak by the strong. This survival of the fittest which I have here sought to express in mechanical terms is that which Mr. Darwin has called 'Natural Selection' or the preservation of the favoured races in the struggle for life."

Herbert Spencer, "Life as Struggle," *1859*

Friedrich Nietzsche

"The herd seeks to perpetuate and protect one type of man while guarding itself on both flanks—against depraved and criminal members of society and against superior spirits who rise above its dead level of mediocrity. Morality in Europe today is herd morality."

Friedrich Nietzsche, The Geneology of Morals, *1887*

Rosa Luxembourg

"The essence of a socialist society is that the great working mass ceases to be a ruled mass and instead lives and controls its own political and economic life."

"The fight against militarism cannot be separated from the socialist class war as a whole....Wars between capitalist states are as a rule the result of their rivalry for world markets....Wars are therefore inherent in capitalism."

Rosa Luxembourg, "Family of Humankind," *1910*

VOICES

THE ANARCHIST AND THE MONARCHIST

Two very different political views of the time were expressed by Emma Goldman, an **anarchist**, and Lord Salisbury, a **monarchist**. The anarchists believed governments were corrupt by nature and should be abolished; people would then live cooperatively with full political and social liberty. The monarchists believed in the importance of a hereditary monarchy as a symbol of national and imperial unity and a focus for loyalty and order. As you read these comments, imagine yourself as an average British citizen in 1900. Which position would you support?

Emma Goldman

"Anarchism, then, really stands for the liberation of the human mind from the dominion of religion, the liberation of the human body from the dominion of property, liberation from the shackles and restraints of government."

"Anarchism is the spirit of youth against outworn traditions."

Lord Salisbury

"The struggle between the English constitution on the one hand, and the democratic forces that are labouring to subvert it on the other, is...a struggle between those who have, to keep what they have got, and those who have not, to get it."

"The classes that represent civilization, the holders of accumulated capital and accumulated thought, have a right to require securities to protect them from being overwhelmed by hordes who have neither knowledge to guide them nor stake in the Commonwealth to control them."

individual freedom. The United States became known as "the land of the free." With its prosperous economy it also became known as "the land of opportunity." Millions of people were drawn to American shores in search of these ideals.

Industrialization led to a new economic freedom. New inventions were transformed into successful business enterprises. Economic freedom led to political freedom as well. A new class of wealthy and influential entrepreneurs emerged to challenge the traditional power of the aristocracy. By the early twentieth century, economic power had shifted from the landowning aristocracy to the new business and manufacturing elite. In England, the factory owners controlled the money while the landowners held the titles. In time, money prevailed. The House of Commons, which represented ordinary citizens and the new business class, emerged as the real source of power, while the House of Lords declined to the position of a symbolic institution.

In the United States and Canada, the giants of industry and commerce—families like the Rockefellers, the Morgans, the Eatons, and the Masseys—wielded the power. In this new economic order, *what* you were was more important than *who* you were. One of the great attractions of America was the opportunity to go from "rags to riches." This dream of wealth was a magnet for the poor and underprivileged of Europe.

PROFILE

PABLO PICASSO (1881-1973)

Many feel that Spanish artist Pablo Picasso revolutionized the visual arts in the twentieth century, demonstrating versatility, imagination and technical brilliance. As you read about this artist and study Les Demoiselles d'Avignon *(shown here), consider why you might agree or disagree with this assessment.*

"I paint objects as I think them, not as I see them."

> *Pablo Picasso, in John Golding,*
> Cubism, *1959*

"Everyone wants to understand art. Why not try to understand the song of a bird? Why does one love the night, flowers, everything around one, without trying to understand them? But in the case of a painting people have to understand....People who try to explain pictures are usually barking up the wrong tree."

> *Pablo Picasso, in Dore Ashton,* Picasso on Art, *1972*

The art of Pablo Picasso first began to earn acclaim during his Blue Period (1901-04), in which the artist combined representational form with emotional subject matter. His subjects were poor social outcasts and the paintings were dominated by cold blue tones. In the Rose Period (1905-06) the blue tones gave way to pinks and greys and the mood was less sombre. His subjects now were dancers and acrobats.

In 1906-07, Picasso created *Les Demoiselles d'Avignon*, which critics have proclaimed as the single most important landmark in the evolution of modern painting. At the time many other artists considered the work incomprehensible. In fact, so revolutionary was *Les Demoiselles d'Avignon* that it was not publicly exhibited until 1937. But this work heralded the beginning of the most influential artistic movement in the twentieth century, **Cubism**.

From 1910 to 1916, Picasso worked closely with Georges Bracque developing and exploring Cubism. In creating abstract images from nature, Picasso and the Cubists released their art from simply imitating reality. The movement established the idea that art exists as an object in its own right.

Later Picasso's work became increasingly filled with a mood of foreboding. He became preoccupied with scenes of despair and turmoil. This period culminated with his second pivotal work, *Guernica* (1937). It symbolically depicts the horrors of war following the bombing of the Basque town of Guernica by German planes during the Spanish Civil War.

Picasso continued to create art throughout his life, exploring a wealth of themes in a variety of styles. His vast array of work is his legacy as the most influential visual artist of the twentieth century.

Nevertheless, **capitalism** was not without its critics. Negative effects of industrialization, such as child labour, poverty, and slums, were being moderated in Britain, but they were just surfacing in nations still in the early stages of industrialization. The notion of class became a powerful idea as wealth accumulated in the hands of a few capitalists while workers struggled in poverty.

THE BIRTH OF MODERN CULTURE

The first decades of the twentieth century represent one of the most tumultuous periods in the history of art, culture, and philosophy. The sweeping advances made in science and technology, coupled with radical new movements in art, literature, music, and theatre, created tension, optimism, and uncertainty.

There are those who believe that art has a special capacity to reflect the essence of society. Others go further, believing that art has an important role to play in social protest. At the turn of the century, the arts were having a powerful impact on society. Audiences broke into riots at concerts and theatres where new and controversial compositions and plays were being performed. Igor Stravinsky's *The Rite of Spring* (1913) was equated with outright anarchy, so radical was its departure from accepted harmonic, melodic, and rhythmic concepts. (To later observers, the images created by *The Rite of Spring* foreshadowed the horrors that would engulf Europe during the First World War.) Satirical farces by the French dramatist Alfred Jarry, which foreshadowed surrealism and the Theatre of the Absurd, caused equally extreme reactions. Ecstatic praise and vitriolic abuse greeted the works of contemporary artists such as Matisse

and Picasso. From the insights of relativity and quantum theory to the striking canvases of the group of French impressionist painters known as *Les Fauves*, the new era of the twentieth century promised change and conflict.

"The mission of art is simply to inspire the vision of a new social dawn."

French artist and anarchist Grandjouan

INTERNATIONAL RELATIONS

As the nineteenth century drew to a close, Europe was at the pinnacle of its power. The European nations were in a race with one another for colonies, mainly in Africa and Asia, and the increased trade these would bring. Britain, France, Germany, Holland, Belgium, Portugal, and Italy all had colonies in Africa. In Asia, Britain, France, Holland, and Russia were enlarging their spheres of influence. To defend and extend their possessions, the European nations built larger armies and navies. As jealousies and tensions mounted, international relations became increasingly dangerous.

The South African War

In 1900, Britain was the world's leading power, controlling an enormous empire stretching from Canada to Africa to India to Australia. So vast was Britain's reach that it was said that "the sun never sets on the British Empire." By the turn of the century, however, Britain's domination was being challenged. The result was armed conflict. In the South African, or Boer, War of 1899-1902, hostilities erupted between the Boers (settlers of Dutch

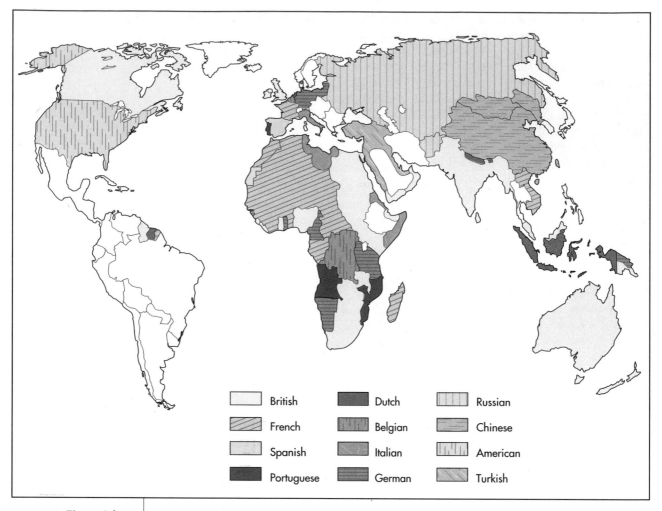

Figure 1.4:
Empires of the World,
1900

Legend:
- British
- French
- Spanish
- Portuguese
- Dutch
- Belgian
- Italian
- German
- Russian
- Chinese
- American
- Turkish

"I would annex the planets if I could."

Cecil Rhodes,
British imperialist and
business magnate

"The British Empire is the greatest engine of evil for the weak races now existing in the world....I should be delighted to see England stripped of her whole foreign possessions."

Wilfred S. Blunt,
English poet and
opponent of imperialism

descent) and the British. The political catalyst for the war was the Boers' refusal to grant equal rights to British immigrants. But essentially the conflict was about imperial domination and the riches this would bring—control of the vast gold and diamond deposits of the Transvaal. It took half a million troops for the British to prevail. In 1902, the Boer republics of the Transvaal and the Orange Free State were defeated and annexed as British Crown Colonies.

The Russo-Japanese War
As a new century dawned, so too did a new force of imperialism. In Asia, Japan, like Britain, was a small island

The Boer War between the white Dutch and British settlers in South Africa was the first of many armed conflicts in the twentieth century.

nation with limited resources. And yet Japan, like Britain, embarked on its own campaign to become a great military and industrial power.

Japan's leaders believed the only way to defend against Western imperialism was to learn the ways of the West. Japanese observers were sent to England to study financial and naval affairs, to France to learn about law and government, and to Germany to study military organization and strategy. They began to develop a strong industrial base. This in turn led to the need to secure raw materials. The Japanese saw how Europeans had pursued their imperialist goals in Asia. If the Europeans could do it, why not the Japanese?

Japan's aspirations in Asia were destined to clash with the imperialist ambitions of other nations. In 1894-95, Japan successfully invaded China and advanced north into Manchuria. But there they encountered the Russians as they moved south. This collision of interests finally led to the outbreak of war between Russia and Japan in 1904-05.

When the battles were over, Japan had prevailed. For the first time, a non-European state had defeated a European power and had exposed as myth the notion of Western invincibility. The victory also gave Japan confidence in its power and influence in Asia. The year 1905 thus marked the beginning of a long and hard struggle to liberate Asia from European colonial control. The repercussions of the war between Japan and Russia would be felt for many decades.

> "To innovate by imitation."
>
> *Japanese motto*

American Imperialism

The turn of the century saw the emergence of the United States as an imperial power. As a former British colony, the US had traditionally

Figure 1.5 Imperial Powers at the Turn of the Century

Country	Reasons for Imperialist Expansion	Spheres of Influence
Britain	• the world's leading power in 1900 • colonial acquisitions provided Britain with an abundance of raw materials as well as markets for its finished products • supported by a large and powerful navy	• empire included 25% of earth's land surface • stretched from Canada to Australia and included India, New Zealand, and parts of Africa and Asia • led to the phrase "the sun never sets on the British Empire"
France	• rivalled Britain as an imperial power • did not need raw materials but desired prestige and power • competition with Britain over colonial territories led to many conflicts and disputes	• empire covered 12% of earth's land surface • controlled one-third of African continent, a large part of South East Asia, and some islands in the South Pacific
Germany	• new German Empire emerging as dominant power on European mainland • desire to increase German power beyond Europe to rival Britain and France • need to access a warm water port for the navy	• challenged France for control of Morocco • seized interests in Asia • prepared to challenge Britain and France on land and at sea
Russia	• need to access a warm water port for the navy	• Trans-Siberia Railway established link to Pacific and access to northern China
Japan	• need to secure raw materials for rapidly developing industrial base • part of new Japanese motto "innovate by imitation" • desire to keep Asia for Asians rather than European imperialists	• occupied Korea and moved north into Manchuria • in Manchuria, collided with the Russians, leading to Russo-Japanese War of 1904
United States	• opposed European imperialism in Western Hemisphere • desire to expand commercial interests • "vital interest" in the Panama Canal	• US economic and military power dominated Latin America • purchase of Alaska in 1867 • annexation of Hawaii • obtained control of former Spanish possessions such as Cuba and the Philippines following Spain's defeat in war of 1898 • controlled 40% of Mexico

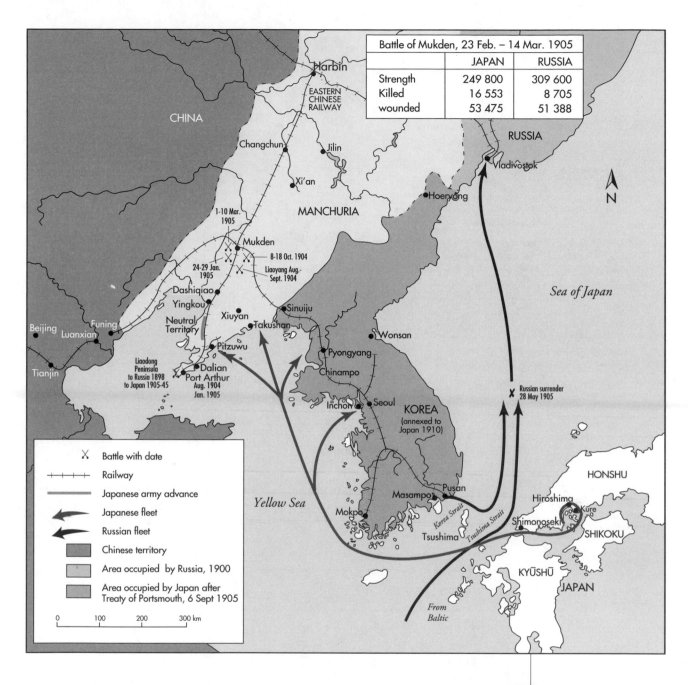

Battle of Mukden, 23 Feb. – 14 Mar. 1905		
	JAPAN	RUSSIA
Strength	249 800	309 600
Killed	16 553	8 705
wounded	53 475	51 388

Legend:

- X — Battle with date
- +++++ — Railway
- ——— — Japanese army advance
- ← — Japanese fleet
- ← — Russian fleet
- Chinese territory
- Area occupied by Russia, 1900
- Area occupied by Japan after Treaty of Portsmouth, 6 Sept 1905

0   100   200   300 km

Figure 1.6:
The Russo-Japanese War, 1904-05

opposed imperialism. The Monroe Doctrine of 1823 had essentially warned the European powers to stay away from the Western Hemisphere. But by the end of the nineteenth century, the US was ready to take a more aggressive stand. New territories like Alaska and Hawaii had been acquired, either by direct purchase, annexation,

"We are a conquering race—we must obey our blood and occupy new markets and if necessary new lands."

*Albert Beveridge
(1862-1927), US Senator*

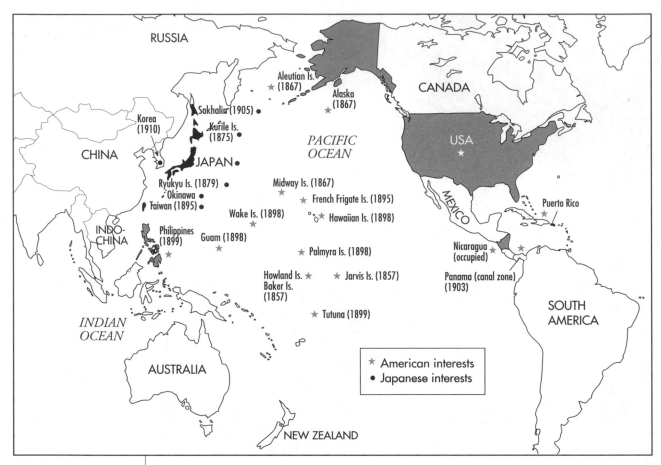

Figure 1.7:
The New Imperialists,
Japanese and American
Possessions, 1910

or war. Economically, Latin America was already dominated by American interests. The expansion of US imperialism marked the beginning of American economic and military domination throughout the world.

In Review

1. In a chart, compare the strengths and weaknesses of the following nations at the turn of the century: Britain, France, Germany, Russia, Japan, the United States.

2. What were the conflicting views and values of Western society at the beginning of the twentieth century. How were these reflected in politics and culture?

3. "We do not desire to put anyone else in the shade, but we want our place in the sun." (Prince Bernhard von Bülow, German Chancellor, 1900-09). What does this statement tell you about imperialism and the attitudes of the European powers at the turn of the century?

SUMMARY

At the dawn of the twentieth century, Europe was the centre of world politics, economics, and culture. The British Empire stood at the zenith of its power. Except for some minor skirmishes, peace had reigned for almost 100 years. The interlude of King Edward VII's reign after the long Victorian age camouflaged the tremendous forces waiting to erupt into the cataclysm of the First World War.

The nineteenth century had somehow been able to contain the forces of imperialism and democracy, liberty and authority, individualism and collectivism, science and religion. The twentieth century would witness the explosion of these forces into open conflict.

To many historians, the First World War marked the true beginning of the twentieth century. It foreshadowed an era of war, revolution, and tremendous social, political, and technological change.

MAKING CONNECTIONS

1. Compare the strengths and weaknesses of these nations today: Britain, France, Russia, Germany, Japan, the United States, Canada. Which countries do you think have seen the greatest changes since 1900?

2. Prepare a picture or word collage showing the differences in lifestyle between 1900 and the present.

3. What impact does culture have on our society at the end of the twentieth century?

DEVELOPING YOUR VOICE

4. Organize a class debate on one of the following topics:
   • Imperialism today is dead.
   • Women have made only modest gains since 1900.
   • Technology has enslaved, not liberated, the world.

5. Role play one of the major figures presented in this chapter and be interviewed by members of the class.

6. Create a poster in support of an idea or personality in this chapter.

RESEARCHING THE ISSUES

7. Research the suffragist movement in Canada. Identify some of the key personalities and events in the movement. What factors contributed to the movement's success? Are there any lasting influences of the suffragists on women's groups today?

8. Research European imperialism at the turn of the century in either Asia or Africa and write a report of your findings.

9. With a partner or in a small group, brainstorm the ways in which life in Canada has changed since 1900. After completing your list, select what you consider to be the three most important changes and explain your choices. Present your selection to the class.

VIEWPOINTS

ISSUE: SHOULD THE UNITED STATES ANNEX FORMER SPANISH COLONIES AND BECOME AN IMPERIAL POWER?

By 1900 the major European powers had acquired vast colonial territories. This grab for colonies was viewed with disdain by most Americans. After all, the US had been a colony of Britain and had fought a bitter revolutionary war to win its freedom. The American War of Independence, which began in 1776, was followed by the Monroe Doctrine of 1823, which warned the European powers to stay out of the Western Hemisphere. In 1898, the US went to war with Spain claiming the high moral purpose of freeing Spanish colonies such as Cuba, Puerto Rico, and the Philippines from their colonial rulers. But with the American victory came the issue of what to do with these newly acquired colonies. Should the US annex these lands and thereby become a colonial power itself?

The following readings present two viewpoints as they were argued in 1899 in the US. While this specific case deals with the US decision to annex the Philippines, these historical readings should provide some understanding of how imperialism was debated and justified at the turn of the century.

In the first reading, US president William McKinley explains his reasons for deciding in favour of annexation. The speech was made to a delegation of prominent Methodists in 1899. The second reading is by William Jennings Bryan who was the Democratic presidential candidate for the 1898 and 1900 presidential elections. Bryan used the issue of imperialism as part of his attack on the McKinley administration. His anti-imperialism argument was that a colonial policy would endanger US democracy.

Read these viewpoints carefully and complete the Argument Analysis and Evaluation Summary for each reading.

NOTE: These readings are from 1899 and, reflect the values and attitudes of that period. Compared to the present, how are other races portrayed in these readings?

William McKinley

"I have been criticized a good deal about the Philippines, but I don't deserve it. The truth is I didn't want the Philippines, and when they came to us, as a gift from the gods, I did not know what to do with them. When the Spanish War broke out, Dewey was at Hong-Kong, and I ordered him to go to Manila and to capture or destroy the Spanish fleet, and he had to; because, if defeated, he had no place to refit on that side of the globe, and if the Dons were victorious, they would likely cross the Pacific and ravage our Oregon and California coasts. And so he had to destroy the Spanish fleet, and did it! But that was as far as I thought then.

"When next I realized that the Philippines had dropped into our laps I confess I did not know what to do with them. I sought counsel from all sides—Democrats as well as Republicans—but got little help. I thought first we would take only Manila; then Luzon; then other islands, perhaps, also. I walked the floor of the White House night after night until mid-night; and I am not ashamed to tell you, gentlemen, that I went down on my knees and prayed Almighty god for light and guidance more than one night. And one night late it came to me this way—I don't know how it was, but it came: (1) That we could not give them back to Spain—that would be cowardly and dishonorable; (2) that we could not turn them over to France or Germany—our commercial rivals in the Orient—that would be bad business and discreditable; (3) that we could not leave them to themselves—they were unfit for self-government—and they would soon have anarchy and misrule there worse than Spain's was; and (4) that there was nothing left for us to do but to take them all, and to educate the Filipinos, and uplift and civilize and Christianize them, and by God's grace do the very best we could by them, as our fellow-men for whom Christ also died. And then I went to bed, and went to sleep, and slept soundly, and the next morning I sent for the chief engineer of the War Department (our map-maker), and I told him to put the Philippines on the map of the United States [pointing to a large map on the wall of his office], and there they are, and there they will stay while I am president!"

Source: Richard W. Lespold and Arthur S. Link (eds.), Problems in American History *(2nd ed) Prentice-Hall, Inc. Englewood Cliffs N.J. © 1957, 1963.*

William Jennings Bryan

"Our nation is in greater danger just now than Cuba. Our people defended Cuba against foreign arms; now they must defend themselves and their country against a foreign idea—the colonial idea of European nations....The very foundation principles of our government are assaulted. Our nation must give up any intention of entering upon a colonial policy, such as is now pursued by European countries, or it must abandon the doctrine that governments derive their just powers from the consent of the governed....

"This nation cannot endure half republic and half colony—half free and half vassal. Our form of government, our traditions, our present interests and our future welfare, all forbid our entering upon a career of conquest.

"Jefferson has been quoted in support of imperialism, but our opponents must distinguish between imperialism and expansion; they must also distinguish between expansion in the western hemisphere and an expansion that involves us in the quarrels of Europe and the Orient. They must still further distinguish between expansion which secures contiguous territory for future settlement, and expansion which secures us alien races for future subjugation.

"Jefferson favored the annexation of necessary contiguous territory on the North American continent, but he was opposed to wars of conquest and expressly condemned the acquiring of remote territory....

"In the case of Porto Rico, where the people have as yet expressed no desire for an independent government, we might with propriety declare our willingness to annex the island if the citizens desire annexation, but the Philppines are too far away and their people too different from ours to be annexed to the United States, even if they desired it.

"The forcible annexation of the Philippine Islands is not necessary to make the United States a world-power. For over ten decades our nation has been a world-power. During its brief existence it has exerted upon the human race an influence more potent than all the other nations of the earth combined, and it has exerted that influence without the use of sword or Gatling gun. Mexico and the republics of Central and South America testify to the benign influence of our institutions, while Europe and Asia give evidence of the working of the leaven of self-government. In the growth of democracy we observe the triumphant march of an idea—an idea that would be weighted down rather than aided by the armor and weapons proffered by imperialism.

"The forcible annexation of the Philippine Islands (and, in my judgment, even annexation by the consent of the people) would prove a source of pecuniary loss rather than gain.

"Who can estimate in money and men the cost of subduing and keeping in subjection eight millions of people, six thousand miles away, scattered over twelve hundred islands and living under a tropical sun?

"Among the possibilities may be mentioned an offensive and defensive union between the United States and one or more European nations. Already one may hear an Anglo-American alliance suggested—a suggestion which would have been discarded as a dream a year ago. When this nation abandons its traditions and enters upon a colonial policy, a long step will be taken toward those entanglements against which Washington and Jefferson with equal emphasis warned their countrymen.

"The Monroe Doctrine, too, what will become of it? How can we expect European nations to respect our supremacy in the western hemisphere if we insist upon entering Asia? So long as we confine ourselves to our own continent we are strong enough to repel the world, but are we prepared (or is it worth while to prepare) to wage an offensive warfare in other parts of the globe?

"It is sometimes suggested that the Philippines would furnish homes for those who are crowded out of this country. This argument, too, is without foundation.

"Our people will not flock to Manila: climatic conditions will be as great an obstacle as overpopulation. English supremacy in India has continued for nearly a hundred and fifty years, and yet in 1891 the British-born population of India was only 100 551—less than the total of prisoners confined in the jails of India at the end of 1895....

"But while the Philippines will not prove inviting to Americans, we shall probably draw a considerable number from the islands to the United States. The emigration will be eastward rather than westward.

"It is not strange that the laboring men should look with undisguised alarm upon the prospect of oriental competition upon the farms and in the factories of the United States. Our people have legislated against Chinese emigration, but to exclude a few Chinese and admit many Filipinos is like straining at a gnat and swallowing a camel.

"The farmers and laboring men constitute a large majority of the American people; what is there in annexation for them? Heavier taxes, Asiatic emigration and an opportunity to furnish more sons for the army.

"Will it pay?"

Reprinted in W.J. Bryan and others, Republic or Empire? The Philippine Question (*Chicago, 1899*), *13-15, 33-39, 59-68.*

ANALYSIS AND EVALUATION

Refer to the Arguments Analysis and Evaluation Guide on page viii.

1. Using the Argument Analysis and Evaluation Guide, compare the readings by McKinley and Bryan. On what do they agree? On what do they disagree?

2. Decide which of the viewpoints you tend to support and explain why. Be sure to use specific information from this textbook, the readings, and other sources to support your position.

3. State and support your position on the issue: "Should the United States annex former Spanish colonies and become an imperial power?"

CHAPTER TWO

The First World War: 1914-1918

"Europe, in her insanity, has started something unbelievable. In such times one realizes to what a sad species of animals one belongs".

Albert Einstein, (1879-1955), physicist and winner of the 1921 Nobel Prize for Physics

"Now, God be thank'd, Who has matched us with His hour,
And caught our youth and wakened us from sleeping,
With hand made sure, clear eye and sharpened power,
To turn, as swimmers into cleanness leaping,
Glad from a world grown old and cold and weary ..."

Rupert Brook, (1887-1915), English Poet, from Peace.

"The Great War of 1914-1918 ... created a physical as well as a psychological gulf between two epochs."

Barbara Tuchman (1912-1989), American historian

Left: Over the Top

❖ OVERVIEW

In the early 1900s, the clouds of war were beginning to form over Europe. Stimulated by rising nationalism and the growth of imperialist rivalries, nations sought protection against each other. Most of the major European powers entered into strategic **alliances** and began rebuilding their armies and navies. By 1914, Europe was divided into two heavily armed camps, each poised for conflict.

Yet while many of Europe's leaders saw war as inevitable, no one envisioned the four years of slaughter and horror that were to follow. In reality, the First World War brought to an abrupt end a century of relative peace and stability and introduced a century of conflict, uncertainty, and change.

FOCUS QUESTIONS

- What were the underlying causes of the First World War?
- How did technology change the nature of warfare during the war?
- What were the major outcomes of the First World War?
- What are some interpretations about the causes of and responsibility for the First World War?

THE CAUSES OF THE FIRST WORLD WAR

There were at least four underlying causes of the First World War: **nationalism**, **economic rivalry**, the **arms race**, and the **alliance system**. Within the context of conditions in 1914, these causes help to explain why war broke out. An atmosphere of fear and suspicion among nations had developed. People began to believe war was necessary.

NATIONALISM

The French region of Alsace-Lorraine, alongside Germany's western border, had an abundance of coal and iron ore deposits and a thriving textile industry. When France was defeated in the Franco-Prussian War of 1871, it ceded Alsace-Lorraine to Germany. The region became important to Germany's naval and military power. But German control spawned bitter resentment among the largely French-speaking population. The region became a focus for French nationalism and anti-German sentiment. On the larger stage, France attempted to restore national pride and prestige by focusing on acquiring an empire. Thus France joined the scramble among European nations for colonies in Africa.

German nationalism was stimulated by politics, economics, and a desire to become an imperial power. There was a new pride and optimism after the unification of the German states in 1871. Following unification, German technology, industry, and trade developed rapidly; intense competition for markets contributed to Germany's growing economic nationalism. Germany's imperialist ambitions went unfulfilled, however. By the time Germany entered the race for colonies, Britain and France had already established massive empires that included the most desirable territories. Germany's inability to acquire important new colonies was a source of great frustration. From the German point of view, Britain and France were conspiring to prevent their nation from expanding.

In Austria-Hungary, ethnic nationalism was fragmenting the country. The

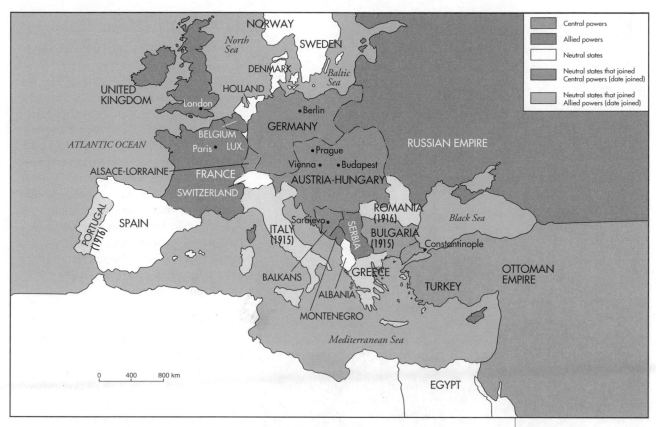

Figure 2.1:
Europe in 1914

old Austro-Hungarian Empire that had once dominated middle Europe was in a state of inner decay. The empire encompassed many nationalities, including Serbs, Croats, Slovaks, Czechs, and Poles. In 1914, local wars were erupting throughout the Balkans as each group fought for its own interests. These conflicts did not go unnoticed by neighbouring powers. Russia saw an opportunity to increase its influence in the region and possibly gain control of the Dardanelles. Russian nationalists called on the Slavic people in the Balkans to unite under their leadership. Within this movement known as **Pan-Slavism**, Russia was supporting the Slavic state of Serbia in its efforts to break free of Austria-Hungary.

Britain was the major economic and imperial power in the world. The country's nationalism was intricately linked with pride in the British Empire. A sense of **noble destiny** permeated

British society. In middle-class England, belief in king and country was intertwined with the concept of duty. Young men enlisted in the army, believing that a **pax Britannia**, or British peace, was the proper order of things in the world and that it was their duty to maintain this order. As the dominant world power, Britain was eager to maintain the status quo. Its leaders were suspicious of the aggressive new nations—Germany and Japan—which sought to increase their territories and power in competition with the British Empire.

Economic Rivalry

Germany and Britain were economic competitors. The unification of Germany and the annexation of Alsace-Lorraine enabled the German economy to flourish. By 1900, many German industries had surpassed those

In 1906, the British introduced a new class of battleship, the dreadnought.

THE ARMS RACE

One of the consequences of nationalism and economic rivalry in the decades preceding the First World War was a determined arms race. The new German monarch, Kaiser Wilhelm II, grandson of Britain's Queen Victoria, wanted to extend German influence as far as possible. He hoped to increase German military and economic power to equal that of Britain. As the world's dominant power, however, Britain was not about to relinquish its favourable balance of power. Both countries, afraid that the other would gain an advantage, embarked on large-scale armament programs.

The Naval Race

Britain depended on its navy for defence and to guarantee the security of its colonies. As a result, the British navy was twice the size of any other power.

After 1898 Germany launched a naval build-up designed to rival Britain's fleet. Forty-one battleships and sixty cruisers were planned for the next two decades. From the British point of view, Germany's naval expansion posed a threat to Britain's naval supremacy and thus constituted a direct challenge to the nation's security.

The British responded by launching their own naval expansion. In 1906 a new class of battleship, the **dreadnought**, was introduced, intensifying the race for naval supremacy. By 1914 Britain numbered twenty-nine battleships of this class, while Germany had eighteen.

What was the major significance of the naval race? Until 1900 Britain's closest ally on the European continent had been Germany. Since the days of Napoleon, France had traditionally been Britain's enemy and imperial rival. But German naval expansion

in Britain. In 1914, for example, Germany was producing twice as much steel as Britain. Because Germany had become industrialized later than Britain, its manufacturing industry enjoyed newer factories with equipment that incorporated the latest technology. British factories, on the other hand, were older and becoming less efficient. In addition, the excellent German education system, with its concentration on science and technology, produced the engineers and scientists needed to foster Germany's developing technology. While the British and French economies continued to . grow after 1900, they could not keep pace with Germany.

Figure 2.2 Economic and Military Potential of the Powers, 1913-14

	Great Britain	**France**	**Russia**	**Germany**	**Austria Hungary**	**United States**
Population (millions)	45.6	39.7	175.1	66.9	52.1	97.3
Military and naval personnel*	532 000	910 000	1 352 000	891 000	444 000	164 000
Warships tonnage*	2 714 000	900 000	679 000	1 305 000	372 000	985 000
Total industrial potential (UK in 1900 = 100)	127.2	57.3	76.6	137.7	40.7	298.1
% shares of world manufacturing output	13.6	6.1	8.2	14.8	4.4	32.0

*Compiled from Paul Kennedy, *The Rise and Fall of the Great Powers* (London: Unwin Hyman Ltd., 1988).

alarmed British leaders and aroused suspicions about their ally's ultimate goals. Rather than face a potential enemy in isolation, Britain sought alliances with its former rivals, France and Russia.

A SYSTEM OF ALLIANCES

Otto von Bismarck, the powerful German chancellor who had brought about the unification of Germany, engineered an alliance system in the 1880s that provided Europe with the illusion of peace and stability. Behind the scenes, however, tensions were mounting.

Bismarck's diplomacy had been aimed at isolating France. In 1879, he signed the Dual Alliance with Austria-Hungary. Three years later, in 1882, he negotiated the Triple Alliance that drew Italy into the pact. Then in 1887, he persuaded Russia to sign a secret Reinsurance Treaty in which both

countries agreed to remain neutral if the other were attacked by a third power. Bismarck avoided conflict with Britain by refusing to pursue a colonial empire and by resisting German naval expansion.

After the death of Wilhelm I in 1888, however, his successor, Wilhelm II, embarked on very different policies. The new kaiser decided to act as chancellor himself and dismissed Bismarck in 1890. In the same year he allowed the Reinsurance Treaty with Russia to lapse. Feeling cast aside by its former ally, Russia turned to France. In 1891, the two countries reached an understanding, and in 1894 they entered into a military alliance. This marked an important shift in European alignments as France and Russia had been enemies since the French invasion of Russia in 1812 during the Napoleonic Wars.

These changes in Europe were a source of concern to Britain. Its leaders were distrustful of the new alliance between Russia and France and dismayed by Germany's growing economic power and increasing imperialism. But of even greater importance was Germany's new policy of naval expansion. Growing insecurity caused Britain to end its century-old policy of "splendid isolation" from alliances with continental powers. By 1907, Britain had joined France and Russia to form the **Triple Entente**.

Europe was now divided into two rival camps—the **Triple Alliance** of Germany, Austria-Hungary, and Italy against the Triple Entente of France, Russia, and Britain. From this point until the outbreak of the First World War in 1914, the arms race intensified, armies multiplied in size, navies expanded their fleets—and international tensions grew.

In Review

1. Summarize the four major underlying causes of the First World War.
2. In your opinion, which of these causes was most important? Why?

The Road to War

As 1914 approached, the international power struggle became more intense. One incident followed another and each contributed to the mounting tension and hostility between the European powers.

Tension in the Balkans

The humiliation of defeat in the Russo-Japanese War in 1905 refocused Russian interests on Europe, particularly the Balkan states. The Balkans included Bosnia, Herzegovina, Serbia, Bulgaria, and part of Greece. They became a focus for European nationalism and imperialism as Turkey, Russia, and Austria-Hungary had conflicting interests there.

In 1908, Austria-Hungary annexed the states of Bosnia and Herzegovina from the Turks. This act of aggression infuriated Serbia because these two states were populated primarily by Serbs. In addition, the annexation effectively cut Serbia off from the Adriatic Sea. Serbia hoped that Russia would intervene on its behalf. But Russia, aware that Germany would back Austria-Hungary, decided not to become involved in the conflict.

In 1912 the situation changed dramatically. A Balkan League was formed under the leadership of Serbia. It declared war on Turkey and succeeded in defeating the Ottoman Turks, thereby reducing Turkish influence in the region. The rise of Serbian power concerned Austria-Hungary. These fears were heightened in 1913 when another Balkan war erupted. After the battles, Serbia had almost doubled its size. Afraid of Austro-Hungarian aggression, Serbia turned to its ally Russia for protection. The situation was becoming increasingly volatile. As Russia and Austria-Hungary took opposite stands in the Balkan conflicts, their allies watched with growing apprehension.

THE MAJOR POWERS IN 1914

Britain

In the decades preceding the First World War, Britain was overtaken industrially by both the United States and Germany. Where the British Empire had been the foremost colonial power of the nineteenth century, by the twentieth century it was facing intense competition in its commercial and colonial interests. Still, Britain remained the foremost power in the world, even if its domination was in decline. The greatest challenge for Britain at this time was to maintain the status quo, or at least to maintain a strong level of control over the unfolding of events. British foreign policy was often ambiguous. Britain's leaders were reluctant to form a military commitment *with* Germany in 1889 and 1898-1901 or *against* Germany in 1906-14.

Germany

In the years leading up to the First World War, Germany was an industrial power led by the authoritarian rule of a monarchy. Unlike the British monarch, the German Kaiser exercised enormous power. His personality, views, and beliefs shaped German foreign policy. The Kaiser challenged the existing order. He directed Germany to flex its muscle, and thereby dramatically alter the European balance of power.

Russia

By 1914, Russia had a rapidly expanding population several times larger than that of either Britain or Germany. The size of its standing army was enormous, with 1.3 million troops and up to 5 million reserves. In addition, Russia had become the fourth largest industrial power. Other European nations were concerned about Russia's emerging might. But this picture of Russian power was misleading. Most of Russia's industrial development was in textiles and food processing, not equipment or armaments. Its status as an industrial power ranked well behind the United States, Britain, and Germany. Russia was still a peasant society, with 80 per cent of its population deriving their livelihood from agriculture.

France

By the eve of the First World War the German industrial giant was eclipsing France's industrial development. Growth in France was hindered by outdated practices and protection of local markets. By 1914 France ranked fifth as an industrial nation among the European powers. Its population growth was almost stagnant compared to that of Germany. Between 1890 and 1914, Germany's population surged by 18 million while the population of France rose by only 1 million. These factors served to increase Germany's power while France's relative position declined. This was a particularly bitter pill for the French given the history of conflict between the two countries.

THE BALKAN CRISIS

The Balkans are deeply divided by geography, history, religion, language, and culture. Historically, Germans, Hungarians, Slavs, and Muslims have made war upon each other. Among the Slavs, several nationalities—Croats, Serbs, Bulgarians, and others—have fought for dominance.

The Balkans had been ruled by the Ottoman Turks from the late fifteenth century, but Turkish rule had been ineffective and revolts were frequent. In the nineteenth century, the Turkish Empire was weakening and other European powers—Austria-Hungary,

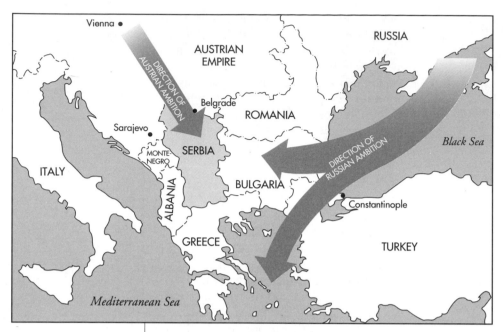

Figure 2.3:
The Balkans in 1914

and hatreds. Observers often noted that the region was like a powder keg ready to explode. The explosion, when it came, not only rocked the Balkans but also Europe and the world.

The incident that ignited the First World War occurred on 28 June 1914. Archduke Franz Ferdinand, heir to the Austro-Hungarian Empire, was assassinated in Sarajevo, the capital of Bosnia. A young Bosnian Serb, Gavrilo Princip, was the assassin. Princip belonged to a secret Serbian nationalist organization known as the **Black Hand**, which was dedicated to obtaining Bosnian independence from the Austro-Hungarian Empire. The assassination gave Austria-Hungary an excuse to re-establish control in the region by blaming the Serbian government for the attack.

Germany had promised to support Austria-Hungary. With this pledge and the belief that Russia would not intervene, on July 23rd Austria-Hungary presented Serbia with a forty-eight-hour **ultimatum**. This set off a chain of events that directly involved the European powers. Russia intervened on behalf of Serbia, demanding that Austria-Hungary guarantee Serbia's independence. In keeping with their mutual defence agreement, France then declared its support for Russia. But even to this point, the situation appeared to be under control. Serbia had agreed to all but two of Austria-Hungary's demands. But as a precaution, Serbia mobilized its troops to protect its borders from a possible invasion. Now the mechanisms for war

Germany, and Russia—began taking an active interest in the Balkans.

At the beginning of the twentieth century, Serbia was gaining power and wanted to unite all Serbs under one great nation, including those in Austrian-controlled Bosnia-Herzegovina. Serbia was encouraged in its goals by Russia, the great Slavic nation to whom Slavs looked for protection.

The juggling for power in the Balkans intensified the deep divisions

"There is nothing to show the complicity of the Serbian government in the direction of the assassination or its preparations in supplying of weapons. Nor is there anything to lead one even to conjecture such a thing. On the contrary, there is evidence that would appear to show that complicity is out of the question."

Friedrich von Wiesner, Austrian investigator, on Serbia's involvement in the assassination of the Archduke, July 1914

Figure 2.4: The Steps to War, 28 June–4 August 1914

June 28: Archduke Ferdinand of Austria assassinated in Bosnian city of Sarajevo by Bosnian Serb nationalist.

July 23: Austrian government gives Serbia 48 h ultimatum. Serbia does not agree to all terms and begins to mobilize.

July 28: Austria-Hungary declares war on Serbia; Serbia turns to Russia for help.

July 29: Czar Nicholas agrees to help Serbia and mobilizes army.

July 30: Germany sends Russia ultimatum to halt mobilization; Russia refuses.

August 1: Germany declares war on Russia; France mobilizes army.

August 2: Germany invades Belgium as part of Schlieffen Plan for attacking France.

August 3: Germany declares war on France; Britain gives Germany an ultimatum to halt invasion of Belgium.

August 4: No reply from Germany; Britain declares war on Germany; Canada automatically at war as part of British Empire; US declares neutrality.

were in motion and events began to spiral out of control. On July 28th Austria-Hungary mobilized its armies and declared war on Serbia. Russia responded by declaring war on Austria-Hungary. Within a month, most of Europe was at war.

THE MOOD OF 1914: A SHORT BUT NECESSARY WAR

Leaders of both alliances gradually came to believe that war was necessary, but that it would be over quickly. The German Kaiser assured the *Reichstag* (parliament) that victory would be won "before the leaves fall"; in Britain, Winston Churchill spoke of a short "cleansing thunderstorm."

In his book *The Origin of the First World War*, historian James Joll claims that "long-term patterns of education, the rhetoric of the inevitability of war,

invasion scares, and downright fear all contributed to the mood of 1914." It was a mood that was in part a revolt against the liberal values of peace and rational problem-solving. According to Joll, this "mood of 1914" made the outbreak of war acceptable to the general populations on both sides. Thus, he notes, when war finally broke out there was a sense of relief, even cele-

"This country has gone wild with joy at the prospect of war with Serbia."

British Ambassador in Vienna, 1914

bration! The British ambassador to Austria described the mood in Vienna when it was announced that relations with Serbia had been broken: "[There was a] burst of frenzy of delight, vast crowds parading the streets and

VOICES

PRE-WAR GERMANY AND BRITAIN: A CLASH OF VALUES

The First World War was not only a clash of armies, it was a conflict of different beliefs and values. Britain and its empire represented the most powerful and successful nation in the world; they looked to the past, to traditional values, and to maintaining the status quo. Germany represented a nation on the rise. Germans looked to the future—to a new world in which German power could expand and be recognized. As you read these statements, compare the beliefs and values of the two societies. In what ways might the differences between the two contribute to rivalry and conflict?

German Attitudes to the War Before 1914
"War was regarded, especially in Germany, as the supreme test of spirit and as such, a test of vitality, culture, and life. 'War,' wrote historian Friedrich von Bernhardi in 1911, was a 'life-giving principle.' It was an expression of a superior culture. 'War,' wrote a contemporary of Bernhardi's, was in fact 'the price one must pay for culture.' In other words, whether considered as the foundation of culture or as a stepping-stone to a higher plateau of creativity and spirit, war was an essential part of a nation's self-esteem and image."

Modris Eksteins, historian, The Rites of Spring: The Great War and the Birth of the Modern Age (*New York: Doubleday, 1990*).

"On August 3, the rectors and senates of Bavarian universities issued an appeal to academic youth: 'Students! The muses are silent. The issue is battle, the battle forced on us for German Kultur, which is threatened by the barbarians from the east, and for German values, which the enemy in the west envies us. And so the *furore teutonicus* bursts into flame once again. The enthusiasm of the wars of liberation flares, and the holy war begins.'"

Modris Eksteins, The Rites of Spring

British Attitudes to the War Before 1914
"If a situation were forced upon us in which peace could only be preserved by the surrender of the great and beneficent position Britain has won by centuries of heroism and achievement, by allowing Britain to be treated, where her interests were vitally affected, as if she were of no account in the Cabinet of Nations, then I say emphatically that peace at that price would be a humiliation intolerable for a great country like ours to endure."

David Lloyd George, British politician and prime minister (1916-22) in 1911

"For the Germans this was a war to change the world; for the British this was a war to preserve a world. The Germans were propelled by a vision, the British by a legacy."

Modris Eksteins, The Rites of Spring

singing patriotic songs till the small hours of the morning."

Why were so many prepared to accept war? Each side came to see a need for war in order to settle their differences, since it appeared that diplomacy alone could not resolve competing and conflicting national goals. Russia wanted to extend its influence in the Balkans, while Austria-Hungary saw Russian goals as a direct threat to its own plans to bring Serbia under its control. Germany wanted to break the powerful Triple Entente which was

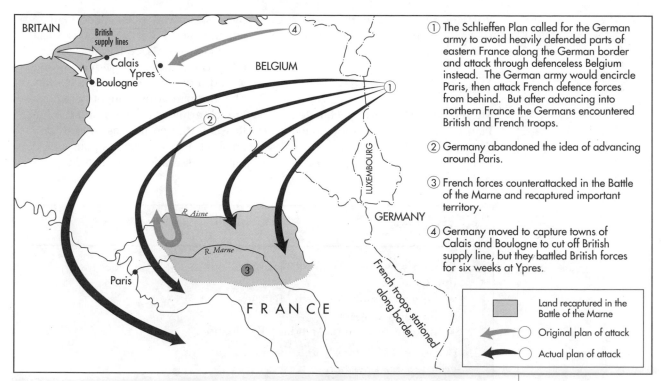

① The Schlieffen Plan called for the German army to avoid heavily defended parts of eastern France along the German border and attack through defenceless Belgium instead. The German army would encircle Paris, then attack French defence forces from behind. But after advancing into northern France the Germans encountered British and French troops.

② Germany abandoned the idea of advancing around Paris.

③ French forces counterattacked in the Battle of the Marne and recaptured important territory.

④ Germany moved to capture towns of Calais and Boulogne to cut off British supply line, but they battled British forces for six weeks at Ypres.

Land recaptured in the Battle of the Marne

Original plan of attack

Actual plan of attack

Figure 2.5:
The Schlieffen Plan

blocking its emergence as a world power. France wanted to maintain and increase its power but felt threatened by Germany. Meanwhile, Britain, as the strongest power, wanted to maintain the status quo, with no nation dominating European affairs.

The hard choice for these competing nations was between going to war or accepting compromises that could be viewed as diplomatic defeat and humiliation. Given this choice, a short war seemed acceptable.

THE SCHLIEFFEN PLAN

German leaders based their military strategy on the quick victory promised by the **Schlieffen Plan**. General Schlieffen believed that a long war was impossible in the modern age where "the existence of nations is based on the uninterrupted progress of trade and commerce." Like many European leaders, he assumed that the enemy would quit rather than risk a long, destructive war.

The Schlieffen Plan called for the concentration of almost the entire German army on one decisive assault. Timing was critical since Germany had to defeat the French army before the

"With the British declaration of war on Germany on August 4, Canada was then automatically at war as well, and most Canadians heartily approved of this arrangement. It was thought that the war would be over and won in short order, would in fact be something of a glorious adventure....There was much display of patriotic fervour as young men...flocked to join up. Everywhere in the Dominion people greeted the war with enthusiasm; crowds sang patriotic songs in the streets."

Roger Graham, Canadian historian, in Andrew H. Malcolm, *The Canadians* (Markham, ON: Fitzhenry and Whiteside, 1979).

Russians attacked from the east. To succeed, France had to be defeated in just six weeks.

PLAN XVII

The French knew of the Schlieffen Plan prior to 1914, but they doubted Germany's ability to execute it because of the huge army that would be required. They had developed their own "short-war" plan, called Plan XVII, which called for a rapid and devastating attack on Alsace-Lorraine. After recapturing these two provinces, they would move at high speed to Berlin. The German army, caught between the French army in the west and the huge Russian army in the east, would be crushed. Part of France's plan included military assistance from Britain.

IN REVIEW

1. Explain why the First World War broke out in 1914. Consider the following:
   - the growing tension in the Balkans
   - the alliance system
   - the assassination of Archduke Ferdinand

2. Compare and contrast British and German attitudes to the war. Outline your personal reaction to these attitudes.

3. What were the objectives of the Schlieffen Plan and Plan XVII? How might the existence of these plans have affected the likelihood of war breaking out in Europe?

THE COURSE OF WAR

When war broke out, each side hoped that the other would quit after the first major battle. Most people were convinced that everything would be over by Christmas. Young men rushed to enlist, afraid that the war would end before they reached the front. No one could have predicted that the battles would rage for four years, and that when it ended a whole generation of young men would be lost forever.

THE WESTERN FRONT

On the night of August 4th, the Germans launched the Schlieffen Plan, crossing the neutral frontier of Belgium without warning. Belgium fell swiftly.

The German army pushed south into France, sending French and British troops into retreat. In early September, an Allied line of defence was established along the River Marne north of Paris. The Germans advanced to within sight of the French capital. But in the critical Battle of the Marne that ensued, the Allied forces held and launched a counterattack. This surprised the German army and stalled their offensive. At Ypres in Belgium, British and Indian troops held back the Germans as they tried to seize control of ports on the English Channel.

By October 1914, both sides had dug a line of trenches from the North Sea to the Swiss frontier. The Allies and the Central Powers now faced each other across mud and barbed wire and the tragic stalemate of trench warfare began. During the four brutal

years that followed, the line of trenches remained virtually stationary, in spite of the massive battles that were fought. Tremendous losses were suffered by both sides in this cruel war of attrition. As millions died, millions more were conscripted or enlisted to take their place. When the war on the western front ended on 11 November 1918, the opposing lines were at almost the same position as they had been when they were first established in 1914. (See Figure 2.6 on page 45.)

THE EASTERN FRONT

On the eastern front, the line was much more mobile. Nevertheless, conditions were deplorable. In August 1914, at the Battle of Tannenberg in Prussia, the Germans outmanoeuvred a much larger Russian force and won a major battle. The Russian supply system had failed, leaving the troops exhausted and half-starved after their long march. Russian communications had broken down, and the Russian high command, unaware of German troop movements, made fatal mistakes regarding the deployment of Russian armies. As a result, the Second Russian Army was surrounded and destroyed. The Germans killed at least 30 000 Russians, took 100 000 prisoners, and captured a vast supply of guns at Tannenberg. The Russian commander, General Samsonov, unable to face his men or the Czar, shot himself.

In November 1917, Canadian troops at Passchendaele held the line in the waterlogged landscape of trenches.

PROFILE

THE ROYAL NEWFOUNDLAND REGIMENT AND THE BATTLE OF THE SOMME

The British-inspired Somme offensive in July 1916 was designed as a smashing breakthrough of German lines. Instead, it turned into a horrific killing field where hundreds of thousands of young soldiers were sacrificed for a few metres of mud. The following reading describes the fate of one regiment, the Royal Newfoundland, after the first day's assault on enemy lines near Beaumont-Hamel on the Somme. As you read about the devastating Battle of the Somme, consider the question of moral responsibility of sending young troops to certain death in a hopeless mission.

"In his H.Q. dug-out, Lieut-Col. Hadow, the English officer commanding the battalion, received his orders by phone from the brigade commander. These were simple. The Newfoundlanders were to leave their present position as soon as possible and advance to the German front line.

"The Newfoundlanders had to go 300 yards before reaching the British front line and then a similar distance across 'No Man's Land.' As soon as they appeared in the open, the German machine-gunners spotted them and opened fire. They concentrated their fire on the 752 Newfoundlanders advancing over the open ground less than half a mile away. Before the men could even get into "No Man's Land," they had to pass through several belts of British barbed wire. As they bunched together to get through the narrow gaps in this wire, the German machine-gunners found their best killing ground. Dead and wounded men soon blocked every gap, but those still not hit struggled on, having to walk over their comrades' bodies.

"Those who survived to reach 'No Man's Land' continued toward the German trenches, but they had no chance. Only a handful of Newfoundlanders reached the German wire. There they were shot.

"The attack had lasted forty minutes. Of those who had attacked, 91 per cent had become casualties—26 officers and 658 men. What had this battalion, which had sailed with such high hopes from St. John's a year and a half earlier, achieved? It is probable that not a single German soldier was killed or wounded by their attack and no Allied unit had been helped to improve its position."

Reprinted from The First Day on the Somme *by Martin Middlebrook, with the permission of W.W. Norton & Company, Inc. Copyright © 1972 by Martin Middlebrook.*

In early September, the Germans took another 125 000 prisoners at the Battle of the Masurian Lakes. The Russians fell back across the border, confused and demoralized. Within the first two months of the war, Russia had lost two armies.

The Russian army was ill-equipped. Russia did not have a strong munitions industry, and arms could not be shipped by its allies, Britain and France, because Germany controlled access to the Black and Baltic seas. Russian soldiers frequently ran out of weapons and ammunition and at times had to fight with pitchforks and swords! It is estimated that one in three Russian soldiers was sent to the front without a weapon. There they waited for someone to be killed or injured and then took his weapon and fought on.

For the next three years, the Russians fought bravely. But by the beginning of 1917, 3 million Russian soldiers were dead or captured. Within Russia, the constant defeats, combined with poverty and corruption, led to a loss of confidence in the czarist regime. Protest groups marched through the streets of St. Petersburg and Moscow demanding "Peace, land, and bread." Finally, in March 1917, Alexander Kerensky overthrew the Czar and established a moderate reform government. It was prepared to continue the war against the Central Powers, but the new government was unable to satisfy the needs of its own people.

In November 1917, Kerensky's government was toppled by the **Bolsheviks**, a radical socialist group of workers and soldiers led by Vladimir Ilyich Lenin. The Bolsheviks, who would become the Russian Communist Party the following year, opposed the war. Once they had established a revolutionary government they proceeded to negotiate an armistice with the Central Powers. The Treaty of

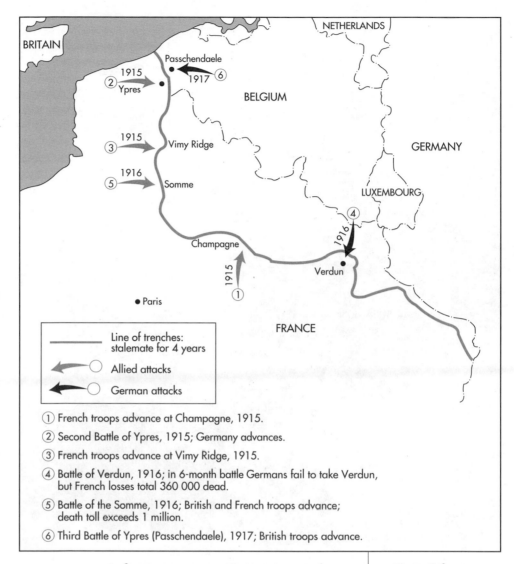

① French troops advance at Champagne, 1915.

② Second Battle of Ypres, 1915; Germany advances.

③ French troops advance at Vimy Ridge, 1915.

④ Battle of Verdun, 1916; in 6-month battle Germans fail to take Verdun, but French losses total 360 000 dead.

⑤ Battle of the Somme, 1916; British and French troops advance; death toll exceeds 1 million.

⑥ Third Battle of Ypres (Passchendaele), 1917; British troops advance.

Figure 2.6:
The Western Front, 1915-18

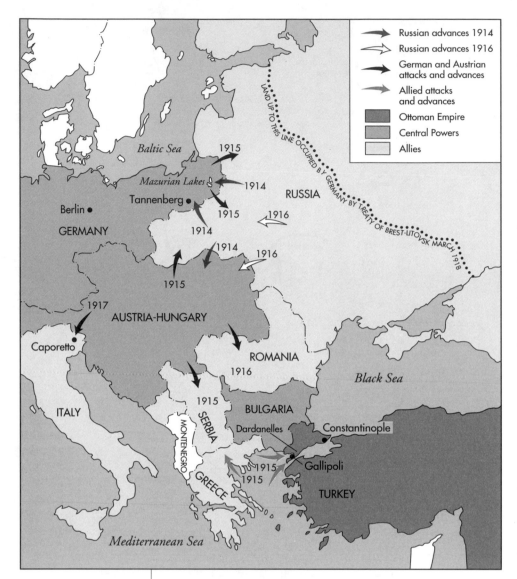

Figure 2.7:
The Eastern Front,
1914-17

TECHNOLOGY AND THE FIRST WORLD WAR

As war clouds gathered, advances in technology were feverishly applied to a new industry—armaments. The types of weapons and the enormous quantities turned out by European, and later American, industries between 1900 and 1918 not only made the war longer and bloodier, but they changed the nature of war.

In September 1916, the battlefields were altered forever when the British introduced the first tanks at the Battle of the Somme. Initially the tanks (primitive by modern standards) were ineffective because the crews were inexperienced and the slow, cumbersome vehicles were frequently caught in the quagmire of the muddy battlefields. Later versions in 1917 and 1918, however, were more effective.

Aviation technology was still in its infancy when war broke out. Military planners saw little use for the weak and unreliable airplanes that were available at the time, except for occasional reconnaissance flights. Nevertheless, military aviation technology made rapid advances over the course of the war, and planes became more numerous, durable, and powerful.

Aerial reconnaissance in particular gained importance in the static warfare

Brest-Litovsk, signed in March 1918, ended Russia's involvement in the war. But the terms were harsh. Russia lost one-third of its population and agricultural land and almost all of its coal reserves. For the time being, Germany dominated eastern Europe.

The Russian armistice was a devastating blow to the Allies. It meant that Germany could relieve food shortages caused by the naval blockade by utilizing the agricultural products of Ukraine. It also allowed Germany to concentrate its forces on the western front against France and Britain.

By the Treaty of Brest-Litovsk, Russia ceded this territory ▮ to Germany and allowed German troops to enter and occupy ▯, including rich wheat lands of Ukraine

① German troops harvest crops of Ukraine, 1918

② German front-line units transferred to western front

Figure 2.8:
The Significance of the Treaty of Brest-Litovsk

of the trenches. Aerial photographs of enemy defences were carefully studied before an attack was launched. Planes were used for observation of enemy movements and artillery, but by 1915 they were taking a more offensive role. The first fighter planes in 1915 were one- or two-seaters armed with forward-firing machine guns. Strategic aerial bombing was carried out by both sides, although it had little serious impact on events. By the end of the war, however, there were dogfights in the air and regular bombing missions. Air power had become a significant military factor. Aviation added a new dimension to the battlefields of war.

On the seas, there were no full-scale naval battles between British and German fleets until the Battle of Jutland in the North Sea in 1916. At the end of May, the British had sailed towards Denmark to intercept the German fleet. The British enjoyed superior naval strength; Germany could only hope to gain victory by isolating part of the fleet and destroying it. This they failed to do. But the British also failed to destroy the German fleet and they suffered the greater losses. Although the Battle of Jutland ended in a draw, both sides claimed victory. But Germany never again directly chal-

lenged the might of the British navy. In the end, the British retained control of the North Sea and the Germans remained confined to the Baltic Sea for the rest of the war.

German submarines, on the other hand, were successful in many of their attempts to destroy British shipping. In

Figure 2.8:
The Significance of the Treaty of Brest-Litovsk

Tank warfare: a British tank mired in the mud

retaliation for a British blockade that prevented Germany from obtaining goods from overseas, Germany announced in 1915 that any Allied merchant ships entering British waters

Germany introduced the Krupp armored car, equipped with airplane guns.

imperialist ramblings of aging European nations. While the war raged on, the United States became increasingly rich and powerful shipping produce and manufactured goods, including war materials, across the ocean. The Americans expected the warring nations to respect the "freedom of the seas" and protested against both British and German blockades.

In 1915, Germany declared the waters around Britain a war zone. They warned that allied vessels would be torpedoed and the safety of neutral vessels would not be guaranteed. On May 7th, a British oceanliner, the *Lusitania*, was torpedoed by German U-boats. Among the 1198 victims were 128 Americans. The incident shocked the United States and served to turn public opinion against Germany. US President Woodrow Wilson warned Germany that another such act would be interpreted as "deliberately unfriendly."

Germany, not wishing to draw the United States into the war, loosened the blockade for two years. In February 1917, however, Germany began a campaign of unrestricted submarine warfare. The German high command hoped that, with supplies cut off, Britain would be forced into a quick surrender before the United States was able to mobilize and send troops. The United States broke off diplomatic relations with Germany and began arming its freighters. During February and March, several American ships were sunk by U-boats. On 6 April 1917, the

would be sunk by German **U-boats**, or submarines. By October 1917, the Germans had destroyed 8 million tonnes of shipping. Britain was in danger of losing its lifeline to the United States and the colonies of the British Empire. Eventually, the submarine war brought the United States into the conflict.

THE UNITED STATES ENTERS THE WAR

The United States was determined to remain neutral, viewing the war as

Between 1914 and 1918, American exports rose from $2 billion to $6 billion annually, largely due to supplying goods to war-ravaged Europe. When the war was over, European countries owed $10 billion to the United States for goods bought on credit.

United States declared war on Germany.

The American entrance into the war ensured a fresh supply of soldiers and materials to the Allied war effort. But the United States was unable to recruit, train, and equip a substantial number of troops to send to Europe until almost a year later. As a result, 1917 was a year of untold hardship and loss for the Allies in Europe.

In the spring of 1918, the armies of both sides were battered and exhausted. Only six divisions of American soldiers had arrived by March. The German army, hoping for a decisive victory before American troops arrived in strength, began a huge offensive on the western front. In March, April, May, and July the Germans attacked Allied troops and advanced to positions not held since 1914. But the casualties on both sides were staggering.

On July 18th, just as the Germans had begun their fourth offensive, the Allies began their counter-offensive, the second Battle of the Marne. The Allies, with French light tanks leading the way and bolstered by eight American divisions, pushed the German lines back over the Marne. The day marked the turning point of the war. From then on the Allies would have the initiative.

In August, Germany suffered its greatest defeat. British, Canadian, and Australian troops launched a surprise attack on the German army near Amiens. The Germans were unable to defend themselves. In one day—called *Der Schwarze Tag* (the black day) by Germany—the Allies took 16 000 prisoners. Germany had run out of reserves. Those soldiers who were still fighting were exhausted, ill-equipped, and demoralized. The Allied forces, on the other hand, were now physically and psychologically bolstered by the constant arrival of American troops.

Germany's collapse was only a matter of time.

In September, at the Battle of Saint-Mihiel, the Americans won their first independent victory. September and October saw more Allied victories from Ypres to Verdun as the Allies kept pressuring the retreating Germans with tanks, airplanes, heavy artillery, and infantry. By October, the Allies had advanced to the German border. On October 28th, the German fleet mutinied at Kiel. The morale of the German forces was cracking.

"It's time to lay the sword and gun away
There'd be no war today,
If fathers all would say,
I didn't raise my son to be a soldier."

Popular anti-war song, 1914

"Over there, over there, send the word, send the word, over there. That the Yanks are coming, the Yanks are coming,
The drums, drums, drumming everywhere.
So prepare, say a prayer, send the word, send the word to beware.
We'll be over, we're coming over, And we won't come back 'til it's over, over there."

Popular pro-war song Over There, *1917*

"There is no other course open to us but to fight it out. Every position must be held to the last man. With our backs to the wall and believing in the justice of our cause, each one of us must fight on to the end."

General Douglas Haig, British commander in chief, April 1918

One by one, Germany's allies bowed out of the war. On October 4th, Germany and Austria-Hungary asked US President Wilson to begin negotiations for an armistice. On November 4th, Austria-Hungary surrendered to the Allies, and on November 7th, the German Kaiser abdicated and fled to Holland. The "war to end all wars" came to a close at eleven o'clock on the eleventh day of the eleventh month of 1918 when Germany accepted peace based upon Wilson's terms. In the words of T.S. Eliot, the end came "not with a bang but with a whimper." But not without a horrendous price: more than 9 million soldiers dead and civilian losses unknown.

In Review

1. Identify and briefly describe a major event for each year of the war.
2. Describe the impact of weapons such as tanks, airplanes, and submarines on the course of the war.
3. What was the significance of the US entry into the war?
4. Outline the major reasons for the defeat of Germany.

Canada and The First World War

Canada entered the war on 4 August 1914, the same day that Britain declared war on Germany. The Canadian government sent this message to the British government: "If unhappily war should ensue, the Canadian people will be united...to maintain the honour of the Empire." Canada's duty seemed clear. Canadians would fight alongside the British.

Despite official support, however, Canada was not united over the war. French-Canadians did not have the strong ties to Britain and they were not as enthusiastic about fighting a war overseas. While they did not object to other Canadians volunteering for duty, they were strongly opposed to **conscription** which required people to enlist.

The Canadian government was able to avoid conscription as long as there were enough volunteers. But as Canadian casualties mounted and enthusiasm for the war waned, fewer recruits enlisted. By the second half of 1916, new enlistments numbered only half of those being lost in battle. Thus in 1917, Prime Minister Robert Borden announced the decision to introduce conscription. While conscription was unpopular in other parts of Canada, in Quebec opposition was especially bit-

The number of Canadians killed in the First World War was 61 326. An additional 172 950 were wounded.

While Canada was not invaded during the war, it did suffer one war-related disaster at home. On 6 December 1917, a munitions ship, the *Mont Blanc*, carrying 6400 t of explosives, collided with the Belgian ship *Imo* in Halifax Harbour. The explosion that resulted destroyed much of the inner city, killing 2000 people and injuring 10 000 more.

ter. The controversy drove a wedge between Quebec and the rest of Canada. For a time, it seemed that the survival of Confederation was in question. Fortunately, the war ended ten months after conscription took effect and few who were conscripted ever saw active service.

THE IMPACT OF THE WAR ON CANADA

One important impact the war had on Canada was to change the status of women. During the war women played a major role on the home front. They replaced male workers in industry, commerce, and agriculture, taking over jobs that had been traditionally reserved for men. Approximately 20 000 women worked in munitions factories and aircraft manufacturing. Thousands more contributed to the war effort through volunteer activities. Overseas, women served as nurses and ambulance drivers, ran canteens, and performed various administrative tasks. By the end of the war opposition to women's suffrage had dissolved. Women won the right to vote in federal elections in 1918.

The war also stimulated Canadian industry. Factories produced guns, ammunition, ships, airplane parts, trucks, and uniforms. The Canadian economy now relied on industry as well as agriculture, lumbering, fishing, and mining. By the end of the war, Canada had been transformed from an agricultural

economy into a growing industrial nation. A stronger and more prosperous Canada had emerged.

Politically, Canada was no longer isolated from the rest of the world, as

Up to 20 000 Canadian women were employed in making shells and aircraft during the First World War.

In 1917, the Canadian government passed the Income Tax Act as a temporary measure designed to generate money needed for the war effort. This "temporary measure" continues to this day!

"No matter what the constitutional historians may say, it was on Easter Monday, 9 April 1917...that Canada became a nation."

D.J. Goodspeed, The Road Past Vimy *(1969)*

After days of heavy bombardment of German lines, Canadian troops attacked at Vimy Ridge on 9 April 1917. By April 14th, they had captured more ground, guns, and prisoners (4000) from the Germans than any previous British offensive. There were 10 602 casualties, of which 3598 were fatalities.

it had been prior to 1914. Canada took its place at the Paris Peace Conference in 1919 and was given representation in the League of Nations, the predecessor to the United Nations, which was formed after the war to promote world peace. This recognition of Canada's war effort contributed greatly to national pride. Canada was no longer a colony of Britain, but a nation.

IN REVIEW

1. Why did the issue of conscription during the First World War divide Canadians?

2. What was the impact of the war on Canada socially, economically, and politically?

3. In your view, should Canada have been involved in the First World War? Explain your answer.

SUMMARY

When war broke out in 1914, the mood was almost festive. Most people believed it would be a short war that would solve many of the problems of the competing nations. As the war dragged on, it became a battle of attrition: who could continue to supply soldiers and weapons in order to outlast the others.

The war cost Europe dearly in terms of human lives and almost ruined the continent economically. The cost of feeding and equipping the military forces was staggering. The destruction left vast areas of Belgium and France in ruins. But while the economies of both the victors and the vanquished in Europe were severely damaged, the American economy was strengthened by the war. Now the international economic balance had shifted in favour of the United States. Even though most European countries recovered by 1924, they faced a new economic order in which the centre of economic power was no longer in Europe.

The First World War caused empires to crumble and the balance of world power to shift dramatically. It set a new direction for the twentieth century.

MAKING CONNECTIONS

1. Review the major causes of the First World War. Identify similar causes that appear to be alive and well in the world today.

2. Compare and contrast the tension in the Balkans in the period before the First World War and in the early 1990s.

3. Identify a modern pro or antiwar song. Present some of the lyrics and discuss their meaning.

DEVELOPING YOUR VOICE

4. Organize a class debate on the topic: The First World War—Whose Responsibility?

5. Assume you are a soldier or battlefield nurse during the war. Write a letter home outlining your experiences, hopes, fears, etc.

6. Write a brief speech stating your views on the First World War to be delivered during a Remembrance Day assembly.

RESEARCHING THE ISSUES

7. Conduct further research into the role played by Canadian women during the war. Your research could include:
    a) activities on the battlefront
    b) activities on the homefront
    c) political gains.

8. Select a major battle of the First World War and prepare a presentation or display showing:
    a) the objectives of the opposing armies;
    b) the basic strategy used by both sides; and
    c) the outcome of the battle.
    You might include maps and statistics.

9. Research the career of one of the key personalities of the war and write a brief biographical profile of this individual.

VIEWPOINTS

ISSUE: WAS GERMANY RESPONSIBLE FOR THE OUTBREAK OF THE FIRST WORLD WAR?

In 1919, the Commission on War Guilt branded Germany and Austria the chief instigators of the First World War. It determined that the Austrian and German governments saw in the assassination of Archduke Ferdinand "a pretext to initiate war" despite the best efforts of Britain, France, and Russia to find a peaceful solution to the conflicts that plagued Europe.

The following viewpoints examine the question of German responsibility for the war. British historian A.J.P. Taylor supports the conclusion of the commission. Revisionist historian Sidney B. Fay argues that this conclusion cannot be supported by the historical evidence. Read these two viewpoints carefully, then complete an Argument Analysis and Evaluation Summary for each reading.

A.J.P. Taylor

"Let me take the events as we know them. The starting-point was the assassination of Archduke Franz Ferdinand at Sarajevo. Why was he there at all? As a gesture of defiance against Serb nationalism; as a demonstration that Bosnia, though inhabited by Serbs and Croats, was going to remain part of the Austrian empire. That explains, too, why Princip and his friends set out to assassinate the Archduke. They were Bosnian Serbs who wanted their national freedom; and far from being encouraged by Serbia, still less acting under Serb orders, their activities were most unwelcome to the Serb government. Serbia was just recovering from the Balkan wars of the previous year; she had not absorbed her new lands; and war with Austria-Hungary was the very last thing that the Serb Government wanted. No one has ever managed to show that the Serb Government had any connection with the plot, though they may have had some

vague knowledge. Indeed it was easy to guess that an Austrian Archduke would be shot at if he visited Sarajevo on 28 June, Serbia's national day.

"...The Austrian government were not much concerned to punish [the assassination]. They wanted to punish a different crime—the crime that Serbia committed by existing as a free national state. The Austrians wanted to prove that they were still a Great Power and somehow to destroy Serbia....This was the first decision which brought about the world war. The man who made it was Count Berchtold, a frivolous aristocrat, but the Foreign Minister of Austria-Hungary.

"He needed the approval of his German ally; and on 5 July he got it. William II, he said, must act against Serbia, even at the risk of war with Russia. Bethmann the German Chancellor...approved also. There was no formal council, no weighty consideration of the issues. Of course the Germans were bluffing. They thought that Russia would let Serbia be destroyed. But, if not, they were ready for war.

"...The Austrians prepared an ultimatum to Serbia....Serbia agreed to nearly all the Austrian demands. It was no use. The Austrians broke off relations and on 28 July declared war. They did this deliberately, to make a peaceful outcome impossible.

"...Could the war of 1914 have been averted? You can make all kinds of conditions: if Austria-Hungary had given her peoples more national freedom; if nationalism had never been thought of; if Germany had relied more on her economic and less on her military power. But in the circumstances of 1914, Great Britain could have kept out of war only if she had been prepared to let Germany defeat France and Russia. France could have kept out of war only if she had surrendered her independence as a Great Power. Russia could have kept out of war only if she had been willing to be strangled at the Straits (the Dardanelles). In short, they could have avoided war only by agreeing that Germany should become the dominant power of the Continent....

From A.J.P. Taylor, "The Outbreak of the First World War," in Europe: Grandeur and Decline *(Harmondsworth, UK: Penguin Books, 1967) pp. 185-189.*

Sidney B. Fay

"None of the powers wanted a European War. Their governing rulers and ministers, all foresaw that it must be a frightful struggle, in which the political results were not absolutely certain, but in which the loss of life, suffering, and economic consequences were bound to be terrible....

"Nevertheless, a European War broke out. Why? Because in each country political and military leaders did certain things which led to mobilization and declarations of war, or failed to do certain things which might have prevented them. In this sense, all the European countries were responsible. It was based on evidence which was incomplete and not always sound.

"Germany did not plot a European War, did not want one, and made genuine, though too belated efforts, to avert one. She was the victim of her alliance with Austria and of her own folly. Austria was her only dependable ally. She could not throw her over, as otherwise she would stand isolated between Russia, where Panslavism and armaments were growing stronger every year, and France, where [past disputes] were not forgotten.

Therefore, Bethmann felt bound to accede to Berchtold's request for support and gave him a free hand to deal with Serbia; he also hoped and expected to 'localize' the Austro-Serbian conflict....When Bethmann realized that Russia was likely to intervene, that England might not remain neutral, and that there was danger of a world war of which Germany and Austria would appear to be the instigators, he tried to call a halt on Austria, but it was too late. He pressed mediation proposals on Vienna, but Berchtold was insensible to the pressure, and the Entente Powers did not believe in the sincerity of his pressure....

"In the forty years following the Franco-Prussian War [1870-71]...there developed a system of alliances which divided Europe into two hostile groups. This hostility was accentuated by the increase of armaments, economic rivalry, nationalist ambitions and antagonisms, and newspaper incitement. But it is very doubtful whether all these dangerous tendencies would have actually led to war, had it not been for the assassination of Franz Ferdinand. That was the factor which consolidated the elements of hostility and started the rapid and complicated succession of events which culminated in a World War, and for that factor Serbian nationalism was primarily responsible.

"But the verdict of the Versailles Treaty that Germany and her allies were responsible for the War, in view of the evidence now available, is historically unsound."

From Sidney B. Fay, The Origins of the World War, *2 Vols. (New York: 1928).*

ANALYSIS AND EVALUATION

Refer to the Argument Analysis and Evaluation Guide on page viii.

1. Using the Argument Analysis and Evaluation Guide, compare the readings by Taylor and Fay.

2. Decide which of the viewpoints you tend to support and explain why. Be sure to use specific information from this textbook, the readings, and other sources to support your position.

3. State and support your position on the issue: "Was Germany responsible for the outbreak of the First World War?"

CHAPTER THREE

Change and Conflict Between the Wars: 1919–1939

"It is easier to make war than to make peace."

Georges Clemenceau (1841-1929), French Premier (1906-09,1917-20)

"This is not peace. It is an armistice for twenty years".

Marshal Ferdinand Foch, French Commander of the Allied Armies, speaking on 28 June 1919, the day the Treaty of Versailles was signed

Left: In the Black Square

❖ OVERVIEW

Ending the First World War had been a long and difficult struggle. Designing a fair peace proved to be equally challenging. The Allies had the difficult task of redrawing the map of Europe and establishing the conditions for a lasting peace. But the process seemed doomed from the start. The defeated nations of Europe were barred from the peace process. The new communist government in Russia was refused representation at the talks. Decision-making power rested in the hands of three governments—Britain, France, and the United States.

The impact of the **Treaty of Versailles** was hardly what the Allies had intended. Instead of an agreement for peace, the treaty seemed more like an **armistice**—a brief respite before the renewal of war.

not recognize its Bolshevik government. The defeated nations were not given any status at the negotiations, so their fate would be decided for them. While all present had a say in the terms of the peace treaty, the real decision-making power lay with the three leading victorious nations: Britain, France, and the United States.

The damage the war had inflicted was horrendous. Ten million lives had been lost. The direct financial costs were estimated at $180 billion, with another $150 billion in indirect costs. Four great empires had crumbled: Hohenzollern Germany, Habsburg Austria-Hungary, Romanov Russia, and Ottoman Turkey. The task that lay before the peacemakers was to establish political and economic stability in Europe and to ensure that the First World War was, in US President Woodrow Wilson's words, truly "the war to end all wars."

The United States was regarded with great hope by millions of war-weary Europeans. President Wilson offered a vision for a new world order, along with the moral authority and economic power to get things done. Wilson joined the American peace delegation in Paris. His personal participation in the peace process and his pledge "to make the world safe for democracy" was welcomed in Europe with great hope and enthusiasm.

FOCUS QUESTIONS

1. What were the terms of the Treaty of Versailles?
2. Was the Treaty of Versailles a just peace settlement?
3. What was the impact of **communism** on the peoples of Russia and Europe?
4. Why did **fascism** gain such appeal in Europe during the interwar years?
5. What factors accounted for the failure of the League of Nations?

THE SEARCH FOR PEACE

The Paris Peace Conference, convened on 18 January 1919, was the largest and most important diplomatic gathering since the Congress of Vienna in 1815. Thirty Allied nations were given seats at the conference. Russia's seat remained empty since the Allies did

WILSON AND THE FOURTEEN POINTS

Wilson believed that war was caused by three major factors: secret diplomacy

Figure 3.1 Wilson's Fourteen Points

I.   Open covenants of peace, openly arrived at, after which there shall be no private international understandings of any kind but diplomacy shall proceed always frankly and in the public view.

II. Absolute freedom of navigation upon the seas, outside territorial waters, alike in peace and in war.

III. The removal, so far as possible, of all economic barriers and the establishment of an equality of trade conditions among all the nations consenting to the peace and associating themselves for its maintenance.

IV. Adequate guarantees given and taken that national armaments will be reduced to the lowest point consistent with domestic safety.

V.   A free, open-minded, and absolutely impartial adjustment of all colonial claims, based on the principle that in determining all such questions of sovereignty, the interests of the populations concerned must have equal weight with the equitable claims of the government whose title is to be determined.

VI. The evacuation of all Russian territory and...assistance of every kind that she may need and may herself desire.

VII. Belgium...must be evacuated [by the Germans] and restored.

VIII. All French territory should be freed and the invaded portions restored, the wrong done to France in the matter...of Alsace-Lorraine...should be righted.

IX. A readjustment of frontiers of Italy should be effected along clearly recognizable lines of nationality.

X.   The people of Austria-Hungary, whose place among the nations we wish to see safe-guarded and assured, should be accorded the freest opportunity of autonomous development.

XI. Romania, Serbia, and Montenegro should be evacuated...Serbia accorded free access to the sea.

XII. The Turkish portion of the present Ottoman Empire should be assured a secure sovereignty, but the other nationalities which are now under Turkish rule...[should be allowed] autonomous development.

XIII. An independent Polish state...should include the territories inhabited by indisputably Polish populations...[and should] be assured a free and secure access to the sea.

XIV. A general association of nations must be formed under specific covenants for the purpose of affording mutual guarantees of political independence and territorial integrity to great and small states alike. "The world must be made safe for democracy."

among nations; the tendency of dominant nationalities to oppress ethnic minorities; and autocratic governments ruled by elites. He believed that these causes of war had to be removed if the world was to have lasting peace. Wilson's **Fourteen Points**, announced on 8 January 1918, addressed these key issues.

Wilson hoped the Fourteen Points would be the basis for a new world order, but as the hard realities of negotiations proceeded, these principles gradually receded to the background. Key decisions were made in secret by the big powers. In time, the high public expectations based on Wilson's idealistic statements would be shattered.

THE PARIS PEACE CONFERENCE: DIFFERENT EXPECTATIONS

The major powers had different expectations at the Paris Peace Conference that began on 18 January 1919. The United States was determined to establish a new world order based on Wilson's Fourteen Points. Added to this idealism was the practical desire to resume the free flow of trade so that American business could continue to prosper. Britain, too, was eager to establish a peaceful atmosphere in which business could flourish. France, where the northern provinces had been a vast battlefield and where the war dead numbered over 1 million, wanted assurances that it would be able to rebuild without threat from Germany, its neighbour. Thus each country had different expectations of the peace treaty.

The United States was a new player in the affairs of Europe. The long tradition of American diplomacy had been one of isolation. Essentially, the Americans were eager to revert to that policy. Their greatest national interest in the peace process was to maintain their robust economy. To that end, the US placed pressure on Britain and France to repay their war loans. These war allies in turn decided to pass on this financial burden to Germany.

"The Allied and Associated Governments affirm and Germany accepts the responsibility of Germany and her allies for causing all the loss and damage to which the Allied and Associated Governments and their nationals have been subjected as a consequence of the war imposed upon them by the aggression of Germany and her allies."

The War Guilt Clause, Treaty of Versailles, 1919

French Objectives

France had two basic goals at the peace conference: national security and financial **reparations**. To ensure national security, France wanted to remove the threat from German military power. In the prewar years, Germany

had developed into a powerful military and economic nation. To keep Germany in check, France had forged an alliance with Russia. Now, however, with Russia in the hands of the Bolsheviks, France had to find other guarantees of security. France demanded the return of Alsace-Lorraine, which had been annexed by Germany following the Franco-Prussian War of 1870. This was accepted by the Allies without question. But France also demanded the German Rhineland to serve as a buffer zone between the two countries. Seizure of this territory clearly violated Wilson's principle of **national self-determination**, and the demand was rejected. However, if France could not have the Rhineland, it demanded that the region be neutralized. The compromise was a **demilitarized zone**. Germany was prohibited from placing troops or fortifications within 50 km of the east bank of the Rhine River. As insurance, the Allies would occupy the west bank for fifteen years. This settlement, combined with other military restrictions and a pledge of immediate military assistance from Britain and the United States in the event of German aggression, satisfied France's security concerns.

The other French goal was to gain financial compensation for losses during the war. Northern France had been devastated after four years of German occupation. Furthermore, the German army had destroyed what was left of the region when they withdrew in 1918. Mines were flooded, railways destroyed, and fields torn apart by shells and trenches. To make up for the German destruction of French coal mines, France was awarded coal rights in Germany's Saar Valley until 1935.

French premier Georges Clemenceau demanded that Germany pay full reparations for war damages. The Americans felt that reparations should be limited to what Germany could afford to pay in thirty years. But the French disagreed, demanding that Germany pay whatever damages were assessed with no time limit. Eventually Clemenceau agreed to the thirty-year limit on the condition that it be extended if necessary. In 1921, Germany was presented with a reparations bill of more than $30 billion, of which the French share was 52 per cent. It was impossible for Germany to pay this amount, and by 1922 the country had already fallen behind in its payments.

The "Big Four"—Italian prime minister Vittorio Orlando, British prime minister David Lloyd George, French prime minister Georges Clemenceau, and American president Woodrow Wilson— signed the Treaty of Versailles.

British Objectives

The key British objective at the conference was to ensure the security of the sea lanes to its empire. This meant that German sea power had to be crippled. This was achieved by reducing the German navy to a token force of six warships, prohibiting German submarines, and redistributing German colonies to the Allies. Britain was not prepared to support French demands for huge reparation payments or territorial gains. If Germany were forced to pay massive reparations to France, the result would be a weak Germany and a strong France. In 1919, Britain was beginning to fear the spread of Bolshevism more than it feared the rise of Germany. Both British prime minister Lloyd George and Liberal Party colleague Winston Churchill felt that if Germany were weakened too much, it could fall into the hands of communist Russia. So Britain began to soften its stand on reparations.

THE PEACE OF PARIS, 1919

When the terms of the peace treaty were established by the Allies, Germany was invited to Versailles for the formal signing on 18 June 1919. Germany signed the treaty, but only under protest. The Germans were particularly incensed by the War Guilt clause that stipulated that Germany accept responsibility for the war. It was a clause that would have serious repercussions in the years to come.

In the months following the signing of the Treaty of Versailles, separate treaties were signed with Austria (the Treaty of St. Germain, 1919); Bulgaria (the Treaty of Neuilly, 1919); Turkey (the Treaty of Sevres, 1920); and Hungary (the Treaty of Trianon, 1920). Seven new countries were created from the former Russian, Turkish, and Austro-Hungarian empires, including Latvia, Estonia, Lithuania, Finland, Czechoslovakia, and Poland. Millions

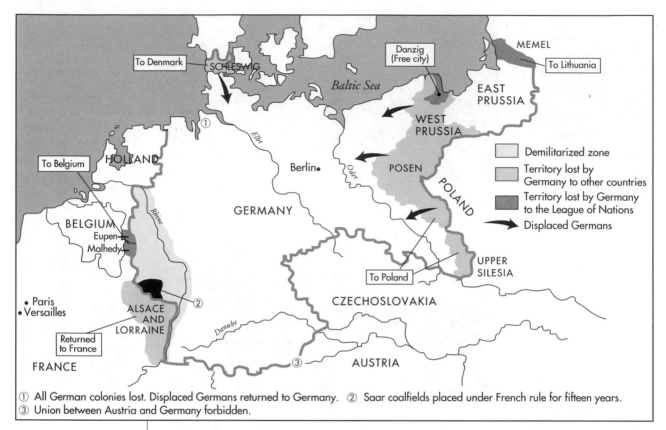

① All German colonies lost. Displaced Germans returned to Germany.   ② Saar coalfields placed under French rule for fifteen years.
③ Union between Austria and Germany forbidden.

Figure 3.2:
The Price of Defeat:
Germany's Losses by the
Terms of the Treaty
of Versailles

of ordinary people found themselves living as minorities in new countries or in different countries after the boundaries were redrawn. The new Europe became a breeding ground for political tension and unrest.

EVALUATING THE TREATY

The Treaty of Versailles created controversy that continues even to this day. It was later used by German leaders to illustrate how unfairly the world was treating Germany.

The League of Nations came into being with the signing of the treaty. This international organization of nations was part of Woodrow Wilson's vision of a new world order. Ironically, the United States Senate rejected the treaty and along with it the League of Nations. Even without American membership, however, the League was a

step towards the establishment of an international arbitrator of disputes, although it came to be seen as a European rather than a world body.

Reparation payments were blamed for Germany's staggering inflation and economic collapse. To make these payments, the German government printed paper money until German currency was worthless. By 1923, the German economy was in ruins. Furthermore, the military restrictions imposed on Germany were seen as harsh and humiliating. Thousands of demobilized German troops, resenting the terms of the treaty and disgruntled with a political system that had been incapable of striking a better deal in Paris, joined right-wing political groups. The groundwork was laid for the emergence of the Nazi movement.

The treaty provided fertile ground for propaganda against the Allies' treat-

VOICES

THE WAR GUILT CLAUSE

When the United States entered the war, US President Wilson said: "We have no quarrel with the German people...we have no feeling toward them but one of sympathy and friendship. It was not upon their impulse that their government acted in entering this war." Wilson's sentiments had given Germans hope that the peace settlement would not be harsh, especially since they had deposed the Kaiser and set up a new government. When the terms of the Treaty of Versailles, signed by Wilson, were made public, however, Germans were shocked. The hardest part of the treaty for Germany to accept was the War Guilt clause, and it caused lasting resentment, as reflected in a speech given at the peace conference by the German Foreign Minister Count von Brockdorff-Rantzau.

Later the Allies admitted that the War Guilt clause was unfair and one-sided, as indicated by historian William Keylor. How does the alleged misunderstanding illustrate the saying "In politics, perception is reality"?

Count von Brockdorff-Rantzau

"It is demanded of us that we confess ourselves to be the only ones guilty of starting the war. Such a confession in my mouth would be a lie. We are far from declining any responsibility that this great world war has come to pass, and for its having been made in the way in which it was made...but we energetically deny that Germany and its people, who were convinced that they were making a war of defence, were alone guilty."

Count von Brockdorff-Rantzau, Paris, 1919

William Keylor

"...this article [the War Guilt clause] was designed to protect Germany against any allied claims for reimbursement of the total costs of the war: Germany was to be held morally responsible for the war and its consequences, but legally liable only for the narrowly defined damages specified in the treaty. Somehow this article was taken to imply the establishment of the principle of Germany's unilateral 'war guilt.' Such an interpretation was entirely baseless. The word 'guilt' does not appear in the article. Nor was there any evidence of a 'unilateral' indictment of Germany: almost identical language was incorporated in the treaties subsequently signed with Germany's allies, Austria, Hungary, Bulgaria, and Turkey. Yet the myth of the 'War Guilt clause,' repeated by successive governments in the 1920s and later used to good effect by Hitler, was to become...a source of resentment in Germany...."

From William Keylor, The Twentieth Century World: An International History, *(New York: Oxford University Press, 1992), p. 85.*

ment of Germany and it was employed with great success. German violations of the treaty grew bolder and more fla-grant until finally Adolf Hitler and the Nazi Party effectively killed the Treaty of Versailles in the early 1930s.

Figure 3.3 The Main Terms of the Treaty of Versailles

1. Territorial Changes
    (a) Alsace-Lorraine to be returned to France
    (b) Belgium, Poland, and Czechoslovakia to receive German border areas
    (c) Poland re-established as an independent state with access to the Baltic Sea (the Polish Corridor to Danzig)
    (d) Danzig to be a free city under the League of Nations
    (e) Germany to give up all overseas colonies to the League of Nations; mandates for administering former German colonies assigned to Britain, France, and Japan

2. Military Terms
    (a) German army reduced to 100 000 troops
    (b) Germany forbidden to have an airforce
    (c) Most German naval vessels, including the submarine force, to be handed over to the Allies
    (d) Germany forbidden to have heavy military frontier fortifications

3. Admission of War Guilt
    (a) Germany forced to accept responsibility for starting the war

4. Reparations
    (a) Germany to pay war reparations to France and Belgium for damages caused during the war
    (b) Germany to pay reparations for shipping damages by turning over part of its merchant marine fleet

5. Other Terms
    (a) Germany to cede Saar coal mines to France for fifteen years
    (b) Allied troops to occupy the Rhineland for fifteen years
    (c) East bank of Rhine to be demilitarized

IN REVIEW

1. What were the key objectives of France, Britain, and the United States at the Paris Peace Conference? In your opinion, which country was most successful in achieving its objectives? Explain your answer.

2. List the major terms of the Treaty of Versailles. Decide which you think were appropriate and which were inappropriate. Give reasons for your assessment.

3. (a) Why did Wilson's idealism not gain much support at the peace conference?
    (b) In your opinion, do Wilson's Fourteen Points have any relevance in today's world?

4. Summarize the two viewpoints on the War Guilt clause. Which viewpoint do you find most acceptable? Why?

5. How did the Treaty of Versailles lead to the rise of Hitler and the Nazi Party?

THE CHALLENGE OF SOVIET COMMUNISM

RUSSIA IN THE FIRST WORLD WAR

Russia entered the First World War with great hopes of victory over Germany. However, an inefficient officer corps, poorly trained soldiers, and inferior equipment led to one disastrous defeat after another. By 1917, Russian soldiers had lost the will to fight. At home, starving citizens began to riot for "peace, land, and bread." The Czar was forced to abdicate, and a moderate social democratic government took power. Yet the protests, strikes, and riots continued to escalate. In November, the Bolsheviks under Vladimir Ilich Lenin seized power.

One of Lenin's first tasks was to end Russian involvement in the war. In March 1918, Russia signed the Treaty of Brest-Litovsk. This forced Russia to acknowledge the independence of Ukraine, Poland, Finland, Latvia, Estonia, and Lithuania and to agree to substantial reparation payments. This treaty cost Russia over 30 per cent of its population and 75 per cent of its coal and iron ore. But with Germany's defeat later that year, the treaty became little more than a piece of paper.

With Russian involvement in the war over, Lenin concentrated on achieving absolute political control for the Communist Party. But the Western Allies launched military intervention in Russia in order to stop the spread of Bolshevism and bring Russia back into the war. The war on Bolshevik forces, which lasted for three years, involved Japan in the east and the Allies, Poland, Czechoslovakia, and the White Russians in the west. The armed conflict and civil war caused chaos in Russia until the Communists were finally able to overcome their enemies. The lasting result was a deep distrust on the part of the Communists towards all Western powers. The atmosphere of hostility and fear would permeate Russian attitudes towards the Western nations for the next seventy years.

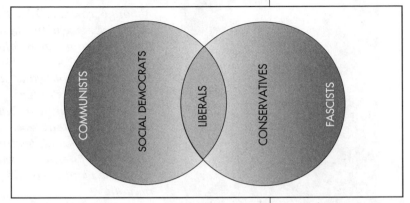

THE NEW COMMUNIST STATE

The First World War, the civil war, and Western intervention had a severe impact on the new communist state. Agricultural regions, particularly Ukraine, had been a battleground for years; food production had collapsed. Industry was completely disrupted; most factories lay idle. Mines had been destroyed and iron production had dropped to 3 per cent of 1913 figures.

The policies of state control introduced by the communist government almost paralysed the economy. The government assumed ownership of many aspects of the economy, such as mines, banks, and the oil industry, as well as any business employing more than ten workers. Foreign trade dried up; transportation broke down. Dissatisfaction spread. Strikes and protests added to the chaos.

The government requisitioned all surplus food to feed the people in the cities. This in turn antagonized the peasants. They retaliated by growing

Figure 3.4:
The Politics of the Right and Left

*The terms **right** and **left** are commonly used in describing political parties. In this diagram conservatives are seen as a party of the right, democratic socialists (or social democrats) as a party of the left, and liberals as a party of the centre. However, in the outer parts of the spheres are two parties that are distinct from others in that they reject democracy and freedom and support totalitarian beliefs. In this sense, fascism is a rightist party and communism a leftist party.*

PROFILE

VLADIMIR ILICH LENIN (1870-1924)

Although conceived in the nineteenth century, the ideas of Karl Marx swept through the twentieth century like a tidal wave, bringing war, revolution, hope, and despair to hundreds of millions of people. Much of the history of the century has been the story of brutal struggles between supporters and opponents of Marx's ideas.

*Marx had argued that all history was the history of class struggle and that eventually the poor, oppressed workers would rise up and destroy their capitalist masters, the **bourgeoisie**. He foresaw a world where no classes would exist and all people would live and prosper in communal harmony and freedom.*

Marx's vision of a world free from hatred, inequality, and oppression inspired dreamers and revolutionaries across the globe. But it was Lenin who put Marxist theory into practice by creating the first communist state. After reading this profile, why do you think Lenin was able to successfully mount a revolution?

"We must now set about building a proletarian socialist state in Russia."
Lenin, November 1917

"While the state exists, there can be no freedom. When there is freedom there will be no state."
Lenin, State and Revolution, *1919*

"It is true that liberty is precious—so precious that it must be rationed."
Lenin, 1919

Vladimir Ilich Ulyanov, or Lenin, the revolutionary name by which he was known, was the architect of the greatest political revolution in the twentieth century. Lenin's story reveals the profound impact that one human being can have on the course of world history.

Lenin was born in 1870 to a family of the lower Russian nobility. His older brother Alexander was arrested, tried, and executed for plotting the

assassination of the Czar when Lenin was still a teenager. This stigmatized the family and Lenin was unable to continue his law studies. Instead he joined a group of Marxist revolutionaries. He was arrested and exiled to Siberia, where he married another revolutionary, Nadezdha Krupskaya, who was equally committed to the overthrow of the Czarist regime.

In 1900, with his term of exile completed, Lenin and Krupskaya travelled to western Europe, where they carried on with their underground revolutionary activities. In 1903, the Russian Marxists held a congress in Brussels and London to unify Russian Marxism. Instead, the congress served to split the Marxists into two groups—the **Mensheviks** and the **Bolsheviks**. Lenin headed the Bolsheviks.

When the First World War erupted, Lenin believed the end of Czarist Russia was imminent. Under mounting pressure from military defeats and internal economic and political chaos, the

Czar abdicated in March 1917. Lenin and other exiled revolutionaries hurried back to Russia.

Lenin skilfully won support for the Bolsheviks with slogans promising peace, land, and bread. In the political chaos of the months following the Czar's abdication, Lenin had a plan for decisive action. He knew the time was ripe. "History will not forgive us if we do not act now," he urged. When the Bolsheviks did strike, in November 1917, they were victorious. The coup was well planned and executed, with simultaneous takeovers by workers, sailors, and soldiers in Petrograd and Moscow. Thus a small group of exiles had engineered the first communist revolution in history.

Consolidating the victory would take years. In 1918, thirty different groups claimed to rule Russia. However, Lenin, with unwavering support from Leon Trotsky and Joseph Stalin, and backed by the Red Army, defeated all rivals. The new secret police, the Cheka, was created and charged with eliminating all opposition in a campaign referred to as the Red Terror. Bourgeoisie, reactionaries, moderate socialists, and proletarians alike were eliminated to establish the communist regime. The Czar, his wife, and five children were murdered in 1918 to prevent counter-revolutionary forces from rallying behind the monarchy.

In 1918, an attempt was made on Lenin's life when a member of a rival left-wing socialist group shot and seriously wounded him. The would-be assassin, Fanny Kaplan, and her collaborators were executed. A few years later, Lenin suffered a series of debilitating strokes, and in 1924 he died. His death set the stage for the emergence of Stalin and a far bloodier chapter in the history of the new communist nation.

only enough food for their own needs. A severe drought ushered in the great famine of 1921-22 in which between 4 and 5 million people died.

By 1921, Lenin realized that the success of the communist revolution was threatened. It was necessary to build in incentives for workers, farmers, and industrial leaders to work harder and more efficiently. Thus the **New Economic Policy**, which incorporated capitalist practices, was introduced in 1921.

The New Economic Policy (NEP), 1921-28

"Two steps forward, one step backward." Lenin realized that to save communism, it was necessary to temporarily step backwards and introduce aspects of private ownership and personal profit—that is, **capitalism**. Lenin announced at the Communist Party Congress in 1921 that the country would move backwards towards a **mixed economy**—socialism blended with capitalism. Under the NEP, some ownership of small industries was per-

mitted. Farmers could once again sell part of their produce for personal profit. Rights of private ownership were reinstated, and foreign investment in Russian industries was invited. As a result, agricultural production gradually increased, although not fast enough to prevent the devastating famine of 1921-22. Industrial production also increased and in the period up to 1927 the Russian standard of living gradually improved. The easing of some of the economic hardships made the new government more acceptable to the people.

In 1922, the Communist Party created the Union of Soviet Socialist Republics. The new Soviet Union at first consisted of the Russian, Ukrainian, White Russian, and Transcaucasian Soviet Socialist Republics. Theoretically this was a voluntary federation of autonomous soviet republics; in fact, however, the federation was dominated by the Russian majority and their Communist Party leaders.

In 1924 Lenin died just as his revolution was taking firm hold. Power was

In the Russian famine of 1921-22, millions of people like these children at the Samara Camp died of starvation.

eventually seized by Joseph Stalin, who created a ruthless dictatorship which was to rapidly transform the Soviet Union.

The Five-Year Plans

Beginning in 1928, the government embarked on a series of Five-Year Plans to greatly increase industrial production. If the USSR was to be strong enough to resist foreign attack, it would have to catch up with the rest of the industrial world. Goals were set and priorities established to increase production—more machinery, greater steel production, new factories, more oil production, and more electrical power plants. The policies were initially successful and the economy began to return to pre-war production levels. However, famine was once again threatening the country. In January 1928, the amount of grain needed to feed urban populations experienced a serious shortfall, due in part to hoarding by farmers. In Stalin's view, several problems were emerging.

First, the success of the NEP had created a new class of successful farmers—the **kulaks**, who were thriving under a semi-capitalist system and who had no use for a communist society.

Second, Stalin recognized the potential danger from foreign intervention or invasion. Throughout Russian history, whenever Russia had been attacked by outside forces, its main weakness had been technological inferiority. In order to preserve the only communist state in the world, the Soviets would have to increase their industrial and military power. The existing rate of industrial expansion was too slow; rapid, large-scale industrialization was needed. But the question was, where would they get the investment capital? They could not rely on foreign investors, and there was not sufficient revenue being generated within the USSR. Stalin concluded that the capital must come from agriculture; therefore agriculture must be totally restructured for maximum efficiency and the profits expropriated for industrial development.

THE RESULTS OF THE FIRST TWO FIVE-YEAR PLANS (1928-38)

Stalin's attempt at creating a **command economy** yielded two opposing results. The first was the collapse of Soviet agriculture as farm labourers who resisted the attempts at **collectivization** were eliminated. Agricultural production dropped sharply. The situation was further aggravated by the famine of 1933. The loss of life was in the millions. Output began to recover slowly in the late 1930s, with the help of improved farm machinery, an army of agricultural scientists, and strict control of the collectives.

The second result was more positive. The Soviet Union was able to invest heavily in industrial development as well as in science, education, and the military. The number of people employed in agriculture declined sharply while educational opportunities

VOICES

STALIN THE TYRANT

The twentieth century has witnessed many dictatorships. Yet perhaps one figure stands out as the embodiment of the dictator: Joseph Stalin, leader of the Soviet Union from 1929 to 1953. Stalin played a minor role in the revolution of 1917. But he caught Lenin's attention and was rewarded with a series of administrative posts, eventually leading to the position of General Secretary of the Politburo. After Lenin's death, Stalin and Leon Trotsky, one of the intellectuals of the revolutionary movement, struggled for leadership of the Soviet Union. After a bitter battle, Stalin ousted Trotsky.

As dictator of the Soviet Union, Stalin embarked on a dramatic policy of economic transformation. He cast aside Lenin's NEP policies and centralized all economic and political power in himself. Those who resisted Stalin's reforms were eliminated. The Soviet Union became a state characterized by repression, fear, torture, threats, mass trials, imprisonment, and execution. Millions died as a result of Stalin's **purges**—Bolshevik comrades from the 1917 Revolution, government leaders, army and police officers, even members of Stalin's own family. No group escaped the terror. As you read about Stalin, consider how his accomplishments should be judged in view of his methods.

George Kennan, historian

"...We know pretty well today what at one time we could only suspect; that this was a man of incredible criminality, of a criminality effectively without limits; a man apparently foreign to the very experience of love, without pity or mercy; a man in whose entourage no one was ever safe; a man whose hand was set against all that could not be useful to him at the moment; a man who was most dangerous of all to those who were his closest collaborators in crime...he liked to be the sole custodian of his own secrets....We are confronted

with a record beside which the wildest murder mystery seems banal. I cannot attempt to list the man's crimes. Trotsky seriously charged that Stalin poisoned Lenin....He evidently either killed his young wife in 1932, or drove her to suicide in his presence. There is every probability...that it was Stalin himself who inspired the murder of his Number Two in the Party, S.M. Kirov, in 1934. How many others...died as a result of Stalin's malignant ministrations, we can only guess. There are at least half a dozen...the writer Maxim Gorky....That the man who split Trotsky's skull with an axe in Mexico City in 1940 did so at Stalin's instigation is beyond question. By way of response, apparently, to what seems to have been some opposition to his purposes on the part of the seventeenth Party Congress in 1934, Stalin killed, in the ensuing purges of 1936 to 1938, 1108 out of a total of 1966 members of the Congress. Of the Central Committee elected at that Congress and still officially in office, he killed 98 out of 139—a clear majority, that is, of the body from which ostensibly he drew his authority. These deaths were only a fraction, numerically, of those which resulted from the purges of those years. Most of the victims were high officials of the Party, the army, or the Soviet government apparatus.

"All this is aside from the stupendous brutalities which Stalin perpetrated against the common people; notably in the process of collectivization, and also in some of his wartime measures...[deaths run] into the millions. But this is not to mention the broken homes, the twisted childhoods, and the millions of people who were half-killed; who survived these ordeals only to linger on in misery, with broken health and broken hearts."

From Russia and the West Under Stalin and Lenin *by George F. Kennan. Copyright © 1960 by James Hotchkiss, Trustee. By permission of Little, Brown and Company.*

In Stalin's Russia, his picture was prominently displayed everywhere.

expanded. As a result, there were more trained and educated professionals. New power plants and manufacturing facilities developed, spurring on the country's surge towards industrialization. The rapid transformation from a peasant agricultural society to a modern industrialized one was unprecedented. By the late 1930s, Russia's industrial output exceeded that of France, Italy, and Japan.

In Review

1. Summarize the terms of the Treaty of Brest-Litovsk. Do you support or reject Lenin's decision to withdraw Russia from the First World War? Explain your answer.

2. Summarize the problems faced by Russians during the period of war communism (1918-21).

3. How did the New Economic Policy attempt to revive the Russian economy?

4. What were the objectives and results of the first Five-Year Plans (1928-32 and 1933-38)?

5. In your opinion, was the economic progress made under Stalin worth the price paid by the Russian people? Explain.

THE RISING TIDE OF FASCISM

THE FASCIST PARTY IN ITALY

The politics of 1920s Europe became increasingly polarized between communism on the left and fascism on the right. The depressed economic conditions in the aftermath of the First World War led to pessimism about the future. People were impatient with moderate policies that did not seem to effectively deal with important issues. In Britain, the Liberal Party faded as a political force in 1924; the Labour Party, a left-wing coalition, took power the same year. In Germany, while the Social Democrats remained strong, the forces of the right were gaining power. The most dramatic change, however, occurred in Italy where the extreme right, under Benito Mussolini, swept aside all democratic institutions and established a dictatorship in just a few years.

Mussolini's opposition to communism won him the support of industrialists and wealthy landowners who feared a communist takeover similar to that in Russia. His claim to be "of the people" and his promise to restore order and greatness to Italy appealed to the working class. Those who opposed the Fascists were beaten and in some cases murdered. Before long the **Blackshirts**, Mussolini's unofficial army, dominated Italy's politics.

Once Mussolini had accepted King Victor Emmanuel's invitation to become Italy's prime minister in 1922, he wasted little time eliminating the opposition through intimidation and violence. By 1925, he had control of the press, the police, and the government. No other political parties were allowed. Strikes and lockouts were illegal. *Il Duce* was

Benito Mussolini ruled Italy for twenty-one years: 1922–1943.

the dictator of Italy. It was a dictatorship that would last for twenty-one years.

Under Mussolini, Italy did experience some economic recovery. Unemployment was reduced by public works schemes in housing, hydroelectric power, highways, and land reclamation. However, after 1929 the Great Depression hit Italy as it did most of the world, causing unemployment and hardship. It was a situation that gave Mussolini justification for total state control of the economy.

With the rise of Hitler, Mussolini's international stature rose. Hitler remained a strong supporter of Mussolini to the bitter end when Mussolini was executed by Italian partisans in 1945.

THE NAZI PARTY IN GERMANY

In Germany, even more than in Italy, fascism found mass support and flourished. Adolf Hitler, who led the German movement, initially admired

> "The great masses of the people ...will more easily fall victims to a big lie than to a small one."
>
> *Adolf Hitler in* Mein Kampf

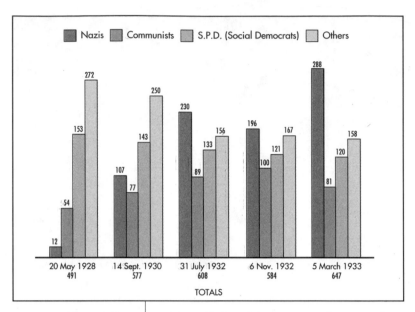

Figure 3.5:
*Nazis at the Polls,
1928-33*

Mussolini and incorporated many of the principles of Italian fascism into his Nazi doctrine. Like the Italian Fascists, the Nazis denounced democracy, liberalism, capitalism, and communism. They called for a powerful German state, strengthened by unity of purpose and decisive action. At every opportunity, they attempted to increase fear of communism and decrease confidence in democracy and the existing government.

> "Whoever can conquer the street will one day conquer the state, for every form of power politics and any dictatorially-run state has its roots in the street."
>
> *Joseph Goebbels in a speech to the National Socialist Party Congress, August 1927*

> "The importance of physical terror against the individual and the masses...became clear to me."
>
> *Adolf Hitler in* Mein Kampf

HITLER'S GERMANY

After becoming Chancellor in January 1933, Hitler took immediate steps to establish a totalitarian state. Within two months, the Reichstag passed the Emergency Decree and the Enabling Law, giving Hitler virtually unlimited power. All political parties, except the Nazis, were abolished. A secret police force—the **Gestapo**—was created. Concentration camps were set up. The judiciary and civil service were purged of possible dissidents. Jews were removed from the universities and public service. Anyone could be arrested without charges and imprisoned without a trial.

Nazi Persecution of the Jews

As Hitler's power was consolidated, the Nazis launched their campaign of persecution against Jews. The **Nuremburg Laws** of 1935 deprived Jews of German citizenship and outlawed marriage between Jews and **Aryans**. Jews were not permitted to practise law or medicine or to perform music. Many Jewish shops were closed, synagogues were shut down, and properties were confiscated.

The situation escalated on 7 November 1938, after a German diplomat in Paris was assassinated by a Jewish youth. Two nights later, on November 9, Jewish communities across Germany were attacked. This night of terror became known as **Kristallnacht**—the night of broken glass. Synagogues, homes, and shops went up in flames. Jews were arrested, beaten, and even murdered. The Jewish community was forced to pay an atonement fine to repair the damages that resulted from *Kristallnacht.* They could no longer own stores or businesses or engage in trade of any kind. Jewish children were banned from attending school. Places of public entertainment, culture, and sports were

PROFILE

ADOLF HITLER (1889-1945)

Adolf Hitler has been called many things—a "genius," "the greatest demagogue in history," "a madman." Whatever the reality, he had a tremendous effect upon the history of the twentieth century. His voice was mesmerizing, strident, and all too prophetic. Hitler was to be the touchstone that unleashed forces that ultimately led to the deaths of 50 million people. As you read this profile, consider how a person like Hitler could rise to power. Was it due to events and desperate times? Or was he a skilled political leader?

"One truth which must always be borne in mind is that the majority can never replace the man."
   Adolf Hitler, Mein Kampf, *1925*

"The Marxists taught—if you will not be my brother, I will bash your skull in. Our motto shall be—if you will not be a true German, I will bash your skull in."
   Adolf Hitler, 1933

Adolf Hitler was not born in Germany, but in a small town in Austria. His early years were marred by the deaths of a brother and sister and the abuse of a drunken, overbearing father. He was a failure at school and left as a drop-out. Afterwards he became a vagrant, working at menial jobs. He was a bitter, desperate young man with a bleak future.

When the First World War broke out, Hitler rushed to join the Austrian army, but was rejected as unfit. He moved to Germany where he successfully enlisted in the army. For Hitler, the war was a great adventure. He had a good war record, earning medals for his service. But the return to civilian life meant a return to poverty and obscurity. At the time, Germany was boiling over with discontent and revolutionary fervour. Hitler threw himself with vigour and determination into this political maëlstrom. He joined a tiny political party of other disenchanted, ruthless young men and soon found an outlet for his energy and ideas.

As leader of the National Socialist German Workers Party (Nazi), Hitler skilfully and purposefully brought his movement into the forefront of German politics. He provided organization, discipline, and a clear political program. He vilified the German democrats as spineless traitors. He attacked the hated Treaty of Versailles and boldly promised to shred it to pieces. Building on long-standing European prejudices, he launched fierce attacks on the Jewish population, blaming them for all of Germany's problems, from disease to defeat in the First World War.

Hitler was a powerful orator able to hold his audiences entranced for hours. His speeches drew larger and larger crowds and the Nazis began to hold spectacular rallies and marches. Many a poor, lost German youth was attracted to the Nazis, who provided a little food, some shelter, an impressive uniform, and pocket money.

Many Germans feared that rising communist strength, strikes, and revolts would lead to a Bolshevik Revolution like that in Russia. Alone among political parties, the Nazis boldly confronted communism. Hitler seemed to be a safe bulwark against the communist threat.

The Nazi Party made great electoral strides when the Great Depression quashed any hopes of a post-war German recovery. Blaming everything on the Jews, communists, democracy, and

Versailles, Hitler gathered increasing attention—and votes. The electoral gains were stunning: in 1928, 13 seats; in 1930, 107 seats; in 1932, 230 seats. In the growing confusion and polarization of German politics, Hitler made strategic alliances with elements in the army and big business who were eager to crush the "red menace" and rebuild German might.

By 1933, Adolf Hitler was the leader of the most powerful political force in Germany, but still not the leader of a majority party. But by skilful negotiation, Hitler had himself appointed chancellor. It was the end of democracy in Germany.

Once in power, Hitler used force to seize all power for the Nazis. Other political parties were banned; opponents were imprisoned or killed. The government was dominated by Nazi philosophy. The press was shackled. Schools began to indoctrinate instead of educate. Employment rose dramatically as Germany began a massive rearmament and public works program.

Hitler's foreign policy was geared towards the destruction of the Treaty of Versailles, the annexation of all German areas in Europe into Germany, expansion to the East, and the destruction of communism. His foreign policy rested on full-scale rearmament which would lead to German supremacy on the battlefield. The stage was set for another world war.

off limits. Driving licences were revoked. All Jews were forced to wear yellow stars, symbolizing the Star of David, on their clothing as identification. Thousands were arrested and imprisoned. Still more were forced into **ghettos**, and then ultimately into the Nazi death camps.

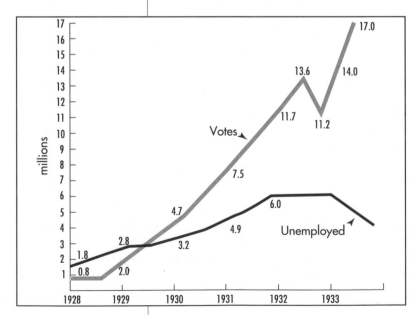

Figure 3.6:
The Relationship
Between Unemployment
and Votes for the Nazis

Hitler's Economic Policies

At the time Hitler rose to power in 1933, Germany was in the midst of the Depression. World trade was at a standstill and the American loans that had allowed Germany to make reparation payments had ended. Hitler immediately set to work to eliminate unemployment and make Germany economically self-sufficient. Vast public works and rearmament programs absorbed the unemployed. German factories started manufacturing war materials; housing programs were begun; highways were built across the country; and, after 1935, the armed forces were greatly increased through conscription. Strict government control aimed at minimizing imports and maximizing exports substantially strengthened the economy. Working to reduce Germany's need to import raw materials, German scientists developed synthetic rubber, plastics, and textiles. These decisive policies and the positive results they yielded won Hitler many supporters, both inside and outside of Germany.

In 1936, Hitler announced his ultimate goal: to mobilize the armed forces and the economy for war within four years. State control of industry, commerce, and the military made sure these aims were implemented.

IN REVIEW

1. What factors explain the rise to power of Mussolini in Italy and Hitler in Germany?

2. Summarize the central beliefs of the Fascists in Italy and the Nazis in Germany.

3. How did the Emergency Decree and the Enabling Law prepare the way for a totalitarian state in Germany?

4. What measures did Hitler take to tighten his grip on Germany?

5. How did the Nazis persecute the Jewish citizens of Germany?

6. What were the results of Nazi economic policies in Germany?

THE UNITED STATES IN THE 1920S AND 1930S

THE RETURN TO ISOLATIONISM

One of the great disappointments in Europe following the peace of 1919 was the American return to isolationism. While Wilson was optimistically forging the League of Nations in France, his support at home was crumbling. Americans were eager to return to peace and prosperity and did not wish further entanglements with European nations. This desire for isolation was due in part to the fact that the United States was a nation of immigrants, many of whom had emigrated in order to escape the corruption, hostilities, and problems of Europe. There was also a long-standing American suspicion about the underhanded politics of the Old World. Membership in the League of Nations was perceived as a permanent tie to the complicated affairs of Europe. Consequently, the United States Senate refused to ratify the peace treaty and rejected the bill to join the League of Nations.

In the US elections of 1920, Warren Harding and the Republican Party won by a landslide. Despite the fact that he won the Nobel Prize for Peace that year, President Wilson was not even renominated to lead the Democratic Party in the election.

THE STOCK MARKET CRASH OF 1929

September 13, 1929 was a day to remember on the New York Stock Exchange. It was the last good day for the booming stock market of the 1920s. Over the next month stock prices fluctuated drastically. No one knew why or what to do about it. Then, on October 24th—"Black Thursday"—the stock prices collapsed as some 13 million shares were sold. Panic set in as everyone wanted to get out of the market before it dropped even lower. The following Tuesday—October 29th—another record was set as 16 million shares were sold and prices dropped even further. The stock market had crashed. Millions of people who had gone from "rags to riches" in the new industrial economy found that the process was indeed reversible.

What treaty is represented by the 'Treaty of Peace'? What is the main point of the cartoon?

THE GREAT DEPRESSION

The effect of the stock market crash was devastating. Thousands of businesses went bankrupt, putting countless people out of work. With rising unemployment and no unemployment insurance, people could not buy goods; consequently, other businesses suffered. As profits shrank, more companies laid off workers, and a vicious downward economic cycle resulted. By 1932, unemployment reached 25 per cent; 15 million American workers were without jobs.

In 1933, Franklin Roosevelt was sworn in as president, reassuring the American public that "The only thing we have to fear is fear itself....I am prepared to recommend the measures that a stricken nation in the midst of a stricken world may require." He proceeded to enlist the services of the best minds in the country to find a way out

of the Depression. During his first term in office, Roosevelt announced the **New Deal**—a comprehensive program of "relief, recovery, and reform" for Americans. Included in the New Deal was legislation dealing with public welfare, agriculture, public utilities, housing, industry, and transportation. Ultimately, however, it was the Second World War and the need for armaments that actively stimulated the economy and brought an end to the Great Depression.

WORLD DEPRESSION

The economic recovery of Europe after the First World War was largely spurred by the strong American economy. The crash of 1929 therefore had international repercussions. In the mid-1920s the United States had only 3 per cent of the world's population. Yet it accounted for 46 per cent of the world's industrial output, 70 per cent of the world's oil, and 40 per cent of the world's coal.

When this powerful engine of growth slowed down, the effects were felt around the world. The most immediate impact was an end to foreign lending and pressure to call in existing loans. Between 1931 and 1938 American banks received $6.6 billion from Europe. This massive withdrawal of funds had a negative impact in Europe. The political implications of the economics of the 1930s were seen in the rise of fascism and the movement towards war.

THE TREATY SYSTEM VS. COLLECTIVE SECURITY

One of the most important political issues following the First World War was how to maintain world peace. Most European leaders maintained a nationalist point of view. They argued that

PROFILE

FRANKLIN D. ROOSEVELT (1882-1945)

Franklin Delano Roosevelt (FDR) was one of the most popular presidents in American history. He struck a powerful chord with Americans from all walks of life, and his years in office resulted in sweeping changes. As you read this profile, think of what factors make FDR one of the most important political figures of the twentieth century.

"I pledge you, I pledge myself to a new deal for the American people."

> *FDR in his acceptance speech at the Democratic Convention in Chicago, 2 July 1932*

"These unhappy times call for the building of plans...that build from the bottom up...that put their faith once more in the forgotten man at the bottom of the economic pyramid."

> *FDR, 7 April 1932*

Roosevelt was born into a wealthy old American family. He attended the best schools and graduated from Harvard and Columbia. While in university, he married Eleanor Roosevelt, a niece of former president Theodore Roosevelt.

Money and family connections soon drew Roosevelt into politics, first as a state senator, then as Assistant Secretary of the Navy. His promising career was almost finished in 1921, however, when he contracted polio. Although he recovered, he was never again able to stand or walk without support.

Roosevelt won the governorship of New York state in 1928. Four years later he won the Democratic presidential nomination. In 1933, during the dark days of the Depression, Roosevelt was sworn in as president of the United States, and he moved swiftly to deal with the economic crisis. He had pledged a New Deal with relief programs, job creation, and financial assistance. He maintained an approachable, down-to-earth image, despite the fact that he came from a world of wealth and connections. His famous radio "fireside chats" endeared him to large segments of the American public.

Increasingly, Roosevelt's attention was drawn to the events unfolding in Europe. As war loomed, he had to balance his country's traditional isolationism against his own convictions that the United States was a great power with global interests and responsibilities. With the outbreak of the Second World War in 1939, Roosevelt promised to help Britain with "all aid short of war." When Japan attacked the American naval base at Pearl Harbor on 7 December 1941, however, the United States was drawn directly into the conflict. The Americans declared war on Japan. On December 11th, Germany and Italy declared war on the United States. Roosevelt was now free to unleash America's industrial and military power on its enemies.

The strain of the war and the pressures of holding down the presidency for an unprecedented twelve years ultimately proved to be too much. In 1945, Roosevelt died suddenly of a cerebral hemorrhage.

Some critics claimed that Roosevelt had not been aggressive enough in his negotiations with Stalin and had given in to too many Russian demands. Nevertheless, Roosevelt's leadership in the Depression and the Second World War contributed greatly to the United States' new superpower status in the world community in 1945.

In Canada, where the economy depended mainly on exports of farm products and raw materials, the Depression hit extremely hard. Wheat prices plunged, markets shrank, and the economy of the prairies collapsed. The situation was made even worse by drought, dust storms, and crop failure. In Saskatchewan, two-thirds of the population was forced to go on welfare. Across Canada, farms and homes were lost and businesses were closed. Soup kitchens and - relief camps were common. Men "riding the rails" on the tops of freight cars became a familiar sight, travelling from one part of the country to another in search of work that wasn't there.

each nation was best able to pursue and protect its own national interests and that national security could best be achieved through individual military power or the forging of powerful alliances. Thus the big powers of Europe would act as a world police force to keep the smaller nations in line.

Woodrow Wilson, the idealist, believed that global collective security should be an international responsibility maintained under the auspices of the League of Nations. The underlying assumption was that the world is interdependent and that national self-interest must give way to the common interests of all nations. Security for individual nations would be achieved through group solidarity. In theory, no nation would dare to attack another because that would violate international law, resulting in punishment or sanctions.

While this argument seemed theoretically sound, in practice there were problems. Perhaps the biggest was the question of enforcement. Who would send troops to stop an attack or enforce a punishment? The League of Nations was a collection of independent states, not an independent body with specific laws or a police force to enforce those laws. The only power it held was the power allocated to it by its members. And how much power would they be willing to give?

The absence of the United States, the Soviet Union, and later Japan and Germany from the League of Nations meant that there was more power *outside* the international organization than inside. Without the major powers to back its decisions, the League had little clout. Nations determined to expand their territory found it easy to ignore the League and simply forge ahead with their plans. Indeed, both Fascist Italy and militaristic Japan challenged the League by invading Abyssinia (Ethiopia) and China with impunity. The League talked but in the end did nothing to force the aggressors to withdraw. This perceived weakness only encouraged Adolf Hitler in his expansionist plans.

In Review

1. Why did Americans reject the League of Nations and return to isolationism?

2. How did the collapse of the US economy affect the world economy and the drift towards war?

3. Explain the main ideas behind the internationalist and nationalist view of maintaining world peace. Outline your reaction to these ideas.

SUMMARY

The period that began with the optimism of Wilson's Fourteen Points and the relief over the end of the First World War ended with the misery of an international depression, the failure of the League of Nations, and the drift towards an even more horrific world conflict. Instead of a new era of progress and co-operation, the years from 1919 to 1939 would become known as "the years between the wars." The early promise of the twentieth century seemed a long way off and for many was growing progressively dimmer.

MAKING CONNECTIONS

1. What evidence is there that fascist principles and leaders still exist in the world? Offer specific examples.

2. Why do economic difficulties often propel people towards leaders and parties with extremist views? Note any current examples of this reaction.

3. What peoples are currently suffering persecution similar to that faced by Jews in Germany?

DEVELOPING YOUR VOICE

4. Prepare a brief position paper on the question: Was the Treaty of Versailles fair? Be prepared to share your findings with the class.

5. Assume you are a young student in Hitler's Germany. In your diary, note reasons why you might be attracted to, or repelled by, Hitler.

6. Assume you are a Jewish citizen living in Nazi Germany. Write a letter to friends in North America about your experiences with the Nazis.

RESEARCHING THE ISSUES

7. Do further research and write a one- to two-page report on the main ideas and influences of one of the following:
   (a) Georges Clemenceau
   (b) Woodrow Wilson
   (c) David Lloyd George
   (d) Leon Trotsky

8. Investigate neo-Nazism in the world today and prepare a brief report.

9. Prepare a collage of pictures and stories on the Great Depression. Display it in the classroom.

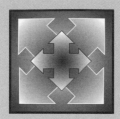

VIEWPOINTS

ISSUE: WAS THE TREATY OF VERSAILLES A FAIR AND REASONABLE TREATY?

Under the Treaty of Versailles in 1919, the victorious allies imposed the conditions of peace upon Germany. The key players in drafting the treaty were American president Woodrow Wilson, British prime minister David Lloyd George, and French premier Georges Clemenceau. The expectations were that a just and fair treaty based on the idealism of Wilson's Fourteen Points would emerge from the Paris Peace Conference. To many observers, however, the true spirit of the Fourteen Points was sacrificed and replaced with a series of draconian measures designed to cripple Germany....

Economist John Maynard Keynes was a delegate at the peace conference. He abandoned the proceedings in protest over the harsh and unrealistic demands of the treaty. In his famous book *The Economic Consequences of the Peace*, Keynes denounced the treaty.

Twenty years after the Treaty of Versailles, the world was engulfed in the Second World War. Historian Paul Birdsall published his review of the Paris Peace settlement. In it, he praised Woodrow Wilson and his idealism as well as the overall peace settlement he had inspired.

Read each of these viewpoints carefully, then complete an Argument Analysis and Evaluation Summary for each reading.

John Maynard Keynes

"There are two separate aspects of the peace which we have imposed on the enemy—on the one hand its justice, on the other hand its wisdom and its expediency. I was mainly concerned with the second. But there were certain aspects of the first also with which I thought it my duty to deal carefully.

Its Justice

"The nature of the terms which we were entitled *in justice* to impose depends, in part, on the responsibility of the enemy nations for causing so tremendous a calamity as the late war, and in part on the understanding on which the enemy laid down his arms at the time of the armistice. In my own opinion, it is not possible to lay the entire responsibility for the state of affairs out of which the war arose on any single nation; it was engendered, in part at least, by the essential character of international politics and rivalries during the latter part of the nineteenth century, by militarism everywhere certainly in Russia as well as in Germany and Austria-Hungary and by the universally practiced policies of economic imperialism; it had its seeds deep in the late history of Europe.

"But I believe, nevertheless, that Germany bears a special and peculiar responsibility for the war itself for its universal and devastating character, and for its final development into a combat without quarter for mastery or defeat. A criminal may be the outcome of his environment, but he is none the less a criminal.

"The evidence which has become public in the past year has convinced me that, during the weeks preceding August, 1914, persons in power in Germany deliberately provoked the war and intended that it should commence when it did. If this be so, the accepted standards of international justice entitled us to impose, at Germany's expense, any terms which might be calculated to make some part of the destruction done, to heal Europe's wounds, to preserve and perpetuate peace, and to terrify future malefactors.

"Even so, however, it was our duty to look more to the future than to the past, to distinguish between the late rulers of Germany on the one hand and her common people and unborn posterity on the other, and to be sure that our acts were guided by magnanimity and wisdom more than by revenge or hatred....Above all, should not the future peace of the world have been our highest and guiding motive?...

The Treaty's Wisdom

"With these brief comments I pass from the justice of the treaty, which can not be ignored even when it is not our central topic, to its wisdom and its expediency. Under these heads my criticism of the treaty is double. In the first place, this treaty ignores the economic solidarity of Europe, and by aiming at the destruction of the economic life of Germany it threatens the health and prosperity of the Allies themselves. In the second place, by making demands the execution of which is in the literal sense impossible, it stultifies itself and leaves Europe more unsettled than it found it. The treaty, by overstepping the limits of the possible, has in practice settled nothing....

"The treaty's claims for an indemnity may be divided into two parts: those which, in accordance with our pre-armistice engagements, we were entitled to make if we judged it expedient to do so, and those which, in my judgment, we had no right to make. The first category includes as its chief items all the direct damages to civilian life and property for which Germany was responsible, more particularly in the invaded and occupied areas of France, Belgium, and Serbia, by air raids, and by warfare of submarines. It includes also compensation for the improper treatment of interned civilians and for the loot of food, raw materials, livestock, machinery, household effects, timber, and the like; and the repayment of fines and requisitions levied on the towns of France and Belgium....

Indemnity Demands

"This is...the claim which we were entitled to present to the enemy. I believe that it would have been a wise and just act to have asked the German Government at the peace negotiations to agree to a...final settlement, without further examination of particulars. This would have provided an immediate and certain solution, and would have required from Germany a sum which, if she were granted certain indulgences, it might not have proved entirely impossible for her to pay. This sum should have been divided up among the Allies themselves on a basis of need and general equity....

The Blank Check

"No final amount is specified by the treaty itself, which fixes no definite sum as representing Germany's liability. This feature has been the subject of very general criticism that is equally inconvenient to Germany and to the Allies themselves that she should not know what she has to pay or what they are to receive. The method, apparently contemplated by the treaty, of arriving at the final result over a period of many months by an addition of hundreds of thousands of individual claims for damage to land, farm buildings and chickens, is evidently impracticable, and the reasonable course would have been for both parties to compound for a round sum without examination of details. If this round sum had been named in the treaty, the settlement would have been placed on a more businesslike basis....

A Dead Treaty

"Such, in brief, are the economic provisions of the Treaty of Versailles....A year has passed since it came into existence, and authority has already passed from it—not, in my judgment, because there has been much softening of sentiment toward Germany, but because the treaty is no treaty, because it is now generally recognized that in truth it settles nothing. After what has passed, Europe requires above all a *settlement*, and this the treaty has not given it....'

From John Maynard Keynes, "The Peace of Versailles," Everybody's Magazine, *1920 (September) pp. 36-41.*

Paul Birdsall

"The simple thesis of those who oppose the treaty is that the doctrinaire and unrealistic program of Wilson collapsed under the impact of the power politics of Europe. Nationalist aims triumphed over his principles. There was division of the spoils of war...in defiance of his principles of self-determination. The Allied governments had accepted Wilson's program. While violating it, still they must pay it lip-service....Keynes in his disillusionment has fixed the legend of a *Carthaginian Peace in Wilsonian disguise.

"This is caricature, not history, but like most successful caricature it has enough verisimilitude [truth] to be plausible....The 'Reparation' chapter of the Treaty of Versailles, besides being a clear violation of the Pre-Armistice Agreement with Germany, proved in the outcome to be the most disastrous section of the treaty.

"The prosaic [sad] truth is that elements of good and bad were combined in the treaties. There were Carthaginian features like the Reparation settlement and Wilsonian features like the League of Nations. There was actually a distribution of colonial spoils of war, but only after the valuable principle had been established that colonial powers administered their new estates under specified conditions and subject to review and correction by an international tribunal, the League of Nations. The territorial settlement in Europe was by no means the wholesale, iniquitous, [unfair] and cynical perversion of Wilson's principles of self-determination which has been pictured....

"The populations of central Europe are hopelessly mixed and, therefore, simple self-determination is impossible. Any boundary will leave national minorities on one side or the other. Moreover, the history of the past few years has certainly justified the commissioners in taking account of strategic factors in the award of boundaries to the new states of Europe. If the Allies should ever conquer Germany again, the negotiators of the new Versailles will face precisely the same dilemma....

"Finally, the territorial settlement contained in the various treaties negotiated at Paris is still, with all its faults, the closest approximation to an ethnographic map of Europe that has ever been achieved. If the next Peace Conference does better, it will be because of the achievements as well as the mistakes of Versailles.

"The treaty was essentially a compromise between Anglo-American and French conceptions of a stable international order. On the one hand, immediate French concern for military security was taken care of by the limitation of German armaments, demilitarization of the Rhineland area and Allied military occupation for a fifteen-year period, and—finally—an Anglo-American treaty of military guarantee. These were certainly adequate guarantees, granted the full weight of English and American resources to support them, and there could be every hope that they would enlist France in the cause of an effective League of Nations. They represented the minimum price which English and American negotiators had to pay for French abandonment of their traditional policy of entirely dismembering Germany. They were a realistic concession to French needs without violating the Fourteen Points in any important particular. Above all, they were regarded as essentially interim measures to provide the necessary breathing spell for the consolidation of the league....Military occupation of German soil would end in fifteen years, at the very moment when residents of the Saar valley might vote to return to German sovereignty; German disarmament was to be the prelude to general disarmament; and the Anglo-American treaty of military guarantee was to cease when the League itself was thought strong enough to provide general security.

"The Reparation settlement was the chief stumbling block, partly because of impossible financial demands even more because it combined an egregious [flagrant] breach of faith....In both financial and political results it proved disastrous. Yet, even here, American participation in the settlement could be counted upon to exert a moderating influence....The Reparation issue emphasized more than any other the necessity of continuing Anglo-American cooperation to make effective

---

*Carthaginian peace refers to the complete destruction of the city state of Carthage by Rome in 202 BC and 146 BC. A "Carthaginian peace" is one where the enemy is completely destroyed and unable to rebuild.

Anglo-American conceptions of a world order....

"The defection of the United States destroyed the Anglo-American preponderance which alone could have stabilized Europe. It impaired the authority and prestige of the League at its birth and it precipitated an Anglo-French duel which reduced Europe to the chaos from which Hitler emerged to produce new chaos....Practically and immediately, it destroyed the Anglo-American treaty of military guarantee which was to have been one of the main props of French Security....

"English sentiment was already developing the guilt-complex about the whole Treaty of Versailles which, among other factors, paralysed English foreign policy from Versailles to Munich. It would be interesting to speculate as to how much that guilt-complex was the result of the brilliant writing of John Maynard Keynes. Devastatingly accurate and prophetic in its analysis of the eco-nomic aspects of the treaty, his *The Economic Consequences of the Peace* included the whole treaty in one sweeping condemnation as a "Carthaginian Peace," and his caricatures of the leading negotiators at Paris immediately fixed stereotypes which still affect much of the writing about the Paris Peace Conference.

"Only too late did British and French leaders observe that Hitler was les concerned about rectification of the "injustices" of the *Diktat* of Versailles than with the conquest of Europe. The muddle and confusion in liberal and democratic communities about the real character of Versailles contributed to the stupidity of Allied policy from Versailles to Armageddon."

From Paul Birdsall, Versailles Twenty Years After, *(1941), in I.J. Lederer (ed.),* The Versailles Settlement: Was It Foredoomed to Failure? *(Boston: D.C. Heath and Co.)*

ANALYSIS AND EVALUATION

Refer to the Argument Analysis and Evaluation Guide on page viii.

1. Using the Argument Analysis and Evaluation Guide, compare the readings by Keynes and Birdsall. On what do they agree? On what do they disagree?

2. Decide which of the viewpoints you tend to support and explain why. Be sure to use specific information from this textbook, the readings, and other sources to support your position.

3. State and support your position on the issue: "Was the Treaty of Versailles a fair and reasonable treaty?"

CHAPTER FOUR

The Second World War: 1939-1945

"When Hitler attacked the Jews I was not a Jew, therefore I was not concerned. And when Hitler attacked the Catholics, I was not a Catholic, and therefore I was not concerned. And when Hitler attacked the unions and the industrialists, I was not a member of the unions and I was not concerned. Then, Hitler attacked me and the Protestant church—and there was nobody left to be concerned."

Martin Niemöller (1892-1984), German pastor imprisoned for preaching against the Nazis, in the Congressional Record, *14 October 1968*

Left: Infantry Near Numegan

❖ OVERVIEW

The Second World War was the first truly global war. Both the east and the west were swept into the strife that would last for six years. In Europe, the war began on 1 September 1939 when Germany invaded Poland. But the war clouds had been building for several years, perhaps since the Treaty of Versailles in 1919.

War between China and Japan had been smouldering and flaring up throughout the 1930s. Japan had been expanding its economic control and territory in Asia. In 1937, it launched all-out war against China. The United States, Britain, and Holland, all of which had interests in South East Asia, supported China. Most experts expected the conflict to remain localized. But on 7 December 1941, the Japanese attacked the American naval base at Pearl Harbor, Hawaii. Attacks on the Philippines, Singapore, and Hong Kong followed. Declarations of war rang out from continent to continent. A global war had begun.

quickly consolidated power as the undisputed dictator of Germany. He then turned his attention to his goal of establishing Germany as the dominant power in Europe. To achieve this, it was necessary to violate the Treaty of Versailles, which Hitler viewed as humiliating and designed to maintain a weak German state. Hitler embarked on this objective in 1935 by rearming Germany. At the same time, he began to gather personal control of Germany's military and foreign affairs.

Hitler was encouraged in his expansionist foreign policy by the failure of the League of Nations to create international peace and order following the First World War. Weakened by the worldwide economic depression and a lack of commitment and resolve on the part of its members, the League was powerless to prevent aggression anywhere in the world. In 1931-32, Japan occupied Manchuria without challenge. In 1935-36, Italy conquered Abyssinia (Ethiopia) with little protest. Hitler observed that the threat of international action against aggression was virtually non-existent.

In Hitler's vision, a great Germany meant an expanded Germany and this new territory was to be obtained through conquest. The fact that the areas Hitler wanted belonged to other nations was of no concern to him. He believed in the principle of "might is right"—those who are fit survive while those who are weak perish. According to Hitler's outlook, the Germans were a superior Aryan race that should subdue and control "lesser" races, such as the Slavic peoples in eastern Europe. As for the Jews, Hitler felt it was his mission to banish them

FOCUS QUESTIONS

1. What were the major steps on the road to war between 1930 and 1939?
2. What were the key events of the war?
3. What were the major results of the war?
4. What are some of the major interpretations of the basic causes of the Second World War?

HITLER'S AIMS AND FOREIGN POLICY

The rise of Hitler and the Nazi Party signalled the beginning of a new age for Germany and Europe. Upon becoming chancellor in 1933, Hitler

Hitler led a victory parade in Vienna following Germany's occupation of Austria in 1938.

from Europe by whatever means necessary.

Hitler also wanted Germany to be self-sufficient. Trade was not the answer because that would make Germany dependent on others. In order to obtain rich agricultural land and other valuable natural resources, Germany would have to expand into eastern Europe.

THE REOCCUPATION OF THE RHINELAND

The Treaty of Versailles had established a demilitarized zone in the Rhineland between Germany and France. In March 1936, Hitler ordered the army to move into the Rhineland and reclaim it for Germany. The move was risky. Hitler's military leaders opposed the action, fearing it would precipitate war with France—a war for which Germany was simply not ready. As a precaution, German troops were ordered to retreat at the first sign of French resistance. Hitler, however, had gambled that there would be no such resistance. He was right.

ANSCHLUSS

Anschluss (the union of Germany and Austria) was one of Hitler's long-standing dreams. While the union would be an important military advantage, for Hitler it was more personal. He wanted to annex Austria so that he and his fellow Austrians would be officially German. The fact that *Anschluss* was forbidden under the terms of the Treaty of Versailles was of little consequence.

> Hitler believed that Germany needed more *lebensraum* (living space) for its expanding population of pure-blooded Aryans. To encourage the increased birth rate of Aryans, Hitler dismissed women from jobs in industry, exhorting them to devote themselves to *kinder, kirche, kuche* (children, church, kitchen).

Still, there were other obstacles in Hitler's way. First he had to persuade the Italian dictator Mussolini, who had signed a treaty with Austria guaranteeing its independence, to renege on that commitment. Hitler came up with a simple solution: he offered German support to Mussolini, whose troops had just occupied Abyssinia, if Italy would ignore its commitment to Austria.

> "And now before us stands the last problem that must be solved and will be solved. It [the Sudetenland] is the last territorial claim which I have to make in Europe, but it is the claim from which I will not recede...."
>
> *Adolf Hitler, in a speech in Berlin, 26 September 1938*

Next, Hitler pressured Austria to legalize the Nazi Party and appoint a Nazi supporter as Minister of the Interior. Once legalized, the Austrian Nazi Party became increasingly vocal, demanding union with Germany. However, the Austrian Chancellor, Kurt von Schuschnigg, convinced that Austrians would vote for independence, decided to hold a **plebiscite**. Hitler was infuriated. Under the threat of German invasion, Schuschnigg was forced to resign. The leader of the Austrian Nazi Party assumed the office of Chancellor. He invited the German troops massed along the border to enter the country and restore order. As German forces marched into Vienna, the union of Austria and Germany was officially proclaimed. The first step in Hitler's plan was now complete.

WHY ENGLAND AND FRANCE SLEPT

In hindsight, Germany's march of aggression in the 1930s seems obvious. Why, then, wasn't Hitler stopped? Why were Britain and France so timid in their response to Hitler's demands and his territorial conquests? The answers are complex.

In the 1930s, the horrible slaughter of the First World War was still fresh in the memories of most Europeans. A mere fifteen years before, a whole generation of young men had died on the fields of France and Belgium. Most leaders wanted to avoid a repetition of that senseless bloodshed. They believed that another world war would be even more devastating.

Furthermore, the Western world was caught in the Great Depression. Most countries lacked the funds needed to support their unemployed citizens and deal with the social problems arising from the economic crisis. Rearmament and war preparations would only further drain already depleted economies.

Political opinion in Britain and France was deeply divided between

the conservative forces of the right and the labour and social democratic forces of the left. Many people of the right were suspicious of the growth of communism in the USSR and feared communist expansion in the rest of Europe. To some, the strong anticommunist rantings of Hitler and Mussolini were a counter force to the spread of communism. Thus some were prepared to support fascism simply to contain communism. For others, communism seemed to be the movement of the future, a means of overthrowing the oppressive capitalist forces. These conflicting views tended to split nations and made it difficult for governments to establish a strong foreign policy. The result, for both Britain and France, was political paralysis. Where fascist actions did not conflict directly with their interests, the Western powers were prepared to follow a policy of **appeasement**.

CZECHOSLOVAKIA AND THE MUNICH PACT

In April 1938, Hitler issued his directive on his plans for expansion into Czechoslovakia: "It is my unalterable decision to smash Czechoslovakia by

When Neville Chamberlain returned from Munich, he confidently declared "peace for our time."

"We must always demand so much that we can never be satisfied."

Hitler on his strategy during negotiations at Munich

What does this cartoon suggest about the Nazi-Soviet Non-Aggression Pact of 1939?

Chamberlain, the British prime minister, and the French premier, Édouard Daladier, announced that they would agree to give the predominantly German-speaking Sudetenland region of Czechoslovakia to Germany in order to avoid war. They pressured Czechoslovakia to give in to Hitler's demands.

The matter was decided at a conference in Munich in September 1938. Czechoslovakia was not represented. Hitler, Chamberlain, Daladier, and Mussolini signed the Munich Pact, giving Germany the Sudetenland in return for agreeing to make no further territorial demands. Czechoslovakia thereby lost the fortified border the Sudetenland provided; the country was now defenceless. Meanwhile, the exclusion of the Soviet Union from the Munich Conference raised Stalin's suspicions that Britain and France, by appeasing Germany, hoped to turn Hitler's attention away from them and to the east—and the USSR.

Following the Munich Conference, Chamberlain returned to England and proclaimed to a cheering crowd "I believe it is peace for our time." To Hitler, the agreement signified the willingness of the West to let him have his way in order to avoid armed conflict. Now there would be no stopping Germany.

In March 1939, despite Hitler's assurances in Munich, German troops

military action in the near future." Hitler's plan was to isolate Czechoslovakia from its allies, then launch a short but decisive attack. He believed that a massive show of power and a quick victory would discourage outside military intervention. But before Hitler could launch his attack, Neville

"In spite of the hardness and ruthlessness I thought I saw in his [Hitler's] face, I got the impression that here was a man who could be relied upon when he had given his word."

Neville Chamberlain, after meeting with Hitler in September 1938 prior to the Munich Conference

occupied the rest of Czechoslovakia. Not a shot was fired. Hitler was clearly contemptuous of the Allies. Once again, he had gambled and won. Few people in Germany would dare speak out against such obvious success. Now more than ever, Hitler believed that his genius and superior will would enable him to achieve any objective.

THE POLISH GAMBLE

Hitler's successful foreign policy achievements encouraged him to gamble for increasingly higher stakes. Poland was his next target.

The specific dispute between Germany and Poland was over the free port city of Danzig (later renamed Gdansk) and the Polish Corridor, both of which had been part of Germany prior to 1919. Danzig had become a free city by the terms of the Treaty of Versailles, and Poland had been given special trading privileges there. The Polish Corridor, created to give Poland access to the Baltic Sea, cut East Prussia off from the rest of Germany. The predominantly German population in the Polish Corridor clamoured to be reunited with their homeland. Hitler exploited this instability and ordered his generals to develop plans for a Polish invasion. Could Hitler win Poland by bluster and bluff, as he had

won Czechoslovakia, or would this gamble lead to war? Now there was a new ingredient in the mix: Britain and France, realizing they had been fooled at Munich, no longer trusted the Nazi leader. Chamberlain reacted to Hitler's manoeuvres by pledging support to Poland. It was a warning that further expansion would be opposed.

> "England has been offered a choice between war and shame. She has chosen shame and will get war."
>
> *Winston Churchill, in opposition to Chamberlain's policy of appeasement, September 1938*

THE GERMAN/SOVIET PACT

For years Hitler had proclaimed that the Soviet Union, as a communist nation, was the major enemy of Germany. Suddenly, in August 1939, Germany and the USSR announced an agreement of mutual non-aggression. The world was shocked by this agreement. Germany was now free from the danger of fighting a war on two fronts. One week later, on 1 September 1939, Germany unleashed its *blitzkrieg* on Poland. The Second World War had begun.

IN REVIEW

1. What were Hitler's foreign policy objectives?

2. Why did England and France "sleep" while Hitler marched towards war?

3. Outline the results of the Munich Pact.

4. What was appeasement and why was it ultimately unsuccessful?

5. What was the importance of the pact between Germany and the Soviet Union?

6. What event started the Second World War?

THE OUTBREAK OF WAR

THE NATURE OF THE SECOND WORLD WAR

The speed, scale, and destruction of the Second World War were unprecedented in human history. This was no war of the eighteenth and nineteenth centuries in which colourfully dressed professional soldiers met on isolated fields of battle. This was total war, much like the First World War, except that the killing machines were more efficient and more deadly.

The Second World War was characterized by blitzkrieg—lightning war! The principle behind blitzkrieg was that the best way to defeat an enemy was to cut them off from all supplies and communication. This would require swift, massive strikes from the air, coupled with rapid tank invasions on the ground. Hitler successfully employed blitzkrieg tactics to expand Germany's territorial control in the early stages of the war.

THE PHONEY WAR

On 1 September 1939, the German army invaded Poland. Using blitzkrieg tactics, it defeated Poland by the end of the month. Soviet troops moved in to occupy eastern Poland, in accordance with the secret terms of the Nazi-Soviet Pact signed on August 23rd. With the eastern front secure, Hitler turned his attention to the West.

From October 1939 to April 1940 there was little fighting. During this lull in the action, known as the "phoney war," the German army refined its attack plans and trained its troops for the battles that lay ahead. The Allies seemed content to improve their defences and wait for Hitler's next move. French troops waited behind the massive Maginot Line while British and French forces took up positions along the Belgian border where an anti-tank ditch had been prepared and fortified. To the north and west, German troops massed along the Siegfried Line.

THE FALL OF FRANCE

The phoney war came to a sudden end on 9 April 1940 when, without warning, Germany attacked Norway and Denmark, both neutral nations. While Denmark fell immediately, Norway, with the help of the Allies, continued to resist until June.

On May 10th, Germany attacked Holland, Belgium, Luxembourg, and France. Relying on blitzkrieg tactics, the German army conquered Holland in one week and Belgium in three. The main thrust of the attack took place in France as the Germans swarmed into the country through the Ardennes forest. Their position drove a huge wedge between the bulk of the French army stationed behind the Maginot Line and the Allied forces in Belgium.

The Germans then pushed straight for the sea, forcing British and French forces to retreat to the west. In a mighty sweep, the Germans encircled the retreating French troops to the south and the British Expeditionary Force (BEF) to the north, pinning them on the beaches of Dunkirk in northern France. (See Figure 4.1.)

Hitler's victory could have been even more devastating. But while the German ruler fussed over whether the air force or the army should have the honour of completing the victory, an amazing rescue by the British navy and thousands of ordinary citizens was under way at Dunkirk. Tugs, barges, fishing boats, yachts, lifeboats, and naval vessels crossed the English Channel to evacuate the Allied troops on the beach. This heroic effort resulted in the rescue of over 330 000 troops. While heavy arms and equipment were destroyed or abandoned, the British army escaped to fight again.

The German forces continued to press southward, taking Paris by mid-June. On June 17th, the newly appointed French Premier, H. Philippe Pétain, requested an armistice with the Germans. The agreement was signed on June 22nd. France had fallen in just over a month.

THE BATTLE OF BRITAIN

The defeat of France was a severe blow to the Allies. Now continental western Europe was in Hitler's hands. Only the English Channel and the powerful British navy separated Britain from Hitler's empire.

Hitler was convinced that Britain would now have no choice but to seek peace. But the success of the rescue at Dunkirk had made Britain determined to fight to the end. In frustration, Hitler gave orders to launch Operation Sea Lion, the invasion plan for Britain. First,

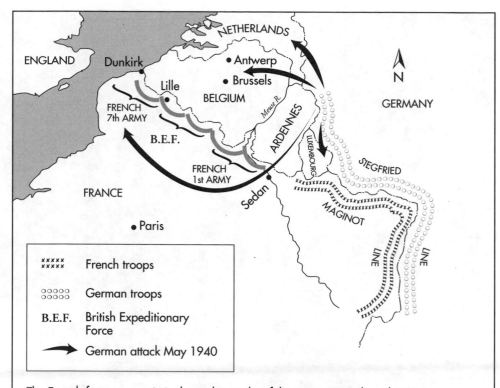

The French front was static in the early months of the war as French and German troops faced each other from the Maginot and Siegfried lines. The British Expeditionary Force and French 1st and 7th armies massed along the border of neutral Belgium to guard against the possibility that the Germans might strike there. On May 10th, Germany attacked the Netherlands, Belgium, Luxembourg, and France.

however, the *Luftwaffe* (the German air force) had to gain control of the air to ensure the safe passage of the German army across the English Channel.

On 10 July 1940, the Luftwaffe began air raids over Britain in preparation for invasion along England's southern coast. The Royal Air Force (RAF) airfields, British ships in the English Channel, and harbours in the south were targeted for destruction by German aircraft. The air assault continued throughout the summer and into the fall. Never before had bombing from the air been so intense.

Although German bombers and fighter planes outnumbered those of the British by four to one, the RAF had great success against the Luftwaffe, losing only one plane for every two

Figure 4.1:
The Battle of France

In the Battle of the Atlantic (top), convoys of supply ships from North America were escorted by British warships and Canadian corvettes. The Battle of El Alamein (bottom) in October-November 1942 marked the beginning of the end of Germany's campaign in northern Africa.

The Battle of Stalingrad (top), from September 1942 until January 1943, ended Germany's success in the Eastern Front. American soldiers stormed the beaches of the French coast directly into fire from Nazi defenders in the D-Day invasion (bottom).

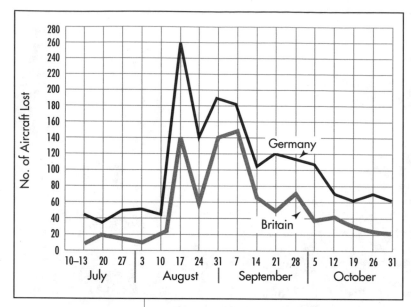

Figure 4.2:
*The Battle of Britain
This chart compares the
number of aircraft lost
by Britain and Germany
each week during the
Battle of Britain.*

German planes. A new invention—radar—allowed the British to detect German bombing missions in advance and to prepare to defend themselves.

In September, Hermann Goering, the commander of the Luftwaffe, decided to change his tactics. Instead of bombing RAF bases, the Germans began bombing industrial and port centres in the hope of breaking British morale. Cities such as London and Coventry were heavily bombed. In London, explosives and incendiary bombs rained down night after night, destroying huge sections of the city. The centre of Coventry was obliterated. But the bombing campaigns only made

"We shall defend our island, whatever the cost may be. We shall fight on the beaches, we shall fight on the landing-grounds, we shall fight in the fields and in the streets, we shall fight in the hills. We shall never surrender."

*Winston Churchill,
addressing Parliament,
4 June 1940*

British civilians more determined to resist defeat.

German losses were so heavy in September that in October the Luftwaffe changed tactics again, switching to night bombing. Although this was much less effective from a military standpoint, the dark of night hampered Britain's defensive plans. This siege, which lasted from July 1940 until May 1941, was known as the **Blitz**.

While German bombs were laying much of Britain to ruins, British bombers were causing similar destruction in German cities. Air raids on centres like Hamburg, Dresden, and Berlin were leaving masses of rubble and debris in their wake. The scale of civilian destruction was unprecedented.

By October 1940, Hitler realized that the Battle of Britain was lost. He postponed his invasion plans and began to refocus his attention eastward towards Russia.

THE ALLIED VICTORY IN EUROPE

In 1945, the Allied forces bombed, torpedoed, and marched their way to victory in Europe. The German forces were outnumbered and outgunned by the vast Allied armies that now swept across the continent. Hitler's empire was crumbling against the pounding from Russian forces in the West. Allied control of the air and seas made victory inevitable. While German soldiers fought desperately and valiantly in defence of their own soil, Hitler refused calls for surrender. With Allied troops about to capture Berlin, Hitler finally committed suicide in an underground bunker in the bombed-out ruins of the city in May 1945. Germany surrendered unconditionally. The war in Europe was over.

PROFILE

SIR WINSTON CHURCHILL (1874-1965)

Long before the twentieth century was even half over, Sir Winston Churchill was being lionized as "the greatest living Englishman" and one of "the greatest figures of the twentieth century." World leader, author, prime minister, soldier, war correspondent, painter—Churchill played all these roles.

Churchill was criticized for his role in the ill-fated Gallipoli raid in the first world war and relegated to back bench or opposition roles for most of the interwar period. However, when England needed a leader in its darkest hour, it turned to him. His leadership provided the inspiration England needed to face Nazi Germany while he forged a powerful alliance with the United States and the Soviet Union to defeat the Axis Powers. As you read about Churchill, consider why he played such an important role in the British resistance.

"We have before us an ordeal of the most grievous kind. We have before us many, many long months of struggle and of suffering. You ask, what is our policy? I will say: It is to wage war, by sea, land, and air, with all our might and with all the strength that God can give us: to wage war against a monstrous tyranny, never surpassed in the dark, lamentable catalogue of human crime. That is our policy. You ask, what is our aim? I can answer in one word: Victory, victory at all costs, victory in spite of all terror; victory, however long and hard the road may be; for without victory there is no survival.

> *Winston Churchill, upon becoming British prime minister, 13 May 1940*

"I expect that the Battle of Britain is about to begin. Upon this battle depends the survival of Christian civilization. Upon it depends our own British life and the long continuity of our institutions and our Empire. The whole fury and might of the enemy must very soon be turned on us. Hitler knows that he will have to break us in this island or lose the war. If we can stand up to him all Europe may be free and the life of the world may move forward into broad, sunlit uplands; but if we fail then the whole world, including the United

States, and all that we have known and cared for, will sink into the abyss of a new dark age made more sinister, and perhaps more prolonged, by the lights of a perverted science. Let us therefore brace ourselves to our duty and so bear ourselves that if the British Commonwealth and its Empire lasts for a thousand years, men will still say 'This was their finest hour.'"

> *Winston Churchill, to the House of Commons when the invasion of Britain seemed imminent, 18 June 1940*

"The gratitude of every home in our Island, in our Empire, and indeed throughout the world, except in the abodes of the guilty, goes out to the British airmen who, undaunted by odds, unwearied in their constant challenge and mortal danger, are turning the tide of world war by their prowess and by their devotion. Never in the field of human conflict was so much owed by so many to so few."

> *Winston Churchill paying tribute to the RAF, 20 August 1940*

Winston Churchill was a member of one of England's most illustrious noble families. He was educated at the prestigious institutions of Harrow and Sandhurst and could have lived a life of ease and comfort, but his pugnacious personality and the events of the twentieth century were to provide nearly a century of adventure, challenge, and singular achievement.

In 1900, Churchill entered Parliament and embarked on a dramatic political career that saw the independent-minded politician switch parties—twice! During the First World War, Churchill served as First Lord of the Admiralty, where he used navy funds to develop a new weapon, "the land battleship"—the modern tank.

After the First World War, Churchill served in a variety of cabinet positions. During the 1930s, he became increasingly alarmed by the spread of fascism and the rise of Adolf Hitler. But his dire warnings found few listeners in a world preoccupied with economic depression.

As the Second World War ignited, Churchill was once again admitted to the British cabinet as First Lord of the Admiralty. In the wake of successive Nazi victories on the continent, Chamberlain resigned as British prime minister. In May 1940, Churchill took his place. While much of the world was stunned by the speed and power of the Nazi blitzkrieg, Churchill seemed defiantly confident and unwilling to buckle under to the Nazi war machine. As prime minister, Churchill came to symbolize the indomitable will of the British people and their allies to survive and defeat Axis aggression.

In 1945, Churchill was defeated at the polls but he returned to office from 1951 to 1955, finally retiring as Conservative Party leader at the age of eighty. However, he did not leave politics even then, but served as a Member of Parliament for nine more years. He also found time to write the six-volumes of *The Second World War*, which earned him the Nobel Prize for Literature in 1953.

When Churchill died in 1965, a grateful nation gave him a grand state funeral. This man, with such a powerful sense of self, history, and destiny, had his own explanation for his perceived greatness: "I have never accepted what many people have kindly said, namely that I inspired the nation. It was the nation and the race dwelling all around the globe that had the lion's heart. I had the luck to be called upon to give the roar."

IN REVIEW

1. What was the blitzkrieg? What effect did it have on German success in the early years of the Second World War?

2. What was the "phoney war"?

3. Briefly describe the campaigns waged by Hitler against England and France. Why was England able to survive?

4. Why was Hitler unable to conquer Britain?

5. Review the excerpts of three of Churchill's speeches. What made these speeches so important in their day? Explain your answer.

THE ASIAN PACIFIC CONFLICT

As an industrialized nation, Japan needed raw materials and export markets. With the economic crisis of the 1930s, international trade with the West was drastically reduced. The strong militarist element in Japan believed that if Japan had a colonial empire, it would have access to raw materials and could control its own markets. The more liberal element, composed of industrialists and bankers, felt that Japanese trade should be carried out peacefully. They worried that acquiring territory by force would result in trade reprisals from the West.

THE CHINA INCIDENT: MANCHURIA

Manchuria, in northern China, had an abundance of rich mineral and timber resources that Japan wanted to exploit. In September 1931, Japanese troops guarding the South Manchurian Railway alleged that Chinese saboteurs had attempted to blow up a section of the track. On the pretext of protecting the railway, they seized control of the nearby cities of Mukden and Changchun. Within a few months, the Japanese army, acting on its own initiative, had captured all the main cities of Manchuria.

The Chinese leader, Jiang Jie Shi (Chiang Kai-shek), appealed for help to the League of Nations. In 1933, after a lengthy investigation, the League recommended that Japan withdraw from Manchuria. But while the League condemned Japan it was not prepared to act and Japan simply withdrew from the League. The militarist element in Japan gained great prestige from this successful and profitable gamble. As a result, expansion by conquest became a preferred Japanese policy.

With Manchuria conquered, expansion in South East Asia was the next goal. But first Japan needed to secure its northern flank from a possible attack by the Soviet Union. This was achieved through the Anti-Comintern Pact Japan signed with Nazi Germany in 1936. Germany and Japan agreed to co-operate against the **Comintern** (the world communist movement led by the Soviet Union). With this agree-

ment, the USSR was threatened on two fronts—by Japan in the east and Germany in the west.

WAR WITH CHINA

In the summer of 1937, the Japanese launched an all-out attack against Beijing, Shanghai, Nanking, and much of the coastal areas. They soon occupied most of China. As it had in the Manchurian conquest, the League of Nations condemned Japan, but took no action.

In 1939, the United States announced its intention to cancel its commercial treaty with Japan, which had been in effect since 1911. This allowed the US to impose trade restrictions against Japan, which seriously affected industries that depended upon American petroleum, steel, iron, copper, and industrial machinery. While the Japanese government pondered the problems trade restrictions created, events in Europe provided new opportunities. The German invasion of Poland focused the attention of the European powers and the United States on Germany. Japan took advantage of the situation by occupying the northern part of French Indochina in 1940. Now Japan posed a direct threat to the British naval base at Singapore and the vast oil supplies in the Dutch East Indies.

Britain and Holland were fully embroiled in the war in Europe and could not send ships to defend their Pacific colonies. The United States, although not yet directly involved in the war, issued repeated warnings to Japan against further aggression. In May 1940, it reinforced these warnings by stationing its Pacific fleet in Pearl Harbor, Hawaii. In 1941, Roosevelt imposed further economic sanctions in the form of an embargo on aviation fuel, iron, and scrap metal. This

The USS Shaw *exploded during the Japanese raid on Pearl Harbor, 7 December 1941.*

THE ATTACK ON PEARL HARBOR

Japan intended a quick and decisive victory over the United States. In a long war, American industrial power would crush Japan. The most obvious target for the Japanese was the American fleet stationed at Pearl Harbor, Hawaii. With this fleet eliminated, Japan would have naval supremacy in the western Pacific Ocean. Plans for a surprise attack were engineered by Japan's brilliant naval commander and military strategist Admiral Yamamoto Isoroku.

marked a serious blow to Japan's economy.

Refusing to buckle to US pressure, in July 1941 Japan announced a new foreign policy. Called the Greater East Asia Co-prosperity Sphere, the policy was designed to eliminate Western influence in Asia. The plan called for Japanese control of the natural resources of South East Asia; in return, South East Asia would become the market for Japanese manufactured goods. In effect, it was the blueprint for a Japanese empire.

In July 1941, Roosevelt froze all Japanese assets in the United States. All trade between the two nations was now terminated. Japan was faced with a tough choice: to fight or negotiate. But as a condition to any negotiations, the Americans insisted that Japan must withdraw from all the territories it had seized. The Japanese government, now firmly controlled by the militarists led by General Tojo Hideki, chose war.

On 7 December 1941, Japanese bombers took off from aircraft carriers positioned north of Hawaii. Catching the American navy completely off guard, the fleet suffered severe damage and a staggering loss of life. A total of 19 ships were destroyed or disabled, 150 planes were lost, and 2400 military personnel and civilians were killed. That evening, the Japanese officially declared war on the United States.

Japanese hopes that the attack on Pearl Harbor would be the first step towards establishing a lasting empire in the Pacific were short-lived, however. The US navy recovered quickly. Within a year almost all of the vessels damaged in the raid were back in service and in action against the Japanese. The size of the American fleet and the number of personnel, combined with more advanced technology and a faster rate of production, helped the Americans to drive the Japanese from

In the Battle of Midway Island (top) in June 1942, low-flying Japanese torpedo planes bombed US aircraft carriers, but suffered heavy losses in ships, planes, and soldiers. In the Battle of Iwo Jima in February 1945 (bottom), US marines secured the island to use to mount bombing offensives against Japanese cities, but US casualties exceeded 20 000.

In the Battle of Leyte Gulf in October 1944 (top), US forces forced the Japanese fleet to withdraw from Philippine waters. The dropping of the atomic bombs on Hiroshima (bottom) and Nagasaki in August 1945 led to Japan's unconditional surrender.

their possessions in the Pacific. The massive destruction of American bombing culminated with the dropping of atomic bombs over Hiroshima and Nagasaki. In August 1945, Japan unconditionally surrendered. The Second World War was finally over.

In Review

1. Describe the goals of the militarists and liberal groups in Japan.
2. What were the results of the Japanese invasion of Manchuria for China, Japan, and the League of Nations?
3. Why did Japan decide to attack the United States?
4. What were the results of the attack on Pearl Harbor in 1941?
5. What accounted for the defeat of Japan in the Second World War?

THE TRAGEDIES OF WAR

SOVIET PRISONERS OF WAR

The German invasion of the USSR in 1941, called Operation Barbarossa, resulted in millions of prisoners of war as entire Soviet divisions were overrun by the blitzkrieg. Nazi propaganda presented these defeated soldiers as evidence of Slavic inferiority in contrast to German superiority. Photographs of Soviet prisoners of war, in which the captives were described as *untermensch* (subhuman) were distributed throughout Germany. One booklet concluded with the shrill warning "The *untermensch* has risen to conquer the world.... Defend yourself, Europe!" Routinely, Russian prisoners were starved, beaten, and worked to death. Many were murdered outright. By the time the war ended, 2 500 000 Soviet prisoners of war had died.

THE KATYN FOREST MURDERS

The Katyn Forest, located near the Polish city of Smolensk, was the site of a grizzly discovery in June 1941. The German army reported finding mass graves containing over 10 000 Polish officers. The Germans claimed this was a Soviet atrocity; the Soviets in turn denied responsibility, claiming the murders were the work of the Germans. It was not until an investigation was conducted in 1951-52 that the Soviets were charged with the crimes. Evidence indicates that when the Soviet army occupied part of Poland from September 1939 to June 1941, they sent Polish officers and intelligentsia to Russian prison camps. Later, under Stalin's orders, the prisoners were murdered. Although the exact reasons for the massacre are uncertain, it is possible that Stalin wanted Poland's military and intellectual leaders eliminated in order to weaken Polish nationalism and military capability after the war.

THE ALLIED BOMBING OF DRESDEN

The massive Allied bombing of the historic German city of Dresden on 13 February 1945 resulted in more than 40 000 civilian deaths. The city was a railway distribution centre, but was of little strategic value. The strategy behind the Allied bombing of German cities was to break civilian morale. After the war, however, many people questioned the morality of destroying cities that were of minor military significance and inflicting such human suffering during the last months of the war.

ALLIED PRISONERS IN ASIA

Cultural differences may explain in part Japan's harsh treatment of civilian and military prisoners. The Japanese believed that surrender was dishonourable; those who surrendered were held in contempt. Japanese soldiers themselves were expected to die rather than surrender. Hundreds of Japanese pilots volunteered for **kamikaze** missions, flying planes laden with explosives directly into American ships. In Japanese culture, to die in combat was glorious.

The Japanese also wanted to dispel the myth of white superiority. These two factors led to harsh treatment of Allied prisoners. In the Philippines, 70 000 soldiers were forced to march 100 km under a blazing tropical sun with almost no food or water. Only 54 000 survived. Prisoners of war were frequently used as slave labour; it is estimated that 13 000 POWs died building the Burma-Siam Railway.

THE CANADIAN DEFENCE OF HONG KONG

In the autumn of 1941, Japanese armies were routinely defeating poorly equipped Chinese forces. North of Hong Kong, Guangzhou had been taken by the Japanese. Would Hong Kong be next?

Some British leaders believed that Hong Kong could not be defended in the event of a Japanese attack, therefore it would be pointless to station additional troops there. Others argued that reinforcing the base at Hong Kong would provide moral support for the Chinese and act as a deterrent to invasion by the Japanese.

In September 1941, Churchill made the controversial decision to ask Canada to provide the troops needed to increase Allied military presence in Hong Kong. On November 16th, two battalions—Quebec's Royal Rifles and the Winnipeg Grenadiers—arrived in Hong Kong to begin their first mission. On December 7th, the Japanese attacked, first from the air and two days later from the ground. On Christmas Day, with no air force, no navy, and heavy casualties, the British commander surrendered.

Nearly 300 of Canada's 2000 troops were killed in the battle. The rest were sent to Japanese prisoner-of-war camps, where over 260 died, some from malnutrition and disease, others from the harsh living conditions. Canadian veterans and historians have questioned why unprepared Canadian troops were sent into a dangerous war zone to protect what many had acknowledged was a defenceless position.

THE ATOMIC BOMBING OF HIROSHIMA AND NAGASAKI

The devastation of atomic war was clearly demonstrated in August 1945. On August 6th, the United States dropped the newly developed atomic bomb on Hiroshima, Japan. The impact was devastating: 80 000 people died instantly; 100 000 people were injured; another 60 000 died within a year. When Japan failed to surrender, a second bomb was dropped on Nagasaki on August 9th, killing another 40 000 people.

American president Harry S. Truman justified the use of the A-bomb by arguing that it would force an end to the war, thereby saving American and Allied lives. Casualties were heavy in the Pacific. The Japanese aversion to surrender meant that many battles were literally fought to the last soldier. Based on such strong resistance, Allied military leaders estimated that half a million to a million troops would be lost in an invasion of Japan by ground forces.

The decision to use atomic weapons on civilians continues to cause controversy. There are those who believe that the bombings were carried out for political rather than military reasons. They argue that the bombs were really intended to intimidate the Soviet Union, which was taking a hard line at the peace negotiations at the Potsdam Conference. Others believe that the bombings were racially motivated, arguing that atomic force would never have been used on a European city. While it is impossible to settle this debate with any certainty, one point seems clear: after spending several billion dollars developing the ultimate weapon, it seemed only logical to use it. The atomic bomb achieved its goal. Five days after the bombing of Nagasaki, Japan unconditionally surrendered.

In Review

1. In your own words, describe three of the tragedies you have just read about. In your opinion, which event was the most senseless? Give reasons for your answer.

2. What lessons can all societies learn from the tragedies of war you have read about here?

The Holocaust

During the Second World War, the Nazis set out to eliminate all Jews—about 11 million people—from Europe. The process began in the 1930s when Jewish citizens were stripped of their rights and possessions. Eventually, Jews were forced to live in urban **ghettos** and then in **concentration camps**. In January 1942, Hitler gave orders to apply "the **final solution** of the Jewish question"—the systematic extermination of all Jews under German control.

At first, firing squads carried out the mass murders. Later, other techniques were used. Jews were transported by railway cattle cars and trucks from all over Nazi-occupied Europe to death camps such as Treblinka, Auschwitz, Belsen, Dachau, and Buchenwald. At the camps, those who could work were spared the gas chamber temporarily. Then, along with thousands of other Jews who arrived at the camps daily, they were herded to their deaths in the gas chambers. By 1945, 6 million Jews had been murdered in the death camps—over 65 per cent of the Jewish population of Europe.

When the Allied armies arrived to liberate the camps, the true horror of Hitler's final solution was revealed to the world. While rumours had circulated during the war, many people believed a policy of **genocide** (the deliberate extermination of a group of

Figure 4.3: The Extermination of Jews

	Country	Previous number of Jews	Losses Lowest estimate	Highest estimate
1	Poland	3 300 000	2 350 000	2 900 000 = 88%
2	USSR	2 100 000	700 000	1 000 000 = 48%
3	Romania	850 000	200 000	420 000 = 49%
4	Czechoslovakia	360 000	233 000	300 000 = 83%
5	Germany	240 000	160 000	200 000 = 83%
6	Hungary	403 000	180 000	200 000 = 50%
7	Lithuania	155 000	—	135 000 = 87%
8	France	300 000	60 000	130 000 = 43%
9	Holland	150 000	104 000	120 000 = 80%
10	Latvia	95 000	—	85 000 = 89%
11	Yugoslavia	75 000	55 000	65 000 = 87%
12	Greece	75 000	57 000	60 000 = 80%
13	Austria	60 000	—	40 000 = 67%
14	Belgium	100 000	25 000	40 000 = 40%
15	Italy	75 000	8 500	15 000 = 26%
16	Bulgaria	50 000	—	7 000 = 14%
17	Denmark	—	(less than 100)	— —
18	Luxemburg	—	3 000	3 000 —
19	Norway	—	700	1 000 —
	Total		4 194 200 app.	5 721 000 = 68%

Hans Jacobsen, Der Zweite Weltkrieg, 1965

people) was inconceivable in the "enlightened" atmosphere of the twentieth century. Now, with the horrific evidence before them, they realized—too late—that genocide had been all too real. Official photographs and films were taken at each camp as proof of Nazi atrocities for the war crimes trials that would follow and as permanent reminders of the extent to which hatred begets tragedy.

In the Nuremberg Trials following the war, twenty-two high-ranking Nazi officers were charged with various crimes, including crimes against humanity. Twelve were condemned to death. Seven received prison sentences. Three were found not guilty. The trials continued until July 1949, as ninety-nine other defendants were tried and sentenced to prison. Many Nazi war criminals escaped, however. Some were eventually captured and brought to trial. Others managed to hide from their pasts and never had to answer for their actions.

RESPONSIBILITY FOR WAR CRIMES

The Nuremberg Trials were based on the principle, affirmed by the United Nations, that "the fact that a person acted pursuant to the order of his government or a superior official does not relieve him from responsibility under international law...."

The decision to prosecute individuals for war crimes was a historic event. It brought into focus the competing values of personal and public responsibilities. The trials made it clear that individuals cannot avoid personal responsibility for their actions. Soldiers who shot civilians or herded them into death camps could not excuse their personal responsibility by claiming they were simply following orders.

Many suspected Nazi war criminals were hunted down by famous Jewish concentration camp survivor Simon Wiesenthal. In 1961, Adolf Eichmann, the infamous Nazi leader directly responsible for implementing Hitler's final solution, was captured in Argentina and brought to trial in Israel. After a trial that lasted four months Eichmann was convicted of crimes against humanity and sentenced to death. Some feel that the victors also committed war crimes and have gone unpunished because, as victors, they made the rules. Critics point to the decision to firebomb Dresden and to drop the atomic bomb as evidence of war crimes that have gone unprosecuted.

FORCES OF RESISTANCE

Raoul Wallenberg

A Swedish diplomat stationed in Hungary during the war, Raoul Wallenberg worked tirelessly and fearlessly to help 95 000 Hungarian Jews escape the death camps. Through

bribes, threats, bluffs, and false passports, he confounded the local fascist authorities, often risking confrontation with armed soldiers.

Sempo Sugihara

As Japanese consul in Lithuania, Sempo Sugihara defied his own

Over 6 million Jews were deliberately and systematically killed as part of Hitler's final solution. This figure is based on the carefully kept records of the SS officers who ran the death camps.

In Canada, the Criminal Code was amended in 1987 to allow trials in this country for war crimes committed by individuals elsewhere. By 1992, there were forty-five cases of suspected Nazi war criminals under review for possible prosecution. The Justice Department set 1994 as the target date to complete all investigations.

VOICES

THE HORROR OF THE DEATH CAMPS

The horror of the Nazi death camps has been recorded and preserved for the historical record. Testimony during the Nuremberg Trials presented the grim details of the Nazis' plan for the genocide of all European Jews. Survivors of the Holocaust have recorded their horrific memories of life in the camps. These quotations present vivid descriptions of the death camps, from opposing perspectives—that of a commander and that of a survivor. As you read these descriptions, reflect on the question of individual responsibility in carrying out crimes against humanity.

Rudolf Hoess, Nazi commandant

"I was ordered to establish extermination facilities at Auschwitz in June 1941. At that time there were already three other extermination camps [in Poland]. I visited Treblinka to find out how they carried out their extermination. The camp commandant at Treblinka told me that he had liquidated 80 000 in the course of half a year. He was principally concerned with liquidating all the Jews from the Warsaw ghetto. He used monoxide gas and I did not think that his methods were very efficient. So when I set up the extermination building at Auschwitz, I used Zyklon B, which was a crystallized prussic acid which we dropped into the death chamber from a small opening. It took from three to fifteen minutes to kill the people in the death chamber....We knew when the people were dead because their screaming stopped. We usually waited about a half hour before we opened the doors and removed the bodies. After the bodies were removed our special commandos took off the rings and extracted the gold from the teeth of the corpses....I estimate that at least 250 000 vic-

tims were executed and exterminated there by gassing and burning, and at least another half-million succumbed to starvation and disease."

From the Nuremburg Trials

Elie Wiesel, survivor of the Holocaust

"We did not yet know which was the better side, right or left; which road led to prison and which to the crematory. But for a moment I was happy, I was near my father. Our procession continued to move slowly forward.

"Another prisoner came up to us."

" 'Satisfied?' "

" 'Yes,' someone replied."

" 'Poor devils, you're going to the crematorium.' He seemed to be telling the truth. Not far from us, flames were leaping from a ditch, gigantic flames. They were burning something. A lorry drew up at the pit and delivered its load—little children. Babies! Yes, I saw it—saw it with my own eyes...those children in the flames....I pinched my face. Was I still alive? Was I awake? I could not believe it. How could it be possible for them to burn people, children...and...my father's voice drew me from my thoughts: 'It's a shame...a shame that you could not go with your mother....I saw several boys of your age going with their mothers....' "

"My forehead was bathed in cold sweat. But I told him that I did not believe that they could burn people in our age, that humanity could never tolerate it....'Humanity? Humanity is not concerned with us. Today, anything is allowed. Anything is possible, even these crematories.' "

From Elie Wiesel, Night *(New York: 1970, pp. 41-42).*

government, which was allied with Germany. In a dramatic nineteen-day period in 1940, he bravely signed exit visas allowing Jews to find transit out of Lithuania, a few steps ahead of the rapidly advancing German forces. Some historians credit Sempo Sugihara with saving 600 lives personally; others note that up to 25 000 may have left using his forged visas.

Oskar Schindler

Not all Germans were Nazis. Even those who flirted with the Nazis and profited from their activities sometimes found the courage to change their course. Early in the war, Oskar Schindler used forced Jewish labour in Poland to ring up huge profits working on behalf of the Nazi war machine. As the atrocities increased, Schindler had a change of heart and began to use his own money and cunning to save Jews. He purchased a list of 1100 Jewish workers to take to a new factory in Czechoslovakia where they could survive the Nazi killing machine. His actions are all the more remarkable because he had been a willing collaborator with the Nazis and had profited handsomely from his connections. Schindler's story was presented in the powerful film *Schindler's List*.

IN REVIEW

1. What was the Holocaust?

2. What was meant by the term *the final solution*?

3. Who should be held responsible for atrocities committed in war—the person issuing the orders? the person carrying them out? both parties? Explain your answer.

4. Read the quotation by Martin Niemöller (page 85). What was his message? Does it have meaning for you today in your community, in Canadian society, or in the world?

5. Sometimes when people have a problem they "pick on" someone less powerful than themselves. This is called **scapegoating**.
   (a) In what way did the Nazis use the Jews as scapegoats in Germany in the 1930s?
   (b) Describe another situation in which a person or group has been made a scapegoat.

TECHNOLOGY AND WAR

Scientists joined forces with military strategists to create a range of new weapons in the Second World War. On both sides of the battlefront, thousands of researchers applied scientific techniques to the special problems of war. In the United States alone, 30 000 scientists and engineers were employed in the development of new weapons and machines and new medical techniques.

BREAKING THE CODES

Science played a key role in breaking German and Japanese secret communications codes. The British were able to crack the German code in April 1940.

They used this knowledge to help the RAF during the Battle of Britain and throughout the war. The Americans were successful in breaking the Japanese secret codes, which helped them locate and track the Japanese fleet. As a result, the Americans were able to win critical naval battles and begin the destruction of the Japanese navy.

In 1938, a Polish mechanic working in a factory in eastern Germany discovered that the plant was secretly manufacturing signalling machines for the German army. The man carefully observed the parts being made and turned over the information to a British agent in Warsaw. With help from the Polish Secret Service, he was smuggled out of Poland to Britain. There he created a model of the machine, called Enigma, from memory. British scientists realized that Enigma was the key to breaking the German communications code. The Polish Secret Service stole a complete working machine from the factory, then British scientists began the complicated task of solving the puzzle of Enigma. By April 1940, the code was broken. For the rest of the war the Allies were able to read secret German messages.

MEDICAL TECHNOLOGY

New or improved drugs and medical techniques made an important contribution to the war and saved the lives of one out of every two wounded soldiers. In the war in the Pacific, malaria was a constant threat to the troops. The principal source of the traditional cure—quinine—was the island of Java. When Java was captured by the Japanese in 1942, the Allies successfully developed a synthetic form of quinine. This new drug was critical to the success of Allied troops in both the Middle East and Asia.

RADAR

Radar is used to detect the nature, position, and movement of an object. Electromagnetic waves are beamed out, reflected from the target, and picked up by the radar unit, which then converts the signals into images on a screen. This technology was being developed by Britain, Germany, and the United States prior to the war, but it was the British who made the most rapid progress. Radar provided them with an early warning system for the German air raids and played an important role in winning the Battle of Britain.

JET PLANES

Germany produced the first jet airplane in 1939. By 1941, they had developed a jet fighter plane. These jet planes could fly at speeds much greater than propeller-driven aircraft and would have given Germany air superiority. But when the new plane was presented to Hitler in November 1943, he demanded that it be adapted for bombing. This delayed production of the aircraft until the fall of 1944; as a result, they were too late to play an important role in the German war effort. The Allies were also developing their own jet planes and had their fighters ready for use in Belgium by 1945.

ROCKETS

As the Allies invaded France and Russian forces moved against Germany from the east, Hitler announced that the German people would be saved by new "miracle inventions." The first of these, the V-1 (Vengeance), was a pilotless monoplane that carried an explosive warhead. Almost 10 000 of these **buzz-bombs** (so called because of the noise they produced) were fired at British cities beginning in 1944. But while the V-1 inflicted serious damage, the more advanced V-2 rockets that followed gave Britain cause for far greater concern. The V-2 flew at supersonic speed, giving no warning and offering no opportunity for defence. Fortunately, British intelligence discovered where these bombs were being developed. An Allied bombing raid on the production plant in August 1943 delayed its manufacture until the following year. In September 1944, however, V-2s were fired on Britain. Still, the delay was an important one for Britain. Had the V-2 been available to the Germans earlier, it might have changed the course of the war.

THE ATOMIC BOMB

In 1939, Albert Einstein, a physicist who had emigrated from Germany to the United States in 1933, wrote a letter to President Roosevelt advising him that German scientists were working on an atomic bomb that would be capable of mass destruction. In response to this German threat, Roosevelt established the **Manhattan Project** to develop an atomic bomb for American use. Robert Oppenheimer led a group of American and Allied scientists in developing the bomb. Following its successful testing in New Mexico in July 1945, the United States was ready to use the ultimate weapon of destruction.

IN REVIEW

1. Give three specific examples to show the role science played in the war effort.

2. Develop arguments for and against the following statement: "Wars encourage technological improvements for society."

3. In your opinion, what was the most significant technological invention of the Second World War?

THE CANADIAN WAR EFFORT

Canada was in a unique position to contribute to the Allied war effort. Like the United States, it was protected from direct conflict on its own shores by the Atlantic Ocean. This position of relative safety enabled the country to turn its resources and industries to the production of war materials. Canadian industries produced combat aircraft, tanks, and motor vehicles. The Canadian forces supplied thousands of troops and support personnel who were directly engaged in the conflicts overseas. In addition, the Canadian military provided other services, such as naval escorts for supply convoys across the Atlantic and pilot training facilities for the British Commonwealth Air Training Plan.

WOMEN IN WARTIME

Canadian women played a large role in the armed forces. By the end of the war, 6000 women had joined the auxiliary forces of the air force and army; 16 000 served in the women's division of the air force; 6600 served in the Women's Naval Service; 21 000 served in the Women's Army Corps; 2500 joined the Nursing Service; and 38 signed up as doctors. Although they were not assigned to combat duty, women served in many essential positions, such as aircraft spotters, wireless operators, drivers, signallers, nurses, and doctors. A new role for women in the war was ferrying all types of aircraft, sometimes in transatlantic flights. While they played vital roles, however, some women felt that the mottoes of the various women's services, such as "We are the women behind the men behind the guns" and "We serve that men might fly," unfairly cast them in a subordinate role.

On the home front, as men enlisted in the services, women stepped in to fill their places in the workforce. As wartime production increased, more jobs were created. By 1942, women were recruited to work on farms, to drive transports and buses, and to labour in factories as welders, riveters, and machinists. Over 260 000 women worked in manufacturing, producing everything from machine guns to ships and airplanes.

After the war most married women returned to their homes and assumed their traditional roles. In fact, married women were barred from the civil service, a regulation that remained in effect for the next ten years. Single women were not discouraged from working but they were channelled back into their traditional jobs as domestics, office workers, nurses, and teachers. Despite pressure to maintain the women's divisions of the armed forces, the government disbanded them as soon as the war was over. The gains women made in the workforce during the war were temporarily lost when the men returned home.

IN REVIEW

1. What was Canada's military and industrial contribution to the war effort?

2. What role did women play in the war? Did their role have any long-range effect on Canadian society?

SUMMARY

The world that emerged from the ashes of Berlin and Hiroshima was radically different from that which had gone to war in 1939. Europe was no longer the centre of the world. A bipolar world dominated by the United States and the Soviet Union had emerged after the first half of the twentieth century.

The second half of the century would be dominated by the Cold War between these two new superpowers in which every crisis could mean the total destruction of human society.

MAKING CONNECTIONS

1. How was the world that emerged from the Second World War different from the world that entered it?

2. What current evidence is there that the brutality revealed during the Second World War is still a part of life today? Offer specific examples.

3. Should Canada continue to prosecute suspected Nazi war criminals? Explain your answer.

DEVELOPING YOUR VOICE

4. Select one student to be US president Harry Truman. The rest of the class should prepare brief arguments for and against the dropping of the atomic bomb on Japan. Organize a council of war to debate the issue. The final decision rests in the hands of the president.

5. Working in small groups, rank order the following in terms of their responsibility for the tragedies of war: a) government; b) military leaders; c) society; d) the nature of war; e) specific individuals; f) other (specify). Discuss your ranking with the class.

RESEARCHING THE ISSUES

6. Select a major battle of the Second World War. Research the battle and prepare a presentation for the class. Include:
   (a) the objectives and tactics of the battle
   (b) the key factors that affected the outcome of the battle
   (c) the significance of the battle to the outcome of the war.

7. View the CBC videotape *The Valour and the Horror*, particularly Part III, which examines the role of bombing raids in the Second World War. What questions does this program raise about the Allied and Axis bombing raids?

8. Research the Manhattan Project. Look particularly for details about Canada's contribution. Prepare a written report of your findings.

VIEWPOINTS

ISSUE: WAS HITLER RESPONSIBLE FOR THE OUTBREAK OF THE SECOND WORLD WAR?

The conventional historical interpretation is that Hitler and Nazi Germany bear the primary responsibility for the Second World War. While Britain and France were lax and should have taken a firmer stand against Hitler long before 1939, these nations were not responsible for Hitler's invasion of Poland. In his controversial book *The Origins of the Second World War*, British historian A.J.P. Taylor challenged this traditional view. Taylor claimed that Hitler did not plan to go to war but was simply a politician trying to solve the historic German problem of security and to right the wrongs of the Treaty of Versailles. Taylor's viewpoint is countered by historian H.R. Trevor-Roper. He argues that Taylor's analysis and interpretation of the events leading to war are historically false. Read these two viewpoints carefully, then complete an Argument Analysis and Evaluation.

A.J.P. Taylor

"Most people think that the Germans wanted international equality—a state free from all restrictions on its armed forces and including all Germans. This is correct. But the inevitable consequence of fulfilling this wish was that Germany would become the dominant state in Europe. Again, many people, including many Germans, said that Germany merely wanted to reverse the verdict of the First World War. This also is correct. But they misunderstood what was implied. They thought that it meant only undoing the consequences of defeat—no more reparations, the recovery of the European territory and the colonies lost by the Treaty of Versailles. It means much more than this: not only that things should be arranged as though Germany had not been defeated, but that they should be arranged as though she had won."

"We now know...what the Germans would have arranged if they had won the First World War. It was a Europe indistinguishable from Hitler's empire at its greatest extent, including even a Poland and a Ukraine cleared of their native inhabitants. Hitler...was a gambler in foreign, as in home, affairs; a skilful tactician, waiting to exploit the opportunities which others offered to him. His easy successes made him careless, as was not surprising, and he gambled steadily higher...."

"I fear I may not have emphasized the profound forces. Of course there was a general climate of feeling in Europe of the nineteen-thirties which made war likely. Everyone talked about the coming war. In particular, military men—in Great Britain and France as much as in Germany—treated war as inevitable. This was quite right from their point of view. It is the job of military men to prepare for war and indeed to assume that it is coming. But their talk washed over on to the politicians, as it still does, and they, too, began to regard war as inevitable...."

"We do right to ask: why did war seem likely in the nineteen-thirties? But wars, however likely, break out at a specific moment and presumably over some specific issue. On 1 September 1939 the German armies invaded Poland. On 3 September Great Britain and France declared war on Germany. These two events began a war, which subsequently—though not until 1941—became the Second World War....I think we are entitled to ask: why did Hitler invade Poland when he did? why did Great Britain and France declare war on Germany? These questions may seem trivial, but historians spend much of their time on trivialities, and some of them believe that only by adding up trivialities can they safely arrive at generalizations...."

Reprinted from Past and Present *(April 1965), by permission of the author and* Past and Present.

H.R. Trevor-Roper

"The thesis of [A.J.P. Taylor's book *The Origins of the Second World War*] is perfectly clear. According to Mr. Taylor, Hitler was an ordinary German statesman in the tradition of [chancellors] Stresemann and Bruning, differing from them not in methods (he was made chancellor for 'solidly democratic reasons') nor in ideas (he had no ideas) but only in the greater patience and stronger nerves with which he took advantage of the objective situation in Europe. His policy, in so far as he had a policy, was no different from that of his predecessors. He sought neither war nor annexation of territory. He merely sought to restore Germany's "natural" position in Europe, which had been artificially altered by the Treaty of Versailles: a treaty which, for that reason, 'lacked moral validity from the start.' Such a restoration might involve the recovery of lost German territory like Danzig, but it did not entail the direct government even of Austria or the Sudetenland, let alone Bohemia. Ideally, all that Hitler required was that Austria, Czechoslovakia and other small Central European states, while remaining independent, should become political satellites of Germany."

"Of course it did not work out thus. But that, we are assured, was not Hitler's fault. For Hitler, according to Mr. Taylor, never took the initiative in politics. He 'did not make plans—for world conquest or anything else. He assumed that others would provide opportunities and that he would seize them.' And that is what happened....The last thing [Hitler] wanted was war. The war of nerves was 'the only war he understood and liked.'..."

"...The real determinants of history, according to Mr. Taylor, are objective situations and human blunders. Objective situations consist of the realities of power; human intelligence is best employed in recognising these realities and allowing events to conform with them; but as human intelligence seldom prevails in politics, the realities generally have to assert themselves, at greater human cost, through the mess caused by human blunders...."

"But is this general philosophy true? Do statesmen really never make history? Are they, all of them, always 'too absorbed by events to follow a preconceived plan'?...Certainly Hitler himself did not think so. He regarded himself as a thinker, a practical philosopher, the...evil creator of a new age of history. And since he published a blueprint of the policy which he intended to carry out, ought we not at least to look at this blueprint just in case it had some relevance to his policy? After all, the reason why the majority of the British people reluctantly changed, between 1936 and 1939, from the views of Neville Chamberlain and Mr. Taylor to the views of Winston Churchill was their growing conviction that Hitler meant what he said: that he was aiming...at world conquest. A contemporary conviction that was strong enough to change the mood of a nation from a passionate desire for peace to a resolute determination on war surely deserves some respect from the historian...."

"Let us consider briefly the programme which Hitler laid down for himself. It was a programme of Eastern colonisation, entailing a war of conquest against Russia. If it were successfully carried out, it would leave Germany dominant in Eurasia and able to conquer the West at will. In order to carry it out, Hitler needed a restored German army which, since it must be powerful enough to conquer Russia, must also be powerful enough to conquer the West if that should be necessary. And that might be necessary even before the attack on Russia. For in order to reach Russia, Hitler would need to send his armies through Poland; and in order to do this—whether by the conquest of Poland or in alliance with it—he would need to break the bonds of treaty and interest which bound the new countries of Eastern Europe, the creatures of Versailles, to their creator, Britain and France. Hitler might be able to break those bonds without war against the West, but he could not be sure of it: it was always possible that a war with the West would be necessary before he could march against Russia. And in fact this is what happened."

"Now this programme, which Hitler ascribed to himself, and which he actually carried out, is obviously entirely different from the far more limited programme which is ascribed to him by Mr. Taylor, and which he did not carry out. How then does Mr. Taylor deal with the evidence about it? He deals with it quite simply either by ignoring it or by denying it as inconsistent with his own theories about statesmen in general and Hitler in particular: theories (one must add) for which he produces no evidence at all...."

"I think Mr. Taylor's book utterly erroneous. In spite of his statements about 'historical discipline,' he selects, suppresses and arranges evidence on no principle other than the needs of his thesis; and that thesis, that Hitler was a traditional statesman, of limited aims, merely responding to a given situation, rests on no evidence at all, ignores essential evidence, and is, in my opinion, demonstrably false...."

"Basically, the problem is that of the outbreak of world wars. According to Mr. Taylor, the Second World War had a double origin: first, it was 'implicit' in the general situation; secondly, it was made explicit by the particular blunders of statesmen in the face of that situation. The general situation was created in 1918 when the victorious Allies did not carve Germany up, and so made the ultimate recovery of its 'natural weight' inevitable. The particular blunders lay in the failure of Western statesmen to draw the logical conclusions and yield to the inevitable. If only they had shown 'realism' and yielded to all Hitler's demands, they would have found them limited and reasonable: it was only victory which surprised him by the size of his winnings and made him think of world conquest."

From E.M. Robertson (ed.), The Origins of the Second World War: Historical Interpretations, *(London: Macmillan Press Ltd., 1978) pp. 83-104.*

ANALYSIS AND EVALUATION

Refer to the Argument Analysis and Evaluation Procedure on page viii.

1. Using the Argument Analysis and Evaluation Procedure, compare the readings by Taylor and Trevor-Roper.

2. Decide which of the viewpoints you tend to support and explain why. Be sure to use specific information from this textbook, the readings, and other sources to support your position.

3. State and support your position on the issue: "Was Hitler responsible for the outbreak of the Second World War?"

Unit Two:
THE COLD WAR

❖ 1946 - 1959   1960 - 1969

POLITICS/MILITARY

1946 - 1959

- Churchill's "Iron Curtain" speech (1946)
- Nuremberg Trials (1946)
- Truman Doctrine (1947)
- Marshall Plan (1947)
- First Arab-Israeli War (1948)
- UN signs Declaration of Human Rights (1948)
- Gandhi assassinated (1948)
- Independent state of Israel declared (1948)
- Berlin Blockade (1948)
- NATO formed (1949)
- Communists win civil war in China (1949)
- Newfoundland joins Canada (1949)
- Korean War begins (1950)
- Korean War ends (1953)
- Warsaw Pact (1955)
- Soviets crush Hungarian Revolution (1956)
- Egypt seizes Suez Canal (1956)
- W. European nations launch EEC (1957)
- Castro becomes leader of Cuba (1959)

1960 - 1969

- Soviets shoot down US spy plane (1960)
- Sharpeville massacre in South Africa (1960)
- Berlin Wall built (1961)
- US Bay of Pigs invasion (1961)
- Cuban Missile Crisis (1962)
- US establishes military presence in Vietnam (1962)
- Nuclear Test Ban Treaty (1963)
- Start of détente (1963)
- Assassination of JFK (1963)
- US enters war in Vietnam (1964)
- PLO formed (1964)
- US begins bombing of North Vietnam (1965)
- Americans walk in space (1965)
- France withdraws from NATO (1966)
- Arab-Israeli Six-Day War (1967)
- Canada's Centennial Year (1967)
- European Community formed to promote political unity (1967)
- Soviets invade Czechoslovakia (1968)
- Tet offensive in Vietnam (1968)

CULTURE/SOCIETY

1946 - 1959

- Spock, *The Commonsense Book of Baby and Childcare* (1946)
- Robinson first black player in US baseball (1947)
- *Diary of Anne Frank* (1947)
- Miles Davis produces first cool jazz
- Orwell, *1984* (1949)
- First credit card (1950)
- Salinger, *Catcher in the Rye* (1951)
- Contraceptive pills introduced (1952)
- de Beauvoir, *Second Sex* (1953)
- First scaling of Mt. Everest (1953)
- Tolkien, *Lord of the Rings* (1954)
- Rock 'n' roll (1955)
- Disneyland opens (1955)
- Presley, "Hound Dog" (1956)
- Galbraith, *The Affluent Society* (1958)
- Stereophonic records introduced (1958)

1960 - 1969

- *Psycho* (1960)
- Eichmann trial in Jerusalem (1961)
- Freedom riders test racism in southern US (1961)
- Thalidomide tragedy—deformed babies worldwide (1962)
- The Beatles become international sensation (1963)
- Martin Luther King leads civil rights campaign in US (1963)
- Kodak Instamatic camera (1963)
- Le Carré, *The Spy Who Came in from the Cold* (1963)
- Thousands arrested in US race riots (1964)
- Colour TV widely enjoyed (1966)
- Rise of black power in US (1967)
- 100 million telephones in US (1967)
- Worldwide student unrest (1968)
- Woodstock music festival (1969)

SCIENCE/TECHNOLOGY

1946 - 1959

- ENIAC the first computer (1946)
- Yeager breaks sound barrier (1947)
- Invention of the transistor (1947)
- Land develops Polaroid camera (1947)
- LP record invented (1948)
- Soviets detonate first atomic bomb (1949)
- Einstein, General Field Theory (1950)
- First commercial jet (1952)
- US launches first nuclear submarine (1952)
- Watson-Crick decode DNA structure (1953)
- USSR explodes H-bomb (1953)
- Salk develops anti-polio vaccine (1955)
- First use of atomic-generated power in US (1955)
- Transatlantic cable telephone service (1956)
- USSR launches first satellite (1957)
- US produces first ICBM (1958)
- US enters space race with USSR (1958)
- USSR lands satellite on moon (1959)

1960 - 1969

- France explodes first nuclear bomb (1960)
- Yuri Gargarin (USSR) first person in space (1961)
- Britain and France agree to build world's first supersonic airliner (1962)
- Telstar satellite (1962)
- Valentina Tereshkova (USSR) first woman in space (1963)
- First compact disc (1963)
- China explodes A-bomb (1964)
- American doctors use plastic heart to keep patient alive (1966)
- First heart transplant (1967)
- US astronauts on the moon (1969)
- First test flight of Concorde (1969)
- First human egg fertilized outside of woman's body (1969)

❖	1970 - 1979	1980 - 1995
POLITICS / MILITARY	• National Guard in US fires on student demonstrators at Kent State (1970) • People's Republic of China enters UN (1971) • US détente with China (1971) • US and China establish diplomatic relations (1972) • Great Britain joins Common Market (1973) • Arab-Israeli Yom Kippur War (1973) • Arab oil embargo (1973) • Watergate scandal forces Nixon to resign (1974) • Vietnam falls to communist forces (1975) • Egypt's Sadat visits Israel (1977) • Carter pardons American draft dodgers (1977) • Vietnam conquers Cambodia (1979) • Thatcher first woman PM in UK history (1979) • SALT II signed in Geneva (1979) • Soviets invade Afghanistan (1979)	• Solidarity formed in Poland • Iran-Iraq War (1980) • US invades Grenada (1983) • USSR and Eastern bloc boycott LA Olympics (1984) • Gorbachev elected Soviet General Secretary (1985) • US and USSR limit long-range nuclear missiles (1987) • Canada-US Free Trade Agreement (1988) • Iran-Iraq War ends (1988) • Berlin Wall falls (1989) • Collapse of E. European communist regimes (1989) • Iraq invades Kuwait (1990) • Unification of East and West Germany (1990) • START Treaty on Nuclear Disarmament (1991) • Dissolution of Soviet Union (1991) • Middle East Peace Talks (1991) • Civil war in former Yugoslavia (1991) • UN peacekeepers sent to former Yugoslavia (1992) • European Union (1992) • Czechs and Slovaks dismember Czechoslovakia (1993) • Israel-PLO peace agreement (1993) • Mandela wins first free elections in S. Africa (1994)
CULTURE / SOCIETY	• Huge wave of American student protest against war in Vietnam (1970) • Billie Jean King first female athlete to earn $100 000 in a year (1971) • US army ends draft (1972) • Global energy crisis (1973) • Airlift of Vietnam refugees to US (1975) • Japan introduces first video game (1975) • Start of punk rock (1977) • Cardinal Karol Wojityla first non-Italian Pope in 450 years (1978) • Nobel Peace Prize to Mother Theresa (1979)	• Rubik's Cube craze (1981) • *ET* (1982) • Jackson, *Thriller* (1983) • Wall Street stockmarket crash (1987) • UN ranks Canada as best country in world in which to live (1994) • Outbreak of Ebola virus in Africa (1995)
SCIENCE / TECHNOLOGY	• Boeing 747 jumbo starts service (1970) • First heart pacemaker (1970) • Discovery of two new neighbouring galaxies (1971) • Leakey discovers 2.5 million-year-old fossil (1972) • US Skylab space mission (1973) • India sixth nation to explode A-bomb (1974) • US and Soviet craft link up in space (1975) • *Viking I* lands on Mars (1975) • *Viking II* orbits Mars (1975) • First solar-powered calculator (1977) • World's first test-tube baby born (1978)	• US *Voyager 1* travels past Saturn and transmits dramatic photos (1980) • Stealth bomber deployed by US (1980) • US launches first space shuttle (1981) • AIDS identified (1981) • Early success of first permanent artificial heart (1982) • Nuclear accident at Chernobyl (USSR) (1985) • Space shuttle *Challenger* explodes (1986) • Hawking, *A Brief History of Time* (1988) • Hargreaves first woman to scale Everest alone, without oxygen cylinders

CHAPTER FIVE

The Cold War: 1945–1990

"This war is not as in the past; whoever occupies a territory also imposes on it his own system as far as his army has power to do so. It cannot be otherwise."

Joseph Stalin (1879-1953), Soviet leader (1929-53)

"From Stettin in the Baltic, to Trieste in the Adriatic, an iron curtain has descended across the continent....Behind that line lie all the capitals of the States of central and Eastern Europe—all are subject in one form or another not only to Soviet influence but to a very high and increasing measure of control from Moscow."

Winston Churchill (1874-1965), British prime minister (1940-45, 1951-55)

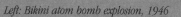

Left: Bikini atom bomb explosion, 1946

❖ OVERVIEW

With the end of the Second World War, a new and even more dangerous era began—the **nuclear age**. The spotlight now focused on the fundamental differences between the United States and the Soviet Union. A new era of tense rivalry between the former allies—now the world's foremost military superpowers—had emerged. The spectre of nuclear war cast a long shadow over the globe.

The atmosphere of suspicion, distrust, rivalry, and hostility quickly became known as the **Cold War**. The hopes of people around the world for peace, co-operation, and security were dashed by the continuous threat of confrontation and conflict between the superpowers. The Cold War often erupted into open conflict involving third parties or in **flashpoints** that brought the United States and the Soviet Union to the brink of direct confrontation. Despite the devastation of two world conflicts, it seemed that humanity had yet to learn the lessons of war.

FOCUS QUESTIONS

1. What were the origins of the Cold War?
2. How were international relations affected by the Cold War?
3. What were some of the causes and results of the major flashpoints of the Cold War?

THE SUPERPOWERS: FROM FRIEND TO FOE

Although the Cold War began after the Second World War, its origins lie earlier in the century. The swift and effective communist takeover in Russia in 1917 shocked the Western democracies.

They tried to overthrow the new regime by backing anti-Bolshevik forces between 1918 and 1920.

In the 1920s and 1930s, the West feared that communism would spread throughout Europe. As a result, the Soviet Union was politically isolated by the Western powers. No Soviet representatives were invited to participate in the peace talks at Versailles. The United States refused to recognize the Soviet government until 1933. And the Soviet Union was not invited to join the League of Nations until 1934.

During the 1930s, while the rest of the industrialized world was mired in economic depression, the Soviet Union was forging a new industrial order. Under Stalin's reforms, sweeping social and economic changes were transforming the country. The West watched with a great deal of uneasiness.

BITTER ALLIES

In August 1939, the Soviet Union and Germany secretly negotiated a Non-Aggression Pact. At the same time, however, Stalin had been looking towards an alliance with the West. The Allies were stunned by Stalin's deception. For his part, Stalin was convinced that the Allies were unwilling to stop Hitler. He believed that they hoped Hitler's aggressive territorial ambitions would be diverted from Western Europe towards the Soviet Union. Consequently, Stalin felt a pact with Germany was in the best interests of the USSR because it would buy time in which to prepare for a German attack.

That attack came in June 1941, ending the Nazi-Soviet pact and bringing the Soviet Union into the war on the side of the Allies. But it was an uneasy alliance. The common purpose —the defeat of Germany—fostered co-operation, but there were fundamental conflicts over strategy.

The Soviet Union suffered terrible losses in 1941-42. The Soviets appealed to the Allies to open a second front in Western Europe to divert some of the German forces and relieve some of the pressure on the Soviet Union. Promises of an Allied invasion of Europe were made but not kept. In June 1943, Stalin was told by Roosevelt that the second front had been postponed until 1944. Stalin suspected the Allies were deliberately delaying a European invasion to give the Nazis and the Soviets more time to destroy one another.

The Battle of Stalingrad (1942-43) ended with a decisive victory for the Red Army. It marked a turning point in the war and the beginning of the German defeat. But fighting on the Eastern Front remained intense. Throughout 1943 and well into 1944, 75 per cent of Germany's ground troops were engaged there.

As the Soviet army steadily advanced westward in 1943, the Allies began to envision a new scenario, one in which the Soviet Union would liberate not only Eastern Europe but Western Europe as well. German occupation of the continent would be replaced with Soviet domination. Determined to prevent this, the second front became a reality in June 1944 when the Allies landed in Normandy. Russia had forced the Germans back as far as Poland. Now the race was on to reconquer Europe.

YALTA

At the Yalta Conference in February 1945, Churchill, Roosevelt, and Stalin met to decide the fate of postwar Europe. They agreed that, once defeated, Germany would be temporarily divided into three zones, with Britain, the United States, and the Soviet Union each controlling one zone. The former German capital of Berlin, although deep within the Soviet zone, was also to be divided. It would prove to be a prime flashpoint of the Cold War era.

"I cannot forecast to you the action of Russia. It is a riddle wrapped in a mystery inside an enigma: but perhaps there is a key. That key is Russian national interest."

Winston Churchill, in a radio address, 1 October 1939

The key issue of the conference was the future of Eastern Europe, particularly Poland. Soviet troops already occupied most of the region and Stalin was determined that the Eastern European states would have pro-Soviet governments. His position reflected the long Russian tradition of establishing a buffer zone along its extensive western border. This zone included Poland, Czechoslovakia, Hungary, and Romania. In the Soviets' view, countries they recaptured from the Germans should remain under their control. Twice within thirty years, Russia had been attacked via Poland. As soon as Soviet troops had liberated Poland,

"If we see that Germany is winning we should help Russia and if Russia is winning we ought to help Germany and that way let them kill as many as possible, although I don't want to see Hitler victorious under any circumstances."

Harry S. Truman, then Democratic senator, commenting on Germany's invasion of the Soviet Union, June 1941

Churchill, Roosevelt, and Stalin determined the fate of postwar Europe at Yalta.

spheres of influence. The Soviets conveniently interpreted this plan to mean that they would police Eastern Europe, thereby effectively establishing their much-desired sphere of influence.

Churchill favoured the sphere of influence approach to world security. In 1944, he met with Stalin to propose a system of control in Eastern Europe that would benefit both the Soviet Union and Britain. Churchill agreed to recognize Soviet domination in Romania and Bulgaria; in return Stalin was to recognize Britain's right to control Greece.

Stalin installed a pro-Soviet government there.

Roosevelt and Churchill were reluctant to allow Poland to fall under the Soviet umbrella. After all, Britain had entered the war to guarantee Poland's independence. With the fall of Poland, a government-in-exile was formed in London—the so-called "London Poles"—which claimed to be the legitimate government of Poland. Clearly Poland was a test case: American and British recognition of Soviet control would signal their recognition of Stalin's right to establish a **sphere of influence** in Eastern Europe. Churchill strongly opposed the spread of Soviet influence and he urged the American president to be firm. Roosevelt, however, favoured a global approach to world peace. He proposed a co-operative undertaking, with China, the Soviet Union, the United States, and Britain acting as international enforcers in their own

At the insistence of Roosevelt and Churchill, Stalin pledged that free elections would be held in the Eastern European states as soon as possible. This promise was given great significance by Roosevelt and Churchill. But in reality when Stalin left Yalta he believed that Soviet domination in Eastern Europe would not be challenged.

TRUMAN TAKES OFFICE

In April 1945, Roosevelt died. Harry S. Truman, vice-president for little more than a year, assumed the presidency. On the international scene, Truman was a relative unknown. Most observers believed he would quietly serve out FDR's term and then fade from the political scene. But Truman was determined to take a hard line with the Soviet Union. He angrily rebuked the Soviet Foreign Secretary V.M. Molotov for breaking the Yalta agreement on Polish self-determination. Truman demanded a new government for Poland. But in June 1945 he was forced to accept a compromise when the Soviets agreed to install a few pro-Western Poles in the government. Truman's "get tough" policy was hardening Soviet resistance. His belief that the Soviets would yield to American pressure was a critical misconception.

POTSDAM

Between 17 July and 2 August 1945 another conference was held, at Potsdam outside Berlin. Two of the key players had now changed: Truman represented the US and, part way through the conference, Clement Atlee replaced Churchill as Britain's leader. Stalin still presided over the Soviet delegation.

The Potsdam Conference, although marked by arguments and accusations, began the long process of cleaning up after the war. To establish peace treaties with Italy, Romania, Bulgaria, Hungary, and Finland and to finalize boundaries, the powers agreed to establish a Council of Foreign Ministers. As for Nazi Germany, several conditions were established. It was agreed that all Nazi institutions would be dismantled and Nazi war criminals would be tried and punished. Reparations would be paid in machinery and equipment, with the Soviets having the right to take what they wanted from the eastern sector of Germany and 35 per cent from the western sector. The Allies could not agree on the future of Germany so the "temporary arrangement" to divide Germany and Berlin remained in effect.

The question of Poland, however, continued to be hotly debated. The West wanted to reinstate the "London Poles." Stalin, however, would recog-

At the Potsdam Conference, Stalin faced new negotiators in Atlee and Truman.

nize only the pro-Soviet government—the "Lublin Poles"—already in place and backed by the Red Army. The Western powers finally backed down and accepted Soviet control of Poland.

The conflicts, arguments, and misunderstandings of the Yalta and Potsdam conferences provided a glimpse into the Cold War to come. The American perception was that

In a meeting in Moscow in October 1944, Churchill and Stalin unofficially—and secretly—agreed on the division of the Balkans after the war. Churchill wrote these "percentage agreements" on a piece of paper and gave it to Stalin. Stalin had the paper translated, then placed a large checkmark on the paper. The deal was done. The Soviet Union would control 90 per cent of Romania and 75 percent of Bulgaria. Britain would control 90 per cent of Greece. Yugoslavia and Hungary would be divided up fifty-fifty.

Soviet control of Eastern Europe was temporary. The Soviet perception was that Eastern Europe was now its sphere of influence. With the defeat of Japan in August, the need for co-operation between the Soviet Union and the West evaporated and the Cold War began in earnest.

IN REVIEW

1.   What is meant by the term *Cold War*?

2.   What were some of the background causes of the Cold War?

3.   How did the Second World War both unite and divide the Soviet Union and the West?

4.   State the key areas of agreement and disagreement between the Soviet Union and the Western Allies at (a) Yalta and (b) Potsdam.

5.   Explain why the former allies had opposing views about the future of Poland.

THE COLD WAR DECLARED

The deterioration of Soviet-American relations in 1945 was little known out-side official government circles in Moscow and Washington. The citizens of the Soviet Union were preoccupied with the enormous task of restoring their country after the ravages of war. The Americans were content to return to their traditional isolationism. After their victories in two theatres of war, they felt secure in the knowledge that they possessed, in the words of Truman, "the greatest strength and the greatest power" the world had ever known.

Washington's attention, however, was riveted on Moscow. Every Soviet move was viewed with suspicion, every utterance from the Kremlin analysed for hidden meaning. The countries occupied by the Soviet army were becoming increasingly en-trenched in communism, and further expansion of the Soviet sphere of in-fluence seemed likely.

Many American politicians con-sidered the US monopoly of atomic weapons a useful deterrent to Soviet expansion and a lever against Soviet domination of Eastern Europe. While the atomic bombs dropped on Japan ended the war, they may also have been intended as a demonstration to the Soviet Union of American power. Between 1945 and 1949, there is little doubt that Truman used American atomic power as a threat against the mighty Soviet army. This contributed to deteriorating American-Soviet relations and hastened Soviet development of their own atomic weapons. By 1949, the Soviet Union equalled the playing field by exploding its own atom bomb.

THE OPENING SHOTS OF THE COLD WAR

Two speeches in 1946 alerted the world to the mounting tensions between the West and the Soviet Union. In February 1946, Stalin addressed voters in Mos-cow, predicting that, because of "the unevenness of development of the capitalist countries," they would split into "two hostile camps," with war the inevitable result. He exhorted the Soviet people to prepare for a situation similar to the 1930s by sacrificing consumer goods in favour of industrial production. He warned that the future would bring neither internal nor external peace. In Washington, Stalin's words were interpreted to mean that war with the West was inevitable. The atmosphere grew heavier with suspicion, distrust, and hostility.

Churchill's "Iron Curtain" Speech

Winston Churchill had always been distrustful of Stalin's intentions. He took the threat of communist expansion seriously. At Truman's invitation, Churchill travelled to the United States to warn the Americans of the Soviet threat and the need for an "association of the English-speaking peoples" acting outside of the United Nations to reorder the world. His "Iron Curtain" speech, which received massive press coverage, had a great impact on American public opinion. It convinced many Americans that Truman's "get tough" approach to the Soviets was the right one.

Stalin reacted angrily to the speech. He accused Churchill of embracing racial theories not unlike Hitler's and of wanting English-speaking people to "rule over the remaining nations of the world." Labelling Churchill a "firebrand of war," Stalin reminded him that the Allies had agreed to the Polish settlement in Potsdam. If communism was expanding, it was because "Commu-

nists have showed themselves to be reliable, daring, and self-sacrificing fighters against Fascist regimes for the liberty of peoples."

THE TRUMAN DOCTRINE

A year after Churchill's Iron Curtain speech, on 12 March 1947, Truman delivered his declaration of Cold War. He called on the nation to resist communism throughout the world. His speech was designed to garner support for an American pledge of hundreds of millions of dollars to prevent the spread of communism in Europe. Greece was in the throes of a civil war in which rebel forces, including communists, were challenging the pro-Western government. Britain could no longer afford to provide military aid to Greece. While the rebels were supported by Yugoslavia, not Moscow, Truman feared that without Western military support Greece would fall to communism. In reality, however, Stalin recognized Britain's position in Greece; he went as far as to warn Yugoslavia not to provoke a confrontation with the

In a speech in Fulton, Missouri, Churchill warned that "a shadow has fallen" over the Allied victory in the Second World War.

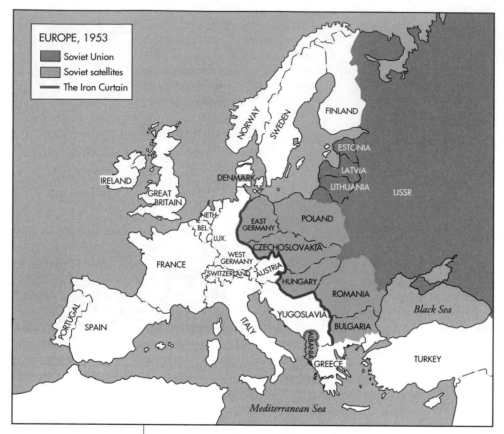

EUROPE, 1953
- Soviet Union
- Soviet satellites
- —— The Iron Curtain

Figure 5.1:
Europe and the
Iron Curtain

extended to a host of regimes, including right-wing dictatorships, in an effort to block communist takeovers. Thus the United States committed itself to sacrificing money and lives to halt the growth of communism anywhere in the world. It was a policy that would have serious implications for the entire world.

THE POLICY OF CONTAINMENT

George Kennan, a prominent American diplomat and respected expert on Soviet affairs, warned Washington in 1946 that the combination of "the traditional and instinctive Russian sense of insecurity" with communist ideology, secretiveness, and conspiracy would inevitably create an explosive situation. He argued that Stalin's policies were shaped by a communist ideology that called for revolution in order to overthrow capitalist governments. Since the collapse of capitalism was inevitable, according to communist theory, Moscow would be in no hurry. The Soviets would slowly chip away at the capitalist world.

Kennan believed that if the United States could contain the spread of communism, the Soviet system would eventually crumble. He did not advocate military confrontation; his was strictly a defensive strategy. His ideas formed the basis for the new American policy of **containment**.

While Kennan was realistic about the establishment of spheres of

West. For Truman, however, in order to win congressional approval for $400 million in aid, the communist threat had to appear overwhelming.

The policy of fighting communism around the world became known as the **Truman Doctrine**. In the years that followed, American aid was

On 5 September 1945, Igor Gouzenko, a Soviet citizen employed at its embassy in Ottawa, defected to Canada. He brought with him documents that proved that the Soviet Union was spying on its allies. An investigation revealed a widespread spy network operating in Canada. This incident gave credence to reports about the Soviet threat.

influence by both the Soviets and Americans, Truman's administration was not prepared to tolerate a Soviet sphere of influence in Eastern Europe. Consequently, Kennan's strategy of "firm" containment, when incorporated with Truman's "get tough" policy, lost its defensive character. It was replaced with an aggressive anticommunist policy that called for reducing Soviet influence around the world rather than simply containing it.

AMERICAN FOREIGN POLICY

By 1947, and for the next twenty-five years, American foreign policy was founded on the fear of communism, not only abroad but within the United States itself. Intervention in the affairs of independent nations was considered justified if the forces of communism could be presented as a threat. Anyone challenging the legitimacy of such intervention could be conveniently branded a communist sympathizer.

The assumption in most of official Washington was that *any* action by the Soviet Union was aimed at expanding world communism. Yet there were some who disagreed. They believed that Soviet determination to control Eastern Europe and the Black Sea region was a traditional Russian goal aimed at ensuring national security, an objective that dated back to czarist Russia. They suggested that Stalin wanted to control the countries on the USSR's western frontier to provide a buffer zone against German aggression. But in the suspicious atmosphere of the Cold War, simplistic assumptions about superpower conduct were more readily embraced than more complex political realities.

The prevailing attitude in Washington was that the activities of all communist governments were controlled from Moscow. This was certainly true in the satellite countries of Eastern

---

Figure 5.2: The Truman Doctrine

"I believe that it must be the policy of the United States to support free peoples who are resisting attempted subjugation by armed minorities or by outside pressures....

"I believe that our help should be primarily through economic and financial aid which is essential to economic stability and orderly political processes....

"The seeds of totalitarian regimes are nurtured by misery and want. They spread and grow in the evil soil of poverty and strife. They reach their full growth when the hope of a people for a better life has died. We must keep that hope alive. The free peoples of the world look to us for support in maintaining their freedoms. If we falter in our leadership, we may endanger the peace of the world—and we shall surely endanger the welfare of our own nation."

Europe, where Soviet occupation armies guaranteed that the new leaders were favourable to Moscow. However, in other parts of the world, such as Vietnam and China, communist governments operated independently. Foreign policies in these states reflected nationalist ambitions and frequently differed from policies Moscow might have imposed.

THE MARSHALL PLAN

In 1947, Western Europe was in the midst of a postwar depression. Governments lacked the capital and resources to revive their war-torn economies. Widespread unemployment and social unrest in Europe caused concern in Washington. If Western European states were to remain outside the orbit of the Soviet Union, they would have to regain their economic and political strength. American financial aid was the key. Yet there was another reason for European economic recovery on the American agenda. As an exporting nation, the United States depended on a prosperous Europe to purchase its products. There was wide-

How do these cartoons show how each side views the other side's motives and methods in the Cold War?

spread concern that if the European economies did not recover quickly, the United States might also sink into a depression.

On 5 June 1947, US Secretary of State George Marshall announced the new European recovery program. Known as the **Marshall Plan**, it offered American economic aid to all countries devastated by the war. The offer was not without conditions, however. Countries seeking aid had to open their economic records to American scrutiny, make their financial needs public, and present a plan for the allocation of funds. The Marshall Plan was open to all countries, including those of the Soviet bloc.

Molotov, the Soviet foreign minister, was willing to explore the possibility of accepting aid under the Marshall Plan. He met with British and French officials, but refused to accept the joint approach to economic reconstruction that these former Allies proposed. Perceiving the plan to be an extension of the Truman Doctrine and a tool of American economic imperialism, Molotov finally rejected it. He warned Britain and France that the plan would divide Europe, create a strong

Germany, and give the United States control over European affairs.

To counterbalance the Marshall Plan, Molotov created a recovery scheme for the Soviet bloc. Czechoslovakia, Hungary, and Poland, which had shown interest in the US plan, were obliged to reject it in favour of the **Molotov Plan**. Lacking the funding of the Marshall Plan, Molotov's scheme was founded on bilateral trade agreements within the Soviet bloc. Eventually 70 per cent of the trade of the Soviet bloc nations was among the bloc.

In the fall of 1947, sixteen Western European countries, including Germany, agreed to a four-year recovery plan. As a leading industrial power before the war, Germany was the key to restoring a healthy economy in Western Europe. And with its strong anticommunist tradition, Germany could provide a counter-force to Soviet expansion.

The Impact of the Marshall Plan

More than $13 billion was allocated to the Marshall Plan between 1948 and 1952. As a result, industrial growth in Western Europe flourished. While the plan enhanced economic and political stability, it also produced tangible benefits for the United States. Millions of dollars worth of American goods were sent to Europe. This stimulus to the American economy led to a period of unprecedented growth in the 1950s.

In response to the success of the Marshall Plan, Stalin moved to tighten his hold on Eastern Europe. In the fall of 1947, coalition governments were abandoned. All non-communist parties were dissolved, paving the way for complete communist control of Poland, Bulgaria, Romania, and Hungary. Non-communist leaders fled their countries or faced imprisonment, even assassination.

THE COMMUNIST COUP IN CZECHOSLOVAKIA

After the Second World War, Czechoslovakia returned to a democratic government under the liberal leadership of President Edvard Benes. But in elections in 1946, the Communists won 38 per cent of the vote, more than any other single party. A coalition government was formed under Communist leader Klement Gottwald.

Czechoslovakia, located along the dividing line between Eastern and Western Europe, had maintained a neutral position in the early stages of the Cold War. Stalin, however, wanted to ensure that the Czechs would be firmly positioned on the Soviet side. In December 1947, in a five-year trade deal, the Soviet Union agreed to supply Czechoslovakia with much needed wheat and cotton. In February 1948, with active Soviet support, Gottwald and the Communist Party took control

of the government, expelling all non-communists and eliminating all other parties. Czechoslovakia was now a single-party dictatorship and another Soviet satellite.

The takeover of Czechoslovakia shocked the West. Only ten years earlier in Munich the Allies had handed Czechoslovakia over to Germany. Now the country threatened to be the spark that would ignite new hostilities. Believing that war was possible, Truman called for a resumption of the military **draft**. In June 1948, he signed the **Selective Service Act**, which ordered all males between the ages of eighteen and twenty-five to register for service in the armed forces. The Cold War was beginning to heat up.

The Communist Information Bureau (**Cominform**) was established in September 1947 under Moscow's direction. Together with the Molotov Plan, the purpose of the Cominform was to help consolidate the position of the Soviet Union in Europe and bring the Soviet bloc countries closer together. The Cominform coordinated the work of Communist parties across Europe, including democracies like France and Italy, where communist supporters were ordered to provoke strikes and use labour unions to mount opposition to the Marshall Plan. Their efforts were unsuccessful and the Cominform was disbanded in 1956.

THE BERLIN BLOCKADE AND AIRLIFT

Until 1948, the Cold War had not drawn the two superpowers into open conflict. There had been a war of words, and policies and promises had been made to woo or coerce individual

An American airlift plane approaches the Berlin airport in May 1949 as jubilant Berliners wave welcome.

set in motion. The Soviet Union responded to the West's actions by establishing a blockade of all rail, canal, and road links in and out of West Berlin and by cutting off electric power from East to West Berlin. Since Berlin was located within the Soviet sector of Germany, the 2.1 million inhabitants of West Berlin were left isolated and helpless.

Stalin's motives for blockading West Berlin puzzled the West. On the surface, the blockade appeared to be a protest against the currency reform. But it was more than that. Stalin wanted to prevent the West from establishing a West German state. He wanted the whole of Germany eventually reunified as a communist state under Moscow's control. Stalin may also have been gambling that the West would allow West Berlin to be absorbed into the Soviet sector rather than risk armed conflict. The success of the coup in Czechoslovakia had suggested to Stalin that a gamble might pay off. But it was not to be this time.

Britain and the United States responded to the blockade with a massive airlift. Twenty-four hours a day thousands of tonnes of supplies were flown into West Berlin. Had the Soviet Union tried to block the airlift, it would clearly have been an act of war, and war was not what the Soviets had intended. In fact, the blockade, rather than damaging the West's ties to West Berlin, served to reinforce them. On the other hand, a counter blockade imposed by the British and Americans on Western goods being shipped to the Soviet zone severely damaged the East German economy.

The Berlin Airlift lasted for eleven months. Finally, in May 1949, accepting that the blockade was futile, Stalin reopened surface access to West Berlin. As a precaution, however, the airlift continued until September.

nations into one camp or the other. Still, they had managed to avoid direct confrontation. Germany was about to change all of that.

The partitioning of Germany and Berlin into occupied zones was supposed to be a temporary measure. But the fragile state of relations between the Soviets and the West prevented any permanent solution. The stalemate caused severe economic hardship in Germany. To spearhead an economic recovery, the United States, Britain, and France established economic co-operation and currency reform in their zones. Plans to establish a constitutional assembly that would lead to an independent West German state were

In May, the three occupation zones of the Western Allies became the German Federal Republic (West Germany), with its capital in Bonn. The following October, the Soviet zone of occupation officially became the German Democratic Republic (East Germany), with its capital in East Berlin. Germany would remain divided until 1990.

RIVAL ALLIANCES: NATO AND THE WARSAW PACT

The Truman Doctrine and the Marshall Plan were economic strategies designed to foster the reconstruction of Europe. But events like the coup in Czechoslovakia and the Berlin Blockade suggested to the Americans that economic intervention was not enough to contain communist expansion. A greater deterrent was needed.

NATO

The **North Atlantic Treaty Organization** (NATO) was established on 4 April 1949. It brought together twelve countries—the United States, Canada, Britain, France, Belgium, the Netherlands, Denmark, Norway, Iceland, Italy, Portugal, and Luxembourg—in a mutual defence pact. (Greece and Turkey joined in 1952, Spain in 1982.) The purpose of the alliance was to counter the perceived military threat from the Soviet bloc countries. It indicated the West's intent to meet Soviet expansion with collective resistance and to prevent war through collective defence. By the terms of the treaty, the United States would rearm Western Europe and would assume a leadership role in the defence of the Western world. NATO represented a big step for the US. Never before had the Americans joined an alliance in peacetime. But NATO also signalled that the Western powers did not believe that the United Nations was a sufficient guarantee of peace in a world dominated by two hostile superpowers.

To the West, the formation of NATO seemed all the more justified when, in August 1949, the Soviets exploded their first atomic bomb. This marked the beginning of the biggest threat in the Cold War—the **nuclear arms race**. Truman promptly ordered the development of a new super weapon—the hydrogen bomb.

In 1955, West Germany was allowed to join NATO. The decision was a momentous one. As a member of the alliance, it meant that Germany would be rearmed. France and Britain were especially uneasy about German rearmament. But since they did not have the military power to defend West Germany from a Soviet attack, they had little choice. As a precaution, however, German forces were placed under American control.

The Warsaw Pact

Five days after West Germany joined NATO, the Soviet Union met in Warsaw with representatives of seven Soviet satellites—Albania, Bulgaria, Czechoslovakia, East Germany, Hungary, Poland, and Romania—to sign the **Warsaw Pact**. Modelled after NATO, it set up a military alliance in which members pledged to assist each other in the event of attack. It also established a unified military command, with headquarters in Moscow. The military alliances of the two superpowers were now complete. Both sides were prepared for conflict.

Other Military Alliances

NATO was only one part of the new strategy of international organizations and military alliances designed to contain communism. In 1948, the **Organization of American States** (OAS) was established to achieve "peace and justice and to promote American solidarity." Initially, however, it was an American-dominated vehicle designed to resist communism and limit relations with the Soviet Union.

Another alliance, the **South East Asia Treaty Organization** (SEATO), was created in 1954. This pact included the United States, Australia, New Zealand, the Philippines, Thailand, Pakistan, Britain, and France. It provided for mutual action in the event of an attack or internal subversion. The latter condition would prove to be a key in the American policy of containment.

In 1955, the United States and Britain engineered the Baghdad Pact, renamed the **Central Treaty Organization** (CENTO) after one of the signing members, Iraq, left the alliance in 1958. Initially CENTO offered mutual assistance between members—Turkey, Iraq, Iran, Pakistan, and Britain (with the US as an associate member)—in the event of aggression. But increasingly the pact sought to provide a mutual defence policy against the Soviet Union.

In 1957, Canada and the United States joined together to create the **North American Air Defence Command** (NORAD). It established nuclear tracking, warning, and control stations across the northern Arctic. Eventually, surface-to-air missiles with nuclear warheads were introduced. In 1981, NORAD changed its name to the **North American Aerospace Defence Command** (NAADC).

The USSR and Eastern Europe were almost surrounded by military alliances or mutual defence treaties backed by American arms. The United States was committed to the defence of forty-two nations around the world.

The Spread of Communism in Asia

Civil War in China

China had been embroiled in civil war since 1927. It began when Jiang Jie Shi (Chiang Kai-shek), the leader of the Chinese Revolutionary National Party (the **Kuomintang**) attempted to eradicate the Communist Party. In a three-year purge known as the "White Terror," communists, suspected communists, and communist sympathizers were murdered. Despite the heavy losses of life, however, the Communists, under the leadership of Mao Zedong, continued to be a powerful force. They established a stronghold in northwest China, where they launched repeated attacks against the Kuomintang. The hostilities were suspended when China was attacked by Japan in 1937. During the Second World War, the warring sides cooperated long enough to defeat the Japanese.

When the Second World War ended, the United States attempted to mediate an end to the civil war by negotiating a coalition government between Jiang and Mao. But the attempt failed and civil war resumed in 1946. Substantial American aid in the form of arms, money, and military advisors was provided to Jiang to bolster his fight against communism. Between 1945 and 1949, over $3.5 billion was invested in the nationalist forces. Ironically, Stalin also aided Jiang as part of an agreement with Roosevelt in 1945 before the defeat of Japan. But he had other motives as well. Stalin did not want to see a strong, united China that might oppose Soviet ambitions in Asia.

Mao's policies of land reform and peasants' rights had strong appeal for farmers. The Communist army was disciplined and dedicated. By 1946, they were beginning to make steady inroads. Jiang, on the other hand, headed a corrupt regime. He was uninterested in reform and lacked popular support. The Kuomintang, although larger than the Communist army, lacked efficient leadership and was burdened with low morale. Towards the end of the civil war, many Nationalist soldiers deserted to the Communist side.

By 1948, it was apparent that the Communists would be the victors. Washington now faced a difficult decision: to withdraw support of Jiang, thereby not only losing face but losing the enormous Chinese market as well, or to embark on full-scale intervention, creating resentment on the part of the Chinese people and condemnation by the American public. Reluctantly Truman decided to halt the flow of aid to the Kuomintang.

In Beijing on 1 October 1949, Mao proclaimed the People's Republic of China. Jiang, along with the remnants of his Nationalist army, fled to the island of Taiwan, where he set up the Republic of China. In the years that followed, Taiwan was supported through foreign aid and protected by the US navy. The American government recognized Taiwan as the sole legitimate government of China in the hope that Jiang would eventually liberate the mainland from the Communists.

The United States blocked the People's Republic of China from admission to the United Nations. Instead, the Republic of China held the UN seat. As a result, over 25 per cent of the world's people were not represented in the UN. It was not until 1971 that the People's Republic of China was admitted to the UN, replacing the other China. In 1978, the United States finally recognized the People's Republic as the sole legal government of China.

Mao and Jiang toast their success against Japan in the Second World War at a dinner held in the fall of 1945.

The Korean Conflict

The Cold War turned hot in 1950 with the outbreak of the Korean War. This conflict marked the first face-to-face confrontation between Communist troops and Western forces. The Americans led a UN-sponsored army into combat against the communist forces of North Korea, who were supported by Chinese troops. The guns fell silent in 1953, but no lasting peace was achieved. UN forces continued to patrol the border between North and South Korea, a situation that continued into the 1990s. (The Korean conflict is discussed in greater detail in Chapter 6.)

COLD WAR POLITICS

The atmosphere of suspicion and fear escalated in the 1950s. The United States and the Soviet Union were increasingly distrustful of each other's motives and actions. This was clearly exhibited by the continual wrangling at the United Nations.

But fear and mistrust were evident within the two countries as well, not only in the totalitarian Soviet Union, but in the democratic United States. Dissent or disagreement with government policies was frequently viewed as suspicious or subversive. In the United States, this led to the anticommunist crusade of Senator Joseph McCarthy. From 1950 to 1954, McCarthy and the House Un-American Activities Committee searched for communists everywhere in American society. Often with little or no substantial proof, they accused fellow legislators, civil servants, Hollywood actors, newspaper publishers, US army officers, and even the 1952 Democratic presidential candidate of communist activities. **McCarthyism**, as it became known, destroyed the lives of many innocent people. By 1954, McCarthy's colleagues in the Senate had denounced him and stripped him of his power. But the anxiety and antagonism that was reflected in and intensified by McCarthyism affected American policy for decades and prevented a balanced American appraisal of Soviet aims and Communist leaders.

IN REVIEW

1. Compare and contrast the views of Churchill and Stalin during the early years of the Cold War. In your analysis, whose viewpoint was more accurate? Why?

2. What was the Truman Doctrine? What was its impact on the Cold War?

3. Explain the policy of containment. Do you think this was an effective way to deal with the Soviet Union? Explain.

4. Briefly explain the objectives, terms, and results of the Marshall Plan.

5. Note the impact of the following on the course of the Cold War: (a) the Cominform; (b) the coup in Czechoslovakia; and (c) the Berlin Blockade and Airlift.

6. In your view, which nation bears the greatest responsibility for starting the Cold War? Explain your answer.

7. In your opinion, could the Cold War have been avoided? Explain.

8. Compare the origins, membership, and goals of (a) NATO and (b) the Warsaw Pact.

9. Why were Mao and the Communists able to gain victory in China?

10. What were the results of Cold War anticommunist hysteria in the United States?

COLD WAR FLASHPOINTS!

A series of international incidents between the late 1950s and the 1980s caused the Cold War to heat up. Each of these flashpoints added to the antagonism between East and West and heightened fears that the Third World War was inevitable.

FLASHPOINT: THE CUBAN MISSILE CRISIS

The island of Cuba, 150 km off the Florida coast, had long been an American military, political, and economic stronghold. By 1945, Americans owned 90 per cent of the country's mineral wealth, 80 per cent of its utilities, and 40 per cent of its sugar cane fields. The island was ruled by the corrupt dictatorship of Fulgencio Batista until a young socialist revolutionary named Fidel Castro succeeded in ousting the regime in 1959. In Cuba, Castro was a hero. In the United States, the new Cuban leader was welcomed—until it became clear that Castro was about to radically alter American interests in the island nation.

Cuba was faced with an economic crisis. The economy was foreign-owned and many Cubans lived in poverty. In order to redistribute property to the poor and gain control of the country's economy, Castro decided to **nationalize** most of the American-

owned businesses. The Cuban government seized ownership of key parts of the economy. American investors and their government were outraged. The Soviet Union, on the other hand, saw an opportunity to gain an outpost near

The world was on the brink of nuclear war when the Soviet Union attempted to establish a nuclear missile base in Cuba. U.S. aerial reconnaissance shows Soviet missiles aboard a ship bound for Cuba.

"It shall be the policy of this nation to regard any nuclear missile launched from Cuba against any nation in the Western Hemisphere as an attack by the Soviet Union on the United States requiring a full retaliatory response upon the Soviet Union."

John F. Kennedy, in an address to the nation, 22 October 1961

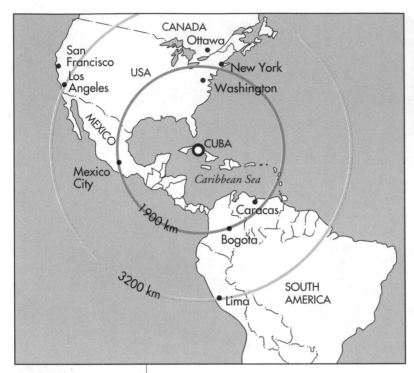

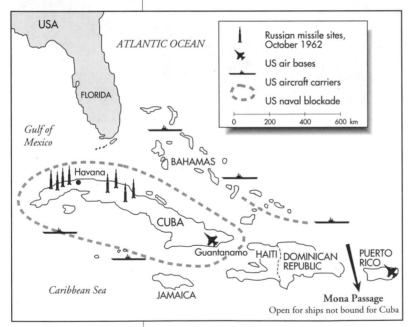

Figure 5.3: US Missile Sites in Turkey (top right); *Figure 5.4:* Range of Cuban Missile Sites if Built (top left); *Figure 5.5:* US Naval Blockade of Cuba During the Missile Crisis (bottom)

was ignited in Cuba. The Central Intelligence Agency (CIA) had trained a small army of Cuban exiles; their mission was to overthrow Castro. On 17 April 1961, 1500 exiles landed in Cuba at the Bay of Pigs. The invasion was a disaster as Cuban troops quickly rounded up the invaders.

The Bay of Pigs incident embarrassed the United States and its new president, John F. Kennedy. Perhaps more significantly, however, the abortive invasion strengthened Cuba's ties to the Soviet Union. Soviet weapons were deployed to defend Cuba from another invasion. But between August and October 1962, American intelligence sources and spy plane photographs revealed that something much more sinister was being shipped to Cuba. On October 22nd, Kennedy announced that the United States had proof that Cuba was building missile sites that could be used to launch Soviet nuclear weapons at the US. Kennedy took a firm stand. He ordered a naval blockade of Cuba. No ships would be allowed into or out of Cuban ports. Ready to launch a nuclear war, the two superpowers were poised, as Kennedy said, at "the abyss of destruction."

The Soviets called the American reaction a "crude form of blackmail" and warned that "if the aggressors unleash

American soil. Threats and economic pressure from the United States only served to push Castro closer to the Soviets. Finally, in 1961, Eisenhower severed diplomatic relations with Cuba.

It wasn't long before armed confrontation between the superpowers

a war, the Soviet Union will strike a mighty retaliatory blow." But in reality the Soviets were in a difficult position. The missile sites had been discovered before they were completed and so posed no real threat to the United States. The Americans would have the advantage, while the Soviets would be caught in a fight far from home on the enemy's doorstep. Their plan had backfired. But now what were they to do about it?

At first Khrushchev threatened retaliation. But behind the scenes, Kennedy's brother Robert, the US Attorney-General, met with the Soviet ambassador to the US on October 27th to present an ultimatum: remove the missiles by the following day or the US would remove them by force. In return, Kennedy guaranteed that the US would not invade Cuba and assured the Soviets that the US had already decided to remove its missiles from Turkey.

In response, Khrushchev wrote directly to the president to negotiate a settlement. He offered to withdraw the missiles if the Americans guaranteed they would not invade Cuba. For Khrushchev it was a face-saving measure. Each side could now withdraw with honour. The missiles were removed.

While each side claimed success, American Secretary of State Dean Rusk expressed the situation accurately when he said "We were eyeball to eyeball, and I think the other fellow just blinked." The crisis had shown the

Kennedy and commanders of the US Navy and Marine forces confer during the Cuban Missile Crisis.

perils of courting catastrophe. Both sides knew there could be no victory in a nuclear war.

The Cuban Missile Crisis highlighted the need for closer international communications. In response, the famous **hotline** was established between the leaders of the two superpowers. In the event of another major crisis, the two leaders would now be able to talk to each other immediately and directly.

"They talk about who won and who lost. Human reason won. Mankind won."

Nikita Khrushchev, 1962

PROFILE

JOHN F. KENNEDY (1917-63)

John Fitzgerald Kennedy was elected the 35th president of the United States in 1960. Although he served only 1000 days before an assassin's bullet ended his life, his presidency claimed to offer a new vision of freedom and social justice. The impact of what came to be known as the "Camelot" years extended beyond the effects of the administration's legislative achievements. Why do you think this was so?

"Let the word go forth from this time and place, to friend and foe alike, that the torch has been passed to a new generation of Americans—born in this century, tempered by war, disciplined by a hard and bitter peace, proud of our ancient heritage—and unwilling to witness or permit the slow undoing of those human rights to which this nation has always been committed, and to which we are committed today at home and around the world."

> *John F. Kennedy, inaugural address,*
> *20 January 1961*

"And so my fellow Americans: ask not what your country can do for you—ask what you can do for your country."

> *John F. Kennedy, inaugural address,*
> *20 January 1961*

John F. Kennedy was the second of nine children born to a wealthy Irish family in Boston. He graduated from Harvard University in 1940 and joined the US Navy. During the Second World War, the torpedo boat he was commanding was hit and sunk in the Solomon Islands. Kennedy helped his crew to escape despite his own personal injuries and he was awarded a medal for gallantry.

After the war Kennedy won a seat in Congress as a Democrat; he was elected to the Senate in 1952. In 1960 he became the Democratic nominee for president and narrowly defeated his Republican rival Richard Nixon. At the age of forty-four Kennedy became the youngest man to be elected president of the United States.

Kennedy's youth and energy created a spirit of hope and enthusiasm. Together with his young and elegant wife Jacqueline, JFK brought a sense of glamour to the White House and created a new self-image for the American public.

In 1961, as a direct challenge to the Soviet space program, Kennedy announced his intention that an American would land on the moon "before this decade is out." Congress enthusiastically approved appropriations for Project Apollo and the space race was on. As Kennedy had hoped, an American took the first steps on the moon in 1969.

During his term as president, Kennedy enjoyed increasing popularity. But his time in office was not without challenges. The Bay of Pigs fiasco in 1961 was a personal humiliation. His leadership was challenged again in 1962 during the Cuban Missile Crisis. This time, however, Kennedy took control and skilfully manoeuvred the situation through the threat of nuclear war.

The assassination of John F. Kennedy in Dallas on 22 November 1963 is engraved in the minds of many people who heard the startling news and later witnessed the event on television. The assassination left unanswered questions about the future course the United States might have taken under Kennedy's leadership. It also left lasting questions about the assassination itself. Lee Harvey Oswald is officially named as the man who killed JFK. But controversy continues to swirl around this theory. Many people believe that the truth behind Kennedy's assassination is yet to be revealed.

PROFILE

NIKITA KHRUSHCHEV (1894-1971)

Nikita Khrushchev, as Soviet leader, sought to effect internal reform while maintaining Soviet parity with the United States. He brought his nation to the brink of nuclear war in the Cuban Missile Crisis, yet he also promoted a policy of peaceful co-existence with the United States. He rose to power under the wing of Stalin, but he also transformed Soviet politics, ridding the system of the worst Stalinist excesses.

"Anyone who believes that the worker can be lulled by fine revolutionary phrases is mistaken....If no concern is shown for the growth of material and spiritual riches, the people will listen today, they will listen tomorrow, and then they may say: 'Why do you promise us everything for the future? You are talking, so to speak, about life beyond the grave. The priest has already told us about this.'"

Nikita Khrushchev, 19 September 1964

"We say this not only for the socialist states, who are more akin to us. We base ourselves on the idea that we must peacefully co-exist. About the capitalist states, it doesn't depend on you whether or not we exist. If you don't like us, don't accept our invitations and don't invite us to come to see you. Whether you like it or not, history is on our side. We will bury you."

Nikita Khrushchev, 18 November 1956

Born into a poor mining family in Kalmkova, Ukraine, Khrushchev received a sporadic education. He first became a shepherd before becoming a metal worker. In 1918, he joined the Bolsheviks and served in the Red Army during the First World War. During the 1920s and 1930s, he steadily advanced in the Stalinist bureaucracy. By 1935 he had become first secretary of the Moscow region, and by 1939 he was a member of the Politburo. During the Second World War Khrushchev saw active duty at Stalingrad. Shortly before the war's end he returned to Ukraine, where he assumed the position of first secretary. With Stalin's death in 1953, Khrushchev emerged as leader of the Soviet Communist Party. In 1956, he launched an attack on the extremes of Stalinism and the "cult of personality" during the Twentieth Party Congress. In a three-hour speech, an avalanche of criticism poured forth revealing the darkness of Stalin's era.

In 1958, Khrushchev became premier of the Soviet Union. He introduced dramatic schemes to transform and modernize Soviet industry and agriculture. The challenge of the space race was launched, and the Soviets enjoyed great early success. Internationally, Khrushchev alternately heated up and cooled down the Cold War. He clashed with the United States over Berlin and Cuba. Yet he also instigated the notion of peaceful co-existence, travelling to the United States, Western Europe, China, and other foreign countries on goodwill missions.

By 1964, Khrushchev's image was tarnished within the Soviet Communist Party. His aborted confrontation with Kennedy during the Cuban Missile Crisis cost him both popularity and credibility at home. Poor harvests and economic stagnation seemed to signal a failure of his domestic policies. In 1964, Khrushchev was forced to resign. He lived the remaining years of his life in relative obscurity outside Moscow.

FLASHPOINT: THE WAR IN VIETNAM

The French had controlled the colony of Indochina (Vietnam, Laos, and Cambodia) since the 1860s. During the Second World War, however, nationalism swept through this corner of South East Asia. The British and Dutch reluctantly accepted the inevitability of their colonies gaining independence. The French, on the other hand, were determined to fight the local nationalist forces.

The Indochinese were led by Ho Chi Minh, a popular nationalist and communist leader who had been seeking Vietnamese independence for over twenty-five years. He led his forces in a classic **guerrilla war** against the French, controlling the countryside, fighting hit-and-run battles, and winning the support of the local people. In 1954, the main French forces were surrounded at Dienbienphu and forced to surrender. This marked the end of French control in the region. But it would prove to be far easier to win a victory on the battlefields than to create a lasting peace.

Following the Vietnamese victory, a peace conference was held in Geneva, Switzerland. It was agreed that Vietnam would be divided temporarily at the 17th parallel. Elections to reunite the country were to be held by 1956. North Vietnam, under Ho Chi Minh, established a communist state. The South established a government under Ngo Dinh Diem, an ardent anticommunist

and willing puppet of American policy. The 1956 elections and reunification never happened. Vietnam remained divided into two separate and hostile states.

North Vietnam realized that an invasion of the South would provoke foreign intervention, as had happened in Korea in 1950. Instead, North Vietnamese infiltrated the South to bolster the local communists, the Viet Cong. By 1959, their guerrilla forces were launching major attacks throughout the South.

At first the Americans stayed on the sidelines of France's Indochina conflict. However, the communist victory in China, the strengthening of the communist regime in North Korea, and tensions with the USSR in Europe led the Americans to adopt a more aggressive stance. Fearing the spread of communism, the United States gradually became more involved in the conflict. Initially, this was limited to financial aid to France. But with France out of the conflict, the United States gradually assumed responsibility for the war. In 1960, the US sent 800 military advisors to help the South Vietnamese army. Under Kennedy, the number of personnel was expanded to 16 000. However, the South Vietnamese army was still unsuccessful in containing the communist forces.

With Kennedy's assassination on 22 November 1963, Lyndon Johnson assumed the presidency. Johnson did not want to be accused of being "soft" on communism, nor did he want to be the only American president to lose a war. He was determined to take a hardline approach. In 1964, American naval vessels in the Gulf of Tonkin were allegedly fired upon by the North Vietnamese. (Recent documents indicate that American naval forces may have provoked the incident.) Johnson used the Gulf of Tonkin incident as justification "to take all necessary

"As Ed Murrow once said about Vietnam, anyone who isn't confused doesn't really understand the situation."

Walter Bryan, The Improbable Irish *(1969)*

measures to repel armed attack and to prevent further aggression." Though no formal declaration of war was ever issued, the conflict escalated into a full-scale war. By 1965, over 500 000 American troops were in Vietnam, accompanied by squadrons of helicopters, fighters, and bombers.

The North and South Vietnamese forces were not evenly matched. South Vietnam was hindered by corruption throughout its ranks. It was never able to mount an effective fighting force. The North Vietnamese, however, were trained and equipped by China and the Soviet Union. The Viet Cong were backed by troops from the regular North Vietnamese forces. Massive American bombing raids on the North killed nearly 2 000 000 civilians, but they could not stop the flow of troops and equipment southward along the Ho Chi Minh Trail. When the Viet Cong lost large numbers of fighters in the Tet Offensive in 1968, North Vietnamese regular troops assumed a larger role in the fighting. In spite of their losses, North Vietnam was determined to continue the fight, believing time was on its side.

In the end, the United States, the most powerful military force in the world, lost the war in Vietnam. The reasons lie in the nature of the conflict. Ho Chi Minh and his followers were fighting a traditional war of liberation. They had fought the Japanese, the French, and now the Americans. They were fighting for their homeland and their culture. The Americans, on the other hand, were fighting for the abstract idea of "stopping communist aggression." The American people were divided over the war. Many simply didn't understand why US troops were in Vietnam in the first place. They found it hard to believe that the American way of life was somehow threatened by a small country thousands of kilometres away.

North Vietnamese president Ho Chi Minh (right) sought and received aid from Communist China's leader Mao Zedong.

American Division Over the War

It was evident that the conflict in Vietnam would not be resolved quickly or easily. As the war escalated, so too did the anti-war protests at home.

> "Television brought the brutality of war into the comfort of the living room. Vietnam was lost in the living rooms of America—not on the battlefields of Vietnam."
>
> *Marshall McLuhan, Canadian communications theorist and cultural critic*

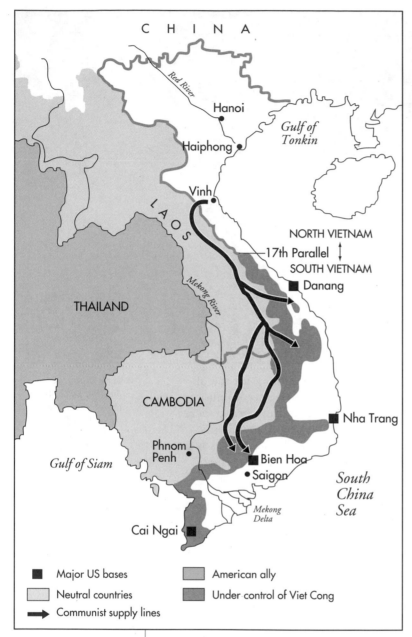

Figure 5.6:
Vietnam

"I regard the war in Indochina as the greatest military, political, economic, and moral blunder in our national history."

George McGovern, Democratic candidate for US President, 1972

Sit-ins at army recruiting offices and demonstrations at military bases often turned violent. Demonstrators burned their draft cards and the American flag. Police were pelted with rocks and bricks; often they used clubs and tear gas to control the crowds. Organized marches like that in October 1967 on the Pentagon brought hundreds of thousands of protesters into riotous confrontations with police and National Guard troops.

Tens of thousands of Americans fled the country as **draft dodgers**, many settling in Canada. Others went to jail rather than serve in Vietnam. Those who did fight felt betrayed and discarded by Americans at home. The war in Vietnam was taking its toll on American society at large.

The Protest Movement

The postwar baby boom generation was the largest group of young people the Western world had ever known. Born in a time of affluence and growth, they were generally well educated and conscious of the power of their sheer force of numbers. Emerging from the relative repression of the 1950s, this wave of youth was drawn into politics by the most dramatic events. Inspired by a new-generation leader like John F. Kennedy, they were shocked by his assassination. The later assassinations of Robert Kennedy and Dr. Martin Luther King only deepened their sense of disillusionment and alienation.

When the Cold War exploded into hot war in Vietnam, it was the baby boom generation that was called upon to fight and die for a vague cause in jungles far from home. The savagery of the war was repeated nightly on television screens. People were horrified by what they saw.

Spurred on by the protests of folk singers like Joan Baez and Bob Dylan, young people marched and demonstrated in the streets and on college campuses. At first, the goal was simple—end US involvement in Vietnam. But "the Movement," as it became known, soon turned its attention to broader issues—poverty, civil rights, racism, and feminism. Time-honoured institutions such as school, church, and business were called into question. Traditional American society was under siege. An American **counterculture** was emerging.

Some elements of the Movement shifted from marches and demonstrations to more militant action. The Yippies (Youth International Party) harassed political supporters of the war and rioted in the streets during the Democratic Party's 1968 convention. Bombings, kidnappings, arson, riots, and other forms of terrorism served the causes of such protest groups as the Black Panthers and Weather Underground. To many, it seemed as if the United States had descended into a kind of civil war that would eventually lead to its destruction and collapse.

In 1970, the depth and tragedy of this clash of generations and values came to a tragic climax. At Kent State University in Ohio, National Guard troops panicked and opened fire on unarmed student protesters, in clear view of reporters and TV cameras. Four students were killed. The incident showed just how far the fabric of American society had unravelled.

The Costs and Consequences of Vietnam

In 1973, the United States joined North Vietnam in signing the Paris Peace Accords. They called for a withdrawal of all American troops, the exchange of all prisoners of war, the withdrawal of foreign forces from Laos and Cambodia, and consultations between North and South Vietnam regarding general elections. The two Vietnams

Anti-war protesters march through the streets of San Francisco, ca. 1968.

Robert McNamara served as US secretary of defense from 1961-68. He was one of the chief advocates and architects of American involvement in Vietnam. In 1995, McNamara created considerable controversy when he publicly proclaimed that the war in Vietnam had been a horrible mistake and expressed his personal remorse and sorrow for his role in it.

VOICES

The music of Bob Dylan voiced many young people's opposition to the war in Vietnam. What is the message in this song?

The Times They Are A-Changin'

Come gather 'round people
Wherever you roam
And admit that the waters
Around you have grown
And accept it that soon
You'll be drenched to the bone.
If your time to you
Is worth savin'
Then you better start swimmin'
Or you'll sink like a stone
For the times they are a-changin'.

Come writers and critics
Who prophesize with your pen
And keep your eyes wide
The chance won't come again
And don't speak too soon
For the wheel's still in spin
And there's no tellin' who
That it's namin'.
For the loser now
Will be later to win
For the times they are a-changin'.

Come senators, congressmen
Please heed the call
Don't stand in the doorway
Don't block up the hall
For he that gets hurt
Will be he who has stalled
There's a battle outside

And it is ragin'.
It'll soon shake your windows
And rattle your walls
For the times they are a-changin'.

Come mothers and fathers
Throughout the land
And don't criticize
What you can't understand
Your sons and your daughters
Are beyond your command
Your old road is
Rapidly agin'.
Please get out of the new one
If you can't lend your hand
For the times they are a-changin'.

The line it is drawn
The curse it is cast
The slow one now
Will later be fast
As the present now
Will later be past
The order is
Rapidly fadin'.
And the first one now
Will later be last
For the times they are a-changin'.

were left to determine their own destinies. In 1975, North Vietnam occupied South Vietnam and reunited the country by force of arms.

What did Vietnam cost the world? Most people would say it cost far too much. Over 3 million American military personnel served in South East Asia; 57 000 were killed in action; 300 000 were wounded; 2500 were listed as "Missing in Action" and have never been accounted for. Tragically, an estimated 50 000 American Vietnam veterans have committed suicide since their return from the war; even larger numbers still battle the substance abuse problems or psychological wounds they brought back from Vietnam. In material terms, the US spent over $150 billion on the war effort.

Among the Vietnamese on both sides, the losses were even more

staggering, although more difficult to verify. Certainly more than a million Vietnamese were killed; half the dead were civilians. Hundreds of thousands of uprooted people sought refuge in other, often unfriendly, countries. The economies of both North and South Vietnam were drained. Agriculture, forestry, and fishing industries were devastated.

American involvement in Vietnam did not contain communism in that country or anywhere in South East Asia. In fact, the war proved that the policy of containment through the use of force was unworkable and that American military power was not invincible. Furthermore, American prestige, popularity, and support was forever diminished in the eyes of nations around the world.

But perhaps the most serious consequences of the Vietnam War were experienced within the United States itself. The astronomical defence expenditures distorted the American economy, making it heavily dependent on defence contracts for jobs and profits. With the end of the war, the economy slid into recession. But the greatest consequences were felt in the collective American psyche. The war transformed many people's vision of themselves as a nation and undermined their trust in government, in politicians, and in their country.

At Kent State University in Ohio, the National Guard fired into crowds of anti-war demonstrators, killing four students.

"Who since Vietnam would venture to say of America in simple belief that she was the 'last best hope of earth'? What America lost in Vietnam was, to put it in one word, virtue."

Barbara Tuchman, American historian

VOICES

THE DEBATE OVER VIETNAM

The war in Vietnam deeply divided the American people. Many of the younger generation denounced the war and even their own country. But many veterans who had fought in the Second World War or in Korea stood behind any American military action. The conflict crossed all generations. As you read these voices, consider the arguments on both sides. Would you have been a "hawk" or a "dove"?

Hawks and Doves

"Past experience provides little basis for confidence that reason can prevail in an atmosphere of mounting war fever. In a contest between a hawk and a dove the hawk has a great advantage, not because it is a better bird, but because it is a bigger bird with lethal talons and a highly developed will to use them."

Senator William Fulbright, 1964

The Case for American Involvement in Vietnam

"We should declare war on North Vietnam. We could pave the whole country and put parking stripes on it and still be home by Christmas."

Ronald Reagan, candidate for Governor of California, October 1965

"The reasons we must fight for Vietnam have little to do with making Saigon safe for 'democracy' or 'freedom.' There has been far too much cant on this point, far too much effort devoted to trying to establish a politically legitimate South Vietnamese Government after our own image. Nor does it do much good to argue the past, debating whether or not we should have become involved in Vietnam in the first place. The facts are that Communist expansionism in Asia has been consistent, related, and progressive, that the end of the Korean war, without a simultaneous settlement in Vietnam, gave Peking and North Vietnam's Ho Chi Minh the opportunity in South East Asia they have so well exploited....

"Vietnam is a nasty place to fight. But there are no neat and tidy battlefields in the struggle for freedom; there is no 'good' place to die. And it is far better to fight in Vietnam—on China's doorstep than fight some years hence in Hawaii, on our own frontiers."

Hanson W. Baldwin, "We Must Choose (1) 'Bug Out' (2) Negotiate (3) Fight." Copyright © 1965 by The New York Times Company. Reprinted by permission.

The Case Against American Involvement in Vietnam

"...the conflict in Vietnam remains a Vietnamese conflict, and in the end it must be resolved by the Vietnamese themselves. We have given extraordinary support to two successive governments in Vietnam. We can do no more and should try to do no more for a third. We have teetered for too long on the brink of turning the war in Vietnam which is still a Vietnamese war into an American war to be paid for primarily with American lives."

US Senator Mike Mansfield, 1964

"So I would have the United States get out of South Vietnam and save the American people the hundreds upon hundreds of millions of dollars that our Government is pouring down that rat hole—and I use the descriptive phrase 'rat hole' advisedly.

"Also, it would save many precious American lives. There are places in this city that do not like to hear that said....But I shall continue to speak it. On the basis of the present policies that prevail there, South Vietnam is not worth the life of a single American boy....[I]...will not vote to continue to sacrifice the lives of American boys in South Vietnam."

US Senator Wayne Morse, 1963

FLASHPOINT: WAR IN AFGHANISTAN

Afghanistan occupied a strategic position between the Soviet Union, Pakistan, and Iran. For nearly a century before the Second World War, the British Empire competed for influence in the region, first with imperial Russia and later with the USSR. In the process, Afghanistan was invaded many times. But no foreign power ever succeeded in controlling the fervently independent people of Afghanistan for long.

Between 1945 and 1978, Afghanistan had been first a monarchy and then, following a coup, a republic. Both governments were dependent on Soviet aid, but they also sought ties with pro-Western governments in Iran and Pakistan. The government of Mohammed Daoud, from 1973 to 1978, was dictatorial and repressive. It was strongly opposed by factions on both the political right and left.

In 1978, the Communist Party in Afghanistan seized control and banned all other political groups. The Soviet Union immediately recognized the government and sent in 85 000 troops to support the new state. But the Communist government was unpopular, partly because of its radical reform policies, which alienated small landowners and offended the religious beliefs of the Muslim Afghans. While rival factions among the Communists struggled for supremacy, non-communist rebels launched a revolution in the surrounding mountains. Units of the Afghan army began to join the rebels. It became clear that the Afghan communists could neither control the rebellion nor be relied upon to follow Moscow's orders.

Refugees from the Soviet invasion of Afghanistan crossed snow-clogged mountain passes into Pakistan.

The Soviets invaded the country in December 1979 and promptly installed their own choice for leader, Babrak Karmal. At the time, Islamic fundamentalists were sweeping into power in Iran and Pakistan. The Soviets were concerned that these neighbouring countries would offer support to Islamic fundamentalists in Afghanistan, which might create instability in the southern republics of the Soviet Union, where over 50 million Muslims lived. They also considered the People's Republic of China a potential rival and wanted to preserve their domination of the area.

For the next ten years anti-government *Mujahidin* ("fighter in a holy war") guerrillas waged war against Afghan troops armed and supported by Soviet tanks, aircraft, and equipment. In 1982, the Soviets launched a massive attack against the rebels, but with little success. The Soviet Union sent hundreds of thousands of troops into the country in a futile attempt to put down—or at least outlast—the rebellion. While Soviet troops controlled the country's few cities, the Mujahidin controlled most of the countryside. The conflict became known as the Soviet Union's Vietnam.

The war in Afghanistan renewed tensions between the Soviet Union and the West. The United States unofficially supported the rebels, and by 1986 had provided over $3 billion in military aid. In protest against the Soviet's intervention, the US cut grain exports to the USSR and, along with Canada and over thirty other countries, boycotted the 1980 Olympic Games in Moscow.

By the late 1980s, the new Soviet President, Mikhail Gorbachev, initiated a dramatic change in Soviet foreign policy. With growing opposition to the war at home and domestic problems mounting, Gorbachev announced that the Soviet Union had no desire to impose its policies on its neighbours and that Soviet forces would be withdrawn from Afghanistan. The Communist government was quickly overthrown by the rebels. Afghanistan was left to sort out its long-standing religious, ethnic, and political conflicts on its own.

IN REVIEW

1. Why were Soviet missiles installed in Cuba?

2. What measures did Kennedy use to force removal of the missiles?

3. What were the results of the Cuban Missile Crisis?

4. Why did the United States become involved in Vietnam?

5. Why was it difficult for the United States to win a military victory in Vietnam?

6. (a) Why were Americans so deeply divided over Vietnam?
   (b) What role did young people play in opposition to the war?

7. In your opinion, what did American involvement in Vietnam accomplish?

8. Why did the Soviet Union deploy troops to Afghanistan?

9. To what extent can the Soviet Union's role in Afghanistan be compared with the United States' role in Vietnam? Explain your answer.

Figure 5.7: Détente Highlights

Year	Treaty	Terms/Description
1963	Nuclear Test Ban	• banned nuclear tests in the atmosphere, space, and under water
1963	Hotline	• direct communications link between the Kremlin and the White House to prevent accidental nuclear war and speed up diplomatic messages during crises
1967	Outer Space Treaty	• agreement that the moon and planets to be used for peaceful purposes only
1968	Nuclear Non-Proliferation Treaty	• banned the nuclear powers from providing nuclear weapons or technology to non-nuclear nations • participating non-nuclear powers pledged not to develop nuclear weapons
1971	People's Republic of China Enters UN	• US agrees to bring China into UN with a seat on the Security Council
1972	Beijing and Moscow Summits	• Nixon travels to Russia and China and establishes new spirit of détente
1972	SALT I	• Nixon and Brezhnev agree to a Strategic Arms Limitation Treaty (SALT I) • first arms limitation agreement since start of Cold War • restricted number of missiles held by superpowers • paved way for more arms limitations talks
1973	East and West Germany Enter UN	• Soviet-American co-operation pave way for "two Germanys" to take their place in UN
1975	Helsinki Conference	• 35 European nations plus Canada, the US, and the USSR sign pact on European security and co-operation 30 years after end of WWII • recognizes Europe's postwar boundaries (Soviet demand) • Soviets pledge support for greater freedoms and human rights (American demand) • increased co-operation in trade, science, and technology
1979	SALT II	• renewal and expansion of landmark SALT I agreement • return of Cold War tensions after Soviet invasion of Afghanistan leads US Congress to refuse final ratification

DÉTENTE

For fifteen years after the Cuban Missile Crisis, there was a period of **détente**—a peaceful co-existence. Détente did not end the Cold War, for the Americans and Soviets continued their competition for supremacy around the world. The key difference, however, was the absence of any direct confrontation between the superpowers. During this period the United

Figure 5.8: Nuclear Delivery Vehicles of the Powers, 1974

	USA	USSR	Britain	France	China
Intercontinental ballistic missiles	1054	1575	–	–	–
Intermediate ballistic missiles	–	600	–	18	c. 80
Submarine-based ballistic missiles	656	720	64	48	–
Long-range bombers	437	140	–	–	–
Medium-range bombers	66	800	50	52	100

Figure 5.9: NATO and Warsaw Pact Naval Strengths

	Warsaw Pact			NATO		
	Non-Soviet	USSR	Total	US	Non-US	Total
Nuclear submarines	–	105	105	85	12	97
Diesel submarines	6	168	174	5	132	137
Major surface warships	3	184	187	1496	227	376
Naval aircraft	52	755	807	2250	283	2533

Tables from Paul Kennedy, *The Rise and Fall of the Great Powers*, (London: Unwin Hyman, 1988) pp. 395 and 511.

USSR did not have a powerful navy or air force, nor did it have nuclear missiles to match American power and capability. In response, the Soviets adopted two strategies, one diplomatic and the other military. On the diplomatic front, the USSR promoted détente to avoid another direct confrontation with the Americans. On the military front, the Soviets set out to establish greater power at sea and in the air.

The lesson of the Cuban Missile Crisis for the United States was quite different. The Americans were convinced that the Soviets were extremely powerful. The firing of a Soviet **intercontinental ballistic missile** (ICBM) and the launching of the *Sputnik* satellite in 1957 supported this myth. But the reality was that the Soviets were unable even to shoot down the American U-2 spy planes that regularly scrutinized their country at 25 000 m. In four years, only one plane was shot down (in May 1960) and that was only after it developed engine trouble and lost altitude. It is uncertain why American intelligence failed to gain an accurate assessment of Soviet military strength. What is certain, however, is that the resulting increases in American military spending would benefit what Eisenhauer had called the **military-industrial complex**.

States and the Soviet Union opened the lines of communication and signed a number of significant treaties. There was a tacit acknowledgement of each other's sphere of influence.

THE ARMS RACE AND ARMS CONTROLS

The Cuban Missile Crisis taught the Soviets that they were far behind the United States in terms of military strength. The Red Army was powerful, but it was only a threat in Europe. The

VOICES

TWO AMERICAN VIEWS OF THE SOVIET UNION

In the 1980s, there was a growing difference of public opinion over the Cold War and efforts at détente. On one side were the traditional hardliners who believed that military might was essential in maintaining stable relations with the Soviet Union. On the other side were those who sought a more conciliatory approach to the tensions that plagued the world. As you read these two points of view, consider which person you believe to have had a better understanding of the complex relationships among nations.

George F. Kennan, American international relations advisor

"In this day of another great political-emotional preoccupation, when the image of the Soviet leaders has replaced that of Hitler in so many Western minds as the centre and source of all possible evil, it is perhaps particularly desirable that we should remember these things. Let us not repeat the mistake of believing that either good or evil is total. Let us beware, in future, of wholly condemning an entire people and wholly exculpating others. Let us remember that the great moral issues, on which civilization is going to stand or fall, cut across all military and ideological borders, across peoples, classes, and regimes—across, in fact, the make-up of the human individual himself. No other people, as a whole, is entirely our enemy. No people at all—not even ourselves—is entirely our friend."

From Russia and the West Under Lenin and Stalin *by George F. Kennan. Copyright © 1960 by James Hotchkiss, Trustee. By permission of Little, Brown and Company.*

Ronald Reagan, President of the United States, 1983

"Soviet leaders have openly and publicly declared that the only morality they recognize is that which will further their cause, which is world revolution....Morality is [for them] entirely subordinate to the interests of class war....

"Well, I think the refusal of many influential people to accept this elementary fact of Soviet doctrine illustrates a historical reluctance to see totalitarian powers for what they are. We saw this phenomenon in the 1930s. We see it too often today.

"Let us pray for the salvation of all those who live in [the] totalitarian darkness....let us be aware that while they preach the supremacy of the state, declare its omnipotence over individual man, and predict its eventual domination of all peoples on the earth, they are the focus of evil in the modern world....

"I urge you to beware the temptation of pride—the temptation of blithely declaring yourselves above it all and label both sides equally at fault, to ignore the facts of history and the aggressive impulses of an evil empire, to simply call the arms race a giant misunderstanding and thereby remove yourself from the struggle between right and wrong and good and evil...."

From Ronald Reagan, An American Life *(Simon and Schuster, 1990).*

The Cold War in the 1980s: The Reagan Era

Ronald Reagan was elected president of the United States in 1980. He had little faith in the process of détente preferring to meet the Soviet challenge from a position of overwhelming strength. His administration would pursue a policy of strengthening America's military might.

In Reagan's first three years of office, military spending increased by 40 per cent. By 1985, the American defence budget was $300 billion—bigger than the entire GNP of many poor nations and larger than Canada's entire federal budget. Reagan launched a massive high-tech campaign to develop a *Star Wars*-type defence system to permanently assure American military superiority over the Soviet Union. Yet the effect of these grandiose plans on what Reagan referred to as the "evil empire" was simply to push the Soviets into increasing *their* military spending. As the military expenditures escalated, other leaders in both the United States and the Soviet Union began to question the astronomical amounts of money being devoted to the mass destruction of the planet. As the 1980s progressed, the Cold War began to thaw out. The end of the Cold War is analysed in detail in Chapter 7.

In Review

1. What were the Soviet Union's strategies during the Cold War?

2. In what way did the Americans overestimate Soviet military strength?

3. In what way was the Reagan era a return to the early days of the Cold War?

4. Assess Reagan's strategies for dealing with the Soviet Union.

Summary

By 1950, the world had split into two hostile camps, divided by ideology and armed for the destruction of the world. Over the next forty years, the superpowers confronted each other indirectly, as in Vietnam and Afghanistan. At other times, they confronted one another directly, as in the Cuban Missile Crisis. Détente created a more conciliatory atmosphere between the superpowers. Yet the possibility of nuclear annihilation was always present. The knowledge that the Third World War would leave few survivors was never far from the minds of the superpower leaders.

MAKING CONNECTIONS

1. Compare each of the major flashpoints in this chapter in an organizer under the following headings: Dates; Causes; Events; Key Personalities; Results.

2. Compare young people in the 1960s with your own generation in terms of appearance, values, activities, and power.

3. Working with a partner, list the major conflicts threatening world peace today. Is your world more or less peaceful than the Cold War world? Explain.

DEVELOPING YOUR VOICE

4. Debate the topic: The Cold War—Who Was Responsible?

5. Write a letter to the editor of your local newspaper expressing your views on world conflict and peace.

RESEARCHING THE ISSUES

6. With a partner, do research to prepare an interview that examines the viewpoints of one of the following people:
   (a) Joseph McCarthy
   (b) Nikita Khrushchev
   (c) John F. Kennedy
   (d) Fidel Castro
   (e) Ronald Reagan

7. Using this text and other sources, collect ten to fifteen quotes by key figures in the Cold War. Display your quotes in a collage on a class bulletin board.

8. Working in groups, design three "Cold Warrior" trading cards. For each person you select, write a brief biography, perhaps with important quotations or relevant statistics, and some illustrations.

VIEWPOINTS

ISSUE: WAS THE UNITED STATES RESPONSIBLE FOR THE DEVELOPMENT OF THE COLD WAR?

Following the end of the Second World War, the victorious Allies faced a new world. The European powers were replaced by two new superpowers, the United States and the Soviet Union. The fundamental differences between the two former allies quickly gave rise to misunderstanding and friction. Within two years, hostility had replaced friendship and the world began to divide into two camps. The long period of the Cold War had begun.

What caused the rapid deterioration of relations between the two superpowers? Did the Americans provoke the Soviets to take an aggressive stance or were they provoked by the Soviets? The following viewpoints shed some light on this question. In the first reading, John Lewis Gaddis argues that unilateral behavior by the Soviets was the cause of the Cold War and that the United States was reactive and defensive. In the second article, Thomas G. Paterson argues that the United States was to blame by first exaggerating the Soviet threat then launching the policy of containment against the USSR.

Read these viewpoints carefully and complete an Argument Analysis and Evaluation Summary for each reading.

John Lewis Gaddis

"Wartime lack of concern over the powerful position the Soviet Union would occupy in the postwar world had been predicated upon the assumption that the Russians would continue to act in concert with their American and British allies. So long as the Grand Alliance remained intact, Western statesmen could assure each other, Moscow's emergence as the dominant Eurasian power would pose no threat. But during the final months of the war, there began to appear unsettling indications of a determination on Stalin's part to secure postwar interests without reference to the corresponding interests of his wartime associates. It was these manifestations of unilateralism that first set off alarm bells in the West about Russian intentions; the resulting uneasiness in turn stimulated deeper and more profound anxieties...

"Estimates of Moscow's intentions...consistently discounted the possibility that the Russians might risk a direct military confrontation within the foreseeable future. Several considerations contributed to that judgment, not least of which was the damage the Soviet Union itself had suffered during the war and the still relatively primitive character of its air and naval forces....

"But these estimates also suggested that the Russians would not need to use force to gain their objectives, because of the ease with which war-weakened neighbours could be psychologically intimidated....

"It was the psychological implications of an extension of Soviet influence over Europe that probably most concerned American leaders. Although the term 'domino theory' would not come into currency for another decade, administration officials worried deeply about the 'bandwagon' effect that might ensue if the perception became widespread that the momentum in world affairs was on the Russians' side. And despite the United States' own history of isolationism, despite its relative self-sufficiency, there was a very real fear of what might happen if the nation were left without friends in the world. In one sense, this fear grew out of the tradition of American exceptionalism: the United States had always viewed itself as both apart from and a model for the rest of the world; it could hardly have regarded with equanimity evidence that its example was no longer relevant. But, in another sense, it was precisely the unexceptional character of Americans in relation to the rest of the world that was at issue here: who was to say that, buoyed by success in Europe, the totalitarian instinct might not take hold in the United States as well?...

"The strategy of containment brought together the new American interest in maintaining a global balance of power with the perceived Muscovite challenge to that equilibrium in a part of the world that could hardly have been more pivotal—Western Europe. It sought to deal with that danger primarily by economic rather than military means; its goal was not so much the creation of an American hegemony as it was a re-creation of independent centers of power capable of balancing each other as well as the Russians....

"Suffice it to say that the strategy could not have evolved without the perception of vulnerability brought about by the war, and the all-too-successful—if inadvertent—efforts of the Russians to give that abstraction an alarming reality.

"Soviet historians have argued with unsurprising consistency through the years that the United States over-reacted to the 'threat' posed by the USSR in the wake of World War II. During the late 1960s and early 1970s, a number of American students of the early Cold War expressed agreement with that conclusion, though not with the methods that had been used to arrive at it....These accounts portrayed official Washington as having in one way or another fabricated the myth of a hostile Soviet Union in order to justify its own internally motivated drive for international hegemony. The difficulty with this argument was the impossibility of verifying it, for without access to Soviet sources there could be no definite conclusions regarding its accuracy....The intervening years have brought us no nearer to a resolution of that problem, but they have witnessed the emergence of several new lines of historical interpretation that appear to call into question the thesis of American 'over-reaction.'

"It may well be, as William Taubman has argued, that the West gave up on the possibility of cooperation with the [Russians]...that any such cooperation would have been on the Kremlin leader's terms and for his purposes: it would have been designed to foster Soviet control of Eastern Europe whether directly (in the case of Poland, Romania, and Bulgaria) or indirectly (in Hungary and Czechoslovakia); to expand Soviet influence in Western Europe, the Near East and Asia; to position the USSR for even greater gains. Western statesmen may perhaps be pardoned for not having shared this particular vision of the postwar world.

"Nor are they condemned...for having resorted to a strategy of containment....Containment no doubt reinforced Stalin's suspicion of the West, but it can hardly be said to have created it; without containment, according to this new line of interpretation, the fears Western statesmen held at the time regarding Soviet expansionism might well have become reality.

"History, inescapably, involves viewing distant pasts though the prism of more recent ones. The incontestable fact that the United States over-reacted more than once during the subsequent history of the Cold War to the perceived threat of Soviet and/or 'communist' expansionism has, to an extent, blinded us to the equally demonstrable fact that in the immediate postwar years the behaviour of the Russians alarmed not just Americans but a good portion of the rest of the world as well. How well-founded that alarm was—how accurately it reflected the realities that shaped Soviet policy— are issues upon which there are legitimate grounds for disagreement. But to deny that the alarm itself was sincere, or that Americans were not alone in perceiving it, is to distort the view through the prism more than is necessary. Fear, after all, can be genuine without being rational. And, as Sigmund Freud once pointed out, even paranoids can have real enemies."

From The Long Peace *29-47, by John Lewis Gaddis. Copyright © 1987 by John Lewis Gaddis. Reprinted by permission of Oxford University Press.*

Thomas G. Paterson

"Presidents from Eisenhower to Reagan have exalted President Harry S. Truman for his decisiveness and success in launching the Truman Doctrine, the Marshall Plan, and NATO, and for staring the

Soviets down in Berlin during those hair-trigger days of the blockade and airlift.... Some historians have gone so far as to claim that Truman saved humankind from World War III. On the other hand, he has drawn a diverse set of critics....Many historians have questioned Truman's penchant for his quick, simple answer, blunt, careless rhetoric, and facile analogies, his moralism that obscured the complexity of causation, his militarization of American foreign policy, his impatience with diplomacy itself, and his exaggeration of the Soviet threat....

"To study this man and the power at his command, the state of the world in which he acted, his reading of the Soviet threat, and his declaration of the containment doctrine to meet the perceived threat further helps us to understand the origins of the Cold War. Truman's lasting legacy is his tremendous activism in extending American influence on a global scale—his building of an American 'empire' or 'hegemony.' We can disagree over whether this postwar empire was created reluctantly, defensively, by invitation, or deliberately, by self-interested design. But few will deny that the drive to contain Communism fostered an exceptional, worldwide American expansion that produced empire and ultimately, and ironically, insecurity, for the more the United States expanded and drove in foreign stakes, the more vulnerable it seemed to become—the more exposed it became to a host of challenges from Communists and non-Communists alike....

"Why did President Truman think it necessary to project American power abroad, to pursue an activist, global foreign policy unprecedented in United States history? The answer has several parts. First, Americans drew lessons from their experience in the 1930s. While indulging in their so-called 'isolationism,' they had watched economic depression spawn political extremism, which in turn, produced aggression and war. Never again, they vowed. No more appeasement with totalitarians....

"Another reason why Truman projected American power so boldly derived from new strategic thinking. Because of the advent of the air age, travel across the world was shortened in time. Strategists spoke of the shrinkage of the globe....

Airplanes could travel great distances to deliver bombs. Powerful as it was, then, the United States also appeared vulnerable, especially to air attack....

"These several explanations for American globalism suggest that the United States would have been an expansionist power whether or not the obstructionist Soviets were lurking about. That is, America's own needs—ideological, political, economic, strategic—encouraged such a projection of power. As the influential National Security Council Paper No. 68 (NSC-68) noted in April 1950, the 'overall policy' of the United States was 'designed to foster a world environment in which the American system can survive and flourish.' This policy 'we would probably pursue even if there were no Soviet threat.'

"To Truman and his advisers, the Soviets stood as the world's bully, and the very existence of this menacing bear necessitated an activist American foreign policy and an exertion of American power as a 'counterforce.'

"But Truman officials exaggerated the Soviet threat, imagining an adversary that never measured up to the galloping monster so often depicted by alarmist Americans. Even if the Soviets intended to dominate the world, or just Western Europe, they lacked the capabilities to do so. The Soviets had no foreign aid to dispense; outside Russia Communist parties were minorities; the Soviet economy was seriously crippled by the war; and the Soviet military suffered significant weaknesses.... A Soviet *blitzkrieg* invasion of Western Europe had little chance of success and would have proven suicidal for the Soviets, for even if they managed to gain temporary control of Western Europe by a military thrust, they could not strike the United States. So they would have to assume defensive positions and await crushing American attacks, probably including atomic bombings of Soviet Russia itself....

"Why then did Americans so fear the Soviets? Why did the Central Intelligence Agency, the Joint Chiefs of Staff, and the President exaggerate the Soviet threat? The first explanation is that their intelligence estimates were just that—estimates. The American intelligence community was still in a state of infancy, hardly the well-developed system it would become.... So Americans lacked complete assurance that their figures on Soviet force deployment or armaments were accurate.... When leaders do not know, they tend to assume the worst of an adversary's intentions and capabilities....

"American leaders also exaggerated the Soviet threat because it was useful in galvanizing and unifying American public opinion for an abandonment of recent and still lingering 'isolationism' and support for an expansive foreign policy....The military particularly overplayed the Soviet threat in order to persuade Congress to endorse larger defense budgets....

"Why dwell on this question of the American exaggeration of the Soviet threat? Because it oversimplified international realities by under-estimating local conditions that might thwart Soviet/Communist successes and by over-estimating the Soviet ability to act. Because it encouraged the Soviets to fear encirclement and to enlarge their military establishment, thereby contributing to a dangerous weapons race. Because it led to indiscriminate globalism....

"American policies were designed to roll the Soviets back. The United States reconstruction loan policy, encouragement of dissident groups, and appeal for free elections alarmed Moscow, contributing to a Soviet push to secure the area. The issue of free elections illustrates the point. Such a call was consistent with cherished American principle. But in the context of Eastern Europe and the Cold War, problems arose. First,

Americans conspicuously followed a double standard;...that is, if the principle of free elections really mattered, why not hold such elections in the United States' sphere of influence in Latin America, where an unsavory lot of dictators ruled? Second, free elections would have produced victories for anti-Soviet groups. Such results could only unsettle the Soviets and invite them to intervene to protect their interests in neighbouring states— just as the Unites States had intervened in Cuba and Mexico in the twentieth century when hostile groups assumed power....And third, the United States had so little influence in Eastern Europe that it had no way of insuring free elections....

"The story of Truman's foreign policy is basically an accounting of how the United States, because of its own expansionism and exaggeration of the Soviet threat, became a global power. Truman projected American power after the Second World War to rehabilitate Western Europe, secure new allies, guarantee strategic and economic links, and block Communist or Soviet influence. He firmly implanted the image of the Soviets as relentless, worldwide transgressors with whom it is futile to negotiate. Through his exaggeration of the Soviet threat Truman made it very likely that the United States would continue to practice global interventionism years after he left the White House."

From Meeting the Communist Threat: Truman to Reagan, *by Thomas G. Patterson. Copyright © 1988 by Thomas G. Patterson. Reprinted by permission of Oxford University Press.*

ANALYSIS AND EVALUATION

Refer to the Argument Analysis and Evaluation Guide on page viii.

1. Using the Argument Analysis and Evaluation Guide, compare the readings by Gaddis and Patterson. On what do they agree? On what do they disagree?

2. Decide which of the viewpoints you tend to support and explain why. Be sure to use specific information from this textbook, the readings, and other sources to support your position.

3. State and support your position on the issue: "Was the United States responsible for the development of the Cold War?"

CHAPTER SIX

The United Nations

"We have our last chance. If we do not devise some greater and more equitable system, Armageddon will be at our door."

General Douglas MacArthur, United States Army, 1945

"Our instrument and our hope is the United Nations, and I see little merit in the impatience of those who would abandon this imperfect instrument because they dislike our imperfect world."

President John F. Kennedy, State of the Union Message, 1962

"At the UN everybody wins a few, loses a few, settles for half a loaf. No one, not the US, not the USSR, not Japan, not China, not India, can get away with playing the Big Bully or the Lone Ranger."

Natarajan Krishnan, India's Ambassador to the UN, 1985

Left: The United Nations Headquarters

❖ OVERVIEW

After 1945, two new superpowers, the United States and the Soviet Union, emerged from the wreckage of the Second World War to dominate international relations. Between them they set out to carve up the world into new alliances. A new age was dawning. While the world was now at peace, it was uncertain how to maintain it.

Amidst the confusion of the new world order, the United Nations was founded on 24 October 1945. Fifty-one nations joined together to establish the United Nations Charter calling for international peace, security, and co-operation. Their efforts mark one of the great collaborative achievements of humankind.

boldly declared that "This time we shall not make the mistake of waiting until the end of the war to set up the machinery of peace." Long before the guns were silent, the foundations for a new world order were being laid. In a series of meetings between Roosevelt and Britain's Winston Churchill, and later with Soviet leader Joseph Stalin and Chinese leader Jiang Jie Shi (Chiang Kai-shek), the Allied powers planned the structures and built the consensus on which a lasting peace could be made.

The League of Nations had been too weak to stop aggression by the Axis powers. Roosevelt realized that the lack of American participation was one of the main reasons for that weakness. He was determined to make the United Nations a strong organization by ensuring that all the major powers —especially the United States—were actively involved. To ensure ongoing American commitment to the UN, it was decided that the headquarters would be in the United States. A gift of prime land on the Hudson River, from American entrepreneur J.D. Rockefeller, helped determine that the UN site would be in New York City.

FOCUS QUESTIONS

1. Why was the United Nations created?
2. How does the structure of the UN accommodate the realities of national self-interest with the goals of world peace?
3. What are the purposes of the United Nations?
4. How did the UN meet early postwar challenges to world peace and security?
5. How effective is the United Nations as peacekeeper?
6. Should the UN use military force for peacemaking?

CREATING THE UNITED NATIONS

One of the Allied goals during the Second World War was to create an international organization to ensure peace and security in the postwar world. US President Franklin Roosevelt wanted to avoid repeating the tragic failure of the League of Nations. He

THE STRUCTURE OF THE UNITED NATIONS

The creation of the United Nations was an exercise in compromise and negotiation. The lessons learned from the failure of the League of Nations were applied to the new organization. The key issue was how to accommodate the realities of national self-interest of both large and small powers. What was required was a formula that would give the major powers a greater role in the direction of the UN while still recognizing the need for all countries to have their voices heard. The solution was to divide the UN into two parts: a **General Assembly** in which each country had one vote, and a **Security Council** controlled by the major powers. In addition, the Secretariat, the Economic and Social Council, the Trusteeship Council, and the International Court of Justice were created to address other areas of concern to the international body.

THE GENERAL ASSEMBLY

The General Assembly is the forum for all member states. It holds an annual session in September, but meets throughout the year for emergency debates. The Assembly is a meeting place where world leaders or their representatives, from nations large and small, present their positions on various issues.

The General Assembly divides its responsibilities among six standing committees. Reports from the committees are presented to the Assembly for debate. Most decisions are reached by a simple majority vote; resolutions on questions of peace and security, expulsion of member states, and approval of the budget require a majority of two-thirds. The Assembly appoints the **Secretary-General** and elects a President to preside over Assembly meetings.

Some critics dismiss the General Assembly as an ineffective "talking shop" where nations simply play politics. Others argue that such a forum, in which all nations are recognized and given the opportunity to express their views, serves a valuable purpose in today's hostile world. It provides an

"A FINE TEAM — BUT COULD DO WITH A DASH OF UNITY...."

What is British cartoonist David Low's view of the conflicting interests of the major powers in the UN?

opportunity for the peaceful resolution of conflicts and provides a stage on which to focus world opinion.

THE SECURITY COUNCIL

The real power behind the United Nations lies in the Security Council. The Council is made up of two groups. One group consists of five permanent members—China, France, Britain, the United States, and Russia—each of which has veto power over any UN decisions. The other group consists of ten non-permanent members (the number was originally six but it was increased to ten in 1966), which are elected for a two-year term.

Matters of peace and security were originally placed exclusively in the hands of the Security Council. Since the Korean War, however, the General Assembly has also been empowered to address these issues. Permanent members of the Security Council have direct control over UN intervention in any conflict. But with their individual veto power, any action considered not to be

The first session of the United Nations Security Council took place on 17 January 1946.

The work of the Economic and Social Council is in many ways the most important and enduring of all the UN's achievements. The council co-ordinates the programs of organizations such as the Food and Agriculture Organization (FAO), the World Health Organization (WHO), the International Labour Organization (ILO), the United Nations Children's Emergency Fund (UNICEF), and the United Nations Educational, Scientific, and Cultural Organization (UNESCO).

THE TRUSTEESHIP COUNCIL

This council provides for an international trusteeship to protect the interests of those territories that are not fully self-governing. These trust territories remain under the council's protection until such time as they become independent. The Trusteeship Council consists of the United States, China, France, Russia, and Britain.

in a member's national interest may be thwarted. This has often led to deadlock in the Security Council and provides a ready target for those who question the UN's effectiveness. But it is the power of the veto that ensures the continuing support and commitment of the major powers.

THE ECONOMIC AND SOCIAL COUNCIL

The Economic and Social Council (ECOSOC), with a membership of fifty-four nations elected by the General Assembly, is the branch of the UN entrusted with the fulfilment of the UN's international economic, social, cultural, educational, and health responsibilities.

THE INTERNATIONAL COURT OF JUSTICE

The International Court of Justice forms an integral part of the United Nations Charter and all UN members are automatically parties to the Statute of the Court. The Court is composed of independent judges who possess the necessary qualifications to preside over the

Figure 6.1:
The United Nations Organization

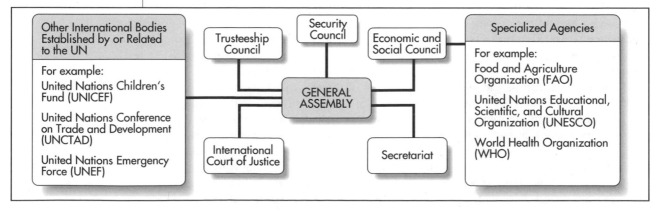

Figure 6.2: The Purposes and Principles of the United Nations

Purposes

1. To maintain international peace and settle disputes
2. To develop the principle of equal rights and self-determination of peoples
3. To solve international social, economic, and humanitarian problems and promote human rights and fundamental freedoms
4. To be a centre for harmonizing the actions of nations to achieve these common goals

Principles

1. The Organization is based on the "sovereign equality" of all members.
2. All members are expected to fulfil "in good faith" all UN obligations.
3. All members should settle their international disputes by peaceful means so that "international peace, security, and justice are not endangered."
4. All members are to refrain from the threat or use of force against any state.
5. All members are to assist the UN in any actions taken and are not to assist any state against which the UN is acting.
6. The Organization seeks to ensure that non-member states act in accordance with these principles to promote peace and security.
7. Nothing in the Charter authorizes the UN "to intervene in matters essentially within the domestic jurisdiction of any state."*

*Ironically, principle 7, which prevents UN intervention within any state, limits purpose 3, which aims to promote human rights and freedoms. In many cases it is the state government itself that violates human rights and freedoms. **Apartheid**, or absolute racial segregation, in South Africa is a case in point. This was an official policy of the white government from 1948 until 1991. While many nations demanded UN action against apartheid, the South African government legally argued that apartheid was an internal matter and was outside the jurisdiction of the UN.

---

high courts of their home countries or who are recognized for their expertise in international law. These fifteen judges (no two of whom may be from the same country) are elected by the Security Council and the General Assembly.

THE SECRETARIAT

The chief executive officer of the United Nations is the Secretary-General. Described as the most important public service job in the world, the Secretary-General is the top-ranking administrator and diplomat in the UN. The Secretariat supports a staff of more than 15 000 (larger than the civil services of many small countries) from over 140 nations. The Secretary-General reports on international problems and progress to the General Assembly, asks the Security Council to deal with matters that threaten international peace and security, and acts as a mediator in international disputes. In addition, the Secretary-General must maintain complete independence free of any influence by any member of the UN.

Choosing a Secretary-General is a complex process. The candidate must be acceptable to the different blocs in the UN and cannot be too closely identified with either superpower.

The six Secretaries-General have been from across the globe: Trygve Lie of Norway (1946-52); Dag Hammarskjöld of Sweden (1953-61); U Thant of Burma (now Myanmar) (1961-72); Kurt Waldheim of Austria (1972-82); Javier Pérez de Cuéller of Peru (1982-91); and Boutros Boutros-Ghali of Egypt (1992-).

The goal of UNICEF is to improve the quality of life for children around the world, including the elimination of child labour.

THE UNITED NATIONS AND THE COLD WAR

The world after 1945 was increasingly **bipolar**. As two opposing blocs formed, one around the US and the other around the USSR, the United Nations was caught in the middle. The Security Council became an arena in which the two blocs competed for influence and undermined one another. The Western democracies brought their Cold War battles to the UN and tried to mobilize world opinion on their respective sides. Nations of the Soviet bloc charged that the UN was dominated by the United States and its allies, which did in fact constitute a majority of UN members until the 1960s. To protect their interests, the Soviets began to use the veto consistently. This paralysed the Security Council, preventing it from making decisions or taking effective action in times of crisis.

THE CHANGING FACE OF THE UNITED NATIONS

The early years of the United Nations were decidely preoccupied with Cold War issues. By the mid-1950s, however, pressures for decolonization of Africa and Asia pushed the organization to broaden its focus. As former colonies became independent and joined the UN, it changed from a body dominated by European and American members to an organization representing over 160 diverse countries, many of them developing nations. As membership changed, the UN took on a new focus. Organizations under the UN umbrella, such as the Food and Agriculture Organization (FAO), the United Nations Educational, Scientific, and Cultural Organization (UNESCO), and the World Health Organization (WHO) began to take on more prominent roles on the international scene.

Conflicting Cultural Values

In 1948, the United Nations passed the Universal Declaration of the Rights of Man. Known today as the Declaration of Human Rights, it is a cornerstone of UN policy. This all-encompassing document calls for universal human rights, including the right to fair government and freedom to vote, equal rights for men and women in marriage, the right to fair employment, the right to protect

Figure 6.3: Key UN Agencies

Organization	Date	Purpose
Food and Agriculture Organization (FAO)	1945	To raise levels of nutrition and standards of living; to improve the production and distribution of food and agricultural products; and to eliminate hunger
United Nations Educational, Scientific, and Cultural Organization (UNESCO)	1946	To promote collaboration among nations through education, science, and culture in order to further universal rights and freedoms
United Nations Children's Emergency Fund (UNICEF)	1946	To provide development assistance aimed at improving the quality of life for children and mothers in developing countries
World Health Organization (WHO)	1948	To obtain the highest levels of health for all the world's citizens through improved health services, the eradication of diseases, improved health training and education, and better working conditions
International Monetary Fund (IMF)	1947	To promote international monetary co-operation and international trade and to offer monetary assistance
General Agreement on Tariffs and Trade	1948	To establish a common code of conduct in international trade and trade relations and to provide a forum for trade negotiations and the reduction of trade barriers
International Labour Organization (ILO)	1946	To formulate international standards of labour conventions

children, the right to freedom to travel, and the right to private ownership of property. But universal human rights is primarily a Western philosophy. Many of these principles are not shared by some non-Western nations. They may conflict with cultural traditions and religious values or with other political, economic, and legal systems. Where reality clashes with ideals, establishing a universally accepted standard of human rights is not a straightforward task.

It is also important to remember that the West has not always embraced the concept of universal human rights. In 1946, both the United States and Britain opposed the establishment of the UN Commission on the Status of Women as well as Article 8 of the UN Charter guaranteeing both women and men the right "to participate in any capacity and under conditions of equality" in all UN organizations. The Western nations, including the United States and Canada, bear the scars of sanctioned injustices against many people throughout their histories. Values change with time and place. They will continue to do so as the world in which we live continues to evolve.

In spite of its cultural biases, the United Nations has developed an important moral leadership in the world. It has improved world health, economic and social welfare, and education, and addressed many important issues, such as refugees and disarmament. The UN has helped to create a better life for millions of people.

PROFILE

ELEANOR ROOSEVELT (1884-1962)

Eleanor Roosevelt, the wife of US President Franklin Roosevelt, has been called one of the great women in history. In her years in the White House, she transformed the traditional role of a political wife and established a remarkable career for herself as champion of social causes. As you read about her life, consider why she was known to many as the "conscience of America."

"When we look upon the failures of the United Nations, we should not be disheartened, because if we take the failure and learn, eventually we will use this machinery better and better. We will also learn one important thing, and that is, no machinery works unless people make it work.

"And in a democracy like ours, it is the people who have to tell their representatives what they want them to do. And it is the acceptance of the individual responsibility by each one of us that actually will make the United Nations machinery work. If we don't accept that, and if we don't do the job, we may well fail—but it lies in our hands. And I think that is the main thing for us to remember today."

Eleanor Roosevelt, 1946

"When will our consciences grow so tender that we will act to prevent human misery, rather than to avenge it?"

Eleanor Roosevelt, 1948

The niece of President Theodore ("Teddy") Roosevelt, Eleanor Roosevelt endured an unhappy childhood. Both parents died before her tenth birthday. As a teenager, she was sent to study abroad. In 1905, at the age of twenty-one, Eleanor married a distant cousin, Franklin Delano Roosevelt.

After her husband was stricken with polio in 1921, Eleanor Roosevelt assumed a more active role in his political career. At the same time, she forged an independent course for herself as a champion of the underprivileged. Roosevelt's confidence and public stature blossomed. During the Depression in the early years of FDR's presidency, she became an inspiration for millions of Americans. She was actively involved in the administration of subsidized housing. She promoted female equality and succeeded in having FDR appoint the first woman to the federal cabinet. During the Second World War she visited Allied forces around the globe, offering her personal support and encouragement.

When FDR died in 1945, Roosevelt's political and social activism expanded to even greater heights. She was a delegate to the first meeting of the United Nations General Assembly. In 1946 she was appointed to chair the UN Human Rights Commission. Shepherding eighteen nations in the chilling atmosphere of the Cold War, Roosevelt led the group in drafting what she termed "a magna carta for mankind." After long, tedious, and contentious meetings, the United Nations passed the Universal Declaration of the Rights of Man in 1948. This landmark document has been the foundation for human rights around the world. Roosevelt continued to serve in the UN until 1952, and again from 1961 until her death the following year.

IN REVIEW

1. Why was the United Nations created?

2. How was America's role in the UN different from its role in the failed League of Nations?

3. Describe the work and membership of the General Assembly and Security Council. Which has the most power? Why?

4. Why has the Security Council often been unable to take effective action?

5. What are the duties of the Secretary-General? Why might this position be viewed as an "impossible" job?

6. Rank order the seven principles of the UN from most important to least important. Be prepared to defend your ranking.

7. Summarize the intentions of purpose 3 and principle 7 of the UN Charter. Explain how one can be used to limit the other.

8. What specific evidence is there that the UN has fallen short of its mission to defend and protect human rights around the world?

9. What criticisms do some non-Western nations have of the UN?

THE ROLE OF THE UN: PEACEMAKING AND PEACEKEEPING

In the 1950s, two crises emerged to threaten the world's security. The United Nations was put to the test in bringing peace and order to these explosive situations. The first conflict was the Korean War, in which the UN acted as **peacemaker** through military action. The second incident was the Suez Crisis, in which the UN assumed a new role as **peacekeeper**.

THE UN AS PEACEMAKER: THE KOREAN WAR

From 1910 to 1945, Korea had been a Japanese colony. At the conclusion of the Second World War, the USSR declared war on Japan, attacking on several fronts, including northern Korea. With the defeat of Japan, Soviet troops held the northern half of Korea while American troops occupied the south. As with the "temporary" partition of Germany, the Allies agreed to divide Korea at the 38th parallel. The two Koreas were to be reunited following a peace settlement. But as with the two Germanys, the Cold War intervened. Korea remained divided.

In 1947, when the United States was unable to obtain Soviet co-operation to hold a general election in Korea, the issue was turned over to the United Nations. The General Assembly voted to establish a commission to oversee a free election and to assist officials in setting up a unified and independent government. The Soviets, however, held their own "election" in the north and established the Democratic Republic of Korea under Kim Il Sung. The Americans did the same in the south and formed the Republic of Korea under President Syngman Rhee.

Both governments claimed to speak for all Korea. Each of the leaders had ambitions to unify the country under his own rule by force of arms. Neither North nor South Korea was able to gain admission to the UN because each was opposed by one of the superpowers. Instead of moving towards unification, North and South Korea became even more deeply divided, and increasingly hostile. By 1950, tensions had reached a boiling point. War erupted on June 25th when Northern forces crossed the 38th parallel and invaded South Korea.

The Outbreak of War

Once US President Harry Truman learned of the attack he ordered his military commander, General Douglas MacArthur, who was stationed in Japan, to send supplies to the South Koreans. At the same time, the United States Seventh Fleet was dispatched to protect Taiwan from possible Chinese invasion. The following day Truman pledged American military intervention against any act of communist expansion in Asia.

At the UN Security Council, the United States introduced a resolution branding the North Koreans as the aggressors and demanding that they withdraw their troops from the South. There was no Soviet veto because the Soviets were boycotting the UN over American refusal to allow the People's Republic to take China's seat in the organization.

In 1949, the defeated Chinese Nationalist government of Jiang Jie Shi was allowed to keep China's seats in the Security Council and the General Assembly. The Soviets argued that the seats should be held by the new Communist government of the People's Republic of China. In protest, they refused to participate in any UN sessions for six months.

At first the military campaign went well for the Communist forces. By September 1950, they controlled all of Korea except a small area around Pusan in the southeast. Then, on September 15th, MacArthur executed a daring attack at Inchon, splitting the North Korean army in half. (See Figure 6.4) North Korea lost 35 000 soldiers. What had seemed like an easy victory was turning into a disaster.

With the North Koreans in retreat, MacArthur and President Rhee decided to take advantage of the opportunity to conquer North Korea. Rhee pressured MacArthur to cross the 38th parallel in pursuit of the enemy. But the conflict was still a UN operation. Coalition members, including Canada, questioned the ultimate goals of the operation. The UN resolution called for the restoration of South Korea; it did not include the right to invade North Korea. Sensing a total victory was at hand, however, a confident Rhee declared: "Where is the 38th parallel? It is non-existent: I am going all the way to the Yalu [river] and the United Nations can't stop me."

The UN forces crossed the 38th parallel early in October and advanced rapidly towards the Yalu. MacArthur proposed pursuing the Communists into China, bombing the bridges and even laying nuclear waste along the river to prevent the enemy from using China as a safe base of operations. MacArthur believed that the Americans should invade mainland China and restore Jiang Jie Shi to power. Truman was not prepared to launch a third world war over Korea, however, and he ordered the troops to halt at the Yalu. As a concession to MacArthur, he allowed limited bombing of the bridges, but "only on the Korean side." This mixed message convinced MacArthur that, for all his tough talk, Truman was actually "soft" on communism.

At the same time, Truman had received a message from the Chinese government, through the Indian Ambassador via the British, that if UN troops joined the South Koreans in combat north of the 38th parallel, China would intervene. Truman's objective in Korea was a limited victory—to repel the North Koreans' invasion, thereby demonstrating the effectiveness of collective action by the UN. MacArthur's objective, on the other hand, was to defeat Asian communism. With their objectives clearly incompatible, a showdown between the two was inevitable.

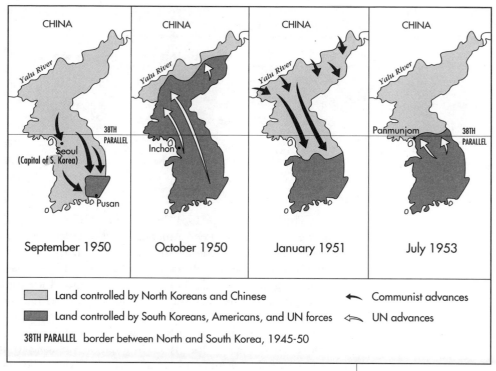

Figure 6.4:
Korea, 1950-53

China Enters the Conflict

As the Americans and the United Nations debated the course of action, the People's Republic of China mobilized half a million troops on the Korean border. In late October 1950, UN and South Korean units advancing towards the Yalu River were halted by Chinese forces. Yet just as suddenly as they had appeared, the Chinese troops vanished. Then, on November 25th, the day after the Americans and South Koreans resumed their offensive, six Chinese armies counterattacked. Within a month, they pushed the surprised UN coalition troops back beyond the 38th parallel into South Korea.

For several months the battle lines shifted back and forth. A stalemate was developing. MacArthur urged an all-out war, including the use of nuclear weapons. Fortunately cooler heads prevailed. Yet this setback did not temper MacArthur's political interference. He continued to clash with Truman until finally on 10 April 1951 he was fired. Truman was determined to enforce one of the basic principles of the American Constitution—that the government determines policy, and it is the responsibility of the military to carry out that policy. American policy was now officially to secure a unified and independent Korea by "political, as distinguished from military, means."

The Canadian government joined the coalition of sixteen nations fighting in Korea under the UN flag. As the war dragged on, Canada increased its contribution until it was exceeded only by that of the United States and Britain. When the guns fell silent in 1953, 26 791 Canadians had served in Korea; 516 had been killed in action.

Figure 6.5: United Nations Forces in Korea

	USA	Other UN*	South Korea
Ground force	50%	10%	40%
Naval force	86%	7%	7%
Air force	93%	2%	5%

*Includes Canada and fourteen other countries; South Korea was not admitted to the UN until 1991

provided medical units, hospital ships, food, and other supplies and equipment. But as Figure 6.5 shows, the majority of the forces in the Korean conflict were American.

The Lessons of the Korean War

The Korean War demonstrated the United Nations' limitations as a peacemaking organization. The UN was directly involved in Korea only because the United States had decided it should be and the Soviet Union had not been in a position to use its veto. So it was more by luck than design that the Security Council was able to authorize any action in Korea. The conflict also highlighted the disadvantages of relying on voluntary military assistance. Technically all UN members are obliged to provide military forces. But in Korea only sixteen nations participated in actual combat, and these were all friends of the United States.

The enduring legacy of the UN experience in Korea was the **Uniting for Peace resolution** passed in November 1950. This gave the General Assembly responsibility for dealing with international aggression if the Security Council is deadlocked. It was passed by the Security Council during the Soviet boycott as a means of countering future Soviet vetoes. Once the Soviet Union returned to the Security Council, it used its veto 103 times before the United States used its veto once. But because of the Uniting for Peace resolution the UN was able to take action in a variety of hot spots around the globe. (When Iraq invaded Kuwait in 1991, it was the Uniting for Peace resolution that enabled the UN to

Throughout June 1951, behind-the-scenes contacts between American and Soviet diplomats at the UN finally resulted in a cease-fire. Peace talks officially began on 10 July 1951. Yet throughout the negotiations sporadic outbursts of fighting continued. A truce between North and South Korea was not reached until 27 July 1953. In total, between 3 and 4 million casualties resulted from this "limited" war. Of the dead, wounded, and missing, more than half were Korean civilians. In the United Nations Command 94 000 soldiers were killed.

Was the effort in Korea an American or a UN military operation? In spite of the immediate American response to lend air support to the South Koreans, Truman intended to use the United Nations to stop communist aggression. Sixteen nations sent combat forces to the war zone; thirty others

With its involvement in Korea, Canada's foreign policy shifted. American influence replaced the traditional British connection. Sending troops to Korea set a pattern for continued Canadian participation in the peacemaking and peacekeeping efforts of the United Nations.

launch a massive attack to drive the Iraqi troops out of Kuwait.)

THE UN AS PEACEKEEPER: THE SUEZ CRISIS

The Korean War demonstrated that the United Nations could be a military peacemaker, but at a high price in terms of money and human life. In addition, although the shooting had stopped, Korea was no closer to peace than it had been before the armed conflict began. Many middle and small powers were not keen to be pawns in conflicts stage-managed to promote the interests of the major powers. It was clear that if the UN was to succeed, a new and more flexible formula for an independent peacekeeping force would be needed. It was the Suez Crisis of 1956 that brought about the first multinational, voluntary peacekeeping force in the history of international relations.

Nasser and the Emergence of Egypt as an Arab Power

Colonel Gamal Abdel Nasser emerged as the leader of Egypt following the Arab defeat in the 1948 Arab-Israeli war. Nasser had two main goals: to create an independent Egypt free from colonial rule and to destroy the newly formed nation of Israel.

To achieve his goals, Nasser needed money, and lots of it. The fastest way to obtain funds was to let the superpowers bid for Egypt's allegiance. Nasser had no ideological preference for dollars or rubles. He accepted both American and Soviet aid in the form of cash, military equipment, technical expertise, and food.

Egypt needed a modern army to destroy Israel, so Nasser's long-term solution was to industrialize. The first requirement was electricity. Nasser

announced ambitious plans to expand the Aswan Dam on the Nile River as a power source. He opened negotiations with both superpowers for financing of the project. In 1955, Nasser signed an arms deal with Czechoslovakia, a Soviet bloc nation. By 1956, he was ready to conclude an agreement with the United States to help finance and build a $1.3 billion dam at Aswan. It appeared that Nasser had successfully manoeuvred the Soviets into supplying arms and the Americans into supplying money and technical expertise. But this delicate balancing act was soon to crumble.

> "We want independence for our country. We want to preserve our nationalism and our dignity."
>
> *Gamal Abdel Nasser, 1956*

Nationalizing the Suez Canal

The Americans were concerned about Nasser's brand of non-aligned nationalism. The continued conflict with Israel, which had close ties to the US, also cost Nasser Western support. Contrary to international and UN agreements, Egypt had been preventing Israeli ships and all ships bound for Israeli ports from using the Suez Canal. When the United States refused financial and technical aid for the Aswan Dam project, Nasser's reaction was immediate and dramatic; on 26 July 1956 he seized control of the Suez Canal and

> "Imperialism is the great force that is imposing a murderous, invisible siege upon the whole region."
>
> *Gamal Abdel Nasser, 1956*

turned to the Soviets for help in building the dam. This accomplished two goals. It signalled the end of Egypt's colonial status and provided funds for building the Aswan Dam and modernizing Egypt.

Nasser's takeover of the canal was a peaceful one; the British and French were offered compensation at the July 25th market value and full use of the facility. Nevertheless, the sudden expropriation increased global tensions. Only two years before, Egypt had assured the UN that international management of the canal would continue. The British and French were determined to regain their 97 per cent share of the canal's profits and reassert their status as ranking powers in the Middle East. Their military leaders plotted with Israel to recapture the Suez and bring about Nasser's downfall in the process.

Together, Britain and France devised an elaborate scheme. Israel was to attack Egypt as part of the ongoing dispute between the two nations. Britain and France would land troops at the canal zone on the pretence of protecting international shipping during the conflict. The plan would allow Britain and France to repossess the Suez Canal and would enable Israel to expand its territory; Nasser would be overthrown and replaced with a leader more favourable to Anglo-French inter-

ests. But the conspirators miscalculated the reaction of the United States and the world community.

The United Nations' Response

On 29 October 1956, Israel attacked Egypt. Britain ordered the Egyptians and Israelis to withdraw from both sides of the Suez Canal. Egypt refused; but five days after the Israeli attack the fighting had already stopped. Even so, Anglo-French paratroops and commandos landed as planned, attacking Egyptian positions along the western side of the canal and securing the canal itself. The invasion stunned the world. The Soviet Union threatened to launch missiles on Paris and London. The United States was outraged. How would the UN deal with this act of aggression by two of the permanent members of its Security Council?

The day after the attack, the US introduced a resolution in the Security Council. It called for Israel to withdraw its troops and for all members to "refrain from the use of force." But France and Britain used their vetoes to kill this motion as well as a Soviet proposal that the Americans and the Soviets jointly intervene. Deadlocked, the Security Council considered taking the matter up in the General Assembly. Only Britain and France voted against the motion. Since the veto does not apply in procedural matters, the motion carried and the Suez issue was brought before the General Assembly.

On November 2nd, an American resolution calling for a cease-fire and UN action to ensure international passage through the Suez Canal was passed. Only five nations (Israel, France, Britain, Australia, and New Zealand) opposed; six others (including Canada) abstained. On November 4th, Canada's UN representative, Lester B. Pearson, proposed that the Anglo-French force in the canal zone be

The Suez Crisis divided Canadians. The Liberal government opposed British actions. The Conservative opposition supported the British, arguing that Britain and France had not only the right but a duty to act. The public was equally split. But the fact that officially Canada opposed Britain and supported the United States confirmed the country's changing relationship with Britain and closer ties with the US.

PROFILE

GAMAL ABDEL NASSER (1918-70)

Gamal Abdel Nasser was an important spokesperson for the Arab nationalism that swept the Middle East after the Second World War. Although unpopular with Western leaders, in the Arab world Nasser was viewed as a hero and a saviour. As you read about his life, consider why this might be so.

"[The Egyptian revolution] has brought about the evacuation of British imperialism and the independence of Egypt. It has defined Egypt's Arab character, fought the policy of spheres of influence in the Arab world, led the socialist revolution and brought about a profound change in the Arab way of life. It has affirmed the people's control of their resources and the product of their national action....

"More important than all this, it has given a place to the workers in the leadership of political action."

Gamal Abdel Nasser, 1952

"I will continue to dream of an enlightened African consciousness sharing with others from all over the world the work of advancing the welfare of the peoples of this continent."

Gamal Abdel Nasser, 1956

Gamal Abdel Nasser was one of eleven children. As a student, he protested against British domination of Egypt. Eventually his actions landed him in jail before he joined the military.

Arab pride and Egyptian nationalism sparked growing criticism of Egypt's monarchy, widely viewed as corrupt and repressive, under King Farouk (himself a Turk rather than an Egyptian). Egypt's defeat by Israel in the war of 1948 caused humiliation among Egyptian soldiers. Pledging to restore Arab pride and dignity, Nasser and others formed a Free Officers movement aimed at ousting the old regime and driving out foreign powers. In 1952, army officers revolted, forcing Farouk to abdicate. The monarchy was abolished and a new republic proclaimed. Nasser became prime minister of Egypt in 1954 and president in 1956.

Nasser had several objectives. First he wanted to free the Arab world from foreign influence. He hoped to weld all Arab peoples into one great Arab nation. He knew that the redistribution of wealth and land was critical if he was to improve the lives of the peasants. He hoped to initiate a vast program of public works and industrialization to provide money and muscle for the Arab revival. Finally, he pledged to restore Palestine to the Palestinians and demolish the state of Israel.

Britain and France viewed Nasser as a dangerous revolutionary and war-monger. Egypt's takeover of the Suez Canal only reinforced their suspicions. But Nasser was celebrated in Egypt and throughout the Arab world for standing up to the Europeans.

In his years as leader of Egypt, Nasser tried to forge Pan-Arabian alliances. He brought Soviet influence into the country as a counterbalance to the West. The Egyptian education and health systems were expanded and reformed, and there was some redistribution of land and wealth. By modernizing and enlarging the Egyptian army, Nasser continued Arab pressure against Israel.

In 1967, Nasser demanded the withdrawal of the United Nations Emergency Force, which had been present since the Suez Crisis. At the same time he pledged a new war of extermination against Israel. In the Six Day War that ensued, Egypt suffered massive losses of territory. Nasser tried to resign, but his offer was rejected. He spent his final years struggling to rebuild Arab confidence and unity. He died in 1970 at the age of fifty-two of heart failure.

replaced by a peacekeeping force charged with protecting the canal and keeping Israel and Egypt apart. Pearson's diplomatic skills succeeded in getting the motion passed unanimously, with nine nations abstaining.

The Significance of the Suez Crisis

The lasting significance of the Suez Crisis was the establishment of an international police force, the UNEF. Since 1956 UN peacekeeping forces have been called into service around the world. Unfortunately, however, they are not the solution for maintaining international peace and security. The reason is **national sovereignty**. When Nasser agreed to accept the UNEF on Egyptian soil in 1956, it was on the condition that the force would leave whenever, in the opinion of the Egyptians, its work had been accomplished. Eleven years later, the UNEF was unceremoniously kicked out of Egypt. A new Arab-Israeli war promptly followed. An international police force can be effective only if the nations involved agree that peace should be maintained.

UN PEACEKEEPING FROM 1956 TO 1995

Since the Suez Crisis, the United Nations has continued its role as peacekeeper. UN forces have had a variety of forms and purposes: as unarmed observers monitoring cease-fires (Kashmir, 1965-66); as armed forces overseeing the withdrawal of belligerent forces (Afghanistan, 1988); and as enforcers of free elections (Nicaragua, 1989). Sometimes, lightly armed troops have not only had to keep the opposing sides apart or prevent the renewal of battles (Lebanon, 1978), but have acted as a police force to maintain law and order (Cyprus since 1964). On a few occasions, UN land and air forces have had to fight, not only to prevent civil war but to save their own lives under attack (the Congo from 1960-64). Peacekeeping forces have been as small as a few hundred and as large as several thousand.

Peacekeeping forces have been drawn primarily from small and middle powers like Canada. (Canada is the only country to have contributed to every UN peacekeeping mission). The United States, Britain, France, and the other major powers have occasionally sent troops, but most often they have provided transportation, equipment, and funds.

Financing peacekeeping operations is becoming increasingly difficult. Canada and other smaller nations can no longer afford to take on new assignments or even to maintain existing forces. Some peacekeeping operations, like that in Cyprus and several in the Middle East, have continued for decades, with costs escalating beyond the reasonable ability of the countries involved to pay.

The Effectiveness of Peacekeeping

Is peacekeeping successful? It is true that in almost every part of the world to which peacekeeping forces have been dispatched, sooner or later there has been renewed fighting. This does not mean that peacekeepers have failed to do their job. It does indicate, however, that the process of creating a lasting peace requires time and a variety of strategies. Peacekeepers minimize confrontations and uphold cease-fires and truces while diplomats and politicians attempt to negotiate a permanent end to the hostilities.

The peacekeepers' successful role in this larger process has been recognized outside the United Nations. In awarding the 1988 Nobel Prize for Peace to UN peacekeeping forces, the Nobel committee declared that these forces "represent the manifest will of

PROFILE

LESTER PEARSON (1897-1972)

Canada's commitment to the development and expansion of the United Nations was mirrored in the career and philosophy of, perhaps, Canada's greatest diplomat, Lester Bowles Pearson. During the early challenges of the United Nations, Pearson laboured tirelessly to protect and enhance the goals of international order and co-operation. In what ways do you think Pearson's work earned Canada international recognition and trust?

"Diplomacy is letting someone else have your way."

> *Lester B. Pearson, 1957*

"The grim fact is that we prepare for war like precocious giants and for peace like retarded pygmies."

> *Lester B. Pearson, 14 March 1955*

Lester Bowles Pearson was born and raised in southern Ontario, the son of a Methodist parson. Pearson served in the medical corps during the First World War. At war's end, he completed his education at the University of Toronto and at Oxford, England. After brief forays into business, law, and teaching, Pearson found his niche in the Department of External Affairs. In 1928, he began a brilliant career as an international diplomat, serving in London and Washington and representing Canada at many conferences, including the one that founded the United Nations in 1945. As deputy Minister of External Affairs, Pearson exhibited great diplomatic skill and expertise in building the foundations of this organization.

In 1948, Pearson was elected to Parliament and appointed Secretary of State for External Affairs. He continued to be involved in the United Nations, serving as President of the General Assembly in 1952. Pearson believed that military alliances during the Cold War were essential. But he continued to push for non-military solutions and preferred that the will of the United Nations rather than the interests of the United States should be the determining force in world affairs.

The Suez Crisis in 1956 stunned the world. Britain and France were being condemned by the UN as well as the United States. Amidst the turmoil, Pearson developed a bold plan to end hostilities, reduce tensions, and reaffirm the purposes and principles of the United Nations.

He promoted the idea of a multinational force of peacekeepers from the middle and smaller powers to serve as a United Nations "police force." Pearson skilfully persuaded UN members to endorse this United Nations Emergency Force (UNEF). Its first mission was the Middle East. It was a radical new approach to keeping the peace among nations. Pearson was awarded the Nobel Prize for Peace in 1957, the only Canadian ever to be so honoured.

Upon retiring from service at the United Nations, Pearson was elected leader of the Liberal Party in 1958. He served as Prime Minister from 1963 to 1968. He pursued policies of **co-operative federalism**, seeking to improve Ottawa's relations with the provinces, and **bilingualism and biculturalism** to ease growing English-French tensions. In 1967 Pearson presided over nationwide celebrations of Canada's Centennial Year.

Pearson retired from politics in 1968 and died four years later. He is remembered by many as a person who combined the realism, practicality, and flexibility of the politician with the highest ideals of humanitarian principles.

VOICES

THE UN: KEEPING THE PEACE

When he was elected as Secretary General in 1992, Egypt's Boutros Boutros-Ghali envisaged a more active and powerful United Nations. He produced a document, Agenda for Peace, in which he called for permanent peace enforcement units designed for rapid deployment to world hot spots. Boutros-Ghali firmly believed that the UN should be prepared "to take coercive action against cease-fire violators."

This vision of a more forceful UN was not shared by all. Critics felt the cost in personnel and material would be too high. Some felt the UN was acting like a world government and trampling national sovereignty. Whatever the objectives, however, the UN has been increasingly involved in crises around the globe. In fact, the UN entered into more operations in the first five years after the Cold War ended than it had undertaken in its first forty years. Boutros-Ghali was clearly prepared to pursue a more activist international role and challenge old ideas about the UN.

Toronto Star columnist Richard Gwyn interviewed Boutros-Ghali in 1993. As you read the following excerpts from the interview, consider whether international authority should take priority over national sovereignty, and if so, under what circumstances.

"**Q:** Is the UN not now trying to do too much in too many places?
A: During the Cold War, the UN suffered a crisis of credibility. Today, we are suffering a crisis of an excess of credibility....We are over-stretched, overloaded. But we cannot refuse to respond, any more than a hospital can refuse a patient.
Q: Does this mean the UN is beginning to become a kind of quasi-world government long before it in fact is ready to be one?
A: We are in a transition period and we are trying to find new concepts on which we can build our actions.

Q: In this trend for the UN to become a quasi-world government, is the key to it the globalization of human rights so that what a national government does to its citizens is no longer its affair alone but the world's?
A: Human rights is one case and an important one. But so is the environment. Or that you have AIDS spreading all over the world. Or the international traffic in drugs. You will have more and more global problems and global problems can only be solved by an international forum.
Q: In the corridors here you'll get people who'll say all this 'global' stuff is just rhetoric. That in reality it's the US that runs the UN. True?
A: That is not the reality, it is an exaggeration. I assure you that decisions are taken by consensus and that is often not easy to reach.
Q: You've said you'll stay for just one five-year term and you're now about one-third the way through that...[Boutros-Ghali interrupts: "Three years and nine months to go"]...When it's done, what would you like to say you've achieved?
A: If I had helped prepare the UN to cope with the new problems of international society, I would have achieved the objective of my mandate. The real problem is the continuous globalization of all forces, from disease to communications to the military and the environment. For this, we need new concepts, a new approach.

"The UN is the unique international forum that can think about and contribute to the solutions of the global problems of tomorrow. The problems of today matter, of course, but the preparation for the problems of tomorrow, because they are global problems, must be the work of the UN and this is my real ambition."

Excerpted from "We Need New Concepts, A New Approach," in the Toronto Star*, 23 March 1993. Reprinted by permission of the Toronto Star Syndicate.*

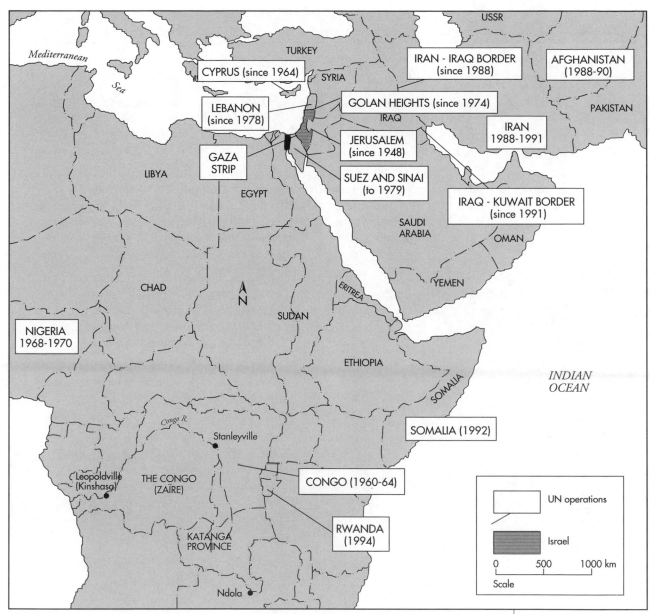

the community of nations to achieve peace through negotiations and the forces have, by their presence, made a decisive contribution toward the initiation of actual peace negotiations."

Changes in Approaches to Peacemaking and Peacekeeping

Despite its many peacemaking and peacekeeping efforts, the United Nations had little expectation of making or keeping peace in conflicts that directly involved the United States or the Soviet Union. The Security Council could do little about crises involving the Soviets in Eastern Europe (the Berlin Blockade, 1949; Hungary, 1956; Czechoslovakia, 1968) and the Americans have had a free hand in Latin America (Guatemala, 1954; the Bay of Pigs, 1961; Grenada, 1983). Nor did the United Nations override the principle of non-intervention "in matters essentially within the domestic

Figure 6.6:
UN Peacekeeping Forces in Northern Africa and the Middle East Since 1960

Figure 6.7: Major Deployments of UN Peacekeeping Forces Since the Suez Crisis

Date	Place	Combatants	Peacekeeping force and its mission
1958	Lebanon	Opposing Lebanese factions and Syrian/Egyptian infiltrators	UN Observation Group in Lebanon (UN-OGIL): 600 observers to ensure no outside arms or personnel entered area of conflict and later to supervise withdrawal of intervening American and British troops
1960-64	Congo (now Zaïre)	Competing Congolese factions and foreign military advisors, agents, and mercenaries	Operation Nations Unies du Congo (ONUC): up to 19 000 UNEF air and land troops to verify Belgian troop withdrawal, maintain law and order, prevent civil war, and secure removal of non-United Nations foreign personnel
1962-63	West New Guinea; Netherlands and Indonesia	Indonesian nationalists and Dutch government	United Nations Temporary Executive Authority (UNTEA): 1600 ground and air personnel to provide security during transition from Dutch to Indonesian rule
1964-present	Cyprus	Greek vs Turkish Cypriots; in 1974 troops from Turkey	United Nations Forces in Cyprus (UNFICYP): 6400 troops and other personnel to supervise cease-fires, patrol buffer zones, maintain law and order, and provide humanitarian aid
1965-66	Kashmir	India and Pakistan	United Nations India-Pakistan Observation Mission (UNIPOM) and United Nations Military Observer Group in India and Pakistan (UNMOGIP, functioning from 1948): up to 200 military observers to supervise cease-fires and troop withdrawals
1973-79	Suez and Sinai	Egypt and Israel	UNEF II: up to 700 United Nations troops to supervise cease-fires and troop withdrawals and patrol buffer zones
1974-present	Golan Heights	Syria and Israel	United Nations Disengagement and Observer Force (UNDOF): up to 1300 troops and observers to supervise cease-fire and establish and patrol buffer zone
1978-present	Lebanon	Israel, Lebanon, and Palestinian infiltrators	UN Interim Force in Lebanon (UNIFIL): up to 7000 land and air forces to ensure Israeli withdrawal, restore Lebanese civil authority in border areas, and establish and patrol security zone

Figure 6.7: Continued

Date	Place	Combatants	Peacekeeping force and its mission
1988-90	Namibia	South West African Peoples Organization vs forces from South Africa, Angola, and Cuba	United Nations Transition Assistance Group (UNTAG): 7000 military and civilian personnel to maintain law and order during supervised elections in Namibia and repatriation of refugees
1989-present	Central America	Nicaraguan Contras vs Sandinistas and El Salvadorean government vs rebels and infiltrators	United Nations Observer Group in Central America (UNOGCA): military and civilian observers from UN to supervise elections and disarmament in Nicaragua, assist diplomatic efforts to end civil war in El Salvador, and monitor area governments' agreements not to interfere in one another's internal affairs
1991-present	Iraq and Kuwait	Forces of Iraq vs Kuwait and twenty-eight nation United Nations coalition	United Nations Iraq-Kuwait Observation Mission (UNIKOM) and other United Nations security missions: over 2000 troops and military and technical observers to patrol security zones at the border and around Kurdish refugee camps in northern Iraq and within Iraq to monitor destruction of chemical, biological, and nuclear weapons and facilities
1992-present	Cambodia (Kampuchea)	Four Khmer factions, including the government in Phnom Penh and the Khmer Rouge	United Nations Transitional Authority in Cambodia (UNTAC): to verify reduction of factions' armies, supervise elections, maintain some government ministries, and assist in repatriation of 350 000 refugees
1992	Somalia	Civil war among competing warlords	United Nations Operation in Somalia II (UNOSOM II): US peacekeeping troops deployed to safeguard delivery of food supplies in country without government; replaced by 30 000 UN forces to monitor distribution of relief aid
1992-present	Bosnia-Herzegovina	Ethnic battles involving Serbs, Croats, and Muslims	United Nations Protection Force (UNPROFOR): over 20 000 peacekeeping forces to protect civilians amidst warring factions in the former Yugoslavia
1994	Rwanda	Ethnic strife between the government and Tutsi-led rebels	United Nations Observer Mission in Uganda-Rwanda (UNOMUR): French observer troops stationed in southwest Rwanda along Ugandan border to establish a safe zone for refugees; replaced by small African peacekeeping force

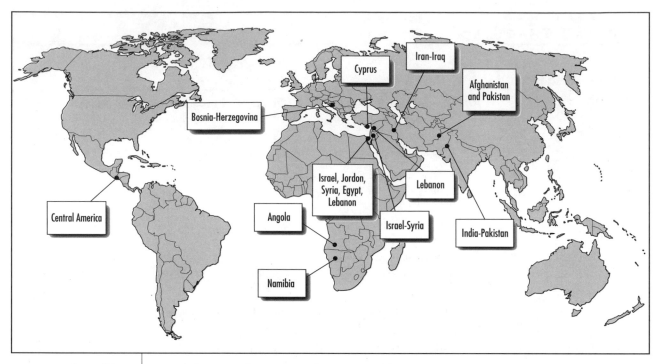

Figure 6.7:
Where UN Forces Keep
the Peace in 1995

jurisdiction of any state" (Britain's crisis in Northern Ireland; China's conflict with the Soviet Union over Tibet).

After the embarrassment of Britain and France in the 1956 Suez Crisis, the major powers were left to sort out their own disputes through diplomatic and political means. But when these efforts did not produce the desired results, the superpowers were willing to fall back on military intervention, as the US did in Vietnam and the USSR did in Afghanistan.

In the 1980s, however, the patterns of peacemaking and peacekeeping began to change. The Soviets accepted UN observers to monitor their withdrawal from Afghanistan in 1988. In 1989, for the first time since the Monroe Doctrine of 1823, the United States co-operated with foreign observers in Central America through the Organization of American States (OAS). Other regional alliances began playing a role more consistent with UN peace initiatives in the late 1980s.

A more fundamental change emerged in the United Nations' reac-tion to Iraq's attacks upon its Kurdish and Shiite Muslim minorities after the Persian Gulf War of January and February 1991. The Security Council declared that the masses of refugees fleeing the region constituted a threat to international peace and security. As the *New York Times* reported on 6 April 1991: "Never before has the United Nations Security Council held that governments threaten international security if their actions force thousands of their citizens to flee to other lands."

Since the end of the Cold War in the 1990s, peacemaking has replaced peacekeeping as the dominant feature of UN interventions. In 1991, the United Nations authorized the use of military force to drive Iraqi invaders out of Kuwait in the Gulf War. (See page 344.) In 1992, for the first time the UN authorized the use of massive military force to ensure that humanitar-ian aid reached the people of Somalia. It sent a smaller force with the same purpose to Bosnia-Herzegovina. (See pages 236-37.) In 1994, the UN strug-gled to contain the overwhelming human misery resulting from civil war in Rwanda, but played almost no role in ending the fighting.

As the world political scene changes from the Cold War alliances, the role of the United Nations will also be redefined. New questions will be raised: Should the UN take an aggressive role in fulfilling its mission of peace and security and solving social, economic, and humanitarian problems throughout the world? Will strong and weak nations alike rely on the UN for security? Will the United Nations continue to create piecemeal forces to undertake peacekeeping missions? Or will a permanent UN peace force be established?

Part of the role of the UN in Kampuchea (formerly Cambodia) is to assist in the repatriation of over 350 000 refugees.

IN REVIEW

1. How did the onset of the Cold War affect the work of the UN?

2. What were (a) the underlying and (b) the immediate causes of the Korean War?

3. Was the Korean conflict more a UN or a US military operation? What was the outcome of the conflict?

4. What was the Uniting for Peace resolution? What purpose did it serve?

5. In what ways is the Korean war an example of UN peacemaking?

6. What was the national interest of each of the following nations in the Suez Crisis: Egypt, Israel, Britain, France?

7. Why did the Suez Crisis divide Canadians? Which side would you have supported? Why?

8. What critical role was played by Lester Pearson in helping to end the Suez Crisis?

9. What was the lasting significance of the Suez Crisis?

10. Which UN peacekeeping operations were most successful, and why?

11. What is the difference between the concepts of peacekeeping and peace-making?

12. Should Canada participate in peacekeeping and/or peacemaking operations? Explain your answer.

SUMMARY

The United Nations was created with a General Assembly to represent all nations and a Security Council that gave powerful nations a dominant role. With the development of the Cold War, the Security Council became deadlocked and matters of peace and security grew more difficult to manage. In the Korean War, the principle of military peacemaking was applied as the United States led a coalition of UN forces to fight North Korean aggression. In the Suez Crisis, the UN was successful in providing a forum for discussion and resolution of the problem.

One major outcome of the crisis was the establishment of a UN peacekeeping force and Canada's role as an important peacekeeper and middle power. Lester Pearson's proposal for the UNEF, which was introduced at Suez, has been the model for UN peacekeeping activities since then.

As Cold War tensions have subsided, there has been renewed interest in the United Nations. Increasingly, the UN has become more active in conflicts around the globe as the organization appears willing to use both its peacekeeping and peacemaking options in a still troubled world.

MAKING CONNECTIONS

1. Working with a partner, determine whether the UN today is stronger or weaker than it was in the 1945-54 period.

2. Compare the roles played by the UN and the results it achieved in (a) the Korean War and (b) the Suez Crisis.

3. Identify the current Secretary-General of the UN and the major concerns that person faces.

DEVELOPING YOUR VOICE

4. Organize a small group discussion on one of the following topics:
    (a) Should Canada continue to participate in UN peacekeeping and peacemaking activities?
    (b) Is the world at the end of the twentieth century any safer than it was at the beginning of the century?
    (c) Is world government possible, or even desirable?

5. If possible, invite a member of a local UN association to visit your class for a presentation/interview session.

6. Write a letter to your MP or the Secretary of State for External Affairs expressing your views on Canada's future role in the UN.

RESEARCHING THE ISSUES

7. Research the role played by the UN and its organizations. What are some of the notable accomplishments and failures? What are some of the issues facing the UN today?

8. Identify a current example of a UN peace*keeping* operation and a UN peace*making* operation. Research to answer the following questions: In what ways do these operations differ? What is the justification for these interventions? How do the national interests and the domestic problems of the disputants affect the ability of the UN to make peace or to keep it?

9. Complete a brief biography of one of the UN Secretaries-General. Focus on background, goals, challenges, and achievements.

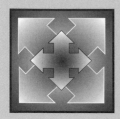

VIEWPOINTS

ISSUE: IS THE UNITED NATIONS A USEFUL AND EFFECTIVE ORGANIZATION?

The United Nations has been the subject of debate since its inception more than fifty years ago. Since that time the UN has changed. As the nations of Africa and Asia gained independence, they joined the UN and gave greater representation to the developing countries of the world. The United Nations has broadened its commitment to the medical, social, cultural, and educational welfare of the developing world. UN peacekeeping missions have increasingly been deployed in political hotspots around the globe.

Yet there is no consensus on the effectiveness of the United Nations. The viewpoints presented here examine two perspectives on the UN. Professor Gerald Segal believes that while the UN is flawed, generally it is a useful organization that provides a valuable forum for the poor and weak nations of the world. Author Phyllis Bennis, however, sees the United Nations as an undemocratic institution that serves only to reflect, rather than challenge, the world power elite, and in particular the United States, that has been in effect since the end of the Second World War. Read these two viewpoints carefully, then complete an Argument Analysis and Evaluation Summary for each reading.

Gerald Segal

"To be sure, there is much that is very wrong with the UN. It is often out of touch with reality, unwieldy and run by incompetents. But, as the most universal of the proliferating international organisations...it continues to serve useful, if mundane functions. It remains a mirror of the world it is meant to help and, despite the adverse publicity the UN has earned in recent years, the cracks in the mirror are not larger than they ever were.

"The ritual incantations of support for the UN have roots in the odd mixture of idealism and realism that existed when the organisation was created. The idealism was rooted in the horror of the Second World War and the carnage that followed the failure of the previous world organisation, the League of Nations, to confront the aggression of Japan, Italy and Germany. The UN was supposed to overcome these failings by operating a system of collective security where aggression would be repelled by the common action of a concerned world. What is more, to help prevent conflict breaking out at all, the UN would take an active role in furthering economic and social progress.

"These twin, idealistic principles were qualified by the realities of power politics—the great power concert. The UN would give greater power to five great powers who would be able to veto any action they disliked. In addition, the UN would be barred from becoming involved in the domestic affairs of states, even though a number of threats to international stability came from the breakdown of government inside states.

"So long as the United States and its western allies retained a majority in the United Nations, western states placed greater stress on the idealism than on the realism. In the early years of the UN, the large number of Commonwealth and pro-United States Latin American states ensured that the West remained in charge....

"Washington's advantage began to fade by the early 1960s when more decolonised states were admitted. In 1960, sixteen new African members were seated and, despite United States opposition, Communist China replaced the Chiang Kai-shek régime in the Chinese chair in October 1971. By the 1980s the organisation had become genuinely universal, with thirty-one members from Europe, thirty from the Americas, fifty-one from Africa and forty from Asia and the Middle East. Taiwan, the two Koreas and Switzerland are notable non-members.

"This rapid increase in members not only wrested the control of the UN from the United States; it also raised the second major issue for the organisation—North-South relations. The UN had been an early participant in the decolonisation process; helping the Netherlands out of Indonesia and the British out of Palestine. UN 'peacekeeping' forces in the Congo (1960-64) were engaged in combat and helped manage the fiasco of Belgium's withdrawal from this colony. But when North-South relations moved beyond the broadly popular issue of ending rule, the UN became the setting for the damaging, extremist rhetoric of North-South relations. The South demanded various 'new orders', meaning the transfer of resources from North to South. The South, encouraged by the Soviet Union and funded by OPEC dollars, sponsored absurd attacks on Israel and in 1975 the UNGA declared Zionism to be 'a form of racism.' The picture of gun-toting Yasir Arafat of the Palestine Liberation Organisation (PLO) addressing the General Assembly made a mockery of the high idealism of the UN. It was no wonder that the United States (by far the largest backer of the UN) responded by cutting back its funding and began decrying the one-state-one-vote principle in the UNGA that had given it so much power back in the 1950s.

"But, for all its obvious excesses, the UN has its good points, First, its various types of peacekeeping have been useful. By now we are familiar with the strange mixed-race, multi-lingual, blue-helmeted soldiers, lightly armed and operating in squalid or remote places under bewildering acronyms like UNFICYP, UNIFIL, or ONUC. They have to carry out difficult, if not impossible, tasks because the UN itself is rarely sure about what it is doing and does not give its forces much authority. These soldiers have been described as 'false teeth' or an umbrella taken away the moment it rains. Nevertheless, enough states have seen fit to make use of UN troops in a wide range of passive and active roles....

"Second, UN-organised international co-operation has also been evident in the various moves, only some of which were effective, to impose sanctions on Rhodesia (later Zimbabwe) and latterly on South Africa. Third, the UN serves a passive role as a venue for traditional diplomacy. In the more obscure, smoky corridors or small back rooms, enemies can meet, signals can be sent and talks can begin. Even in a shrinking world of modern communications, there is still a need for face-to-face contacts.

"Fourth, the UN has established a wide range of specialised agencies and associated organisations that are of practical use. The World Bank and the International Monetary Fund (IMF) are perhaps two of the best-known suppliers of funds to states in economic need. The UN International Children's Emergency Fund (UNICEF) and the High Commission for Refugees (UNHCR) provide essential help for individuals in need. The International Telegraph Union (ITU) and International Civil Aviation Organisation (ICAO) assist modern means of communication....

"Finally, the UN is simply a place where the poor and weak, in a world so dominated by the Superpowers and the developed states, can feel they are being heard. To be sure, this has too often deteriorated into absurd and outrageous proposals, childish antics and shrill speeches. The impotent may feel better for upbraiding the powerful but their actions only undermine the ability of the UN to act effectively. The UN has become much more an arena for conflict than co-operation. Clearly the organisation can do better but that is no reason simply to ignore or deride the place. If the UN did not already exist it would certainly have to be invented."

From Gerald Segal, The Stoddart Guide to the World Today. *Reprinted with permission of Stoddart Publishing Co. Limited, Don Mills, Ontario.*

Phyllis Bennis

"The visibility of UN failures...along with the growing international disfavor in which the UN was viewed in the countries where it was deployed, often masked the real power relations behind the UN decisions and deployment. Since its origins almost fifty years ago, the United Nations was created, and continues to reflect, not challenge, the power relationships of its member states. The Perm Five gave themselves veto-power in the Council not because they were the most representative of nations, but because they were the most powerful—and the UN was designed to perpetuate the power of the victorious World War II allies.

"There was a popular notion that Desert Storm was a "UN war," ignoring Washington's stranglehold on real power. Similarly, as the UN is stretched thinner and thinner in hot spots around the world, it becomes easy to blame "the UN" for peacekeeping failures; praising instead, for example, the arrival of a few platoons of red-blooded young US Marines.

"What gets lost is the issue of who determines success or failure for the UN. Certainly the 500 Pakistani troops sent to Somalia in the summer of 1992 arrived too late, stayed too close to the airport, accomplished very little and quickly failed. But who determined that their mandate should only include defense of the Mogadishu airport? Who decided only 500 should be sent? Why did they have to wait over six weeks because their own logistics people did not have the requisite equipment and no other country would provide it? And given the predominance of US influence in the Council, can a full distinction between "UN" and "US" responsibility be made?

"The ambitious profile of the UN has spurred new interest in many countries in following Washington's lead and seeking out a center of power within the global organization. Japan, for example, has staked out a leading position in humanitarian operations, despite its constitutional ban on sending troops abroad. Visiting Tokyo in February 1993, Boutros Ghali urged Japan to reverse its long-standing ban to participate fully in UN peacekeeping, implying it would help Japan's goal of securing a permanent seat on the Council.

"This was not the only such move. The myriad of failures and/or uncertain outcomes brought new visibility to once-whispered calls for a variety of structural changes designed to rework the UN's relations of authority. Because the focus of real power in the United Nations, the power to wage war or impose peace, lies in the Security Council, most reform proposals focus on expanding its membership.

"Both Germany and Japan claim the right to permanent Council seats, by virtue of their economic clout. The Non-Aligned Movement, seeking to redress the Council's historic North-South imbalance, has discussed adding three of the largest and most powerful countries of the Southern continents—usually mentioning India, Nigeria and Brazil—to the Council's permanent members. The U.S. has been on record (albeit quietly) since 1974 in support of Germany's claim; Japan used its two-year rotating stint on the Council in 1992-93 and its escalating financial support of peacekeeping operations to lobby for a similar position.

The key challenge facing the South in the new UN is the question of democracy. As long as the democratic side of the organization, the General Assembly, is kept strategically powerless, and the least democratic organ, the Security Council, remains the real center of power, the UN will be unable to retain independence of action in the face of US decisions. Structural changes to integrate power and democracy are required.

"An important, though unlikely, start would be a move to realize and empower the Assembly's role of overseeing all Council activity. Democratizing the Council itself requires ensuring a permanent voice for the countries of the South—not expanding and consolidating the North's grip by adding Germany and Japan to the permanent members.

"The Clinton administration entered a UN in which Washington was both preeminently powerful, and the target of deep-rooted antagonism for its heavy-handed enforced consensuses and its double standards. It entered a UN desperately short of cash, while the US still owed hundreds of millions in back dues. It entered the UN to direct the organization's multilateral forms of diplomacy towards the legitimation of its own unipolar projection of power.

"But despite its new credibility in Washington, in certain aspects the UN has not changed since its founding: it continues to reflect, rather than challenge, the basic priorities and power relations of its strongest member states. Resources are still scarce, and the stark reality is that the only UN programs being expanded are those involving peacekeeping forces.

"But key changes are taking place in the broadening definition of international peacekeeping efforts. Historically, international involvement was balanced against the right of nations to maintain their sovereignty. Now, with a notion gaining wider acceptance that national sovereignty might be just a bit passé, UN activism is becoming more and more explicitly interventionist—on the side of the North.

"In a world where the vast majority of conflicts now rage *within*, rather than between nations, increased UN activism may at times be the only viable alternative to the world standing in mute witness to mass slaughter. But that activism cannot be defined solely in military terms, and success in the long term will depend on a currently out-of-reach independence of action on the part of the UN. If its role in the world is to defend democracy, the UN's own democracy must be reclaimed. Otherwise, with the reality of a US dominated United Nations torn by North-South divisions, UN intervention, under the guise of peacekeeping, peacemaking or peace-enforcing, will be indistinguishable from the US interventions it is so often used to legitimate."

From Phyllis Bennis and Michel Moyshabeck (eds), Altered States: A Reader in the New World Order *(New York: Olive Branch Press, 1993) pp. 46-48.*

ANALYSIS AND EVALUATION

Refer to the Argument Analysis and Evaluation Guide on page viii.

1. Using the Argument Analysis and Evaluation Guide, compare the readings by Segal and Bennis.

2. Decide which of the two viewpoints you tend to support and explain why. Be sure to use specific information from this textbook, the readings, and other sources to support your position.

3. State and support your position on the issue: "Is the United Nations a useful and effective organization?"

CHAPTER SEVEN

Death of a Superpower: The End of the Cold War

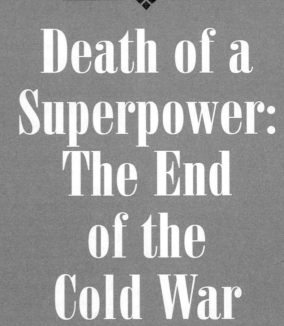

"It is given to very few people to change the course of history. But that is what Gorbachev has done. Whatever happens today, his place in history is secure."

British prime minister John Major, commenting on Gorbachev's resignation, 26 December 1991

"The era of the bipolar division of the world is over....The old orders are falling apart, and it is our task to build new ones."

Václav Havel, president of Czechoslovakia, 1990

Left: Germans celebrate reunification

❖ OVERVIEW

The 1990s began with prospects for peace that had not seemed possible for more than forty years. The Cold War had ended as the communist grip on Eastern Europe was released.

The end of the Cold War came with Soviet leader Mikhail Gorbachev's announcement that the people of Eastern Europe were free to choose their own political and economic systems. The communist totalitarian regimes, left without the power of the Soviet military or the support of the people, foundered and were toppled. By 1990, free elections were the order of the day. The Berlin Wall fell and the two Germanys were reunited.

With the collapse of communism in Eastern Europe, the communist system in the Soviet Union also started to unravel. Once the process began, it continued at a dizzying pace. One by one the Soviet republics declared their independence. The political map of Europe was redrawn almost overnight.

The end of the Cold War created a new, and in many ways, an unfamiliar world. But is this a new world order—or disorder?

rapid—so rapid, in fact, that the West was caught off guard. After forty years of rivalry and hostility the West was reluctant to put much faith in the promises of the new Soviet leader Mikhail Gorbachev. Was this just another period of détente or was this fundamental change? As Gorbachev proposed one peace initiative after another, the United States cautiously tried to analyse these new Soviet policies. The traditional Cold War attitudes expressed by US president Ronald Reagan and his successor, George Bush, no longer seemed appropriate. The Soviet Union was no longer the enemy and the world was no longer divided into two armed camps. Cooperation seemed to be the new order for Soviet-American relations.

PEACE INITIATIVES

At fifty-four, Gorbachev represented a younger, better educated, and more progressive generation of Communist Party officials. Upon assuming the leadership of the Soviet Union in March 1985 he began a startling peace initiative. Until then the typical Soviet-American approach to international security had been to talk about peace while both sides continued to increase their arsenals. Gorbachev challenged the West to stop the arms race and extend a hand of friendship instead.

At the United Nations, Gorbachev announced the unilateral reduction of Soviet armed forces, including a substantial number in Eastern Europe. In 1988, the Soviet Union began to withdraw its troops from Afghanistan. Arms talks that had begun

---

FOCUS QUESTIONS

1. What caused the collapse of the Soviet Union?
2. What was the impact of Gorbachev's policies on the Soviet bloc?
3. What consequences do changes in Eastern Europe have for the new world order of the 1990s?
4. Is the world a safer and more secure place now that the Cold War has ended?

THE GORBACHEV REVOLUTION

The sweeping changes in the Soviet Union were remarkably peaceful and

in 1986 now led quickly to agreements. The United States and the Soviet Union signed a treaty agreeing to destroy all their intermediate- and short-range nuclear missiles. In 1990, Warsaw Pact and NATO members signed the Conventional Forces in Europe treaty which substantially reduced their arms and armies in Europe.

ECONOMIC REFORM

As revolutionary as Gorbachev's peace initiatives were, his program of reform did not end there. When he took office in 1985, Gorbachev was faced with a rapidly deteriorating economic situation. The Cold War emphasis on military strength and the need for a military presence in the Soviet satellites and other parts of the world had drained the economy. An estimated 25 per cent of Soviet production was devoted to the military. This financial burden threatened the stability of the Soviet Union. It was obvious to Gorbachev that the main threat to Soviet security was economic collapse, not invasion from the West.

The deteriorating economic situation was made worse by the communist system itself. Its program of guaranteed employment combined with a lack of incentives did little to encourage technological innovation, competence, or efficient management in either industry or agriculture. In the agricultural sector, for example, government officials, most of whom lacked any agricultural background or expertise, made the decisions. As a result, the industry was unproductive. A comparison of private plots versus collective farms revealed that the private plots produced 25 per cent of the country's total crop output on only 4 per cent of the country's arable land. It was clear that the private agricultural operations were performing significantly better than the government-operated farms.

In 1988, the Soviet Union pulled its troops out of Afghanistan as Gorbachev reduced Soviet military forces.

In 1986, Gorbachev announced to the 27th Communist Party Congress that the country was facing economic disaster. In spite of economic policies intended to improve the Soviet standard of living, little progress had been made. Gorbachev argued that the present system was too inefficient and inflexible to meet the needs of domestic consumers or to allow the Soviet Union to compete in the global marketplace. The remedy was **perestroika**—to accelerate the country's socioeconomic development through vigorous leadership, greater discipline, and economic restructuring. For Gorbachev, restructuring meant moving away from **state socialism** towards a freer market economy. This called for the removal of government subsidies on food products and consumer goods—a measure that was not popular with the Soviet

Figure 7.1: The Decline in the Rate of Growth of Soviet GNP

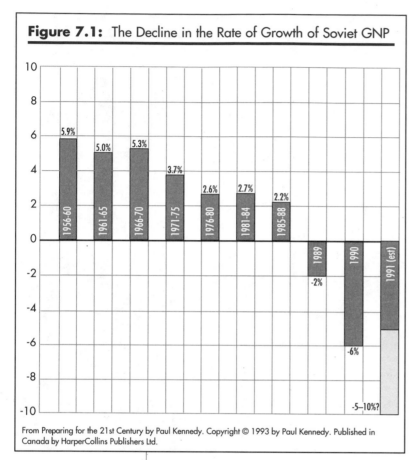

From Preparing for the 21st Century by Paul Kennedy. Copyright © 1993 by Paul Kennedy. Published in Canada by HarperCollins Publishers Ltd.

in establishing a freer market system with private ownership. This was in part because of fierce opposition to the reforms by conservative Communist officials and in part because of the sheer magnitude of the changes. There was widespread dissatisfaction and frustration with the slowness of the reform program and with the soaring inflation that had accompanied the restructuring. Strikes, which had been forbidden under communism, were now common occurrences as people protested their poor working and living conditions. In this time of economic hardship and instability, food became one of the most valuable commodities and it was used to trade for other goods.

Boris Yeltsin, president of the Russian republic and Gorbachev's chief political rival, was also committed to reform. But he favoured a much faster pace than Gorbachev was willing to set. Yeltsin wanted Russia to move to a market economy as quickly as possible and he was supported by popular opinion. People needed food, housing, and medical supplies and were willing to support a radical program of reform.

In 1991, industrial production had fallen a further 20 per cent, famine was threatening many northern regions, and inflation was increasing by 2-3 per cent a week. (See Figure 7.1.) Gorbachev was forced to approach the Western industrial nations for help in rescuing the deteriorating Soviet economy. The United States and Germany were willing to extend credit and aid, but the political situation was so unstable within the USSR that they decided to deal with the Soviet republics on an individual basis.

SOCIAL PROBLEMS IN THE USSR

As the Soviet economy deteriorated, so too did social conditions. Everything

people who had grown accustomed to the lower prices these subsidies ensured.

In spite of Gorbachev's initiatives, by 1990 little headway had been made

In April 1986, a reactor at the nuclear power complex at Chernobyl broke down, bringing the facility to the brink of a nuclear meltdown. The explosion, fire, and resulting radioactive debris caused hundreds of deaths and injuries. The causes of the disaster were identified as faulty designs and inadequate staff training. By 1993, 8000 people had died from radiation-induced diseases and 1 000 000 more cases of serious illness had been diagnosed.

that contributed to the quality of life seemed to be in decline. Corruption was everywhere and a crime wave was sweeping the country.

The health-care system was unravelling, and with it the standards of public health. Infant mortality rates were rising. Life expectancy was declining. Staggering pollution levels were creating health hazards for much of the Soviet population. High levels of industrial waste, toxic chemicals, and radioactive waste—the result of the Communists' demand for economic growth at all costs—had poisoned the environment.

Alcohol consumption, a tradition in Soviet culture, was becoming a serious problem. Between 1970 and 1980, alcohol sales rose 77 per cent. By the 1980s, alcoholism had become the third most common cause of death and was a contributing factor in the escalating divorce and crime rates. Gorbachev campaigned to control alcohol consumption by reducing production and sales of vodka. These measures made him even more unpopular with producers and consumers alike.

The deteriorating social conditions in the Soviet Union created even greater hardships for women. Although most women worked outside the home, traditional roles had not really changed. Women were still responsible for domestic chores and child care. Their responsibilities were compounded as the economy worsened. Women now found themselves spending long hours after a full day's work waiting in food lines for the scarce commodities that were available.

Gorbachev's policy of **glasnost** was intended to reform Soviet life by making society more stimulating and rewarding. By opening up the channels of communication, more information would be available, making informed dialogue possible, which would ultimately lead to a better society.

Food rationing in the Soviet Union resulted in long lineups for limited supplies.

Removing censorship to allow freedom of information and giving the media the right to criticize authority were major steps taken under Gorbachev's leadership. The works of previously silenced dissident writers resurfaced, the policies and actions of former leaders were examined, and social issues such as homelessness, unemployment, drug and alcohol abuse, and prostitution were openly discussed by the media. In addition, Gorbachev ended the ban on Western broadcasting, allowing the Russian-language broadcasts of the Voice of America and the BBC to be heard by Soviet citizens.

While communist ideals supported gender equality, women's pay averaged only 65 per cent of men's, even though women were well represented in professional fields. This figure is comparable to that in most capitalist democracies.

PROFILE

MIKHAIL GORBACHEV (1931–)

Mikhail Gorbachev's years in power transformed the Soviet Union and inspired much of the Western world. He moved international relations beyond détente and brought an end to the Cold War which had cast such a long and chilling shadow over the globe. As you read this profile, consider the importance of Gorbachev in ending the Cold War.

"The use or threat of force no longer can or must be an instrument of foreign policy....All of us, and primarily the stronger of us, must exercise self-restraint and totally rule out any use of force."

> *Mikhail Gorbachev in a speech to the United Nations, December 1988*

"It is...quite clear to us that the principle of freedom of choice is mandatory. Its nonrecognition is fraught with extremely grave consequences for world peace."

> *Mikhail Gorbachev, in a speech to the United Nations, December 1988*

Mikhail Gorbachev was born into a peasant family in the Russian province of Stavropol in 1931. A clever and ambitious young man, Gorbachev was not content to be a farm labourer. In 1953, he entered Moscow University, where he studied law, and joined the Communist Party. Upon graduating from university, Gorbachev returned to Stavropol and began his political career. To broaden his education and to increase his chances of promotion within the Communist Party, he earned a college degree in agronomy by correspondence. He returned to Moscow in 1978 as agriculture secretary.

From 1982 to 1985, a succession of old and progressively weaker Soviet leaders died: Leonid Brezhnev in 1982; Yuri Andropov in 1984; and Konstantin Chernenko in 1985. Gorbachev was named the new Soviet leader (officially the General Secretary of the Communist Party) in 1985. He promptly embarked on a new era in Soviet politics, introducing radical social, economic, and political changes. Two words came to symbolize the new Soviet Union—*perestroika* (restructuring) and *glasnost* (openness).

In January 1986, Gorbachev demonstrated his commitment to disarmament and world peace by proposing a plan for the elimination of nuclear arms by the year 2000. His proposals culminated in the historic Soviet-American arms control treaty in 1987 and effectively brought an end to the Cold War.

Believing that a communist monopoly of power in the Soviet Union obstructed the reform process, Gorbachev introduced free elections to the Supreme Soviet (national parliament) in 1989. He created the new position of president of the USSR so that the country would be run by an elected government rather than by a communist dictatorship. He acquiesced to the dismantling of communist regimes in Eastern Europe. To revive the failing Soviet economy, Gorbachev encouraged a free market system. The transformation seemed to create even greater economic despair, however. Criticism of Gorbachev and his reforms mounted. In 1991, after the failure of a conservative coup, Gorbachev resigned as leader of the USSR.

For the enormous contribution he made towards ending the Cold War, Gorbachev won the Nobel Prize for Peace in 1990. Although he was in office less than seven years, he is considered by many to be one of the most important political leaders of the twentieth century.

IN REVIEW

1. a) What did Gorbachev believe to be the basic problems in the Soviet Union?
    b) What was his strategy for remedying these problems?
2. List the social problems the Soviet Union faced. In what ways did these problems contribute to the slow rate of reform?
3. What did Gorbachev hope to achieve with glasnost?

THE DISMANTLING OF AN EMPIRE

POLITICAL REFORM

In the late 1980s the heady atmosphere of reform spread throughout the Soviet Union. Believing that the one-party system was destroying the country, Gorbachev called for free elections to the Supreme Soviet in 1989. His hope was that the Communist Party would be seen as a party of reform, which would enable it to maintain its control. But the electoral results resembled a tidal wave as Communist officials were swept out of office and new reform-oriented candidates from other parties were voted in.

For the satellite states of Eastern Europe, events in the Soviet Union came to mean the destruction of the communist system. Eager to seize the opportunity, the countries of Eastern Europe asserted their independence after more than forty years of tight Soviet control. Free to decide their own destinies, Hungary, Czechoslovakia, and Poland rejected communism and introduced democratic reforms with market economies. Romania, Bulgaria, and Albania chose to retain a communist system of government. Yugoslavia rejected communism but was immediately plunged into a devastating civil war. (See Chapter 8.) But perhaps nowhere were events more dramatic at the time than in East Germany.

THE UNIFICATION OF GERMANY

The Berlin Wall long symbolized the division of the world into opposing Cold War camps. On 10 November 1989 the world was captivated by the sight of Berliners from east and west perched atop the wall celebrating its dismantling. At points throughout Berlin sledgehammers were busy reducing the wall to rubble. This event more than any other signified the end of the Cold War.

The division of Germany had always been a central issue of the Cold War. The Soviet Union had held East Germany firmly in its grip since after

"In every border post
  there's something insecure
Each one of them
  is longing for leaves and for
  flowers.
They say
  the greatest punishment for a tree
is to become a border post...."

Excerpt from a poem by Evgenii Evtushenko that appeared in a Soviet literary magazine in September 1985

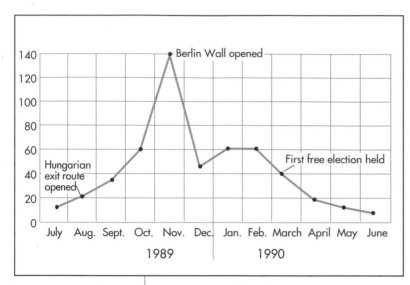

Figure 7.2:
Immigration from East Germany to West Germany.

officials paid little heed to these demands, however, and ignored Gorbachev's calls for glasnost and perestroika.

In 1989, a tide of East German people flowed to the West, travelling through Hungary and crossing the newly opened border into Austria and then into West Germany. As discontent in East Germany spread, Communist Party chief Erich Honeker, a hardliner devoted to maintaining the status quo, was forced out of office. He was replaced by a reform-minded government that opened the borders and eased travel restrictions on East German citizens. This led to the dismantling of the Berlin Wall in November. While this contained the emigration exodus somewhat, thousands of East Germans continued to flee the country. (See Figure 7.2.) West German chancellor Helmut Kohl proposed a unification plan that was conditional on East Germany holding free

the Second World War. After 1985, however, the Soviet Union withdrew its military support for satellite Communist governments. This raised East German hopes for reunification with West Germany. Demonstrations calling for reform became more and more common in East Germany. Government

Figure 7.3: The Soviet Satellite States Achieve Independence

Country	Dates	Key Events
Poland	1980-89	Free elections held after a series of strikes in 1989 by labour movement Solidarity. Solidarity forms the government under Lech Walesa.
Hungary	1988-90	New leadership liberalizes laws and allows multi-party elections. Communists defeated in free elections and coalition government formed.
Czechoslovakia	1989-93	Mass demonstrations and a general strike force Communist government to agree to multi-party rule. Václav Havel becomes president. Free elections held and Communists defeated. Ethnic divisions lead to division of Czechoslovakia into two states, the Czech and Slovak republics.
Romania	1989-92	Mass demonstrations and economic pressures topple Communist dictatorship of Nicolai Ceauçescu. Free elections held.
Baltic states (Part of USSR)	1987-91	Mass demonstrations in Latvia, Estonia, and Lithuania. Free elections defeat Communist governments. Baltic states secede from Soviet Union.

elections. Demonstrators in East Germany took up the call for "one Germany," but the East German government was lukewarm in its response. By December, however, the Communist Party in East Germany could no longer maintain power and free elections were set for the following year.

Amidst all of these changes massive demonstrations for unification accelerated. When free elections were held in March 1990, the people voted for a government that supported reunification. In July, Kohl met with Gorbachev to eliminate Soviet objections to a united Germany. West Germany agreed to pay US $9.5 billion to finance the withdrawal of 370 000 Soviet troops from East Germany. On September 12th, the four nations that had participated in the division of Germany at the end of the Second World War—Britain, France, the United States, and the Soviet Union—signed a reunification treaty. East and West Germany were reunited on 3 October 1990.

PROBLEMS OF REUNIFICATION

The new united Germany faced serious domestic problems. There were huge discrepancies between the standards of living in the two parts of the country. While the economy was prosperous in the west and the people enjoyed a high standard of living, in the east consumer goods were rare and businesses were obsolete, overstaffed, and mismanaged after four decades of centralized planning. Most of the eastern businesses could not compete and up to 35 per cent fell into bankruptcy. By 1992, 30 per cent of workers in the former East Germany were unemployed or underemployed. Wages were purposely set at 60-70 per cent of those in the west to encourage investment and to reflect the lower productivity of the region.

East and West Germans celebrated the dismantling of the Berlin Wall in November 1989.

Neo-Nazis have resurrected Hitler's racist slogans and the Nazi salute. The rise of the Neo-Nazi movement has created concern both in Germany and the world community.

East Germans faced a unique set of problems. On unification West Germany's laws and practices were applied to the whole country, including banking, the welfare system, taxes, and environmental standards. Gone were many aspects of the communist system the East Germans had come to enjoy, such as guaranteed employment and subsidized food. There was a new and disorienting insecurity for the East German people.

Many West Germans were unhappy with the united nation as well. Much higher spending on social welfare in the east was largely being financed by working- and middle-class people in the west. Many resented that an estimated US $775 billion would be spent over five years improving the infrastructure of the east using the money of the west.

Ethnic Tension and Violence

While East and West Germans harboured resentment towards one another, many were united in their hostility towards the influx of refugees and immigrants into the country. Between 1989 and 1991, 2.5 million immigrants and refugees arrived in Germany. These non-Germans were accused of taking jobs away from German citizens.

Incidents of violence began to erupt, at first in the former East Germany where unemployment was highest but then throughout the country. Most often the attackers were young, right-wing **skinheads** who adopted Nazi jargon and insignias as symbols of hatred and rebellion. These neo-Nazis, though small in number, were responsible for thousands of brutal assaults on immigrants and refugees, many of which resulted in death. Even more troublesome, however, was the fact that at times neighbours and even the police cheered the skinheads on as they chased and attacked their victims.

In response to the actions of the skinheads, hundreds of thousands of Germans took part in marches, rallies, and candle-lit vigils to condemn the violence and demand that the government put a stop to it. In November 1992, on the anniversary of Kristallnacht, the night of violent Nazi attacks against Jews in 1938, 300 000 people protested in Berlin. By 1993, however, the German government was forced to bow to pressure from the right. The country's liberal asylum laws were revoked, stemming the flow of refugees.

VOICES

THE NEW GERMANY

The reunification of Germany profoundly affected the political and economic character of Europe. Some viewed the new Germany with suspicion. Others recognized the difficulties that the new Germany faced in the years after reunification. Read the two opinions expressed here and consider the reasons Europeans might be suspicious of a reunified Germany. Do you think there is justification for these suspicions?

Madelaine Drohan

"Until the Berlin Wall fell and their lives changed forever, West Germans proudly described their country as *ein Musterknabe*—a model child. The term conveyed an image of a bright, industrious and generally unassuming nation that excelled, during four decades of postwar occupation, through the hard work of its people.

"In that time, West Germany developed a powerhouse economy and became a responsible member of the new world order through its membership in the North Atlantic Treaty Organization, the European Community and the Group of Seven.

"Then the world order changed. The Berlin Wall came down. The Cold War ended. And West Germany became enmeshed in the unexpectedly expensive and troublesome unification with East Germany that has left both sides feeling sour.

"No longer the model child, Germany is now more like a troubled adolescent. It is uncomfortably aware that its European neighbours view it with apprehension after two bloody wars this century. Former British Prime Minister Margaret Thatcher put into words what many other Europeans feel when she warned recently that plans to tie down 'the German Gulliver' by binding it more tightly into the European Community were doomed. 'With the collapse of the Soviet Union and the reunification of Germany, the entire picture has changed. The problem of German power has again resurfaced.'"

Madelaine Drohan, The Globe and Mail, *4 July 1992. Reprinted by permission.*

Flora Lewis

"The most important difference now dividing Germans from their allies and neighbors is that while most everyone else talks of projection of a greater new German strength from the center of the continent, the Germans feel suddenly weak and uncertain. No one foresaw the emotional, psychological and political problems that unification would bring, let alone the staggering economic and social difficulties that are still only beginning to be understood.

"...There remains a kind of lace curtain where the Iron Curtain stood, separating an 'us' and a 'them,' the genteel and the distressed. People look through it and resent or disdain what they see. From the other side, the 'Wessies' look smug, arrogant, righteous, colonizing, greedy; and 'Ossies' look incompetent, whiny, demanding, lacking initiative and civic spirit. What to do about it is the great preoccupation of German leaders and opinion-makers, so heavy and urgent a concern that they find it hard to see why others cavil at German power. The more they advance with the totally unexpected task that was only an abstract hope for so long, the more they discover they must do and the more the target date for successful conclusion recedes. At this point they feel overwhelmed, not rambunctious; burdened, not burdensome."

Flora Lewis, excerpt from "A European Germany or a German Europe?", reprinted from New Perspectives Quarterly, *Winter 1993, by permission.*

IN REVIEW

1. a) What factors led to the dismantling of the Berlin Wall?
   b) In what way did the dismantling of the Berlin Wall mark the end of the Cold War?

2. What were some of the problems facing Germany following reunification?

3. a) What group is believed responsible for acts of violence against immigrants and refugees in Germany?
   b) Why did this group behave in this manner?

RIVALRY AND CRISIS IN THE SOVIET UNION

POLITICAL RIVALRY

One of the ironies of Gorbachev's leadership was that he was more popular in the West than in his own country. With his wife, Raisa, he toured the world, charming the public and winning the admiration of the press. To the West, Gorbachev represented new hope for a peaceful world. His decision in 1988 to withdraw Soviet troops from Afghanistan, where they had been locked in conflict for eight years, was a convincing demonstration of his commitment to world peace.

Gorbachev's reputation as a progressive leader was undisputed outside the Soviet Union, but at home there was growing criticism of the slow pace of his reforms. By 1991, many people felt he was trying to slow down the process of reform rather than lead it, while Communist hardliners felt he had already gone too far. Leaders of the Soviet republics did not hesitate to exploit Gorbachev's vulnerable position for their own advantage.

Gorbachev's main rival was Boris Yeltsin. Both men were committed to a program of reform but their approaches were different. Gorbachev aspired to introduce major reforms within the Soviet Union by reforming the communist system. Yeltsin, on the other hand, believed that the communist system was the source of the problem and that communism itself had to be abolished. Reforms, he argued, must be quick and radical.

As president of Russia, the largest of the Soviet republics, Yeltsin was able to move swiftly with reforms to create a market economy. But a "war of laws" broke out when Gorbachev tried to block Yeltsin through legislation. Yeltsin countered by legislating that Russian laws took precedence over Soviet laws.

In 1991, Yeltsin was elected president of the Russian republic by popular vote in a democratic election, winning a landslide victory over his Communist Party rival. Yeltsin now had the support of the Russian people. Gorbachev, on the other hand, had not

"Your dearest wish is for our state structure and our ideological system never to change, to remain as they are for centuries. But history is not like that. Every system either finds a way to develop or else collapses."

Aleksandr Solzhenitsyn, excerpt from his Letter to the Soviet Leaders, 1973

The people of Moscow took to the streets during the attempted coup in August 1991, pleading with army soldiers to retreat with their tanks.

been elected by the people in a democratic election. His rise to power had been through the Communist Party. Furthermore, he had lost popularity because of the declining economy and his inability to improve living standards. Politically, too, he had lost favour. The conservatives claimed he had sold out to the radicals while the radicals claimed he had sold out to the conservatives. It was clear that reconciliation of the two sides was impossible. Gorbachev would have to move to one side of the political spectrum or the other. The political appointments he made in the first half of 1991 signalled that his position had shifted towards the conservative hardliners.

THE MOSCOW COUP

For one week in August 1991, dramatic events unfolded in Moscow and the world was on edge awaiting the outcome. A small group of hardline Communists—all of them in powerful positions through Gorbachev's support—attempted a coup to overthrow Gorbachev and the reform movement.

It began on Sunday, August 18th. Gorbachev was placed under house arrest at his Crimean *dacha* (vacation home) by the Communist leaders of the coup. Realizing they would also have to eliminate the radical reform group headed by Yeltsin, the hardliners ordered army tanks to roll through the streets of Moscow and surround key buildings, including the Russian

> "He opened the dam and hoped he could control the water flow. Instead, the dam burst."
>
> *Ivan Laptev, Gorbachev associate, December 1991*

ВНЕОЧЕРЕДНОЙ СЪЕЗД
НАРОДНЫХ ДЕПУТАТОВ
СССР

Following the failed coup, Gorbachev presented a proposal to the Congress of Peoples' Deputies to transform the Soviet Union into a loosely knit confederation.

parliament where Yeltsin and his supporters had taken refuge as soon as the coup began. Before a violent confrontation could take place, however, Yeltsin emerged from the building and climbed up onto one of the tanks. In a bold stroke of public image-making, he stared defiantly at the soldiers and militia around him and announced that the army supported the people and would not attack the defenders of democracy. The tank crews then broke ranks and disbanded.

The hardliners' tactics signalled a return to the repressive style of the Stalinists. In protest, thousands of people rallied in front of the Russian parliament. For two days unarmed Soviet citizens who supported Yeltsin and democracy faced down heavily armed riot troops. Finally the coup leaders lost their nerve and the coup collapsed.

Gorbachev returned to Moscow on Thursday, August 22nd. But his power had been seriously undermined by the week's events. Now it was Yeltsin who was the real leader in the eyes of the people. He took control of the situation immediately, praising those who had defended democracy and promising punishment for those who had aided the coup. Yeltsin laid the blame for the coup squarely on the Communists and announced measures to remove Communist influences from Russia, including replacing the Soviet flag with the traditional Russian flag. On the streets, the overjoyed crowds chanted Yeltsin's name.

Betrayed by his own party, Gorbachev announced his resignation as General Secretary on Saturday and recommended the dissolution of the Communist Party.

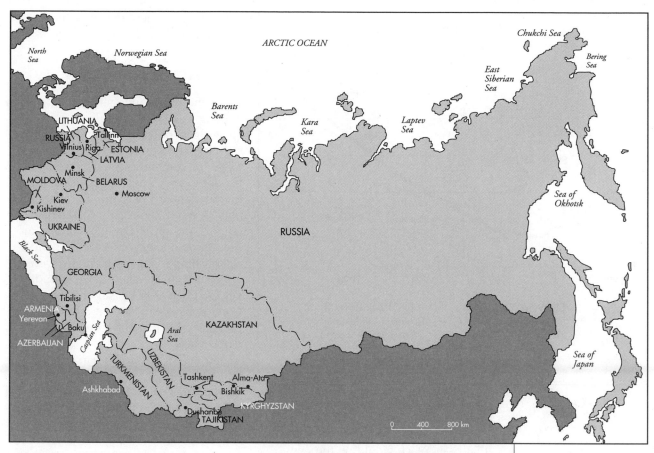

THE EFFECTS OF THE MOSCOW COUP

The effects of the coup attempt were dramatic. Prior to the coup, conservative Communist leaders had been intent on blocking the new Union Treaty, due to be signed on August 20th. Gorbachev had reasoned that the only way to keep the Soviet Union together was to give the republics greater control over their internal affairs. This treaty was designed to give the republics much more authority and end centralized power in the Kremlin. The conservative Communists opposed this relinquishing of power for fear of weakening the Soviet Union. But the coup attempt exposed the weakness of the central government and unleashed a flood of nationalism in many of the republics. By the end of August most

of the republics had declared their independence from the Soviet Union.

The coup also undermined the central government of the USSR. Gorbachev had lost face and the confidence of the people. He had been betrayed by his own party and had been replaced by his political rival. Yeltsin emerged as the hero, having defied communism and successfully defended democracy. He wasted no time capitalizing on the opportunity to discredit Gorbachev. More than any other single event, the coup brought about the end of Soviet communism, the Soviet Union, and Gorbachev's leadership.

THE COMMONWEALTH OF INDEPENDENT STATES

On 7 December 1991, Yeltsin met with the leaders of Ukraine and Belarus in

Figure 7.4:
The Former Soviet Union. The Soviet Union was made up of fifteen republics, or soviets, controlled by a central Soviet government in Moscow. Today the former Soviet republics are independent states.

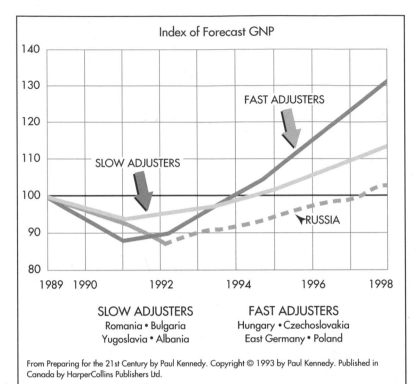

Figure 7.5:
Adjusting to Economic Reform in Eastern and Central Europe

survival in the new global economy was doubtful.

LIFE AFTER COMMUNISM

All of the newly independent states, including Russia, faced three serious challenges: political reform, economic stability, and ethnic relations. The overthrow of communism led to demands for democracy and expectations of a higher standard of living. But after seventy years of communist totalitarian control, the problems encountered in putting democracy into practice and establishing a market economy were enormous. In Russia, a wide split developed between Yeltsin and the old Communist parliament, a conflict that presented problems for the fragile democracy.

In addition, the Russian people had no experience with competitive capitalism. The rapid and sweeping changes involved in introducing a market economy caused economic chaos. The introduction of a market system resulted in spiralling inflation, escalating unemployment, and widespread poverty. Accustomed to the security of subsidized prices, a controlled market, and guaranteed employment, some people rejected the new capitalist system. The majority, however, did not want to return to communism, believing the long-range promise of a higher standard of living was worth the short-term suffering.

ETHNIC DIVERSITY AND CONFLICT

The former Soviet Union consisted of fifty different nationalities speaking one hundred different languages, using five different alphabets, and practising many different religions. Many of these groups were small, but their cultures dated back hundreds and even

the Belarus capital of Minsk. The next day the three leaders declared that the Soviet Union no longer existed and that in its place would be the new Commonwealth of Independent States (CIS). On December 21st, eleven republics signed an agreement to become members of the CIS; Georgia and the three Baltic republics of Estonia, Latvia, and Lithuania declined to join. (In October 1992, Azerbaijan voted against remaining in the Commonwealth.) The Soviet Union was officially dissolved on 1 January 1992.

The CIS helped to prevent the former Soviet Union from collapsing into complete economic and political chaos. It was formed as a loose federation to maintain economic and military relationships while permitting national groups to run their own governments. Problems arose, however, over conflicting interests among the various religious and national groups. Yet the smaller states realized that without their participation in the CIS their

thousands of years. For the most part, they were encouraged by the Soviet government to speak their own language and maintain their cultural identity. Their political rights, however, were restricted, and separatist activities were repressed, often ruthlessly, by the centralized Russian-dominated Communist government.

Once Gorbachev was in power and the policy of glasnost was implemented, minorities throughout the Soviet Union became vocal and protested against discriminatory practices. In the late 1980s, as the control of the Communist Party and the Kremlin loosened, local national groups were encouraged by the atmosphere of reform to seek independence. Power struggles and territorial disputes broke out between rival groups in many parts of the Soviet Union.

With the dissolution of the Soviet Union, disputes over boundaries, language rights, and a host of other problems threaten the peaceful co-existence of these ethnic groups. In some areas, such as Chechnya in the southern part of Russia, ethnic rivalries and hostilities degenerated into violence that involved the participation of the Russian army.

In 1995, ethnic tensions exploded in the break-away republic of Chechnya. Thousands of people died in fierce fighting between Russian and Chechen soldiers in the city of Grozny.

IN REVIEW

1. Why did Gorbachev introduce reforms when he took over the leadership of the Soviet Union in 1985?

2. What was the impact of Gorbachev's reforms on:
   a) the Soviet government
   b) the Soviet economy
   c) ethnic minorities in the former Soviet Union
   d) the communist states of eastern Europe
   e) relations with the West
   f) the Cold War?

3. Compare the policies of Gorbachev and Yeltsin under the following headings: Causes of the Problems, Recommendations for Change, Leadership Qualities, Political Power Base.

4. a) Why did Gorbachev decide to loosen the Soviet Union's tight control of the Soviet republics?
   b) How did the republics respond to this action?
   c) What was the result?

5. a) What did the leaders of the Moscow coup hope to accomplish?
   b) In what ways did the Moscow coup bring about the end of the Soviet Union?

A WORLD NOT QUITE SAFE

The end of the Cold War had huge repercussions for the two powerful military alliances that had opposed each other for forty years. Although the role of the military was substantially reduced, forces on both sides remained formidable in size and strength.

DEMILITARIZATION

Like its American counterpart, the military-industrial complex in the Soviet Union was extremely powerful. Some 10 million people were employed in military-related industries, accounting for 25 per cent of the Gross National Product. In the Russian republic, almost 50 per cent of all manufacturing was for the military. With the breakup of the Soviet Union, however, this powerful sector of the Russian economy collapsed, creating more economic chaos in its wake.

The Red Army numbered 4 million troops, about half of whom were from Russia. Soviet troops had begun to withdraw from the satellite nations of Eastern Europe in 1988 and they continued to do so until 1994. This was an enormous undertaking because of the sheer number of troops, weapons, and materials involved. Many of these troops returned home, not to the country they had left, the Soviet Union, but to new countries like Georgia, Estonia, or any of the other newly independent republics. Absorbing these troops back into civilian life presented difficulties for these new and changing societies. Upon their return, many soldiers found themselves competing for housing and jobs. The resettlement of such large numbers of military personnel placed an additional burden on already fragile economies.

The collapse of communism in Eastern Europe and the Soviet Union effectively disbanded the Warsaw Pact. Its Western counterpart, NATO, did not disband but began to search for a new role. With the Cold War over, Canada and the United States questioned the need for their troops to remain in Europe as part of the NATO commitment. Canada gradually removed its troops from Europe while the United States made major reductions in its forces. But the unpredictable nature of politics and the continued instability and tensions in many former Soviet bloc countries have caused NATO members to remain cautious.

NUCLEAR CONTROL AND DISARMAMENT

The most serious question facing NATO in the aftermath of the Cold War was the control of the nuclear weapons amassed by the former Soviet Union. Somewhere in this vast region were some 27 000 nuclear warheads. NATO had hoped that Yeltsin, as leader of Russia, would concentrate all nuclear weapons and keep them under Russian control. But at least four of the former Soviet republics—Russia, Ukraine, Belarus, and Kazakhstan—had nuclear weapons. Ukraine in particular was reluctant to turn over its nuclear arsenal to Russia. Ukraine inherited enough Soviet nuclear weapons to make it the third largest nuclear power in the world. That, plus its declared intention to maintain a large military, has created a new nuclear power on the world stage.

The development of national armies increases the possibility of conflict among former Soviet republics if relations deteriorate. There is also the question of what will happen if cash-strapped republics decide to sell their nuclear weapons to the highest bidder. The prospect of nuclear missiles falling into the hands of countries with territorial ambitions is a major concern for NATO and the world.

Another problem is the high cost of destroying nuclear weapons. The former Soviet republics do not have the money to dismantle the warheads. Even if all parties agreed to the destruction of nuclear weapons, the West would have to pay to get the job done. It is expected this process could take up to ten years.

As a result, the United States has continued to work towards further arms control agreements with Russia. One of the most important, START II, was signed in January 1993. It provides for the destruction of two-thirds of the nuclear arsenal held by the US and the former USSR by the year 2003. This agreement, however, is between former US president George Bush and Russian president Boris Yeltsin. Its implementation will be in the hands of future leaders who may or may not be as committed to the task.

IN REVIEW

1. What problems did the withdrawal of Soviet troops from Eastern Europe create?

2. What is the greatest challenge facing NATO after the Cold War?

3. (a) How has the breakup of the Soviet Union complicated the problem of the nuclear arms stockpile?
   (b) What are the dangers associated with the nuclear arms stockpile?

4. What is the objective of the START II agreement?

SUMMARY

Gorbachev's reform policies and the collapse of the Soviet Union had a profound impact on the world. At first the dizzying pace and scope of change behind the Iron Curtain spurred sweeping optimism about peace, global unity, and world prosperity. But the early euphoria was subdued and overshadowed by the rise of political, economic, ethnic, and military conflicts.

The newly liberated and democratic nations of Eastern Europe found economic and political progress to be slow, painful, and at times divisive. The decline of powerful Communist governments in some cases has fuelled an upsurge in nationalism not unlike that which plunged the world into war in 1914. As the turn of the century drew near, there continued to be uncertainty and caution about the former states of the Soviet empire.

MAKING CONNECTIONS

1. Compare the reforms of Mikhail Gorbachev with conditions in the former Soviet Union today. How did these reforms ultimately lead to the collapse of the USSR?

2. Critique a film about the Cold War and compare it with actual events.

3. In the aftermath of the Cold War, what do you think are the greatest challenges to world peace and security?

DEVELOPING YOUR VOICE

4. The collapse of the East German government and the reunification of Germany dealt a devastating blow to the power of the Soviet Union. Why do you think this was so?

5. Predict the role Germany will play in the new Europe. Consider economic, social, and political factors in your answer.

6. From the perspective of the twenty-first century, will Gorbachev be seen as a valiant reformer or as an inept politician? Give reasons for your opinion.

RESEARCHING THE ISSUES

7. Select one of the following problems faced by the former Soviet republics and research and write a report on its current status:
   a) adjusting to a market economy
   b) ethnic rivalries and conflicts
   c) efforts to move from a totalitarian state to a democratic society.

8. Select one Eastern European country and prepare a current affairs update on events in the country since the collapse of the USSR.

9. On 1 January 1992, Czechoslovakia ceased to exist as a nation. Prepare a report on the rise and fall of Czechoslovakia from 1945.

VIEWPOINTS

ISSUE: SHOULD THE WEST PROVIDE AID TO RUSSIA AND EASTERN EUROPE?

Since the end of the Cold War there has been considerable debate over Western economic aid to the new and struggling free market economies of Russia and Eastern Europe. Some analysts, such as historian Paul Goble, believe that financial aid is essential, but they caution that it must be accompanied by long-term political assistance. Others questions whether generous financial aid will have any lasting benefit. Social scientist Bogdan Denitch argues that the West cannot afford to finance the great expectations of the former communist countries and suggests that they may not feel the political urgency to do so.

Read each of the viewpoints carefully, then complete an Argument Analysis and Evaluation Summary for each reading.

Paul Goble

"Many believe that if the West gives enough, [Russia and the other post-Soviet states] will make a quick transition to democracy and free market capitalism; some have suggested that what is needed is a new Marshall Plan. This is the worse false analogy of all. The Marshall Plan was the perfect American foreign policy effort: it was short term, it was expensive, and it was directed at people who knew how to spend the money...because they had been both democratic and enjoyed free market economies only a few years earlier.

"This is clearly not the situation in the post-Soviet states. With the exception of the Baltic countries, none of these countries has a tradition of either democracy or free market development....Moreover, they have just gone through the trauma of the Soviet system, and the transition out is extremely difficult....

"Clearly...policymakers need to think about long-term programs of technical assistance rather than 'big bang,' short-term efforts. Indeed, the latter are likely to be counterproductive because they will not be sustained and will thus breed resentment when what they hope to achieve does not materialize in two or three years. This is not to say that [the West] should not provide massive humanitarian aid, but rather that it should not confuse it with political assistance...."

Paul Goble, excerpt from "Ten Issues in Search of a Policy," is reprinted with permission from Current History *magazine (October 1993). © 1993, Current History, Inc.*

Bogdan Denitch

"It is questionable if even two or three decades of generous aid from Western Europe would be able to help to clean up the economic and social problems which the post-communist regimes have inherited. It is even more questionable if aid on such a scale will be available. Germany will have its resources tied down trying to integrate an economically and ecologically devastated former East Germany....How much Western aid will be left over for helping other East European states and the former Soviet Union is anyone's guess. The first priority will be aid to Russia, and that will be for security reasons, as well as the massive natural resources which are potentially available.

"All this does not augur well for the immediate economic prospects of Poland, the Czech and Slovak states, Hungary, the former Yugoslavia, Bulgaria and Romania. Albania's prospects are even worse. The trouble is that the relatively better off East European countries cannot expect a fraction of the aid which the wildly aroused expectations of their populations require. The fact that those societies are now far more open only means that the drastic contrast between their living standards and those of Western Europe are now all too clearly visible....

"Unrealistic hopes have been aroused, some quite irresponsibly, that quick solutions can be achieved by an act of political will. It should be reasonably clear that *none* of these countries is likely to become a part of "Europe," if that means entering the European Community, before the end of the century. At best, what is open is the hope for some type of half-way house process where a gradual increase of contacts and ties with Western Europe takes place. The EC *will* almost certainly try to help, but the amount of aid which is probable does not begin to approach what is needed for the expectations of the peoples of former communist countries to be satisfied.

"What they expected was that their living standards would radically improve after commu-

nism. To date they have not; on the contrary, they have dropped, in the European East, in some cases drastically; moreover, it is universally predicted that things will get still worse before they get better. The only debate is, how much worse, and for how long a period of time. With the old communist repressive regimes and the potential military threat of the Warsaw Pact both gone from the scene, Western Europe and the United States have considerably less interest in the former communist countries. Less interest, unfortunately, translates into less urgent pressure for aid...."

From Bogdan Denitch, "Eastern Europe: Prospects After Communism," in Phyllis Bennis and Michel Moushabeck, Altered States: A Reader in the New World Order *(Brooklyn, NY: Olive Branch Press, 1993), pp. 468-69.*

ANALYSIS AND EVALUATION

Refer to the Argument Analysis and Evaluation Guide on page viii.

1. Using the Argument Analysis and Evaluation Guide, compare the readings by Goble and Denitch. On what do they agree? On what do they disagree?

2. Decide which of the viewpoints you tend to support and explain why. Be sure to use specific information from this textbook, the readings and other sources to support your position.

3. State and support your position on the issue: "Should the West provide aid to Russia and Eastern Europe?"

UNIT THREE:
THE GLOBAL VILLAGE

❖	EUROPE	AFRICA
1940s	• WWII ends (1945) • United Nations formed (1945) • Churchill, "Iron Curtain" speech (1946) • Nuremburg Trials (1946) • Marshall Plan (1947) • NATO formed (1948) • Berlin Blockade begins (1948)	• Apartheid system established in South Africa (1949)
1950s	• Tito becomes president of Yugoslavia (1953) • Stalin dies (1953) • Hungarian Revolution (1956) • Six European countries sign Treaty of Rome creating Common Market (1957)	• Mau Mau rebellion in Kenya (1952-56) • Ghana gains independence (1957)
1960s	• Berlin Wall (1961) • UN peacekeeping forces in Cyprus (1964) • European Community formed (1967) • Czechoslovakian revolt brutally suppressed (1968)	• 31 countries become independent (1960-69) • Biafran war breaks out in Nigeria (1967) • African National Congress banned; Nelson Mandela imprisoned (1960) • Organization of African Unity founded (1963)
1970s	• Britain imposes direct rule on Northern Ireland (1972) • Ireland, Great Britain, and Denmark join Common Market (1973) • Worldwide inflation brought on by rapidly rising fuel costs (1974) • Margaret Thatcher becomes prime minister of Britain (1975)	• 5 countries become independent (1970-79) • Biafran war ends (1970) • Idi Amin establishes himself ruler of Uganda (1971) • Fierce fighting between Ethiopian troops and rebels from Eritrea (1975)
1980s	• Soviet Union invades Afghanistan (1980) • Polish government cracks down on unions (1981) • Soviets withdraw from Afghanistan (1988)	• 2 countries become independent, ending colonial era in Africa (1980-89) • Famine threatens millions of Ethiopians (1984) • State of emergency declared in South Africa (1986)
1990s	• East and West Germany unified (1990) • Civil war breaks out in Yugoslavia (1991) • Czechs and Slovaks form separate countries (1992) • UN peacekeepers stationed in former Yugoslavia (1992) • Maastricht Treaty creates European Union (EU) (1993)	• South Africa liberalizes apartheid and frees Nelson Mandela (1990) • Ethiopian rebels defeat government forces and take over the country (1991) • UN begins relief shipments to Somalia (1992) • South Africa holds first non-racial elections; Mandela elected president (1994) • Civil war in Rwanda (1994)

ASIA	LATIN AMERICA	MIDDLE EAST
• WWII ends (1945) • Elected assembly replaces emperor in Japan (1946) • India independent and partitioned into India and Pakistan (1947) • Ghandi assassinated (1948) • Communist Chinese takeover mainland China (1949)	• Perón president of Argentina (1946) • Organization of American States formed (1948)	• WWII ends (1945) • League of Arab Nations established (1945) • Jewish state of Israel (1948) • First Arab-Israeli war (1948-49)
• Start of Korean War (1950) • Communist forces defeat French in Vietnam (1954) • Korean War ends (1953)	• Castro lands in Cuba with small armed force (1956) • Castro premier of Cuba (1959)	• Egypt becomes a republic (1954) • Nasser seizes Suez Canal; Israeli troops invade the Sinai Peninsula (1956) • Israeli forces withdraw from the Sinai; UN peacekeeping forces established (1957)
• US military advisors to South Vietnam (1960) • US financial and economic aid to South Vietnam (1963) • Indira Gandhi prime minister of India (1966) • First US troops withdrawn from Vietnam (1969)	• US breaks diplomatic relations with Cuba (1961) • Bay of Pigs invasion of Cuba (1961) • Cuban Missile Crisis (1962) • British Guiana becomes independent nation of Guyana (1966)	• OPEC formed (1960) • Six-Day War (1967) • Arafat elected leader of the PLO (1969)
• Mainland China admitted to the UN (1971) • War between India and Pakistan (1971) • US withdraws from Vietnam (1973) • Communist forces overrun South Vietnam (1975) • Shah of Iran deposed by Islamic republican government (1979)	• Juan Perón returns as president of Argentina (1973) • Military takes power in Argentina (1976) • Sandinista rebels in Nicaragua fight US-backed government (1978) • Sandinistas win civil war in Nicaragua (1979)	• Yom Kippur War (1973) • OPEC oil embargo (1973) • Israeli-Egyptian peace treaty (1979) • Islamic revolution in Iran (1979)
• Indira Gandhi assassinated (1984) • Iran-Iraq war ends (1988) • Bhutto elected first female prime minister of Pakistan (1988) • Tiananmen Square massacre (1989)	• Falklands War (1982) • US invades Grenada (1983) • Democratic government in Argentina (1983) • Sandinistas and *Contra* rebels agree to ceasefire in Nicaragua (1988) • US invades Panama (1989)	• Iran-Iraq War (1980) • Israel invades Lebanon (1982) • Israel withdraws from Lebanon (1985) • Violent rioting by Palestinians marks beginning of *Intifadah* (1988) • Iran-Iraq war ends (1988)
• Chinese Communist Party adopts capitalist ideas to socialist ideologies (1992) • Afghan guerrillas defeat government forces (1992) • China regains possession of Hong Kong (1997)	• Violetta Chamorro elected president of Nicaragua (1990) • USSR cuts off aid to Cuba (1990) • UN authorizes US to restore order and democracy in Haiti (1994)	• Iraq invades Kuwait (1990); Gulf War (1991) • Iraq withdraws from Kuwait (1991) • Arab states and Israel agree to peace conference (1991) • PLO recognizes Israel's right to exist (1993) • Self-rule to Palestinians in Gaza and Jericho (1994) • Peace treaties negotiated between Israel–Jordan, Israel–Syria (1994)

CHAPTER EIGHT

The New Europe

"Integration is...the only way for Europe to retain any semblance of world stature and significance."

Richard P. Ahlstrom,
"The European Community Faces 1992,"
Current History, *November 1991*

"In the region that used to be Yugoslavia, war is becoming a way of life. Values have been turned upside down. Criminals are turned into heroes and patriots. Adolescents are taught to be killers."

"Appeal to Stop the War in Yugoslavia,"
Helsinki Citizens Assembly,
HCA Newsletter, *Prague, 1992.*

Left: The Louvre, Paris, 1994

❖ OVERVIEW

After the Second World War, Europe's power and influence in world affairs were significantly diminished. In need of financial aid, the countries of Western Europe turned to the world's new superpower, the United States. The nations of Eastern Europe found themselves under the control of the other superpower, the Soviet Union. Over the next forty years the two sides of Europe embarked on radically different paths. While Western Europe worked towards greater economic and political integration, Eastern Europe languished under the repressive control of the Soviet Union.

Britain's fall from power was perhaps the greatest of all the European nations. Financially drained by war, the country experienced years of stagnation before finding new economic life in the 1980s. In contrast, Yugoslavia in Eastern Europe enjoyed a period of relative prosperity under its independent communist regime. But this prosperity masked the dark forces of nationalism that lay waiting to explode. As the twentieth century neared its end, uncertainty once again shadowed much of Europe.

of the twentieth century. While both cost untold hardship, the world was no safer after the wars than before them. The escalating nuclear arms race after 1945 threatened world peace and security even more than had Nazi aggression.

Nationalism, which had played a key role in both wars, continued to fuel disputes and hostilities in postwar Europe. Some leaders in Western Europe, in particular Winston Churchill, believed that the time had come to set aside nationalist interests and to concentrate on fostering the economic and political integration of European states. Believing that a politically and economically strong Europe was the best deterrent to Soviet expansion, the United States supported calls for European unity. The Marshall Plan, which provided American financial aid for postwar reconstruction in Western Europe, stimulated trade and interdependence.

In 1949, at Churchill's instigation, the Council of Europe was created to provide a forum for dialogue. The Council had no legislative or independent power, but it signalled a desire to establish common European values and goals. The first step towards European economic and political unity was taken in 1952 with the formation of the European Coal and Steel Community (ECSC). The organization pooled coal, iron, and steel production, eliminated tariffs on these industries, and created a free labour market among the participants. The idea of economic union was championed by French economist Jean Monnet as a means of preventing war between former adversaries. While West Germany, France, Italy, and the **Benelux countries** all signed on to the ECSC, Britain refused to join.

FOCUS QUESTIONS

1. What important forces shaped Europe after the Second World War?

2. Why did Europe evolve towards a European Union?

3. How has Britain's role in the world changed since the Second World War?

4. What are the underlying causes of the conflict in the former Yugoslavia?

5. What challenges does the new Europe face in the twenty-first century?

TOWARDS A EUROPEAN UNION

Two enormously destructive wars had raged through Europe in the first half

In 1957, the Treaty of Rome formally created the **European Economic Community** (EEC), or **Common Market**. The treaty abolished tariffs and trade restrictions among members and required common trade policies and tariffs towards all non-members. It also allowed for the free movement of people, capital, and services among members and set a common agricultural policy. Britain opposed the EEC because it meant giving up a substantial degree of economic control to the Community and loosening historic ties with the **Commonwealth**. Once the EEC was operating successfully, however, Britain felt isolated economically. In response, British leaders negotiated an economic alliance with other countries that remained outside the EEC. The so-called "Outer Seven" (Britain, Sweden, Norway, Denmark, Switzerland, Austria, and Portugal) formed the more limited European Free Trade Association (EFTA).

Both trading blocs proved very successful. Trade between EEC members rose by 98 per cent between 1958 and 1964, while EFTA trade increased by 72 per cent. It became clear to Britain, however, that membership in the EEC offered a larger market than the EFTA and thereby a greater potential for economic growth at home. In the 1960s, Britain submitted its application for EEC membership, but the move was blocked by French president Charles de Gaulle. De Gaulle believed that Britain was too closely allied with the United States and that American influence would weaken European integration. With de Gaulle's resignation in 1969, however, French opposition dissipated. In 1973, Britain, Denmark, and Ireland joined the **European Community** (EC). Greece joined in 1981, and Spain and Portugal became members in 1986, bringing the total membership to twelve. Associate status and preferential trade agreements were offered to former colonies.

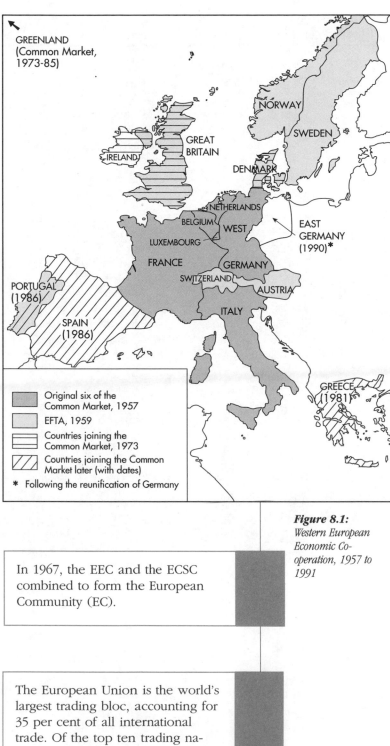

Figure 8.1:
Western European Economic Co-operation, 1957 to 1991

In 1967, the EEC and the ECSC combined to form the European Community (EC).

The European Union is the world's largest trading bloc, accounting for 35 per cent of all international trade. Of the top ten trading nations in the world, six—Germany, France, Britain, Italy, Holland, and Belgium-Luxembourg—are members of the EU.

Figure 8.2: Economic Co-operation Since 1940

Year	Name of Treaty/ Organization	Aims	Members
1949	Council of Europe	To achieve greater co-operation and unity of ten member states	Belgium, Denmark, France, Ireland, Italy, Luxembourg, Netherlands, Norway, Sweden, Britain; later joined by Austria, Cyprus, Greece, Iceland, Malta, Switzerland, West Germany, Turkey
1951	European Coal and Steel Community (ECSC)	To create an integrated market for coal and steel	France, West Germany, Italy, Belgium, Netherlands, Luxembourg
1957	Treaty of Rome: European Economic Community (EEC) the Common Market	To create an integrated economy for member states	France, West Germany, Italy, Belgium, Netherlands, Luxembourg
1960	Stockholm Convention: European Free Trade Association (EFTA)	To establish a rival economic free trade community led by Britain	Britain, Austria, Denmark, Norway, Portugal, Sweden, Switzerland; Iceland and Finland joined later; Britain, Denmark, and Portugal left to join EC
1967	EEC and ECSC combine to form European Community (EC)	To evolve towards greater economic and political unity among members	France, West Germany, Italy, Belgium, Netherlands, Luxembourg; Britain, Denmark, Ireland join in 1973; Greece joins in 1981; Spain and Portugal join in 1986
1991	European Economic Area (EEA)	To merge the EC and the EFTA	EC and EFTA members; Austria, Sweden, Finland, Norway apply for full EC membership
1993	Maastrict Treaty on European Union	To create a unified community with common currency and financial policies, open immigration between members, and further economic and political unity	twelve members of EC; requires ratification by all twelve members; Denmark votes against the Maastrict Treaty in 1992; British opposition mounts

THE MAASTRICT TREATY

A significant step towards "a Europe without frontiers" took place in 1991 when EC members agreed to the Maastrict Treaty during a summit at Maastrict in the Netherlands. The treaty encouraged members to establish the legal and technical means to achieve greater economic and political integration. This included establishing common technical and pollution standards and eliminating restrictions on the flow of capital. While these terms were uniformly accepted, others, such as a central monetary policy and banking system, a common military force, and agricultural subsidies, stirred up great controversy. But before any of the terms of Maastrict could be implemented, each member nation had to ratify the treaty. It wouldn't be a simple task. Maastrict faced fierce opposition in Denmark, France, and Britain. Opposition focused on the excessive centralization of authority that might result from the treaty. In France, the treaty passed with a bare majority in 1992. But in Denmark that same year, Maastrict was rejected in a national referendum, a result that caused Britain to delay its vote on ratification.

In May 1993, a revised treaty exempted Denmark from using the common currency and supporting a common defense policy. The new version of Maastrict was finally ratified by the Danes, but the victory was marred by rioting by anarchists who opposed the EU. That same month, the British House of Commons voted in favour of the treaty, clearing the way for Britain to join the Union.

Opposition to certain aspects of the treaty, particularly the common currency, did not disappear, however. In August 1993, the process by which the EU had planned to introduce a single currency by 1999 was scrapped. This paved the way for German ratifi-

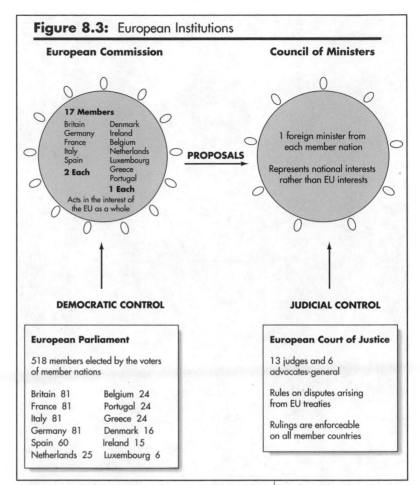

Figure 8.3: European Institutions

European Commission

17 Members

Britain	Denmark
Germany	Ireland
France	Belgium
Italy	Netherlands
Spain	Luxembourg
2 Each	Greece
	Portugal
	1 Each

Acts in the interest of the EU as a whole

PROPOSALS →

Council of Ministers

1 foreign minister from each member nation

Represents national interests rather than EU interests

DEMOCRATIC CONTROL

European Parliament

518 members elected by the voters of member nations

Britain 81	Belgium 24
France 81	Portugal 24
Italy 81	Greece 24
Germany 81	Denmark 16
Spain 60	Ireland 15
Netherlands 25	Luxembourg 6

JUDICIAL CONTROL

European Court of Justice

13 judges and 6 advocates-general

Rules on disputes arising from EU treaties

Rulings are enforceable on all member countries

cation of the treaty in November. Now the ratification process was complete. On 1 November 1993, after two years of political wrangling in twelve countries, the European Union came into effect. On 1 January 1995, three other countries—Austria, Finland, and Sweden—joined the Union, bringing the total membership to fifteen.

The European Union is administered by the European Parliament. Representatives are elected from each member country. While the Parliament does not have the power to set laws, it does debate policies and offer opinions to the European Commission.

Demonstrators in Copenhagen, Denmark, clashed with police during protests against the Maastricht Treaty.

"Poland, 10 years. Hungary, 10 months. East Germany, 10 weeks. Czechoslovakia, 10 days. Romania, 10 hours."

Prague graffiti commenting on the speed with which communism was toppled

THE EUROPEAN UNION AND EASTERN EUROPE

The world order was shattered when the nations of Eastern Europe threw off the cloak of communism they had worn for almost half a century. One by one the communist dictatorships of Eastern Europe crumbled and fell. Free elections installed new leaders committed to democracy and the free market system. But while political change can be rapid and dramatic, economic change takes time.

Switching from a centralized economy to a market economy is a slow and complicated process. In the short term, the new democracies of Eastern Europe experienced severe economic hardships. Inflation and unemployment reached record levels. Food and other essential goods were often in short supply. For many people, especially older citizens who had lived within the communist system most of their lives, democracy appeared to offer few benefits. Unlike the younger generation, who saw the hope for economic prosperity once the transition was complete, many older people believed they would never be as well off as they were before. The effects of the economic hardships began to be reflected at the polls. In 1994, several former Communist Party members were elected in Hungary, Poland, Romania, and Slovenia.

The plight of the new democracies of Eastern Europe raised some troubling questions for the European Union. How should the EU respond to these states? How long can peace in Europe be maintained with the incredible inequities between east and west? As Western Europe moves towards greater integration, the European Union must wrestle with its relationship with Eastern Europe.

IN REVIEW

1. a) On a timeline, plot the key economic changes in Europe since 1945.
   b) In your opinion, which changes were most instrumental in shaping postwar Europe?
2. Why did Europe initially split into two trading blocs?
3. What did the countries of Europe expect to gain from the European Union?
4. What are some of the problems facing the nations of Eastern Europe?

GREAT BRITAIN

At the beginning of the twentieth century, the British Empire encircled the globe. Over 20 per cent of the world's land surface and 25 per cent of its people were within the realm of the British crown. The British navy was considered invincible. The country's wealth, power, and influence were unquestioned. But two world wars and a global depression devastated the British economy and weakened its influence around the world. By the end of the Second World War, the country reflected only a shadow of its former glory. In the second half of the twentieth century, Britain had to struggle to come to terms with its diminished role in Europe and the world at large.

THE LOSS OF AN EMPIRE

As peace at last descended upon Europe in 1945, the British people were forced to recognize that their nation and their place in the world had been altered forever. At home, many industries had either been destroyed by the war or were now obsolete. Postwar reconstruction dictated that much of the country's foreign investment had to be sold in order to finance this enormous challenge.

Britain's vast colonial interests became liabilities. As independence movements gained momentum, the retreat from imperialism began in 1947 with independence in Burma, India, and Pakistan. The process gained momentum throughout the 1950s and 1960s as British colonies throughout Africa and Asia established their independence. By 1980, the process was largely complete. Today more than thirty of Britain's former colonies remain members of the Commonwealth of Nations, a free association of independent states.

THE WELFARE STATE

The two major political forces in British politics are the Labour and Conservative parties. While both parties share a wide middle ground designed to appeal to the middle-class majority, each has distinct—and opposite—roots. Labour's support has traditionally come from labour unions and socialist organizations. It is more closely identified with the **welfare state**—that is, government-sponsored social welfare programs. The Conservative Party, on the other hand, has

In postwar Britain, long lineups for food were common.

care. As part of Britain's economic reconstruction, Labour nationalized the railways, the coal and steel industries, the Bank of England, and all hospitals in the expectation that public ownership of key institutions and resources was in the public interest. Yet the economic recovery was slow. Disillusioned by the unfulfilled promises of the Labour Party, the majority of British voters returned to the Conservatives and Winston Churchill in 1951.

The new government sold some of the nationalized industries back to the private sector and pursued other conservative fiscal policies. The new economic directions produced a few positive results, but overall industries failed to improve their productivity. Britain's economic performance remained sluggish and consistently lagged behind many other European nations. While the 1950s and 1960s brought new prosperity to much of the industrialized world, Britain seemed to stand on the sidelines. Voters blamed government for the country's poor economic performance, but economic analysts suggested a variety of explanations, including the militancy of the trade unions, poor management, and constantly shifting government policies. While many European nations were exporting better designed and more sophisticated products, British industries remained mired in obsolete and unproductive technologies. As a result, they were less competitive in the world market.

traditionally enjoyed the support of business and the upper classes. It favours a limited role for government in both the economy and society in general.

The postwar reconstruction of Britain was launched within this political climate. With the economy in ruins, there was concern that Britain would experience a recurrence of the hardships endured during the Depression of the 1930s. To avoid such economic and social disaster, many people favoured the creation of a social "safety net." Winston Churchill and the Conservative Party, in spite of having led the country to victory in the Second World War, were also associated with the unemployment and poverty of the 1930s. In 1945, the Labour Party, under Clement Attlee, won a sweeping electoral victory.

The new government acted quickly to introduce social welfare programs, including unemployment insurance, old age pensions, and universal health

POSTWAR ECONOMIC DECLINE

Other observers believed Britain's economic problems stemmed more from its leadership role during the Second World War. As the only undefeated European nation, Britain amassed an incredible debt to finance its military operations. After the war enormous sums of money were owed in foreign debt. The Labour Party's move to nationalize many industries and establish the welfare state further drained the economy. Under such circumstances it was perhaps impossible for Britain to share in any postwar prosperity.

ECONOMIC UNCERTAINTY

During the 1960s and 1970s, the economy remained at the forefront of British politics. Promises were made by politicians and parties on both sides that inevitably could not be kept. In 1964, the Labour Party, led by Harold Wilson, won at the polls. It introduced an economic policy of higher taxes and less government spending. But this placed the party squarely on a collision course with its traditional supporters, the labour unions. Labour was defeated in 1970 and the Conservative Party once again took the reins of power. The new prime minister, Edward Heath, tried to reduce spiralling inflation through wage controls, but the labour unions proved to be too powerful. Strikes crippled the economy. In an effort to improve trade,

Britain joined the European Community in 1973. But this was not enough to turn the economy around, and the Conservatives were tossed out of office in 1974.

Wilson and the Labour Party once again had the task of carving a prosperous course for the British economy. The economic chaos that resulted from the 1973 oil embargo by OPEC (the Organization of Petroleum Exporting

Striking postal workers were among various labour unions that disrupted the British economy in the 1960s and 1970s.

Figure 8.4: Britain's Declining Share of World Trade, 1954-78

Britain's share of world trade

%

20
18
16
14
12
10
8

1954 1957 1960 1963 1966 1969 1972 1975 1978
Year

VOICES

DO NOT GO GENTLE INTO THAT GOOD NIGHT

Britain's economic uncertainty after the war created both anger and fear in society. Dylan Thomas, a renowned Welsh poet and writer, captured the people's mood in his poem "Do Not Go Gentle into that Good Night," written in 1952. Read this poem and identify the sentiments Thomas expresses.

Do not go gentle into that good night,
Old age should burn and rave at close of day;
Rage, rage against the dying of the light.

Though wise men at their end know dark is right,
Because their words had forked no lightning they
Do not go gentle into that good night.

Good men, the last wave by, crying how bright

Their frail deeds might have danced in a green bay,
Rage, rage against the dying of the light.

Wild men who caught and sang the sun in flight,
And learn, too late, they grieved it on its way,
Do not go gentle into that good night.

Grave men, near death, who see with blinding sight
Blind eyes could blaze like meteors and be gay,
Rage, rage against the dying of the light.

And you, my father, there on the sad height,
Curse, bless, me now with your fierce tears, I pray,
Do not go gentle into that good night.
Rage, rage against the dying of the light.

Dylan Thomas, "Do Not Go into that Good Night" from The Poems *(J.M. Dent). Reprinted by permission of David Higham Associates.*

Figure 8.5: British Prime Ministers Since 1945

1945-51	Clement Attlee (Labour)
1951-55	Winston Churchill (Conservative)
1955-57	Anthony Eden (Conservative)
1957-63	Harold Macmillan (Conservative)
1963-64	Alec Douglas-Home (Conservative)
1964-70	Harold Wilson (Labour)
1970-74	Edward Heath (Conservative)
1974-76	Harold Wilson (Labour)
1976-79	James Callaghan (Labour)
1979-90	Margaret Thatcher (Conservative)
1990-	John Major (Conservative)

Countries) further hurt the British economy. The embargo raised the price of crude oil by 200 per cent. This in turn caused inflation to skyrocket. At the same time, unemployment was on the rise and strikes by labour unions continued to plague the nation. With the Labour Party unable to solve Britain's economic woes, in 1979 the voters turned back to the Conservatives and their new leader, Margaret Thatcher.

BRITAIN AND THE EUROPEAN UNION

Under Thatcher, the British economy enjoyed a period of substantial growth.

The Eurostar passenger train whisks people between London and Paris via the Channel Tunnel in just over two hours.

It was clear, however, that sustained prosperity would require closer ties with the EC. Thatcher recognized the importance of the European Common Market and the need to eliminate trade barriers within Europe. But she was opposed to expanding Britain's political and economic integration in the new European Union if it meant transferring authority to the EU. She favoured a decentralized union that would be expanded to include other European nations. Consequently, she resisted even her own party's efforts to achieve greater European integration. As a result, Thatcher was ousted as leader in November 1990. She was replaced by John Major, a politician of more moderate views who had no reservations about full participation in the European Union. Proclaiming that he wanted Britain to be at the heart of Europe, Major and the

Conservatives were returned for a fourth term in April 1992. The government then set out to formally link Britain's economy to that of the EU. Major faced a major challenge almost immediately. In September, pressure on the pound forced Major to withdraw Britain from the European Monetary System and to devalue the British currency. The move further delayed Britain's plans to ratify the Maastricht Treaty that was to create the European Union. It was not until May 1993 that the House of Commons voted in favour of Maastricht.

On 6 May 1994, Britain took another historic step towards unity with Europe when the Channel Tunnel linking Britain with the continent was officially opened.

PROFILE

MARGARET THATCHER (1925-)

Margaret Thatcher was Britain's first female prime minister, serving in that capacity from 1979 to 1990, longer than any British prime minister in the postwar era. A determined and decisive politician, Thatcher forged a distinctive path in Britain's domestic and foreign policies. Branded the "Iron Lady" because of her strength and commitment in the pursuit of her policies, Thatcher left an indelible mark on Britain. What characteristics do you think helped her to retain power longer than any other modern British leader?

"We have to get our production and our earnings into balance. There's no easy popularity in what we are proposing, but it is fundamentally sound. Yet I believe people accept there is no real alternative."

> *Margaret Thatcher, in a speech at the Conservative Women's Conference, 21 May 1980*

"We shall not be diverted from our course. To those waiting with bated breath for that favourite media catch-phrase, the U-turn, I have only this to say. 'You turn if you want; the lady's not for turning.'"

> *Margaret Thatcher, in a speech at the Conservative Party Conference, 10 October 1980*

"I am extraordinarily patient, provided I get my own way in the end."

> *Margaret Thatcher, in the* Observer, *4 April 1989*

Margaret Roberts rose from a modest background to become the first female prime minister of Britain, serving with a determined, uncompromising style that gained the respect of some and the indignation of others. Thatcher graduated as a research chemist from Oxford University in 1947. Three years later she began to study law, qualifying as a barrister in 1953. In 1951, Roberts married Denis Thatcher, a manufacturer, and they had twins in 1953.

Always interested in politics, Thatcher ran for a seat in Parliament in 1950. She had no chance of winning and ran simply for the experience, but she did succeed in impressing Conservative Party organizers. In 1959, Thatcher was offered a "safe" Conservative riding and was elected to the House of Commons. Her aggressive style and thorough understanding of the issues gained her attention in the media and in the House. She became the Minister for Pensions and National Insurance in 1962, a junior position in the cabinet. Over the next few years she fine-tuned her political image both as a cabinet minister and as an opposition critic when the Conservatives sat on the other side of the House following their defeat in 1964.

While the Conservative Party clung to social welfare policies in the hopes of gaining the support of the unions and the voters, Thatcher wanted to reduce government intervention in the economy by cutting back on the welfare system and giving more freedom to the private sector. She felt that the welfare state discouraged independence, initiative, and the work ethic. What she wanted instead was a society in which people were self-reliant, worked hard, and took risks—what she called an **enterprise culture**.

After poor results in the 1974 election, the Conservative Party decided on a change of leadership. In the campaign that followed, Thatcher emerged victorious. She led the Conservatives to victory in 1979 on a platform of reducing inflation and limiting government spending.

Thatcher's Conservative Party was in a state of transition. Long the representative of the wealthy establishment, under Thatcher the Conservatives increasingly came to speak for the middle class. The result was a sweeping electoral victory in 1983, fuelled further by patriotic euphoria generated by the Falklands War against Argentina. Thatcher's success was repeated in 1987, making her the first prime minister in 160 years to be elected to a third consecutive term. As the decade drew to a close, however, her critics became more vocal and greater in number.

In an attempt to reduce the deficit, Thatcher privatized a number of nationalized industries, including British Telecom, British Steel, and British Airways, and sold off public housing to tenants. In 1989, she proposed limits on the national health plan and introduced a poll tax that charged a flat-rate tax on all adults instead of on property or income. Thatcher was accused of sacrificing the public good and destroying British institutions for the sake of efficiency and private profit. Yet in reality she did not introduce sweeping reforms to the social welfare system, nor did she substantially reduce government intervention in the economy. When she became prime minister in 1979, government spending stood at 42 per cent of GNP—exactly where it stood nine years later.

Thatcher encountered her greatest opposition within the Conservative Party itself. Opposed to transferring too much authority to the EU, Thatcher resisted the further integration of Britain into the European economy. But her position ran contrary to that of the Conservative Party and resulted in a challenge to her leadership. In November 1990, Thatcher resigned as leader of the party and took a seat as a government backbencher. After eleven consecutive years as prime minister, Margaret Thatcher had served the longest unbroken term in Britain in the twentieth century.

IN REVIEW

1. List the causes of Britain's poor postwar economic performance.

2. To what extent did a) the British people, b) the British government, c) industry, and d) labour contribute to the country's slow economic growth after the Second World War?

3. Suggest how a capitalist and a socialist might judge the success of the Labour and Conservative governments' actions in stimulating Britain's economic recovery.

4. a) What was Margaret Thatcher's position on government economic policy?

    b) Explain Thatcher's opposition to expanding Britain's involvement in the European Union.

YUGOSLAVIA

Yugoslavia was created following the breakup of the Austro-Hungarian Empire at the end of the First World War. The new nation was formed by amalgamating the Balkan provinces of Croatia, Dalmatia, Bosnia, Herzegovina, Slovenia, and Voyvodina, and the independent state of Montenegro.

In 1941, Hitler invaded Yugoslavia, but the Nazi forces encountered a strong resistance movement led by the head of the Yugoslav Communist Party, Josip Tito. His success in resisting the occupying forces earned Tito the support to lead the new Yugoslav government after the war. Although Stalin expected to impose Soviet control, Tito was able to resist domination from Moscow. Instead, he built a strong nationalist and liberal communist society. He established a constitution that recognized the major nationalities within Yugoslavia as separate republics. In foreign affairs Tito adopted a policy of nonalignment. His independent course caused Yugoslavia to be expelled from the Soviet-controlled Cominform in 1948.

Despite relative independence from Soviet control, the disintegration of the USSR released forces for change in Yugoslavia that had a profound impact on the new world order. The collapse of communism led to the disintegration of the Yugoslav federation into competing ethnic and political groups.

YUGOSLAVIA UNDER TITO

Yugoslavian resistance to the Nazis during the Second World War was led by Tito, who was rewarded with the title of Marshal for his efforts. Once the war was over, Tito forced the abdication of Yugoslavia's King Peter II. Elections were held in 1945, and Tito's great popularity enabled him to win an easy victory. Tito was now the head of a new communist regime in Yugoslavia. In 1953, he was elected president, and, in 1974, he installed himself as president for life.

Tito expanded agricultural and industrial production, raising the standard of living for Yugoslavs. With an economic growth rate averaging over 7 per cent throughout the 1950s, 1960s, and 1970s, Yugoslavia was gradually being transformed into a developed country.

Improving the economy was not Tito's most difficult problem, however. That distinction lay in the country's ethnic diversity. Yugoslavia comprised many ethnic groups speaking several different languages. In the northern part of the country were the Croats and the Slovenes; in central Yugoslavia were the Serbs; to the south were the Bosnians, Macedonians, Montenegrins, and Albanians. The north of Yugoslavia was the most economically developed region. But in central Yugoslavia the Serbs enjoyed the greatest political power by virtue of their numbers—36 per cent of the total Yugoslav population.

This ethnic diversity was further complicated by religious differences. Approximately 9 per cent of Yugoslavs were Muslims, living mainly in Bosnia and Herzegovina. Another 30 per cent, primarily Croats and Slovenes, were Roman Catholic. About 50 per cent were Eastern Orthodox. These ethnic and religious groups have long histories of conflict. During the war, Nazi occupation forces declared an independent kingdom of Croatia. Atrocities were committed by Croatian fascists against Serbs, Jews, and communists. In the closing months of the war, there was widespread brutality on all sides. After the war, deep-seated resentment continued. Tito controlled these nationalist rumblings throughout the republics. He kept potentially explosive

PROFILE

JOSIP BROZ TITO (1892-1980)

As president of Yugoslavia for nearly thirty years, Josip Tito steered his country on an independent course free from the dictates of the Soviet Union. His determination to remain independent enabled him to experiment with different styles of communist economics. His strong leadership also contained Yugoslavia's ethnic rivalries. Why might Tito be considered one of the most remarkable figures of the postwar era?

"There can be no independence without an independent foreign policy."
Josip Tito, June 1948

"Let us work as if peace will last a hundred years, but prepare as if war will start tomorrow."
Josip Tito, 1968

Josip Tito was born to a Croatian peasant family in 1892. His attitudes were shaped by his early experiences in Croatia, which included hard work and poverty. His formal education was limited to a few years of elementary school and part-time classes at an apprenticeship school. But Tito had a flair for languages and a love of travel and adventure, and he continued his education on his own.

It was while learning the locksmith trade that Tito became interested in the trade union movement and socialism. At eighteen, he joined a union and the Social Democratic Party of Croatia and Slovenia. When the First World War broke out in 1914, Tito, who had joined the Austro-Hungarian army to serve a mandatory two-year term, accompanied his regiment to the Carpathians to fight the Russians. In 1915, he was captured and detained by the Russian army. The experience gave him the opportunity to witness the Russian Revolution in 1917. It was in Russia that he became familiar with the ideas and writings of Trotsky, Marx, and Lenin.

When Tito returned to Croatia at the end of the war he was a committed communist. His homeland, however, was now united with other Balkan states under the rule of a monarch. Convinced that communism was the best course for Yugoslavia, Tito became an active participant in the Yugoslav Communist Party. He organized unions and encouraged workers to fight for better working and living conditions. By 1928, Tito was one of the leading figures in the party. That same year he was arrested and sentenced to five years of hard labour for his communist activities. In 1929, Yugoslavia became a dictatorship. All political parties were banned, parliament was dissolved, and press censorship was introduced.

Tito emerged from prison even more committed to communism. After his release in 1934, he continued his political activities under various pseudonyms in an effort to escape the notice of the police. In 1937, one of those pseudonyms—Tito—became the name by which the world would know him.

With the German invasion of Yugoslavia in 1941, Tito set about organizing resistance fighters. His ragtag group of partisans not only had to deal with crack German and Italian military forces, but also with the Serbian militia that was run by the German puppet government established in Croatia. Time after time, Tito escaped from overwhelming forces, hiding in the mountains and forests of Yugoslavia where he launched effective guerrilla raids. When the Nazis surrendered on 7 May 1945, Yugoslavia had the distinction of being the only communist nation in Europe to have been liberated without Soviet help.

Tito maintained tight control of the country in the months following the war. Nazi collaborators were rounded up and executed, but Tito was able to contain widespread ethnic hostilities. On 11 November 1945, free elections were held. Tito's popularity helped the Yugoslav Communist Party win a majority. Two weeks later the Constituent Assembly abolished the monarchy and established the Federal People's Republic of Yugoslavia, a communist dictatorship.

Although a communist, Tito resisted Soviet efforts to control Yugoslavia's foreign policy and to intervene in its domestic affairs. He refused to allow the country to become a satellite of the Soviet Union. In 1948, Stalin and Tito quarrelled, causing a formal break in relations. Tito expelled Soviet military advisors and the Soviet Union expelled Yugoslavia from the Cominform. After Stalin's death, Khrushchev tried to woo Yugoslavia back into the Soviet fold. But Yugoslavia, while remaining communist in politics and ideology, preferred to steer a course that was independent of both Cold War superpowers. This allowed it to play a leading role in the nonaligned movement.

When Tito died in 1980, Yugoslavia was prosperous, peaceful, and independent. The Olympic Games in Sarajevo in 1984 were considered a showpiece to mark the nation's entry into the global mainstream. But the optimism that surrounded the games masked deep-seated problems controlled only by Tito's strength of will. Upon his death there was no one of his calibre to take charge. The pent-up pressures of nationalism and political reform were poised, ready to explode.

ethnic conflicts in check through strict rules and regulations. He established a system in which officers in key positions were rotated routinely to prevent any one ethnic group from dominating. He also urged all Yugoslavs to focus their attention and energy on the country's economic development and their own well being. As a result, while there were occasional episodes of violence, Yugoslavia remained relatively calm during Tito's years in power.

POLITICAL CHANGE IN YUGOSLAVIA

After Tito's death in 1980, Yugoslavia's various ethnic and religious groups began raising their nationalist voices and demanding greater autonomy. A deteriorating economy further fuelled their discontent, while a collapsing Communist Party organization was increasingly unable to contain the discord. Within individual groups charismatic leaders began to emerge. The president of the Serbian Republic, Slobodan Milosevic, convinced the Serbs that their interests were not being well served by the Yugoslav federation. In Croatia and Slovenia, reform communists abandoned the old party line in favour of more moderate policies.

The collapse of communism in Poland and the Soviet Union dealt a death blow to the Communist Party in Yugoslavia. In 1990, multi-party elections were held in the republics. In Slovenia, Croatia, Bosnia-Herzegovina, and Macedonia, the communists were defeated by non-communist parties or coalitions. The communists retained power in Serbia and Montenegro, but vocal minorities now held seats in both parliaments. The Yugoslav federation was rapidly disintegrating.

The final breakup of Yugoslavia began in late 1990 when Croatia adopted constitutional reforms proclaiming the republic a sovereign state of the Croats. No mention was made of the 12 per cent of the population that was Serbian. In response, Serbs in Croatia seized control of government facilities, blocked roads, and declared their own ethnic enclaves as autonomous Serb territory. They were supported by the government in Serbia, which applied economic and military pressure on the Croatian government, including the use of the Yugoslav army in Croat-Serb clashes within Croatia. The Serbs demanded that the boundaries of the two republics be redrawn so that Serbian enclaves in Croatia would become part of the Serbian republic.

In June 1991, both Slovenia and Croatia unilaterally declared themselves independent. The Serbian-dominated Yugoslav army attempted to prevent the separations, but they were quickly defeated by the Slovenian forces in a ten-day war. The Yugoslav army retreated into Croatia, where fighting between the Serbs and the Croats intensified. The Yugoslav army was in disarray and was unable to mount a sustained and effective campaign. In the breakaway republics, militias were formed to defend the newly formed nations. Various ethnic communities armed themselves and dug into defensive enclaves. The fighting raged throughout 1991, killing thousands of soldiers and civilians in the slaughter.

SERBIAN OPPOSITION TO THE BREAKUP OF YUGOSLAVIA

The Serbs opposed the breakup of Yugoslavia because they were in a position of power, both politically and militarily. In addition, 25 per cent of the Serbian population was outside of Serbia in the other republics of the nation. If the republics became independent, the Serbs would become minorities in republics dominated by other ethnic groups. The long history of animosity and violence among the various ethnic groups suggested that Serb minorities would face an uncertain future. The government in Serbia

In December 1992, Slobodan Milosevic was returned to power as president of the Serbian Republic with 55 per cent of the vote. The election was monitored by other European countries that reported the process was marred by smear tactics, rigging of electoral lists, and other irregularities.

actively encouraged enclaves of Serbs in the other republics to arm themselves and to use violence to press for their own autonomy.

THE RESPONSE OF THE EUROPEAN COMMUNITY

The European Community was unable to mediate the conflicts in Yugoslavia with any degree of success. Europe was in political chaos. The Cold War had just ended, Eastern European countries were struggling with democracy, and the Soviet Union was

Figure 8.6: Serbian Population in the Yugoslavian Republics During Last Census (1981)

Total Yugoslav Population: 22.4 million
Serbs: 8.1 million (36%)

(millions)

Republic	% Serbs
Serbia	(85)
Croatia	(12)
Bosnia-Herzegovina	(32)
Vojvodina	(54)
Macedonia	(2)
Slovenia	(2)
Kosovo	(13)
Montenegro	(3)

Serbs

Figures in ( ) indicate % Serbs

Source: *Statistical Yearbook of Yugoslavia, 1988*

VOICES

THE CONFLICT IN YUGOSLAVIA

The conflict in Yugoslavia caught many observers off guard. Under Tito Yugoslavia had been a stable and prosperous nation. The diverse ethnic and religious groups had lived in relative harmony. Analysts have questioned what caused the sudden disintegration of a system that appeared to work. As you read these excerpts, consider the reasons each author suggests for the nationalist battles in the former Yugoslavia.

Paul Hockenos

"In Yugoslavia, the violent disintegration of Tito's centralized federal state unleashed a plethora of ultra-nationalist movements. The bitter war that broke out first in Croatia and then in ethnically mixed Bosnia-Herzegovina radicalized the region's many peoples, bringing highly nationalistic, autocratic rulers to power in almost every former republic. The determining characteristic of Yugoslavia's many right-wing ideologies was the nationalism that underpinned the logic of national independence; and, in most cases, nationalist expansion. The war transformed the republics' political cultures into militaristic war cultures, and the governments themselves into virtual dictatorships.

"Yet, as the conflict plunged the south Slavs further into nationalist delirium and economic chaos, markedly more extreme, heavily armed radicals found themselves in positions of power. These extremist groups provided the most vivid example of the way in which tiny radical splinter elements can trigger emotions and movements with far-reaching consequences. Many journalists portrayed the peoples of former Yugoslavia as crazed nationalist zealots, and the conflicts of today as the result of yesterday's hatreds which only the police state had suppressed. But, in fact, the many peoples of the region had lived in relative harmony for over forty years, as friends, neighbors

and often as family. Rather, it was the republics' chauvinistic leaderships and a handful of extremists who successfully manipulated the nationalities' age-old fears of one another, reviving the deep hatreds that flourished prior to 1945."

Paul Hockenos, "Uncivil Society: The Return of the European Right," in Phyllis Bennis and Michel Moushabeck (eds.), Altered States: A Reader in the New World Order *(New York: Olive Branch Press, 1993), p. 159.*

Robin Alison Remington

"For some three decades, Yugoslavs had lived relatively comfortably with the inconsistency implicit in a society that was devoted to participatory, self-managing socialism and dependent on charismatic authority. Before he died in 1980...Tito tried to resolve this 'contradiction'...by spelling out an elaborate power-sharing arrangement in the constitution of 1974....

"...There were three federal players: the party, the government, and the armed forces. On the regional level, eight parties and governments vied with one another and the federal center. In this contest, decision making by consensus gave regional party leaders virtual veto power, while quotas applied to most political jobs undermined any sense of national Yugoslav unity.

"...In short, Tito's successors had inherited a cumbersome political machine that had the unintended consequence of decreasing the federal government's ability to broker solutions among regional politicians who were always tempted to put regional needs above national needs...."

Robin Alison Remington, excerpt from "The Federal Dilemma" is reprinted with permission from Current History *magazine (December 1990). © 1990 Current History, Inc.*

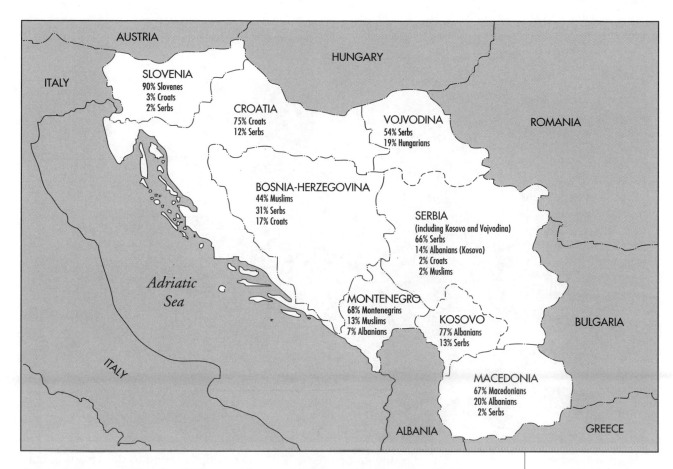

Figure 8.7:
The New States of the Former Yugoslavia, with Ethnic Breakdown Before the Civil War.

disintegrating. Initially, the EC opposed independence for the republics of Yugoslavia, fearing an avalanche of unstable new nations in Europe. However, as it became clear that the armed conflicts would not end without independence, Germany argued that recognition of the new states was the only course of action. Still, other members of the EC, particularly France and Britain, were reluctant to go that far. With dissension within the organization, it was obvious that the EC could not bring about peace in Yugoslavia. Europe now turned to the United Nations for help.

BOSNIA-HERZEGOVINA

The Serbian government had failed to prevent the disintegration of

Yugoslavia and had won only token protection for Serbs in Slovenia and Croatia. The Serbs were determined to be successful in the next stage of the conflict, the separation of Bosnia-Herzegovina.

In February 1992, the population of Bosnia was 44 per cent Muslim, 31 per cent Serbian, and 17 per cent Croatian, with the remainder being of other ethnic backgrounds. The Muslims and Croats voted overwhelmingly in favour of independence in a referendum in February 1992. Unwilling to see the largest group of Serbs outside of Serbia become minorities in a new country, the government of the Serbian republic launched a full-scale assault on Bosnia. Serb forces moved into Serbian enclaves in Bosnia-Herzegovina in an attempt to eliminate all Muslims and Croats from these

Throughout the former Yugoslavia there are scenes of devastation, like this church in a once-quiet neighbourhood in Sarajevo.

regions. Other ethnic groups responded to this policy of **ethnic cleansing** with similar brutality. Civilians of all backgrounds became targets for military offensives.

The EC recognized the independence of Bosnia-Herzegovina on 5 April 1992. The United Nations demanded an end to the violence, but the demands were ignored. Both the UN and the EC imposed harsh economic sanctions against Serbia. UN peacekeeping forces were established in Bosnia to keep the airport in Sarajevo operational and to protect the few civilian relief shipments that were reaching the war-torn region.

Throughout 1992 the fighting in Bosnia escalated. Cease-fires were negotiated but they lasted only a few days. By September, Yugoslavia (now the combined republics of Serbia and Montenegro) was expelled from the United Nations.

By the spring of 1993, Serb forces had continued to make inroads into Muslim territory. The security of the UN peacekeeping forces stationed in the region was threatened. Still, the West was reluctant to launch any military intervention, preferring to wait for

> "A large number of people have died. The Bosnian Muslims and the Bosnian Croats are at one another's throats. They are using artillery, rockets, mortars and small arms. They are in a life-or-death struggle."
>
> *Lieutenant-Colonel Bob Stewart, British peacekeeper, in the* Toronto Star, *25 April, 1993.*

a more permanent resolution of the situation. But a peace proposal that would have divided Bosnia into three ethnic regions was rejected by Bosnian Muslim leaders.

August 1993 marked the beginning of a long-term game of cat and mouse between NATO and the Serbs. Serbian offensives were met with NATO ultimatums to withdraw. Under threat of military retaliation, the Serbs complied, only to reclaim the territory later on. In February 1994, NATO launched its first combat mission since its inception in 1949 with a limited bombing raid against a Serbian stronghold. Throughout it all, UN peacekeeping forces tried to fulfil their dangerous mission of protecting civilians and keeping the supply lines open. UN

personnel frequently found themselves the targets of attack.

Throughout 1994 and well into 1995 the conflict continued. No peace proposal satisfied all groups as each

United Nations relief and peacekeeping operations are continuously under threat from hostilities in the region.

"Countries don't give their troops to the UN in trust to be killed trying to implement a really lousy cease-fire agreement arranged by a bunch of diplomats and politicians. That's what is happening in Yugoslavia."

Major-General Lewis Mackenzie, former officer in command of UN forces in Bosnia, in the Toronto Star, *30 January 1993*

one was considered to give too much territory to a rival group. A history of hostility combined with the recent atrocities created an intense atmosphere of mistrust and tension throughout the region.

In Review

1. a) Why was Yugoslavia able to retain its independence from the Soviet Union?
   b) To what extent was the disintegration of the Soviet Union a factor in the disintegration of Yugoslavia? Explain your answer.
2. Was Tito an effective leader in Yugoslavia? Explain your answer.
3. What are the root causes of the turmoil and conflict in Yugoslavia today?
4. a) Why was the European Community concerned about the breakup of Yugoslavia?
   b) What action did it take?
5. a) What is the role of the United Nations in Bosnia today?
   b) Do you think the UN has achieved any degree of success?
   c) What role do you think international organizations should play in conflicts like that in Bosnia?

Summary

The twentieth century has been a remarkable era of turmoil and change in Europe. For most of the century the continent has been divided by war, either through the direct military confrontations of the World Wars or through the political hostilities of the Cold War. At the end of the twentieth century Europe has entered a new era.

In Western Europe, the European Union promises greater political harmony and economic prosperity. For the nations of Eastern Europe, a more difficult path lies ahead as they try to rebuild their political institutions and their economies following the demise of communism. Amidst the new order in Europe, however, ethnic rivalries continue to be a source of tension and potential violence in some regions.

MAKING CONNECTIONS

1. Outline the important forces that shaped both Eastern and Western Europe in the second half of the twentieth century.

2. Describe the ways in which the European Union integrates its member countries. Consider social, political, and economic ties.

3. Compare political and economic conditions in Eastern and Western Europe since the Second World War. Use a chart to organize your ideas.

DEVELOPING YOUR VOICE

4. In 1991, Belgium's foreign minister, Mark Eyskens, remarked that Europe "is an economic giant, a political dwarf, and a military worm."
   a) What do you suppose Eyskens meant by this comment?
   b) What might be the implications for the rest of the world if this comment is accurate?

5. Do you think that the nations of Europe should form a United States of Europe? Give reasons for your position.

6. Design a logo for the European Union. In a paragraph, describe the symbols you have created and give the reasons for your choices.

RESEARCHING THE ISSUES

7. Research one country in Europe, focusing on how it has responded to either the creation of the European Union or the disintegration of the Soviet Union.

8. Research how five individual nations in Europe have responded to one of the issues below. Before you begin, prepare a research organizer in which you list topics and subtopics that may be important to the issue. Present your conclusions to the rest of the class.
   - terrorism
   - the environment
   - refugees
   - nuclear weapons
   - AIDS
   - illegal drugs.

9. How successful has an integrated European community been? Compile statistical information to document the economic changes since 1990. Determine whether or not the expansion of this trading bloc has been beneficial to the member countries.

VIEWPOINTS

ISSUE: WILL THE EUROPEAN UNION BECOME AN ECONOMIC SUPERPOWER?

The creation of the European Union and the collapse of communism in Eastern Europe has created considerable debate over the role of Europe in the new world order. Some observers argue that Europe could become a major power on the world stage. Economics professor Séamus O'Cléireacáin supports the view that the strength of a single European economy combined with the opportunities presented in eastern Europe will lead to a wealthy and influential super state. Other analysts disagree. Journalist William Drozdiak argues that European companies, buffeted by government subsidies, will be unable to compete successfully on the economic stage of the new world order.

Read each of these viewpoints carefully, then complete an Argument Analysis and Evaluation Summary for each reading.

Séamus O'Cléireacáin

"Just as the European Community's (EC) eight-year effort passed the halfway stage on the way to 1992, the collapse of the last great European imperial power, the Soviet empire, cast the Community's efforts at its own construction in a new light. German unification and the resurgence of democracy in Eastern and Central Europe have not only introduced the need to create new political and security architectures for intra-European and Atlantic relations, but they have altered as well the role of the EC in the international system, placing it on the brink of transformation from a regional to an economic superpower....

"As member states fashion a more assertive EC, superpower status is made more likely by the emergence of new security arrangements in Europe which place greater emphasis on the economic and political, rather than military, dimensions of this security. At the same time, the Community is involved in five important areas of policy development, all of which contribute to its leadership role: (1) completion of the EC's internal market; (2) the EC-European Free Trade Agreement (EFTA) creation of a European Economic Space (EES); (3) new ties with Eastern and Central Europe; (4) German unification; and (5) Economic and Monetary Union (EMU)....

"It may be argued that the roots of future greatness lie in the five current enterprises in which the EC is now engaged, and in the importance that a changed external environment gives to these efforts. Three of these areas of development—the 1992 program, German unification, and EMU—will strengthen the economic union if they prove successful. The other two —EES and new ties with Eastern and Central Europe—could provide the economic union leverage in advancing its already considerable economic influence even further in the international system....

"The program to complete the EC's internal market was conceived during an era...characterized by double-digit unemployment and the... failure of Community industry to compete with the United States and Japan in any areas save limited, niche markets. As a defensive reaction to its slipping global competitiveness, the EC was not considered a likely candidate for the status of an economic superpower. The promise of the 1992 program was one of greater Community competitiveness, faster economic growth, and more jobs. Original estimates of the effects of completing the internal market are now considered underestimates. If the 1992 program raises the EC growth rate permanently by a full percentage point, living standards will triple over the life expectancy of the

Community's citizens rather than doubling as at present.

"In addition to these internal effects, the 1992 program promises to increase the bargaining power of the EC in the international economic system by providing Brussels with the ability to project a more sharply articulated image. Completion of the internal market offers the prospect of 'free circulation' of goods and services. Goods imported into the EC from the rest of the world could be transshipped without hindrance anywhere in the Community. 'Free circulation' will present the rest of the world trading system with a common EC commercial policy. As the dwindling policy gaps in the unified commerce are closed, the 1992 program will provide EC trading partners with a more coherent, unified commercial policy that will be projected outward onto the global trading system....

"Currently, trade with Eastern and Central Europe accounts for less than 4 per cent of extra-EC trade. Some forecasts suggest that this trade will...replace the United States as the Community's second most important export market. Trade may be expected to grow rapidly with the advent of market economies, infrastructure investments, direct private foreign investment, aid from the new European Bank for Reconstruction and Development (EBRD), and the second wave of bilateral trade agreements between the EC and individual countries....

"In the next wave of trade relations with Eastern and Central Europe, two distinct processes are now in motion. First, limited partnerships with Bulgaria, Czechoslovakia, and Romania may be upgraded to full trade and economic cooperation agreements....

"Second, trade and economic cooperation agreements may pave the way for a new class of associated membership agreements announced by the EC in August 1990. While these do not necessarily carry a presumption of eventual full membership and are conditional on political and economic reform, they offer aid, eventual free trade, and entry into the EES. Likely candidates for early associated member status are Czechoslovakia, Hungary, and Poland....

"These new economic relationships will pro-
duce few transitional difficulties for the 1992 program. In particular, new export-oriented investments in Eastern and Central Europe will not be allowed to disrupt EC markets. Industries facing structural damage induced by the 1992 program may even find that openings into Eastern and Central Europe promise to make this transition easier for them....

"Finally, the choice of currency in which to express capitalization of the EBRD represents a further indicator of the growing international status of the EC. The choice between capitalization in dollars and in the European Currency Unit (ECU) pitted the United States against the Community. The choice of the ECU signifies an important break from an earlier era of postwar, multilateral lending agencies. The EBRD is the first, within this family of institutions, where the United States does not have a veto....

"For the United States, the transformation underway in the EC's role presents a challenge. While the role of the EC as a regional power is central to American efforts at encouraging political and economic liberalization in Eastern and Central Europe, the US may not yet have fully come to terms with the prospect of a more assertive EC in the global economic system... Contradictions may be expected to emerge within the American policy-making establishment between the Europe-oriented wing accustomed to viewing the Community as its main ally in fostering change in Eastern and Central Europe, and those charged with dealing with the EC as a potential economic superpower on the wider stage of world economic and political affairs. Although the American ability to influence the policies of this European superpower may be expected to decline, global system management would be made easier by the presence of a coherent EC-centered European perspective, provided the US is prepared to accept further sharing of its leadership position."

An abridged version of "Long-Term Implications of the Unified European Market: Birth of an Economic Superpower?" by Séamus O'Cléireacáin, Mediterranean Quarterly, *Fall 1990. Copyright © 1990*, Mediterranean Quarterly. *Reprinted by permission of Duke University Press, Durham, North Carolina.*

William Drozdiak

"The European Community (EC) [has entered] a brave new world that many of its movers and shakers believe will create an era of unparalleled prosperity and breathtaking historical change.

"On Jan. 1, 1993, all national borders [tumbled] between the 12 member states...creating a single market that will allow their 340 million citizens to travel and change jobs, invest their money and sell their products as freely as Americans can within their own country.

"Even more ambitious plans will follow. By the end of the decade the German mark, English pound, French franc, and Italian lira may become as obsolete as the Edsel. A single currency, known as the 'ECU' and managed by a European federal reserve, would replace all those assorted currencies.

"That, in turn, is expected to build irresistible momentum toward a single European economic policy that would inevitably require full political union. National governments would pool their sovereignty and elected leaders would make all important decisions at a single, European level.

"Those remarkable goals, coupled with the democratic revolution that swept Eastern Europe, have infused Western European countries with a sense of dynamism and ambition that they have lacked since World War II. With the collapse of the Soviet empire and troubled economic conditions confronting America after the profligacy of the Reagan era, Europe has suddenly emerged as the darling of think tankers and moneymen alike, the land of golden opportunity in the 1990s.

"But is it, really?

"Since the Persian Gulf crisis erupted in August 1990, a more sober assessment of Europe's potential has been taking place. Iraq's seizure of Kuwait again demonstrated how both Western and Eastern Europe have become precariously dependent on oil and gas sources in politically unstable regions....Sustained turmoil in any of those areas—coming on the heels of worldwide economic slowdown—would certainly slash growth projections and transform a limitless horizon of affluence into a gloomy scenario of high inflation and high unemployment.

"Such fears are not merely hypothetical; in Europe, it has happened before. In 1972, after a period of steady economic expansion and Britain's entry into the European Community, the EC's leaders agreed to a timetable for an economic and monetary union that was supposed to be achieved by the end of that decade. But a year later, war broke out in the Middle East and an oil embargo sent European governments scrambling to salvage their economies and electoral prospects. The meticulous agenda for European unity in 1980 became a shambles and was not resurrected until recently. Indeed, the history of European integration has shown that the member states make important progress during good times but experience trouble reconciling their myriad national interests during periods of economic downturn....

"Europe dithered while the United States mobilized the troops and firepower to stop Iraqi President Saddam Hussein after he kidnapped Kuwait and turned his gaze toward Saudi Arabia. It was another painful reminder that despite its clout as a leading commercial power, Europe is still not prepared to act decisively and quickly to protect its own security and economic interests. The Gulf crisis has shown, says Belgium's Foreign Minister Mark Eyskens, that Europe 'is an economic giant, a political dwarf and a military worm.'...

"There are other troubling developments that threaten to derail Europe's pretensions of becoming a dominant political and economic power around the world.

"The tremendous difficulties facing Eastern European countries and the Soviet Union in transforming state-run systems into market economies and altering the work habits and consumer instincts of their populations will require massive and sustained assistance from their Western neighbors.

"Investing enough hard cash to rebuild those economies is a big part of the problem, but only part. Increasingly, Western business and political leaders stress that incorporating the economies of the East bloc and Soviet Union will require an infusion of technological, financial, and management talent that is likely to be focused on the integration of Western European economies for most of the decade.

"Still, the EC countries know that they have no other choice but to make this massive investment of money, talent and attention to help the East. For if they allowed those economies to collapse, the material deprivations would drive much of the population toward the West in search of food, work, and shelter....

"Although the immigrants might provide a new source of cheap labor—and, indeed, high labor costs are a central problem for European countries trying to compete with the United States and Japan on world markets—they would also be a serious drain on the generous social welfare benefits, such as six-week paid vacations and subsidized medical care, that are considered sacrosanct in Europe.

"Besides the problem of the East and its preoccupation with the process of integration, Western Europe will also need to undergo important economic reforms.

"For too long, many European firms enjoyed the cozy protection of national governments that were willing to subsidize losses and build barriers to competition because they could not tolerate the political costs of plant shutdowns and job losses. A key question now, as global economic challenges grow more intense, is whether European companies can learn to survive on their own in an open continental market—and world markets—without such aids....

"Despite such daunting hurdles to the creation of a dynamic and united economy, the optimists believe that Europeans realize they can surmount these challenges only by further pooling their sovereignty and their resources. The EC ex-

ecutive commission is touting a study claiming that the introduction of a single currency by itself will create efficiencies worth $130 billion to European companies each year, an amount equal to the entire gross national product of the Netherlands. With the help of such efficiencies, and a big, prosperous market at home, the EC looks to a day when its products and services compete successfully with the best from Japan and the United States....

"The pessimists, however, can point to the collapse of worldwide trade talks in Brussels as fresh evidence that Western Europe is not yet ready to exchange the security of relatively closed economic borders for the efficiencies of consolidation and the possibilities of competing more successfully for business around the world.

"Those talks failed largely because France and Germany would not abandon agricultural subsidies that allow their farmers to sell surplus cereals around the world below the cost of production. And should that stalemate continue, Europe—like the rest of the world—is likely to drift toward protectionism, shunning trade with Asia and North America and increasingly turning its attentions inward...."

William Drozdiak, "Europe's Pretensions Go Back on the Continental Shelf," The Washington Post National Weekly Edition, *February 4-10, 1991. Copyright © 1991,* The Washington Post.

ANALYSIS AND EVALUATION

Refer to the Argument Analysis and Evaluation Guide on page viii.

1. Using the Argument Analysis and Evaluation Guide, compare the readings by O'Cléireacain and Drozdiak. On what do they agree? On what do they disagree?

2. Decide which of the viewpoints you tend to support and explain why. Be sure to use specific information from this textbook, the readings and other sources to support your position.

3. State and support your position on the issue: "Will the European Union become an economic superpower?"

CHAPTER NINE

Africa: After Independence

"Direct political imperialism may have come to an end with the hauling down of colonial flags and the disbandment of colonial armies, but the economic imperialism continues to exist; it appears even to be strengthening its hold and purpose."

S. Moroney, ed., Africa, *Vol. 2 (Facts on File, 1989).*

"The condition of sub-Saharan Africa—'the Third World's Third World,' as it has been described—is… desperate…. Recent reports upon the continent's plight are extraordinarily gloomy, describing Africa as 'a human and environmental disaster area.'"

Paul Kennedy, Preparing for the Twenty-first Century, *(Toronto: HarperCollins, 1993).*

Left: Crowds cheer Nelson Mandela

❖ OVERVIEW

Nationalism swept across the African continent following the Second World War. One by one, the European colonies in Africa launched campaigns for independence. For some it was a peaceful transition; for others the road to independence was one of violent confrontation. In 1945 when the United Nations was founded, only four members were African states. By the end of the twentieth century, forty-six African nations were represented in the UN.

The African continent is a vast land of over 700 million people in almost fifty nations. Each has had its own unique experiences. Ethiopia, which has been independent for thousands of years, faces one of the gravest economic crises in the world. South Africa, a former colonial territory, has experienced a different kind of turmoil as the black majority has struggled to obtain equality in a society dominated by white rule. These two case studies provide a sample of the political, social, cultural, and economic diversity in Africa.

coast of the continent for hundreds of years, relying on African traders to bring them the ivory, spices, minerals, and slaves they sought. All this changed during the era of European imperialism when the nations of Western Europe extended their authority throughout Africa. In the process, local economies and traditional African cultural, social, and political systems were transformed to meet the needs of the imperial powers.

Between 1870 and 1914, most of the continent of Africa fell under European control. Britain, France, Portugal, Belgium, Spain, Italy, and Germany partitioned Africa in their scramble for territory. The motives behind colonial expansion were three-fold. The European powers wanted to establish new supplies of natural resources to fuel their developing industries. In return, they expected Africa would provide an additional export market for their manufactured goods. Ultimately, a prosperous economy enhanced a nation's international power and prestige.

Colonial expansion was also fuelled by the atmosphere of rivalry that existed among European nations. Colonial holdings symbolized international power and provided military outposts to help the European empires maintain their positions in the world order.

The notion of **racial superiority** was an underlying motive behind European imperialism. Many people in Europe believed it was their obligation to spread Western civilization around the world.

FOCUS QUESTIONS

1. What were the conditions in colonial Africa before the Second World War?

2. What factors led to the colonies of Africa gaining independence?

3. What are some benefits and problems resulting from independence?

4. How is Ethiopia dealing with recent political and economic problems?

5. How did the people of South Africa end apartheid and white rule?

THE COLONIZATION OF AFRICA

Europeans knew little of the interior of Africa before the middle of the nineteenth century. They had plied the

THE EFFECTS OF IMPERIALISM

The imperial powers controlled all aspects of life in their colonies. The economy, government, law, education. and social institutions were molded to conform to Western standards and values. In some cases, large numbers of Europeans settled in the colonies, thereby reinforcing the imperial power's control and changing the face of Africa forever.

The colonial powers regulated all economic activities in their African territories. Cash crops destined for European markets were grown on sprawling plantations. Mining and logging operations provided an abundance of valuable raw materials for the industrial processing plants of Europe. Ownership and profits from all economic activities were the exclusive domain of the Europeans while most of the labour was supplied by the Africans, who worked long hours under harsh conditions for little pay. Much of what they earned was paid to the colonial government in the form of taxes. These were used to pay for the soldiers and administrators sent out from the imperial country and for roads, railways, and other facilities that were primarily for the benefit of the colonists.

The Europeans did not value the traditions and customs of African societies. Instead, they imposed their own beliefs through schools, courts, businesses, and government. The minds and cultures of Africans were subjected to colonial domination. Many Africans, impressed by the wealth and power of the Europeans, rejected their traditional lifestyles in favour of Western ways. Colonialism led to a breakdown of traditional African values and village life. African ideas of identity and nation were replaced with vastly different European concepts.

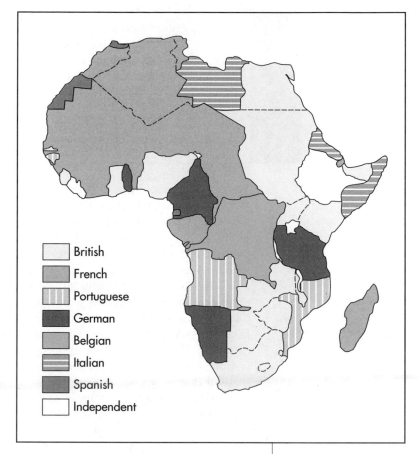

British
French
Portuguese
German
Belgian
Italian
Spanish
Independent

Figure 9.1:
Imperialism in Africa, 1914

THE RISE OF AFRICAN NATIONALISM

The driving force for African nationalism stemmed from opposition to colonial rule. Since the early days of colonial domination there had been sporadic revolts and local organized resistance in many colonies. Most of the leadership at this level came from local chiefs. But sustained and effective opposition to the powerful European interests required a different kind of leadership. Ironically, the colonial powers themselves provided the training for a new generation of African leaders.

During the 1930s and 1940s, large numbers of African intellectuals, writers, artists, and professionals returned home from universities in France, Britain, the United States, and other

Leaders who followed a peaceful path to independence include Nnamdi Azikiwe in Nigeria, Dr. Hastings Banda in Malawi, Antonio Neto in Angola, Jomo Kenyatta in Kenya, Kwame Nkrumah in Ghana, Julius Nyerere in Tanzania, and Leopold Senghor in Senegal.

Western countries. Armed with a Western education and experienced in the ways of Western culture, this new generation was prepared to lead their countries to independence. Some members of this select group emerged as leaders of a host of newly independent states after the Second World War. Other nationalist leaders prepared for their roles through the colonial military or police forces. Key personnel were frequently trained abroad. There they learned European military practices—methods they would later apply against the Europeans. Thus the colonial system played an important part in the events that ultimately led to its own destruction.

From 1945 through the 1950s, African leaders emerged at the head of political parties and armed resistance groups. These organizations united and directed the actions of a widespread and diverse membership. Political organizations like the Rassemblement Democratique Africain, founded in 1946 in the French colonies, and insurgent groups like the Mau Mau in

British Kenya, which was active between 1952 and 1960, challenged colonial rule.

In 1963, the **Organization for African Unity** (OAU) was established at Addis Ababa in Ethiopia. The goals of the organization were to promote African unity and solidarity, to co-ordinate political, economic, defence, and social policies of all members, and to eliminate colonialism in Africa.

INTERNATIONAL SUPPORT FOR INDEPENDENCE

Strong leadership and popular support at home were not enough to ensure the success of Africa's many nationalist movements. African independence needed the support in principle of the United Nations. Perhaps even more importantly, however, it needed the support of the two superpowers, the United States and the Soviet Union.

The United States had both a philosophical and an economic motive for supporting African nationalism. Having staged a revolution for its own independence from the British Empire in 1776, the US was naturally sympathetic to the African colonies' desire to shed the chains of colonialism. They also recognized that newly independent countries would be interested in establishing economic relationships with the US. These relationships could provide American industries with valuable raw materials and new export markets.

The Soviet Union had its own motives for supporting African independence. Philosophically, the USSR supported liberation movements. They also saw independence as a way of weakening the European powers and counteracting the spread of American influence. Without the support of the United States and the Soviet Union it would have been more difficult for

Among those African leaders schooled in the military or police were Idi Amin of Uganda, Jean Bokassa of Central African Republic, Mohamed Siad Barre of Somalia, Sese Seko Mobutu of Zaire, and Ibrahim Babangida and Yaukubu Gowon of Nigeria.

African states to break free from European domination.

Within Europe itself there was considerable support for African independence. The African colonies had made tremendous contributions to the European countries during the Second World War. Many Europeans felt that the reward for such support and loyalty should be independence. These sentiments were reinforced by a growing trend towards more liberal attitudes that favoured nationalist ambitions. Yet in Europe, too, the promotion of African nationalism was not without self-interest. The high cost of postwar reconstruction meant few resources could be spared for the colonies. In addition, Africa was facing severe social and economic problems. The Second World War had stripped the European powers of the economic and military strength needed to enforce their rule over their overseas possessions.

INDEPENDENCE

The imperialist nations of Europe professed to support African independence. Yet racism continued to play a role in colonial policymaking. The Western nations still viewed themselves as a "civilizing" force for African peoples. From their point of view, **self-determination** should be granted to the colonies through a slow and deliberate transition. The African nationalists had a different timetable, however. They blamed colonial rule for the

Figure 9.2: The Organization for African Unity

Algeria*	Gambia	Nigeria*
Angola	Ghana*	Rwanda*
Benin*	Guinea*	Saharan Republic+
Botswana	Guinea-Bissau	São Tomé and Principe
Burkina Faso*	Ivory Coast*	Senegal*
Burundi*	Kenya	Seychelles
Cameroon*	Lesotho	Sierra Leone*
Cape Verde	Liberia*	Somalia*
Central African Republic*	Libya*	Sudan*
Chad*	Madagascar*	Swaziland
Comoros	Malawi	Tanzania*
Congo	Mali*	Togo*
Djibouti	Mauritania*	Tunisia*
Egypt*	Mauritius	Uganda*
Equatorial Guinea	Morocco*+	Zambia
Ethiopia*	Mozambique	Zaïre
Gabon*	Niger*	Zimbabwe

* Original members
+ The Saharan Republic was admitted in 1984. Morocco resigned in protest.

myriad social and economic ills that plagued the continent. One way or another, they were determined to regain Africa for the Africans.

THE TRANSITION TO INDEPENDENCE

There were two very different roads to independence: through peaceful negotiation or violent confrontation. The

"As long as we are ruled by others we shall lay our mistakes at their door, and our sense of responsibility will remain dulled. Freedom brings responsibilities, and our experience can be enriched only by the acceptance of those responsibilities."

Dr. Kwame Nkrumah, first prime minister of Ghana, 1953

Kwame Nkrumah led the former British colony of Gold Coast to independence as the country of Ghana.

"The wind of change is blowing through this continent."

British prime minister Harold Macmillan, 1960

"It is no ordinary wind, but a raging hurricane."

Dr. Kwame Nkrumah, prime minister of Ghana, 1960

first peaceful transition took place in the British colony of Gold Coast. A group of African lawyers and business-people formed the first nationalist movement in 1947. Called the National Gold Coast Convention, its leader, Kwame Nkrumah, was a political activist educated in the United States. Inspired by India's Mahatma Gandhi, Nkrumah organized nonviolent protests and boycotts against British rule. Eventually he was jailed for treason, but this only served to elevate Nkrumah to hero status. In elections to a new legislative assembly in 1951, Nkrumah's party won thirty-four of thirty-eight available seats. Bowing to the public's support of Nkrumah, Britain released the jailed leader and asked him to form a new government. For six years the Gold Coast existed under limited self-rule. In 1957, Britain withdrew from the colony altogether. The new country of Ghana served as a model for peaceful independence movements across the continent.

Not all transitions were peaceful, however. A number of colonies erupted in violence and bloodshed during their drives for independence. In Kenya, the secret society known as the Mau Mau launched violent attacks against colonial institutions. A war of independence raged in Algeria be-tween 1954 and 1962. The Belgian Congo (now Zaïre) was granted inde-pendence in 1960 but civil war erupted almost immediately. Racial violence flared in the colony of Southern Rhodesia before it gained indepen-dence as Zimbabwe in 1980. Guerrilla warfare broke out against Portuguese forces in Angola until Portugal granted that colony independence in 1974. Uganda gained independence in 1962, but the new nation was plagued by famine and violence; conditions only became more dangerous and chaotic during the tyrannical rule of Idi Amin from 1971 to 1985.

VOICES

AFRICAN DEMOCRACY

Julius Nyerere became the first president of the newly independent nation of Tanzania in 1964. He believed that democracy in Africa must be fundamentally different from Western concepts of democracy. Nyerere introduced a one-party system of government in Tanzania based on the principles of socialism, but held elections at regular intervals. He was always re-elected as president with a substantial majority until his resignation in 1985. In the following passage, Nyerere explains why he believes that Western democracy could not be strictly applied in Africa. As you read Nyerere's comments, consider to what extent you agree or disagree with his concept of democracy.

Julius Nyerere

"Democracy is another essential characteristic of a socialist society. For the people's equality must be reflected in the political organization; everyone must be an equal participant in the government of his society. Whatever devices are used to implement this principle, the people (meaning all the members of the society equally) must be sovereign, and they must be able to exert their sovereignty without causing a break-down of the law and order, or of the administration in their society. There must, in other words, be some mechanisms by which the people exert their will peacefully, and achieve changes in the laws which govern them; they must be able to change the personnel in positions of leadership within the framework of the normal workings of the social system. It is difficult to see how this could be achieved without the existence of some system of free elections if the society is so large that direct democracy (the direct government by all the people) is impossible. But elections are not the beginning and end of democracy. The freedom of the people to choose

their own representatives is important, but it is equally important that the people's representatives should possess the freedom and the power to exert effective control over those sectors of the social organization for which they have been given responsibility. And none of these things is possible unless every other aspect of society—its economic, social and legal organization—is such as to emphasize and serve man's equality. A political democracy which exists in a society of gross economic inequalities, or of social inequality, is at best imperfect, and at worst a hollow sham....

"In 1965 Tanzania adopted its own form of democracy—we rejected the Western model and said it was not appropriate for our circumstances despite the fact that all our constitutional development had until then been based on it. We looked at different democratic systems round the world, and studied the work of different thinkers, and we asked ourselves two questions. First, what is the purpose of democratic systems? And second, what are the conditions of Tanzania, and what special problems face the country? Then we worked out a system of one-party Government which seemed to us to include the essential elements of democracy at the same time as it provided for unity and strength in Government, and took account of our poverty, our size, our traditions, and our aspirations. The resultant constitution is not perfect; but it suits us better than any system operating elsewhere, and we believe that it safeguards the people's sovereignty at the same time as it enables the effective and strong Government so essential at this stage of our development."

From Julius K. Nyerere, Freedom and Socialism *(Dar es Salaam: Oxford University Press, 1968), pp. 5, 19. © Julius K. Nyerere 1968.*

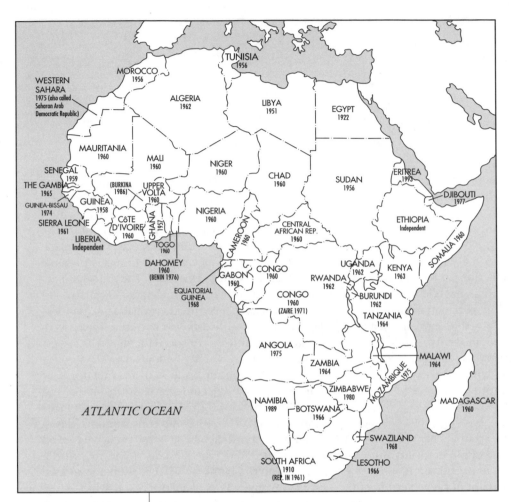

Figure 9.3:
Africa, 1985. Dates of independence and new names included.

ized key industries. Yet they lacked the management expertise to run state-owned operations successfully and many of these businesses quickly failed. Soon the optimism disappeared. Today most Africans are poorer in material terms than they were at the time of independence. Of the twenty-five poorest countries in the world, seventeen are in Africa.

One of the most serious problems African nations face is in agriculture. For years farmers over-used the land in an effort to feed the rapidly growing population. The excessive grazing and planting caused soil erosion. Forests were laid bare as the trees were removed to provide fuel wood for heating and cooking. Combined, these factors led to **desertification**. Recurring drought created even greater loss of vegetation.

The lack of fertile land led to widespread food shortages. In the 1970s and 1980s, famine plagued twenty-two countries and it was estimated that 70 per cent of Africans did not have enough food to eat. Countless numbers of people died of starvation. Malnutrition left those who survived less productive and more vulnerable to disease.

Despite the widespread food shortages, cash crops for export remained the foundation of the African economy. Countries relied on these exports to

ECONOMIC CHALLENGES

Optimism for the future in Africa's newly independent countries was high in the 1960s and 1970s. Many leaders believed that rapid industrialization was the key to economic success. To achieve this goal, many countries took control of their resources and national-

Among the fifty founding members of the United Nations in 1945, only four—Egypt, Ethiopia, Liberia, and South Africa—were African states. By 1992, forty-six African nations sat in the General Assembly, constituting over 25 per cent of UN membership.

generate foreign currency to buy everything from energy supplies and pharmaceuticals to machines and military equipment. But prices for cash crops are highly variable; a modest drop in demand can cause the market price of a crop to plummet. Today there is a growing recognition of the need to move away from this traditional dependence on the exporting of primary products.

Economic problems are intensified by the fact that many African nations must import food to deal with their domestic food shortages. These imports have increased as desertification has spread. As a result, many countries have amassed even greater foreign debt in their efforts to maintain the food supply. Ultimately, the solution to Africa's food shortages lies in long-term policies that promote sustainable development.

POLITICS IN INDEPENDENT AFRICA

Many of Africa's new nations adopted some form of parliamentary democracy once independence was achieved. Yet the people were often ill-prepared for democratic rule. As colonies these nations had been ruled by highly centralized administrations that were anything but democratic. Thus the people had little experience with governing under a western democratic system.

Politics was often made more difficult by the ethnic diversity within countries. When boundaries were carved out by the imperial powers, little consideration was given to traditional ethnic and cultural divisions and territories. These borders often split cultures among different colonies and placed different ethnic groups

Soil erosion leads to desertification. To help combat the problem, erosion barriers are being built.

VOICES

THE CAUSES OF UNDERDEVELOPMENT

There are a variety of opinions that explain the lack of development and continued poverty in Africa. Many people blame the impact of European colonialism for the conditions in Africa today. Others argue that those countries with closer colonial ties are actually the more prosperous nations. Still others blame not the political imperialism of the past, but the economic imperialism that replaced it. Read each of these excerpts and consider which, in your opinion, has the most merit.

Yuli M. Voronstov

"A serious and comprehensive analysis of the economic difficulties prevailing in Africa indicates that their real causes are rooted in the ills inherited from colonialism, in the merciless plunder and selfish policies pursued by the colonial powers towards African countries. Today there is an abundance of studies demonstrating convincingly that the root causes of the African crisis originated in colonial times...."

Yuli M. Voronstov, in a statement to the United Nations General Assembly, 27 May 1986

Carlos Rangel

"The Third World's poorest countries are not those that have had longer and closer exchanges with the West, but, significantly, those whose exchanges had been weaker and shorter—Ethiopia, for instance.... In sharp contrast is Nigeria, where, prior to 1890, there was no cultivation of cocoa, peanuts or cotton. Due to the British development and commercialization of their cultivation, however, Nigeria today exports an enormous proportion of the world supply of these products."

Reprinted by permission of Transaction Publishers. Excerpt from Third World Ideology and Western Reality *by Carlos Rangel. Copyright © 1986. All rights reserved.*

Michael Parenti

"In a word, the Third World is not 'underdeveloped' but overexploited. The gap between rich and poor nations is not due to the 'neglect' of the latter by the former as has often been claimed.... [T]he gap between rich and poor only widens because investments in the Third World are not designed to develop the capital resources of the poor nations but to enrich the Western investors...."

Michael Parenti, The Sword and the Dollar: Imperialism, Revolution and the Arms Race *(St. Martin's Press, 1989).*

under common rule. The new governments were frequently faced with the task of trying to unite diverse cultural groups that may have had little or no attachment to the nation state.

Political instability frequently resulted in military **coups** in which governments were overthrown by force. The new military regimes promised to end political conflict and economic instability through rigid discipline and control. Yet these governments proved to be ineffective in improving the quality of life. Military rule has in turn often been followed by revolution or civil war as dissatisfied social groups and political factions reacted against repressive regimes.

AFRICA'S FUTURE

The people of Africa can be both optimistic and pessimistic about the future. The population is young and has yet to reach its full potential. Literacy rates are rising as spending on education increases. More opportunities are available for people seeking secondary and higher education. The number of health care facilities, staffed by well-trained local professionals, is increasing and more people are receiving medical care. As a result, infant mortality rates, while still high, are declining and life expectancies are rising. However, these positive achievements have added to a growing population problem. In 1994, Africa's population was 701 million; by 2010 it is expected to exceed 1.1 billion. Rapid population growth creates greater demand for health care and social services. Education costs rise annually because of the growing number of children. The need for more food increases the stress placed upon already fragile ecosystems. Growing populations place pressure on the basic infrastructure of water supplies, transportation facilities, and other essential services.

Africa is rich with abundant natural resources. The continent produces large volumes of chromium, plutonium, manganese, and cobalt, and there are still vast mineral resources to be explored. But the mining industry is

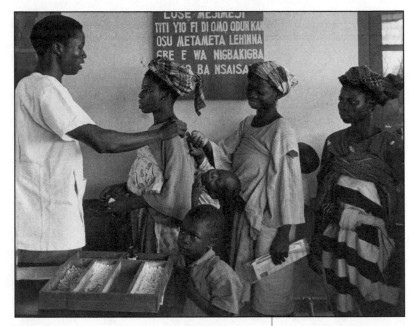

Post-natal health clinics have helped to reduce the infant mortality rate in much of Africa.

primarily foreign-owned. The raw materials are often exported for processing, thereby limiting the opportunities for economic growth in Africa itself.

In Mozambique, 3000 foreign technicians earned $180 million in 1991—three times the total salaries of 100 000 Mozambican civil service employees.

Figure 9.4: Age Pyramids, Canada and Nigeria, 1992

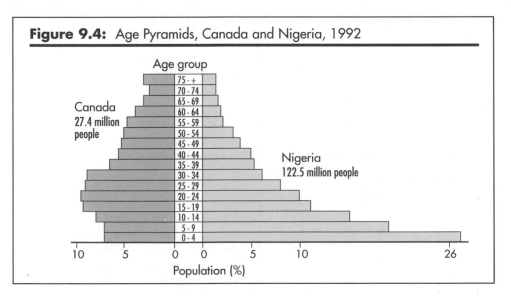

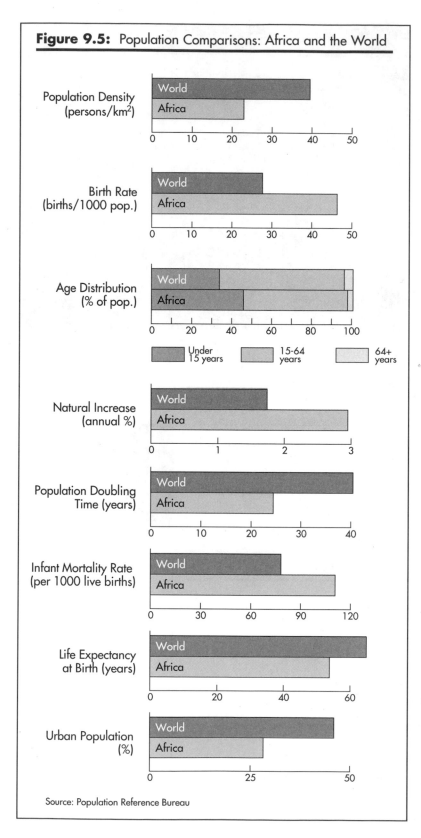

Figure 9.5: Population Comparisons: Africa and the World

Source: Population Reference Bureau

FOREIGN DEBT

The foreign debt crisis is perhaps the greatest obstacle to African development. For many countries the interest payments alone on foreign debts exceed the total value of exports. Money that leaves a country as debt payment is lost as investment capital at home. On a national level, this means there is little money to spend on improving the quality of life. On the local level, it means that consumers have little money to spend and so there is little stimulation of local businesses.

Most governments are required to adopt economic programs established by international lending organizations as a condition of continued support. Often, however, these programs are ill-suited to the economies of these developing nations. The result is often even greater economic chaos. In many countries, for example, governments are required to cut government spending as part of their international loan agreement. Wages are cut and the number of government employees is reduced. Health, education, and other social services are devastated as a result.

AFRICAN INITIATIVES

The end of the Cold War has created a new order in Africa. The United States and the former Soviet Union are no longer jockeying for political advantage in the region. Instead of relying on international programs to direct their economic development, many Africans are now looking for African solutions to African problems. In almost every country in Africa there are new human rights organizations monitoring activities without assistance from international agencies. A conference convened by African ministers of health in 1992 brought together grassroots groups with government officials and health care specialists to address the pressing health concerns in Africa. Many countries are looking at ways to relieve chronic food shortages through long-term reconstruction programs rather than internationally sponsored relief programs. Environmental groups are actively protesting environmentally destructive projects and policies in an effort to reduce the damage being

In Kenya, the activist Greenbelt Movement mobilized 50 000 women in a tree-planting project.

inflicted on this diverse land. In a host of other areas as well, the people of Africa are looking for their own solutions to their unique problems.

In Review

1. a) What were i) the benefits and ii) the costs of colonialism for the imperial countries?
   b) What were i) the benefits and ii) the costs of colonialism for the colonies?
2. What factors led to the independence movements in Africa after the Second World War?
3. What economic problems exist in many parts of Africa?
4. What reasons are there to be optimistic about Africa's future?
5. What initiatives are African groups taking to solve the problems on their continent?

ETHIOPIA

Ethiopia in northeast Africa is one of the poorest countries on earth. Two-thirds of its people live below the poverty level. Famine and drought plague the nation with devastating regularity. Foreign aid is a way of life for a large portion of the population. Ethiopia is a country with a 2000-year history as an independent nation. Yet it has experienced over forty years of continuous internal warfare that began shortly after the Second World War.

Ethiopia defeated Italy's attempt at colonization in 1895-96. It thereby established itself as the only African kingdom to survive intact into the twentieth century. In 1936, Italy succeeded in occupying the country, but the emperor, Haile Selassie, was

restored to power by a combined force of European and African troops during the Second World War.

In 1952, the United Nations made the predominantly Muslim state of Eritrea an autonomous region federated with the largely Christian Ethiopia. In 1962, Selassie, eager for access to the coast, annexed Eritrea as a province of Ethiopia using American military aid. In response, the Eritrean People's Liberation Front (EPLF), armed by the Soviet Union and China, launched a military campaign against the Ethiopian offensive.

The conflict between Ethiopia and Eritrea continued throughout the next decade. Ethiopia maintained its control with repressive measures against the opposition. In the meantime other forces were at work that undermined

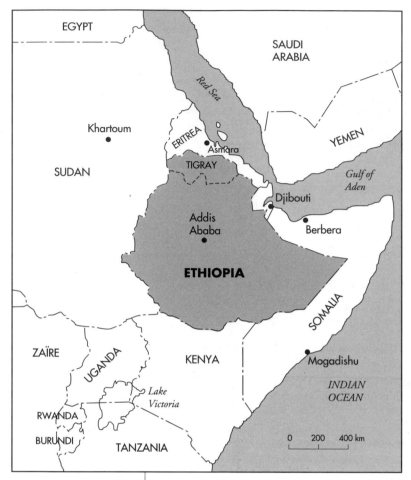

Figure 9.6:
Ethiopia

Ethiopia's war with Somalia illustrates the role played by the superpowers in Africa. Prior to the war, Somalia had been supported by the Soviet Union. But the communist government of Ethiopia had signed a treaty with the Soviets, so the Soviets withdrew their support of Somalia. The United States offered its support to Somalia in an effort to counter Soviet influence. The Eritrean rebels, once supported by the USSR, were now without military aid. They received support from Arab countries. In return, the rebels had to curb their Marxist rhetoric.

Ethiopia's stability. Other ethnic groups began to raise their nationalist voices demanding greater autonomy.

In 1972 and 1973, devastating drought gripped the land, causing widespread famine. Discontent with Haile Selassie's leadership mounted. It reached a peak in 1974 when a group of junior army officers staged a coup that deposed the emperor.

In the years that followed, intense political rivalries created grave instability. Political adversaries were executed in the ongoing struggle for power. In 1977, Colonel Mengistu Haile Mariam wrested control in yet another coup and established himself as the leader of an authoritarian communist regime. He continued to seek a military solution in Eritrea, however, and in return faced continuing guerrilla warfare. Ethiopia's problems were compounded when a border dispute erupted with neighbouring Somalia over the Ogaden Desert. The Ethiopians held off the Somali forces, but cross-border skirmishes continued.

The civil war with Eritrea continued throughout the 1980s. In the meantime, the region experienced a severe drought. With the death toll mounting, Mengistu introduced a resettlement program. Over 1.5 million people from the drought-stricken war zone were forced from their homes and relocated in the south; an estimated 600 000 died before they reached their destination. But the resettlement program was really a thinly disguised scheme to reduce support for the rebels in the region. Under pressure from international agencies and foreign governments, the program was discontinued in 1986.

FAMINE

Drought swept across Ethiopia in 1982, resulting in almost total crop failure in northern and eastern Ethiopia in 1983.

Victims of Ethiopia's famines found shelter at Red Cross relief camps.

The region already housed thousands of refugees who were displaced by the civil war. In May 1984, the Ethiopian Commission for Relief and Rehabilitation appealed for international aid to prevent millions of people from dying of starvation. In response, over 400 000 t of food were sent to Ethiopia between October and January alone. But much of the food failed to reach the famine victims. The civil war made some areas dangerous or even impossible for truck convoys to pass through safely. Food storage facilities were often raided. The challenges of mounting a relief campaign in the middle of a war zone were at times insurmountable.

Famine struck Ethiopia again in 1989-90. During this crisis, Mengistu expelled all relief organizations except the United Nations International Children's Emergency Fund (UNICEF) and the International Red Cross, and announced that only the Ethiopian Red Cross would distribute aid in the country. It was a cruel attempt to use food relief for government purposes, and the policy received worldwide condemnation. It was soon abandoned and new relief efforts were launched. International agencies continued to work to combat famine and prevent future crises. The real solution may lie not in continued food aid, however, but in developing long-term programs aimed at establishing fundamental changes in the agricultural system.

In 1984 and 1985, pop music superstars turned their talents to raising money for African famine relief. Irish rock musician Bob Geldof founded Band Aid in Britain; American and Canadian aid groups followed. The campaign reached its climax in August 1985. Geldof's Live Aid concert, featuring over sixty musicians, raised over US $100 million as they performed simultaneously from London's Wembley Stadium and Philadelphia's John F. Kennedy Stadium. The television audience was estimated at 1.5 billion viewers in 152 countries.

Fans filled London's Wembley Stadium for the Live Aid concert, which raised millions of dollars for famine relief in Ethiopia.

A NEW REGIME

In the late 1980s, Soviet support for the Mengistu government in Ethiopia began to soften. Soviet leader Mikhail Gorbachev favoured a political solution to the civil conflict, largely because the economic problems that plagued the Soviet Union meant there was little money to be invested in foreign military ventures.

With a reduction in the amount of military aid reaching the Ethiopian government, the Eritrean rebels started to make substantial gains and Mengistu's political support began to erode. Despite a treaty resolving the border dispute with Somalia, by 1989 Mengistu had to put down an attempted coup by disgruntled generals. In 1991, facing a major offensive by six rebel groups united as the Ethiopian

People's Revolutionary Democratic Front (EPRDF), Mengistu fled the country. The EPRDF entered the capital, Addis Ababa, and took over the government.

After the overthrow of Mengistu, the new Ethiopian government and Eritrea settled the independence question through a peaceful referendum. Following independence in May 1993, both governments embarked on reconstruction of their war-torn countries, with minimal assistance from international sources.

The EPRDF promised a new beginning for Ethiopia. They moved quickly to establish control and end the political instability that threatened the nation. Committed to what it called **ethnic federalism**, the government opted to share power with all Ethiopians. It encouraged a variety of

political and ethnic parties to participate in new elections and made the humanitarian needs of its people a top priority.

There is no doubt that the transition to a more democratic society has many pitfalls. The country is in a desperate economic condition. The people urgently need food, jobs, health care, and education. There is always the possibility that another military coup will upset long-range plans. Interference from foreign interests and governments remains a danger. Still, the political changes in the early 1990s offer a glimmer of hope for a better life in Ethiopia.

Women and men trained to become guerrilla fighters during the civil war between Eritrea and Ethiopia.

IN REVIEW

1. What factors led to the fall of Emperor Haile Selassie?

2. How did Mengistu hope the resettlement plan would help to solve the civil war with Eritrea?

3. What was the international response to the famine in Ethiopia in 1984-85?

4. What factors led to the downfall of Mengistu's communist regime?

5. What are the priorities of the new government established by the Ethiopian People's Revolutionary Democratic Front?

South Africa

The Dutch were the first Europeans to establish settlements on the southern tip of Africa. They came to the area in 1652, followed by French protestants in 1688. Britain took possession of the area in 1815 following the Napoleonic Wars in Europe. When Britain outlawed slavery in the Cape Colony in 1834, the Dutch Boers (farmers) trekked into the interior to carve out new countries—the Republic of Natal in 1838, the Orange Free State in 1854, and the Transvaal in 1858. The British also expanded into the interior, annexing Natal in 1843 and imposing white domination of native peoples through their military conquests.

With the discovery of diamonds in 1867 and gold in the 1880s, many British people and other Europeans flocked to the Orange Free State and the Transvaal. Their arrival brought them into conflict with the Boers. War was declared between the two sides in 1899; it ended in 1902 with the defeat of the Boers by the British. An act of the British Parliament in 1910 joined the British and Boer colonies in the Union of South Africa. In 1926, South Africa became an independent dominion within the British Empire.

The ruling white minority of the new union was outnumbered by the native black population by more than ten to one. To ensure continued white rule, a series of laws and regulations were introduced. The Urban Areas Act of 1923 established separate residential areas for blacks and whites. Under **pass laws**, non-whites were required to carry documents that proved their residence in special reserves or resettlement camps that had been established for them; they were required to present these passbooks on demand. Over the years the number of restrictions on non-whites increased. As nationalist movements swept across the continent following the Second World War, the white South African government moved to tighten its grip over the largely non-white country.

Apartheid Becomes Law

Apartheid was introduced in South Africa in 1948. This racial policy classified all residents of South Africa into four categories: white, black, coloured (people of mixed ancestry), or Asian. The purpose was to create two separate and distinct classes—a privileged white ruling class and an exploited, dependent, and subservient native class. Whites controlled the political, educational, and economic institutions. Racial groups were forced into separate schools, workplaces, and residential areas. It was illegal for people of different races to marry or even to mix together in public places.

Apartheid was supported by the majority of the white population and by the country's social institutions. The Dutch Reform Church declared that "God divided humanity into races, languages, and nations....Those who are culturally and spiritually advanced have a mission to leadership and protection of the less advanced." This "leadership and protection" included laws restricting blacks to menial and low-paying jobs and forcibly moving them to resettlement camps. To constrain native opposition to apartheid, the government limited the number of blacks who could live in urban areas where they could organize their resistance more easily. Many blacks were forced to live in native homelands. While these regions were granted some degree of self-rule, they were not free of South African control.

Opposition to Apartheid

After the Second World War, nationalist groups such as the African National

Congress (ANC) began to attack racial discrimination in South Africa using passive, non-violent resistance. They used boycotts, strikes, and demonstrations and openly defied segregation laws by entering "whites only" areas and using white facilities. The government's response included arresting leaders like the ANC's Nelson Mandela. Tensions escalated and reached a violent climax on 21 March 1960 during a demonstration outside a police station in Sharpeville. The police opened fire on the demonstrators; 249 people were shot, 69 of them fatally. In response, a crowd of 30 000 Africans marched into the heart of white Cape Town. A state of emergency was declared and 18 000 people were subsequently arrested. In April, other repressive measures were introduced. All public meetings were banned. Suspected dissidents were arrested and held indefinitely without a warrant. Black nationalist organizations like the African National Congress were banned and their leaders were arrested. It seemed that political change through non-violent protest was no longer possible.

Following the government ban on nationalist organizations, resistance groups set up their headquarters in neighbouring countries. From there they launched their attacks against the government. South African-armed forces repeatedly raided Mozambique, Botswana, Zambia, and other border countries in search of the rebels.

During the 1970s and 1980s the violence escalated. Hundreds of demonstrators were killed in clashes

with police and army forces. Violence erupted among different black groups over the most effective means of obtaining equality. In response to the growing unrest, the white government eased some of the apartheid laws. The ban on interracial marriages was lifted and black labour unions were legalized. In 1984 coloureds and Asians were granted the right to vote for representatives to their own separate parliaments with little authority. But blacks, who made up 67 per cent of South Africa's population, were still denied voting rights. They responded with riots, strikes, and acts of sabotage against the white rulers. In 1985, South African president P.W. Botha declared a state of emergency. Police now had sweeping powers to arrest hundreds of black nationalist leaders.

INTERNATIONAL SANCTIONS

In spite of the state of emergency, the South African government continued to ease some apartheid laws after 1985. In 1986, the pass laws were ended and signs identifying separate facilities by race were removed. Non-white workers

Sixty-nine people were killed in the Sharpeville massacre. The incident created an international furor. Many foreign companies withdrew their investments in South Africa and the country withdrew from the Commonwealth.

Figure 9.8: Selected Data on Racial Inequality

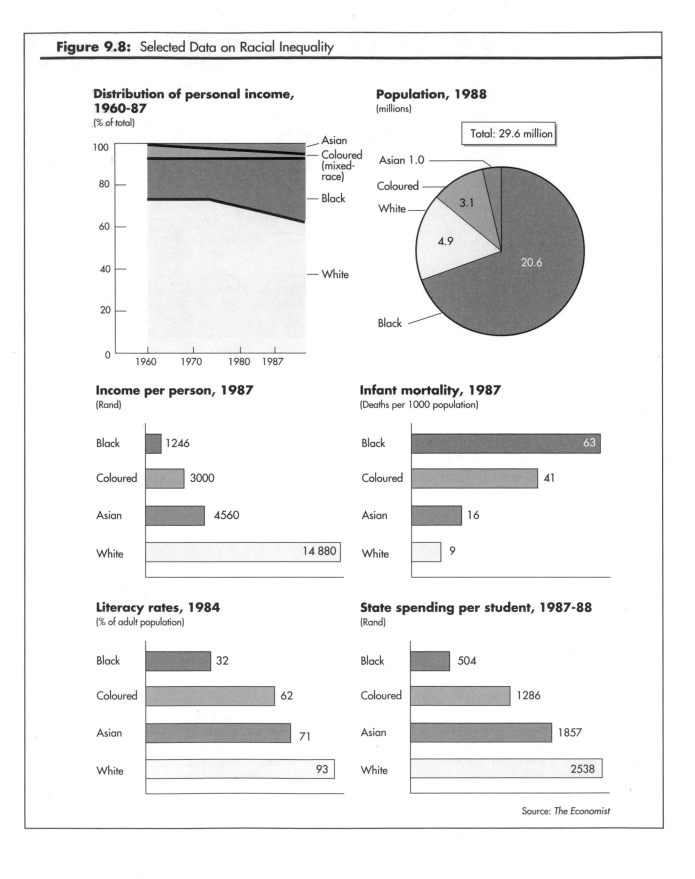

Source: *The Economist*

were no longer forced to pay more taxes than whites, and blacks were allowed to hold skilled jobs. More money was allocated to black education, although the school system remained segregated and unequal.

Many of the reforms in South Africa resulted from the pressure for change created by sanctions imposed by the international community. Many countries, including Canada, restricted business loans and investment in South Africa and reduced trade with the country as a means of applying pressure on the government. Several multinational corporations, such as General Motors and Kodak, withdrew their operations. Such sanctions were supported by some African leaders, including Archbishop Desmond Tutu, the head of the Anglican church in South Africa. As reforms increased, international sanctions were gradually lifted.

THE REFORM MOVEMENT

In 1989, F.W. de Klerk became president of South Africa. He promised a program of gradual reforms aimed at reducing black grievances and ending the civil strife that gripped the country. Within a year, de Klerk repealed laws that maintained racial segregation in public facilities. The ban on the African National Congress was lifted and Nelson Mandela, the ANC leader who had been imprisoned for twenty-seven years, was released. In June 1991, the government ended the hated Population Registration Act, which officially segregated South Africans, and introduced new laws to end the partitioning of South Africa into separate racial states. In return, the ANC agreed to suspend its violent activities and to work towards a negotiated settlement of racial issues.

Many whites opposed de Klerk's initiatives. They feared that democracy,

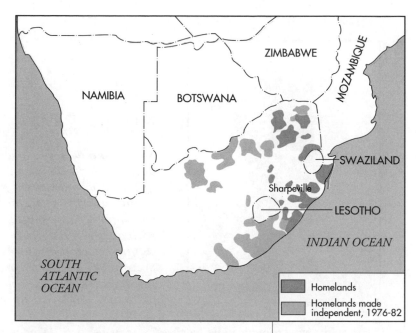

Figure 9.7:
South Africa, 1985

which would place the black majority in a powerful position, would lead to retaliation by blacks against whites. Fears of violence were magnified in the early 1990s when rival black groups clashed, leaving many black Africans dead. In response, extremist white groups launched their own violent campaigns designed to intimidate the reformers.

In 1993, against a background of continuing violence and bloodshed, the de Klerk government and the ANC reached an historic agreement. The country's first democratic elections, with voting privileges for all citizens regardless of colour, were announced for April 1994. The international community supported the decision and took the first steps towards lifting all economic sanctions.

In January 1994, Nelson Mandela launched an historic campaign for the presidency of South Africa against the incumbent de Klerk. But a cloud still loomed on the election horizon as the Inkatha Freedom Party threatened not to participate. Negotiators from the United States and Britain joined the talks in Johannesburg seeking to

PROFILE

NELSON MANDELA (1918-)

Nelson Mandela was once known as "the most famous prisoner in the world." From 1963 until 1990, Mandela was imprisoned in South Africa for leading the black majority's fight against apartheid. During his incarceration he became an international figure with a worldwide following of supporters. By the time of his release in 1990, Mandela had attained the stature of hero for his steadfast refusal to bow to the political pressures of the white government in South Africa. After reading about Nelson Mandela, find out what changes have taken place in South Africa since he became president.

"The white government must legalize us, treat us like a political party and negotiate with us. Until they do we will have to live with the armed struggle. It is useless to simply carry on talking."

Nelson Mandela, 1960

"I do not deny that I planned sabotage. We had to either accept inferiority or fight against it by violence. When my sentence has been completed...I will still be moved to take up again, as best I can, the struggle for removal of injustices until they are finally abolished once and for all."

Nelson Mandela, to the court upon his conviction, 1963

"No serious political organisation will ever talk peace when an aggressive war is being waged against it. No proud people will ever obey orders from those who have humiliated and dishonoured them for so long."

Nelson Mandela, in response to offers of a political deal in exchange for his release from prison, 1989

Nelson (Rolihlahia) Mandela was born a member of the Tembu people of South Africa, the son of a Tembu chief. He attended university in Johannesburg, where he earned a degree in law and set up South Africa's first black legal practice.

Mandela's battle against racial injustice began when he joined the African National Congress in 1944. He helped to co-ordinate the 1952 Defiance Campaign of passive resistance against the white regime's apartheid laws. When the Defiance Campaign was brutally suppressed by authorities, Mandela was arrested. His nine-month sentence was suspended, but he was banned from attending public meetings or taking part in ANC activities. In 1956, after Mandela participated in the Congress of the People's Freedom Charter, which declared that "South Africa belongs to all who live in it, black and white," Mandela, along with 156 other South Africans, was arrested and tried for treason. He mounted his own eloquent defence and was acquitted, along with his co-defendants.

Following the Sharpeville massacre in 1960, Mandela and other ANC leaders decided that non-violent protest was ineffective in the face of such government brutality. Mandela organized the Spear of the Nation movement and led a series of violent acts of sabotage and guerrilla activity. He was forced to go underground but was eventually arrested and imprisoned for five years for incitement. In 1964, after a second trial, he was convicted of sabotage and treason and sentenced to life in prison.

Mandela spent the next twenty-seven years in captivity. While in prison he fought against abuse and brutality, defended prisoners' rights, and confronted authorities. He repeatedly refused offers of freedom in exchange for a political deal with the government. His convictions elevated him to mythical status among many black South Africans.

During Nelson Mandela's incarceration, his wife Winnie, whom he had married in 1958, carried his message to the world. In 1982, an international campaign was launched to free Mandela. The United Nations Security Council demanded his freedom. World leaders applied diplomatic and political pressure for Mandela's release. Musicians, writers, and dramatists championed his cause. Bowing to the pressure, the government offered to release Mandela, but on their terms. Again Mandela refused.

In 1988, the year of Mandela's seventieth birthday, demands for his release escalated amidst much international publicity. Mandela was moved to more comfortable facilities as his health began to deteriorate. Finally, in 1990, in the face of mounting civil unrest and external pressure, President F.W. de Klerk ordered the release of the man who had come to symbolize the future freedom of millions of black South Africans. The ANC was legalized. The government pledged reforms to create an equal and democratic South Africa. Mandela committed his leadership to negotiating a new order for the country. In 1994, Nelson Mandela was elected the first black president of South Africa.

resolve the impasse. A week before the election an agreement was reached that satisfied the demands of Inkatha. The voting began on April 26th. Over the next three days all people of South Africa were free to cast their ballots. More than 300 observers from other nations monitored the election and declared it free and fair.

The results of South Africa's first free elections were announced on May 6th. Mandela's African National Congress captured 63 per cent of the vote, while de Klerk's National Party received 20 per cent; the Inkatha Freedom Party garnered 10 per cent. Seats in the 400-member National Assembly were distributed according to the popular vote, and the Assembly chose the new president. On May 9th, the assembly took office and nominated Nelson Mandela as president.

Public support for Mandela was overwhelming. Heads of state and other dignitaries from around the world joined the celebrations at his inauguration on May 10th. In a spirit of co-operation and harmony, Mandela formed his cabinet. Former president de Klerk was named a vice-president.

Other cabinet appointments included eighteen members from the ANC, six representatives from the National Party, and three members from the Inkatha Freedom Party. Apartheid no longer existed. Now the challenge was to build a new South Africa.

Not all blacks recognized the ANC as the legitimate voice of black South Africa. Violence broke out between the ANC and the Inkatha Freedom Party, another black, primarily Zulu, nationalist group. The animosity threatened to undermine South Africa's transition to democracy.

Between April 24th and 27th a series of election-related bombings rocked South Africa. Twenty-one people were killed. The bombings were linked to extremist groups, and thirty-one people were arrested for the attacks.

Blacks formed long lines at the polls in South Africa during the election process. There was a general air of celebration as the first free elections were held.

IN REVIEW

1. Explain the policy of apartheid in South Africa.

2. Why did the African National Congress abandon its policy of nonviolent protest against apartheid in the 1960s?

3. What reforms were introduced in the mid-1980s?

4. a) What was the purpose of sanctions imposed by the international community?
   b) Why were sanctions gradually eased?

5. What measures did F.W. de Klerk take to end the civil unrest in South Africa?

6. What were the results of South Africa's first free elections?

SUMMARY

Africa faces serious challenges in the twenty-first century. Solutions must be found to the problems of poverty, overpopulation, and environmental destruction. Political instability, ethnic and religious conflicts, and civil strife threaten to impede progress in economic development. Whether the new world order will provide greater opportunities for African nations remains to be seen.

MAKING CONNECTIONS

1. Compare the case studies of Ethiopia and South Africa. Record your points in a comparison organizer under the headings Economic Conditions, Political Climate, and Important Problems.

2. After the fall of Mengistu a newspaper commented: "Mengistu...is a victim of the end of the Cold War. The crutches of the rivalry between the US and the USSR kept [him] standing; the new détente made him fall." (Piero Ostellino, *Corriere della Sera*.) In what ways did Cold War politics contribute to the violence in Ethiopia?

3. What were some similarities between colonialism in Africa and in North America? What were some important differences?

DEVELOPING YOUR VOICE

4. Is the colonial history of Africa responsible for the poverty and economic problems the continent faces today? If so, what obligations do the former imperial powers have towards these countries? Discuss this issue in class.

5. Debate the statement: "Nothing has really changed in Africa. Political imperialism has simply become economic imperialism."

6. Create a role-playing situation in which several students act as government officials in an imperial country and an equal number of students act as African nationalist leaders in a colony. Working together, propose a plan for a smooth transition of power from imperial rule to African self-government.

RESEARCHING THE ISSUES

7. Research an African country of your choice to determine the major issues in its history since the Second World War. Prepare a case study based on your findings.

8. Find several photographs of places and people in Africa in magazines, newspapers, and books. What impressions are created by these photos? Write a one-page essay on the impact of the media on our perceptions of Africa.

9. Research one of the problems facing the countries of Africa today. Possible topics include population growth, desertification, urbanization, and the AIDS epidemic. Prepare a three-page essay detailing the nature of the problem, its impact on countries and people, and possible solutions.

VIEWPOINTS

ISSUE: IS COLONIALISM RESPONSIBLE FOR AFRICA'S PROBLEMS?

Africa is a continent mired in poverty. Much of the region is politically unstable. Repeated droughts threaten the survival of many of Africa's people. Widespread environmental destruction is a constant threat. Africa's continuing crises threaten the region's prospects for long-term economic development.

There is a continuing debate as to what lies at the heart of Africa's problems. Many experts believe the lasting effects of colonialism are to blame. Mai Palmberg, a supporter of black liberation groups in southern Africa, argues that colonialism established the economic and political conditions that continue to keep Africa poor and dependent on the West. P.T. Bauer, a professor at the London School of Economics and Political Science, argues that colonial rule is not the cause of African poverty.

Read each of these viewpoints carefully, then complete an Argument Analysis and Evaluation Summary for each reading.

Mai Palmberg

"The then Prime Minister of England, Harold Macmillan, in a speech in Cape Town on 3 February 1960, said that 'a wind of change' was blowing over the continent and that the main question now was whether the peoples of Asia and Africa would turn to the East or to the West, to Communism or to 'the free world'. In December of the same year Charles de Gaulle, then President of France, spoke to army officers in Blida in Algeria. He asked them to try to understand what was happening in the world, to understand that the old methods of direct control, based on arms and the colonial state apparatus, had become impossible to practice, the new ways had to be found so that 'the activities of France in

Algeria can continue'. In March 1961 the US President John F. Kennedy launched what was called 'The Alliance for Progress' for the Latin American states. To prevent the revolutionary example of Cuba becoming contagious the Latin American states were to embark on some social and economic reforms with the aid of US dollars.

"These three speeches show how the leaders of the Western world understood that new forms for imperialism had to be created when direct colonial control was no longer politically possible. The question was how to continue the exploitation of the Third World as cheaply and as easily as possible, and also to prevent the 'loss' of more countries than China, that is, a change in Socialist direction. Independent Africa became a field of experiments for neo-colonial policies....

Economic Dependence

"The independent African states got their own national flags but they inherited economic dependence. This dependence could be used by the imperialist forces to further their aims. The dependence rests on two pillars, a continued colonial division of labour and foreign control of key sectors of the economy. This pattern can be summarized in three points:

1. As in colonial times a large part of production is sold for export.
2. Most of the goods exported are a few unprocessed raw materials.
3. More than four-fifths of Africa's exports [are] directed to the imperialist states. Three-fourths of Africa's imports originate there.

"The big private companies which have dominated the exploitation of African raw materials are powerful actors on the African scene. For many of them their annual turnover is far larger than the total state budget of the countries where they invest their capital.

"They carefully guard the secrets of their trade. The technical development in modern industry is almost entirely controlled by big multinational companies, which own industries in a large number of countries, and often have near-monopoly in their fields of production....

"Investments and trade are not the only form of dependence. 'Development aid' has become an important instrument for the neo-colonial policies. The words 'development aid' give an impression that it is an unselfish sacrifice from the rich to the poor. But only if we look at it as part of the total economic relations between underdeveloped countries and industrialized capitalist states can we judge the real function of development aid....

"An overwhelming part of all development aid goes to infrastructure, that is to the preconditions for modern production. Infrastructure means, on the one hand, economic investments, such as communications, telecommunications, airports, harbours, energy supply, irrigation projects etc., and, on the other hand, social investments such as schools, hospitals and administrative buildings. Of course, such projects need not be worthless for the receiving country. But, in the first place, they are designed to reinforce export dependence instead of furthering domestic use of the raw materials. In the second place, these investments are, to quote [L.D. Black], a North American spokesman for development aid, 'an indispensable precondition for the capacity to attract foreign private investment'....

Unequal Exchange

"To all this must be added the losses incurred by the Third World countries from deteriorated terms of trade. This means that most raw materials, which we have seen make up the major share of the exports from underdeveloped countries, have decreasing prices on the world market, whereas the prices of manufactured goods, which the underdeveloped countries import, steadily rise....

"This 'unequal exchange' means that for the Third World the loss is often more than what is 'given' in development aid. Another difficulty for the economy of Third World countries is the fact that they do not control the sale of their raw materials, but this is subject to speculation on the raw materials exchanges in New York and London....

"As long as the majority of the Third World countries believe that changes can be made in co-operation with those industrialized countries which have created and maintained the Third World's underdevelopment, the neo-colonial policies have not completely lost the day....

"Political organization is decisive for development in the progressive states. Only through a popular basis and control of political life can the people decide what will be produced and for whom."

From The Struggle for Africa *by Mai Palmberg, published by Zed Books, 1983, London. Reprinted with permission.*

P.T. Bauer

"Acceptance of emphatic routine allegations that the West is responsible for Third World poverty reflects and reinforces Western feelings of guilt. ...The West has come to abase itself before countries with negligible resources and no real power. Yet the allegations can be shown to be without foundation. They are readily accepted because the Western public has little firsthand knowledge of the Third World, and because of widespread feelings of guilt. The West has never had it so good, and has never felt so bad about it....

"About ten years ago a student group at Cambridge published a pamphlet on the subject of the moral obligations of the West to the Third World. The following was its key passage:

> We took the rubber from Malaya, the tea from India, raw materials from all over the world and gave almost nothing in return.

"This is as nearly the opposite of the truth as one can find. The British took the rubber to Malaya and the tea to India. There were no rubber trees in Malaya or anywhere in Asia (as suggested by their botanical name, *Hevea braziliensis*) until about 100 years ago, when the British took the first rubber seeds there out of the Amazon jungle. From these sprang the huge rubber industry—now very largely Asian-owned. Tea-plants were brought to India by the British somewhat earlier; their origin is shown in the botanical name *Camilla sinensis*, as well as in the phrase 'all the tea in China'....

"Far from the West having caused the poverty in the Third World, contact with the West has been the principal agent of material progress there. The materially more advanced societies and regions of the Third World are those with which the West established the most numerous, diversified and extensive contacts: the cash-crop-producing areas and entrepot ports of South-East Asia, West Africa and Latin America; the mineral-producing areas of Africa and the Middle East; and cities and ports throughout Asia, Africa, the Caribbean and Latin America. The level of material achievement usually diminishes as one moves away from the foci of Western impact. The poorest and most backward people have few or no external contacts;....

"Large parts of West Africa were...transformed...as a result of Western contacts. Before 1890 there was no cocoa production in the Gold Coast or Nigeria, only very small production of cotton and groundnuts and small exports of palm oil and palm kernels. By the 1950s all these had become staples of world trade. They were produced by Africans on African-owned properties. But this was originally made possible by Westerners who established public security and introduced modern methods of transport and communications. Over this period imports both of capital goods and of mass consumer goods for African use also rose from insignificant amounts to huge volumes. The changes were reflected in government revenues, literacy rates, school attendance, public health, life expectation, infant mortality and many other indicators.

Massive Transformation

Statistics by themselves can hardly convey the far-reaching transformation which took place over this period in West Africa.... For instance, slave trading and slavery were still widespread at the end of the nineteenth century. They had practically disappeared by the end of the First World War. Many of the worst endemic and epidemic diseases for which West Africa was notorious throughout the nineteenth century had disappeared by the Second World War....

"The role of Western contacts in the material progress of Black Africa deserves further notice. As late as the second half of the nineteenth century Black Africa was without even the simplest, most basic ingredients of modern social and economic life. These were brought there by Westerners over the last hundred years or so. This is true of such fundamentals as public security and law and order; wheeled traffic (Black Africa never invented the wheel) and mechanical transport (before the arrival of Westerners, transport in Black Africa was almost entirely by human muscle); roads, railways and man-made ports; the application of science and technology to economic activity; towns with substantial buildings, clean water and sewerage facilities; public health care, hospitals and the control of endemic and epidemic diseases; formal education. These advances resulted from peaceful commercial contacts.

"Wherever local conditions have permitted it, commercial contacts with the West, and generally established by the West, have eliminated the worst diseases, reduced or even eliminated famine, extended life expectation and improved living standards....

Colonialism Is Not at Fault

"Whatever one thinks of colonialism, it cannot be held responsible for Third World poverty. Some of the most backward countries never were colonies, as for instance Afghanistan, Tibet, Nepal, Liberia. Ethiopia is perhaps an even more telling example (it was an Italian colony for only six years in its long history). Again, many of the Asian and African colonies progressed very rapidly during colonial rule, much more so than the independent countries in the same area. At present one of the few remaining European colonies is Hong Kong—whose prosperity and progress should be familiar. It is plain that colonial rule has not been the cause of Third World poverty.

"Nor is the prosperity of the West the result of colonialism. The most advanced and the richest countries never had colonies, including Switzerland and the Scandinavian countries; and some were colonies of others and were already very prosperous as colonies, as for instance North America and Australia. The prosperity of the West was generated by its own peoples and was not taken from others. The European countries were already materially far ahead of the areas where they established colonies....

"The allegations that external trade, and especially imports from the West, are damaging to the populations of the Third World reveal a barely disguised condescension towards the ordinary people there, and even contempt for them. The people, of course, want the imports. If they did not the imported goods could not be sold. Similarly, the people are prepared to produce for export to pay for these imported goods. To say that these processes are damaging is to argue that people's preferences are of no account in organizing their own lives....

"The exponents of Western guilt further patronize the Third World by suggesting that its economic fortunes past, present and prospective, are determined by the West; that past exploitation by the West explains Third World backwardness; that manipulation of international trade by the West and other forms of Western misconduct account for persistent poverty; that the economic future of the Third World depends largely on Western donations. According to this set of ideas, whatever happens to the Third World is largely our doing. Such ideas make us feel superior even while we beat our breasts."

From Equality, the Third World and Economic Delusion *by P.T. Bauer. Reprinted with permission of the publisher, George Weidenfeld & Nicolson Limited, London.*

ANALYSIS AND EVALUATION

Refer to the Argument Analysis and Evaluation Guide on page viii.

1. Using the Argument Analysis and Evaluation Guide, compare the readings by Palmberg and Bauer. On what do they agree? On what do they disagree?

2. Decide which of the viewpoints you tend to support and explain why. Be sure to use specific information from this textbook, the readings, and other sources to support your position.

3. State and support your position on the issue: "Is colonialism responsible for Africa's problems?"

❖

CHAPTER TEN

Asia: The Awakening Giant

❖

"What I did was a very ordinary thing. I declared that the British could not order me around in my own country."

Mahatma Gandhi, 1947

"It is reasonable to expect...the rise of the Pacific region is likely to continue, simply because that development is so broad-based. It includes not only the economic powerhouse of Japan, but also that swiftly changing giant the People's Republic of China;...the immensely successful Asian newly industrializing countries like Taiwan, South Korea, Hong Kong and Singapore—as well as...Malaysia, Indonesia, Thailand and the Philippines."

Paul Kennedy, The Rise and Fall of the Great Powers (New York: Random House, 1987) p. 441.

Left: Pro-democracy demonstrations in Beijing in 1989

❖ OVERVIEW

In the aftermath of the Second World War, many nations of the South Pacific and South East Asia were left with shattered economies and unstable governments. Out of the chaos emerged a handful of dynamic and prosperous industrial economies—along with some of the poorest nations on earth.

Today Japan leads a string of newly industrialized powers that are not only reshaping the economy of the region but of the world as well. These manufacturing nations are gaining international importance as they challenge the economic supremacy of the West. Yet this prosperity is only one aspect of such a diverse continent as Asia. Many nations remain mired in poverty, their economic development hampered by rapid population growth, political instability, and internal conflicts. Standing out amidst it all is China, the world's most populous nation and the last great bastion of communism, struggling to find its place in the new world order.

in the recent history of Asia. During the age of imperialism, all of South and South East Asia, with the exception of Thailand, was under the control of European powers. Within the region, Japan engaged in its own imperialist expansion in the nineteenth century as it seized control of Formosa and Korea. Japan renewed its imperialist ambitions in the 1930s. By 1942, during the height of the Second World War, Japan dominated most of South East Asia until its surrender to the Allies in 1945.

NATIONALIST MOVEMENTS

The end of the Second World War signalled the end of European colonial rule. The Italian and Japanese empires disappeared as a result of their military defeats. Over the next thirty years, the remaining empires of Britain, France, Spain, Portugal, the Netherlands, and Belgium were dissolved as their colonies gained independence and became sovereign states.

There were several reasons for the dramatic events that brought an end to European domination in Asia. Many colonial regiments served alongside the Allies in the war. Their participation raised the hopes of colonial peoples for political freedom in the postwar world. Hope was also fuelled by the promises of the Atlantic Charter drafted by Churchill and Roosevelt in 1941, which pledged sovereignty and self-government for all nations. This coincided with strong nationalist movements in the colonies. Led by a new generation of European-educated leaders, the colonies demanded the right to rule themselves.

FOCUS QUESTIONS

1. In what ways did the Second World War affect economic development in Asia?

2. What was the role of nationalism in the independence movements in Asia after 1945?

3. Why have some Asian nations experienced economic success while others have not?

4. What factors led to Japan's emergence as Asia's economic leader?

THE END OF IMPERIALISM

The struggle for political and military power has been an overriding theme

Many European leaders supported these independence movements. The experience of the Second World War led many people in Europe to oppose imperialism philosophically; they were also unable to justify it economically as they struggled to rebuild their own countries after six years of war. Britain was prepared to grant independence to new pro-Western governments. The other European colonial powers were in similar economic positions, although France and the Netherlands did not give up their colonies without a struggle.

Following the war, the United States and the Soviet Union emerged as the dominant world powers. Both countries wanted to see the breakup of the European empires. The United States, having waged its own war of independence against the British Empire in 1776, supported independence movements. But the US was also motivated by economic interests: if Europe lost its empires, the United States would have greater access to the former colonies' markets and resources. The Soviet Union, too, opposed European imperialism in principle. But it also recognized that a weakening of European power in Asia would provide greater opportunities for establishing communist rule in the new nations.

Figure 10.1:
The Extent of Japanese Control During the Second World War

INDEPENDENCE GAINED

As nationalist movements gained momentum after 1945, the colonies in Asia gained their independence. Britain, which had the largest empire, withdrew from its empire without serious conflict. In 1947, under the provisions of the Indian Independence Act, India was partitioned and the independent states of India (primarily Hindu) and Pakistan (primarily Muslim) were formed. Ceylon (renamed Sri Lanka in 1972) and Burma (renamed Myanmar in 1989) gained their independence in 1948. Internal struggle in Malaya delayed its independence until 1957; in 1963, Malaya merged with other

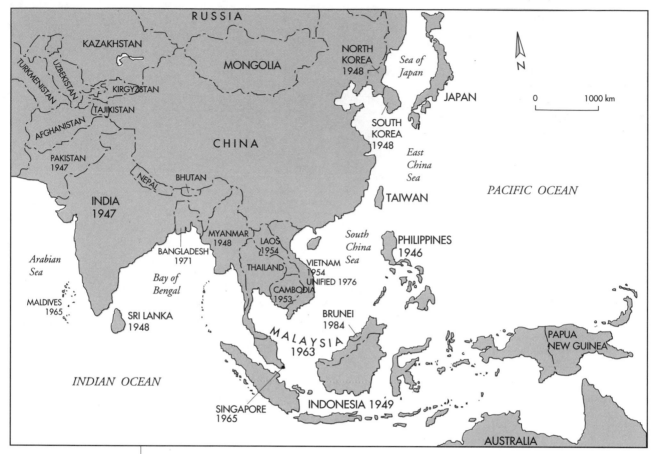

Figure 10.2:
Asia, 1995. The dates represent the year each country gained independence from colonial rule.

colonies to form the Federation of Malaysia.

France was less co-operative in the dismantling of its empire. After seven years of fighting in Vietnam against nationalist forces, France was defeated in 1954. At the Geneva Conference that year France lost control of all of Indochina.

The Netherlands had controlled the Dutch East Indies since 1799, but the islands were abandoned to the Japanese in 1942. After the war, the Netherlands tried to re-establish colonial rule. But after four years of armed conflict, the Dutch government recognized the independent republic of Indonesia in 1949. Nationalist movements continued throughout Asia, Africa, and the Middle East. By the 1970s, most of the European empires had disappeared.

THE PROBLEMS OF INDEPENDENCE

While independence marked the end of European political domination and economic exploitation, it created its own set of problems. Many of the boundaries of the former colonies had been arbitrarily determined by the colonial powers, without consideration to race, culture, or religion. In countries like India, Ceylon, and Vietnam, civil wars erupted from the tensions that lay hidden beneath the blanket of colonial rule. In addition, many of the new nations inherited weak economies with limited resources. Most countries exported raw materials and agricultural products and imported manufactured goods from the home country. Raw materials were at the mercy of fluctuating world prices. Most countries faced declining revenues for the raw products they exported and increasing prices for the finished goods they imported.

Although the Asian nations had a new generation of educated leaders and trained administrators, in many cases the challenges of managing a new economy, society, and government proved difficult. Most countries were experiencing the opportunities and responsibilities of democracy for the first time. In some cases inefficient, unstable, or corrupt democracies were replaced by military dictatorships.

REVOLUTION AND CONFLICT

Most revolutionary movements in Asia were rooted in nationalist campaigns against existing governments. In China, Indochina, the Philippines, and Malaysia, these governments were supported by the West. Nationalist forces, whether or not they were communist, often sought Soviet support in their opposition to these pro-Western governments.

As the Cold War developed, communist expansion in Asia became a source of great anxiety for the United States. While the Americans supported independence, they were concerned about the movement of some Asian nations towards communism. Determined to prevent this, the United States attempted to solidify its influence through direct intervention in Asian affairs.

THE SOUTH EAST ASIA TREATY ORGANIZATION

In 1949, Mao Zedong and the Communist Party won the civil war in China. In 1950, communist forces in North Korea attempted to take over South Korea. In 1954, Ho Chi Minh's nationalist army, supported by China and the Soviet Union, defeated the French army in Indochina. Communist forces in Malaysia and the Philippines led guerrilla wars of liberation there. American leaders feared that the Soviet Union and China were planning to spread communism throughout South East Asia. The US decided that a military alliance similar to NATO was needed to halt communist expansion in Asia. In 1954, the United States founded the **South East Asia Treaty Organization** (SEATO). Members included the United States, France, Great Britain, Australia, New Zealand, Thailand, Pakistan, and the Philippines.

CONFLICT IN SOUTH ASIA: INDIA

For 200 years Britain had ruled the subcontinent of India as one entity in

Figure 10.3:
The Partitioning of India and Pakistan

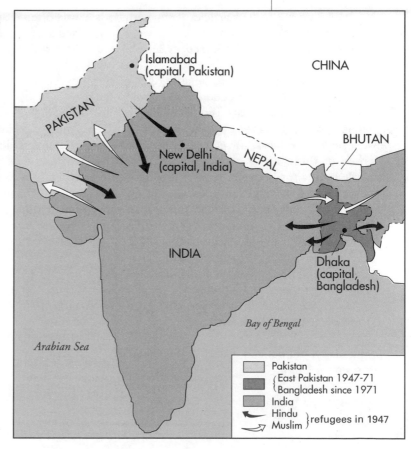

PROFILE

MAHATMA GANDHI (1869-1948)

Mahatma Gandhi was one of this century's most powerful leaders. His words and deeds mobilized millions of people, yet he remained a humble man. Gandhi's religious and political values were a blend of Western and Indian thought. He was influenced by the sacred Hindu book, the Bhagavad-Gita, *by the Indian conviction that meditation is the way to spiritual renewal, by Christ's Sermon on the Mount counselling people to meet violence with love, by socialism as a way to improve the lives of the poor and the oppressed, and by Henry David Thoreau's belief in civil disobedience as a response to unjust laws. He spent his life preaching love, religious tolerance, and non-violence. What leaders in modern history have adopted Gandhi's philosophy?*

"Non-violence is the first article of my faith. It is also the last article of my creed."
  Mahatma Gandhi, 18 March 1922

"We believe that it is the inalienable right of the Indian people...to have freedom and to enjoy the fruits of their toil and have the necessities of life, so that they may have full opportunities of growth. We believe also that if any government deprives a people of these rights and oppresses them, the people have a further right to alter it or abolish it. The British Government in India has not only deprived the Indian people of their freedom but has based itself on the exploitation of the masses, and has ruined India economically, politically, culturally, and spiritually. We believe, therefore, that India must sever the British connection and attain Purna Swaraj, or complete independence...."
  Mahatma Gandhi, in a speech to the Congress Party, 31 December 1931

Mohandas Karamchand Gandhi was born to a prosperous Hindu family in India in 1869. At the age of eighteen, he went to England to study law. Soon after graduating and returning home, Gandhi was offered an assignment in South Africa, which had a large Indian population. Almost immediately he experienced racial discrimination, which led him to mobilize Indians to protest against oppression.

On his return to India in 1915, Gandhi was welcomed as a champion of Indian rights. He became a leader in the National Congress and a prominent activist in the struggle for independence. He abandoned Western clothing, preferring to identify with the Indian masses by wearing a loincloth and living a spiritual life of fasting and meditation. The great Indian poet, Raindranath Tagore, winner of the Nobel Prize for Literature in 1913, called Gandhi "Great Soul (Mahatma) in peasant's garb."

When British troops fired on unarmed demonstrators at Amritsar in 1919, killing or wounding more than 1500 people, Gandhi insisted that his followers not respond with violence. He believed that the British would be defeated not when they had no strength (which was limitless) but when they had no heart to continue the fight against moral, non-violent people who simply would not submit to them. This commitment to peaceful change earned Gandhi respect worldwide.

In 1928 and 1929, nationalism reached a peak in India. Violent protests became common as people grew impatient with the lack of progress towards independence. Gandhi took action by protesting the Salt Laws, which required that salt had to be purchased from the government salt monopoly. On 12 March 1930, Gandhi and seventy-eight followers set off on a long trek to the sea where they could illegally obtain salt. They reached the Indian Ocean on April 5th, having marched nearly 500 km. Along the way their band of protestors had grown to several thousand. At the ocean Gandhi picked up some of the salt from the beach, thereby officially infringing on the government monopoly. Peasants took Gandhi's cue. All along the coast they began collecting salt for sale in the cities. Over 60 000 people were jailed. Despite the arrests, the protest remained peaceful but civil disobedience increased. The British were forced to back down and release Gandhi and many other Indian leaders.

In 1935, Winston Churchill proclaimed that "Gandhism and all it stands for must ultimately be grappled with and finally crushed." Gandhi stood for an independent India; Churchill stood for the British Empire. In 1940, Churchill became prime minister and announced his refusal to "preside at the liquidation of the British Empire." However, when Japan attacked British colonies in Asia, Britain sought to secure Indian loyalty by offering independence following the war.

In 1947, the new states of India and Pakistan were created. Ongoing conflict between the Hindus and the Muslims, however, resulted in violent confrontations. Gandhi tried to quell the violence as he travelled tirelessly throughout India convincing rioters to practise love and tolerance. In January 1948, at the age of seventy-eight, he went on a hunger fast to bring about peace and universal compassion. The disorder in India diminished amidst promises of tolerance and Gandhi ended his fast. Later that month, only five months after independence, Gandhi was assassinated by a group of militant Hindu conspirators who opposed Gandhi's acceptance of Muslims.

Gandhi's funeral was attended by a million mourners. World leaders paid homage to the man who inspired India. The United Nations lowered its flag to half mast. Indian Prime Minister Jawaharlal Nehru said, "The light has gone out of our lives and there is darkness everywhere." But Gandhi's message continues to inspire humanitarians and seekers of peace.

spite of the region's deep ethnic, linguistic, and religious diversity. Britain was reluctant to relinquish its hold on this jewel of the British Empire, but it did grant India limited self-rule between the two world wars. When the Second World War broke out Britain promised full autonomy to India at the war's end in return for India's help in defeating the Axis powers.

Once the war was over, Britain began negotiating an independence agreement between the two main political organizations, the Muslim League and the Indian National Congress. The main obstacle was the fundamental difference between the Muslim minority, which wanted a separate Muslim state, and the Hindu majority, represented by the Indian National Congress,

which opposed the partitioning of India.

British efforts at compromise failed. In 1946-47, waves of violence swept the country. This convinced the British that India should be partitioned and that the date for independence should be moved forward from 1948 to 1947 in order to avert further violence. Under the provisions of the Indian Independence Act of 1947, India was partitioned and two republics were formed. The new Muslim state of Pakistan was created by separating two Indian provinces with large Muslim populations, the Punjab and Bengal, into West and East Pakistan.

Mass migrations of more than 12 million people followed the partitioning of India. Muslims in India fled to

Pakistan while Hindus and Sikhs in Pakistan fled to India. The migrations were not peaceful, however. Approximately 1 million people were killed in the violence; still more died of disease and starvation. Conflicts continued throughout the 1950s and 1960s. In 1971, East Pakistan declared its independence as the new state of Bangladesh. Civil war followed in which thousands were killed and 10 million people were forced to flee to India. Later that year India and Pakistan declared war against each other and Pakistan was quickly defeated.

> Bangladesh is an independent Islamic republic, but it is one of the poorest countries on earth and is constantly plagued by natural disasters.

ECONOMIC PATTERNS

The nations of Asia have chosen radically different paths in their political and economic development. These choices have created vast differences among them in their current economic realities and their prospects for the future. These economic patterns fall into four categories: industrialized economies, resource-based economies, centrally planned economies, and developing economies.

> "Singapore's social order is rather good. Its leaders exercise strict management. We should learn from their experience, and we should do a better job than they do."
>
> *Deng Xiaoping, Chinese Communist leader, 1992*

Industrialized Economies

The "Four Dragons" of Asia—Taiwan, Singapore, South Korea, and Hong Kong—are evidence of the rapid economic change that has swept through some parts of South East Asia. In just a few decades these economies have been transformed from agrarian societies to important manufacturing entities.

What has made these Four Dragons such economic powerhouses in spite of their lack of natural resources? All four have a strong work ethic, placing considerable value on hard work and loyalty to employers and employees. It is common for employees in these countries to work long hours six days a week and for workers and industries to place long-term financial rewards above short-term gain. Because of this, wage rates for skilled workers are lower than in competing countries. Workers also save more of their incomes than North Americans do, creating large capital resources for business ventures.

The Four Dragons modelled their development on postwar Japan, achieving rapid growth by targeting high-tech industries. They have worked to create an attractive environment for export-oriented industries by encouraging their banking systems to provide maximum support for industry and by sponsoring research and development. The positive attitude towards business and industry has encouraged foreign investment. Individual approaches have varied, however. While Hong Kong's development has been pure capitalism, for example, Singapore has developed a modified socialist model of economic development.

Resource-based Economies

Not all nations in Asia have achieved the economic success of the Four Dragons. There are several countries with abundant natural resources that have not enjoyed the same economic development. Indonesia has substantial oil and natural gas reserves, but has been plagued by political instability and ethnic rivalry. Combined with weak global markets for energy and rapid inflation, these conditions have produced widespread unemployment and persistent food shortages. India has a significant natural resource base that could be used to expand its economy. But its rapid population growth, averaging 2 per cent a year, negates the country's economic gains. While harvests have improved due to better agricultural practices, food and other resources must be shared among a growing number of people.

The Four Dragons have targeted manufacturing in high-tech industries to achieve their economic success. Taiwan is one of the world's leading producers of electronic goods.

Centrally Planned Economies

The centrally planned economies of China, Vietnam, Myanmar, and North Korea are founded on the strong centralized control of all aspects of the economy. The emphasis is on heavy industry and agriculture. Frequently the economic policies isolate the countries by restricting foreign interaction, investment, and tourism. As a result, per capita incomes remain extremely low and these economies continue to be mired in out-of-date and inefficient technologies.

Developing Economies

A number of countries in Asia lack any of the economic opportunities afforded by the three other economies. These are some of the poorest nations in the world. Their economic plight is usually further hampered by forces beyond their control. Natural disasters such as floods, typhoons, droughts, and earthquakes frequently devastate these countries. The cost of rebuilding over and over again consumes financial and human resources that might otherwise be used for economic development. These nations are forced to rely on foreign assistance for their very survival.

Other Factors

Ethnic strife is another factor hindering economic development. Sri Lanka, for

Singapore's economic growth rate in 1989 was an impressive 9.2 per cent, while in South Korea it was 6.5 per cent; by comparison, growth rates in Canada and the United States in the same year were 2.9 per cent.

Figure 10.4: Comparison of Selected Asian Countries, 1994

Country	GNP/Capita (US $)	Labour Force in Agriculture (%)	Life Expectancy (Years: male/female)
Japan	19 800	7	76/82
Industrialized Economies			
South Korea	6500	21	67/74
Taiwan	10 000	16	72/79
Resource-based Economies			
India	270	67	58/59
Indonesia	680	55	59/63
Centrally Planned Economies			
China	360	60	67/69
Vietnam	230	65	63/68
Developing Economies			
Bangladesh	200	74	55/55
Papua New Guinea	850	82	56/57

example, is divided along ethnic lines, with the Tamils concentrated in the south and the Sinhalese in the north. Since independence from Britain in 1948, the minority Tamils have fought for recognition of their separate cultural identity while the Sinhalese have asserted control over the nation. Intense ethnic violence has gripped the country since 1985. Similar circumstances exist in other countries where political boundaries have not recognized ethnic divisions. In some cases both communist and Western governments have attempted to influence these conflicts for their own purposes.

Political instability also limits economic growth. Papua New Guinea, for example, achieved independence from Australia in 1975 and adopted a parliamentary system of government. But the government has faced a series of no confidence votes, uneasy coalitions,

civil unrest, and violence. Unable to wield real power, the government has been unsuccessful in dealing with the problems facing the nation, including a lethargic and corrupt bureaucracy, a weak global economy for mineral exports, ethnic conflicts, and increasing violence.

PROSPECTS FOR THE FUTURE

Just as the nineteenth century was the age of Europe and the twentieth century was the age of the superpowers, many observers predict the twenty-first century will be the age of the Pacific. By the year 2000 it is expected that the Asian Pacific region will account for 20-25 per cent of world GNP—equal to that of Europe and North America. In January 1992, the leaders of the **Association of South East Asian Nations** (ASEAN) signed an agreement to create a regional free trade zone by 2008.

Yet obstacles to economic prosperity in Asia remain. While economic issues may be the top priority for many nations, military conflicts cannot be ruled out, particularly in sensitive areas like Korea, Taiwan, and perhaps even Hong Kong. The formation of trading blocs in other regions, such as the North American Free Trade Agreement, may hurt the economies of Asian countries that rely on their exports to consumer nations like the United States and Canada. As in the past, much of the economic development in Asia will depend on the continuing leadership and prosperity of Japan.

Monsoon rains have caused flash floods and landslides in Bangladesh (above in 1988). Such devastating natural disasters contribute to the economic problems of many poor countries.

In Review

1. In what ways did the Second World War both help and hinder Asian efforts to gain independence?

2. Why did violence and unrest often accompany independence in Asia?

3. What were the problems associated with independence in India?

4. Identify the factors responsible for the economic diversity in Asia.

5. List the positive and negative factors that may affect economic development in Asia in the future.

Japan

From the ashes of the Second World War Japan has experienced a miraculous economic transformation. While the island nation failed in its bid to establish itself as a world power militarily, it has succeeded in securing a world role economically.

The Rebuilding of Japan

Japan unconditionally surrendered to the Allied forces on 2 September 1945, ending the Second World War. The country was immediately occupied by American troops under the command of General Douglas MacArthur. MacArthur supervised the dismantling

Although cities like Nagasaki (above) were destroyed at the end of the war, Japan quickly rebuilt its strong industrial base.

and technical assistance from the United States, Japanese industries quickly began to rebuild their devastated factories. Land reform programs broke up large landholdings and allowed small farmers to join the landholding class. The large family-owned businesses called **zaibatsu** were also dismantled to allow greater competition.

It was not enough for Japan to rebuild its industrial base, however. It was critical that manufacturers find new markets for their products. With the horror of war still vividly remembered in the lands Japan had occupied, the defeated nation could expect only meagre trade in South East Asia. The victory of the communist forces in China in 1949 closed off the huge Chinese market to Japan as well.

The United States was willing to help Japan rebuild, primarily because the Americans now needed their former enemy as a Cold War ally to counterbalance the growing influence of China in the region. Thus, with American help, Japan's postwar recovery was extraordinary. American aid included trade access to the US market, the transfer of new technologies, and financial incentives. The Korean War in the early 1950s stimulated $3 billion in manufacturing as Japan's proximity to the conflict zone made it a natural supply area. The country's growth rate was the world's highest in the 1950s, reaching 17 per cent in 1960, largely due to exports to the United States.

of the Japanese military and the establishment of a **constitutional monarchy**. A new constitution called for a revised parliamentary system, called the **Diet**, with two elected houses. Women were given the right to vote and a bill of rights guaranteed freedom of speech and religion and equality of the sexes. The constitution also prohibited Japan from engaging in war or maintaining armed forces.

The Industrial Revolution had reached Japan almost a century before the Second World War. With financial

The Japan Security Treaty was signed in 1951. The treaty guaranteed that the United States would defend Japan against any aggression. In return, the United States had the right to maintain military bases in Japan.

JAPAN'S ECONOMIC SUCCESS

Why was Japan's economic recovery so successful? A number of factors worked together to create this incredible transformation. Part of the answer lay in the Japanese culture. Businesses stressed teamwork and commitment to one's employer. Employees typically worked six days a week, arriving early and leaving late. In return, most people were employed for life and were part of a company culture that extended beyond working hours. The Japanese people also saved 15 to 25 per cent of their wages. This created large cash reserves that were available to finance industrial expansion.

Japan also enjoyed a stable government. One party, the Liberal Democratic Party, governed Japan almost continually after 1945. The government established policies that favoured the development of high-technology industries with great export potential. Industry was further supported through tax incentives for research and development, while trade policies restricted competitive imports from non-Japanese firms.

Japan was always eager to import new technology, however. Industries bought the latest equipment for their factories, which in turn produced high-quality goods for the export market. In time, Japanese manufacturers were able to improve upon many foreign technologies, with the help of government sponsorship for research and development and an education system that emphasized science and math.

With Japan prohibited from maintaining a military, there was no need to pour billions of dollars into defence industries. Instead, Japanese capital was able to focus on industrial development and economic expansion. And so Japan emerged as an economic superpower.

Japan has been very successful in high-tech manufacturing.

THE ENERGY CRISIS

Throughout the 1950s and 1960s Japan enjoyed unprecedented economic growth. But the country was hit by a shock wave in October 1973. The oil-producing Arab nations announced they were cutting off the flow of petroleum to "unfriendly nations"—that is, those countries that refused to support the Arab nations in their war against Israel. Japan, which imported 99.6 per cent of its oil—and 85 per cent of this from the Middle East—was left with an oil reserve of only four days. To support the Arabs against Israel, however, would set Japan squarely against the United States.

Japan lacked a workable network of alliances that would assure its oil supply. As a result, by the end of the year the Japanese government was forced to revise its Middle East policy, demanding that Israel withdraw from the occupied Arab territories. The flow of oil to Japan quickly resumed but the crisis was not over. Oil prices jumped four-fold between October and January, launching a staggering financial crisis. Skyrocketing energy costs forced prices on manufactured goods to rise. The demand for Japanese goods dropped at home and abroad. Inflation ran rampant as wages and prices escalated, but the economy slid into recession as production fell. Japan was not alone, however; all other industrial nations were experiencing a similar crisis.

To reverse inflation, the Japanese government pressured corporations to keep prices as low as possible. Workers were encouraged to restrict their wage demands. A national energy savings plan was implemented. By 1975, inflation was under control and the Japanese economy was outperforming those of other industrialized nations.

By the mid-1980s, energy prices had stabilized, but Japan had learned a lesson from the crisis. Energy sources were diversified to include coal and liquefied natural gas and nuclear power was given a higher priority. The country also set out to forge stronger ties with the oil-rich nations of the Middle East through joint ventures and development assistance. But Japan's economic collaboration with Arab states brought harsh criticism from its US ally.

In 1989, Japan offered $6.1 billion to China for more than forty modernization projects.

DEVELOPING SUPERIOR TECHNOLOGIES

In the early 1970s, Japanese businesses bought most of their semiconductor computer chips from American companies. Recognizing the growing importance of this technology, the Japanese quickly moved to develop superior products. In 1976, a consortium of top electronic companies agreed to work together to design and produce powerful micro semiconductors. This venture was encouraged by the government, which lent huge amounts of capital and established regulations that made it difficult for foreign companies to obtain access to the technology. By the end of the decade, Japan had replaced the United States as the leading manufacturer of powerful semiconductors. The Americans viewed this government-supported co-operation by competitors as an unfair business practice.

This pattern of employing and expanding a borrowed technology was repeated with industrial robots. Robots were first developed by American industry in the 1960s, but by the mid-1980s Japan had over half of all the industrial robots in the world. Several factories were constructed using only these "steel-collar workers." This technology allowed the country's automobile industry to expand from a total production of 3200 cars in 1950 to over 12.5 million vehicles in 1992.

JAPAN'S FOREIGN INVESTMENT

The need for secure markets and sources of raw materials prompted Japanese investors to look outside the country for business opportunities. Beginning in the 1970s, investment capital began to flow out of Japan in an effort to take advantage of cheaper labour in countries like Indonesia and

Singapore and to profit from large, lucrative markets like the United States.

In South East Asia, this injection of capital acted as the catalyst for real economic growth. Private Japanese investment increased from US $1.4 billion in 1985 to $4 billion in 1987 for auto-assembly plants, iron and steel complexes, and similar industries.

Figure 10.5: Patents for Selected Countries, Mid-1980s

Country	Number of Patents	Patents per Million People
United States	104 541	419
Japan	76 984	626
Germany	11 156	141
Britain	8 795	151
France	7 672	135
Netherlands	5 737	382
Switzerland	5 002	735
Canada	1 156	43

JAPAN'S IMAGE PROBLEM

Critics have argued that while Japan encourages teamwork and co-operation from its citizens, the nation itself has not been a team player on the world scene. The government has assisted its business community in increasing exports and limiting imports through trade barriers and restrictions. For many years, Japan has consistently exported more than it imports. This trade surplus has been a source of conflict with the United States and the European Union, which have accused Japan of unfair trade practices. Retaliation in the form of quotas on Japanese car imports and high tariffs on Japanese electronics have resulted in the Japanese government making some concessions.

Critics have also argued that Japan has not accepted its obligation as a rich country to help those countries in need, in spite of the assistance it received only a few decades ago. In response, Japan has reduced some tariffs and removed some trade regulations on developing nations. Japan has also provided financial aid to ease the debt burden of several developing countries.

In spite of attempts to improve its image around the world, Japan is still viewed with a degree of suspicion, especially in countries it occupied during the Second World War. Some of this anxiety stems from the knowledge that Japan has been extremely successful on the business battlefield and has beaten Western producers on many fronts. There is some concern over how the country might use its economic power. But Japan is sending strong signals that it wants a new and improved relationship with the rest of the world. In 1993, the newly elected prime minister, Morihiro Hosakawa, opened a new era in Japanese diplomacy by formally apologizing for the damage and suffering caused by Japan during the Second World War. In 1994,

In 1989, Japan spent US $10.5 billion on foreign aid and announced a new foreign aid and credit package amounting to $43 billion.

By the year 2000, Japan's massive foreign investment program is expected to exceed US $1 trillion.

In 1992, Japan contributed its first contingent of troops to the UN peacekeeping operation in Cambodia.

the government announced a US $1 billion program to fund cultural exchanges and research into wartime atrocities.

THE REARMING OF JAPAN

In 1945, the United States imposed a new constitution on Japan that forbade the country from engaging in war. The United States agreed to defend Japan in return for establishing military bases in that country.

By the 1980s, however, the US was reeling from the high cost of maintaining military forces across the globe. Some American leaders felt a rich, prosperous Japan benefited from

American protection but shared little of the real financial and military burden this protection imposed. As the US sought to withdraw from Asia, increased pressure was applied to Japan to play an active role as a stabilizing force in the region.

Japan also faced increased pressure from the world community to take a more active part in UN operations. In particular, Canada, having contributed one out of every ten peacekeepers across the globe, called for greater Japanese involvement in these costly and difficult operations. During the Gulf War in 1991, Japan was pressured to pay a staggering $13 billion towards the cost of the operation.

In 1992, the Japanese government passed a law that would permit Japan's civilian Self-defense Forces (SDF) to serve in UN peacekeeping operations overseas. The same year, the highest-ranking Japanese official at the United Nations was appointed to direct UN operations in Cambodia, and Japan

> "We expect Japan to shoulder its burden and that's not just writing cheques."
>
> *Canadian External Affairs official, 1993*

 # VOICES

REARMING JAPAN

For some people, a rearmed Japan suggests stability and sharing the burden of world peace. For others, a military role for such an economic giant raises the spectre of war and empire. As you read the following quotations, try to develop your own views on this important issue.

Edward A. Olsen

"Tokyo and Washington know that Japan is not a free rider, but neither does it pay a full fare.... Japan's defence contributions remain decidedly minimalist, parsimonious, and inordinately cautious. Japan is indeed getting a cheap ride. It benefits from an international security system predicated on collective security but refuses to pay its fair share of the costs or bear a fair share of the risks."

Edward A. Olsen, US policy analyst, 1989

Seizabro Sato

"The major purpose of the US-Japan alliance since World War II has been to deter the Soviet Union. But the interesting thing is that in spite of the diminishing of the Soviet or Russian threat, the importance of the US alliance remains almost the same. There is no plan for the US to radically reduce its military presence in Japan...and the reason is very obvious: it nicely fits American interests, and Japan's, and the interests of most Asian countries as well."

Seizabro Sato, Director, International Institute for Global Peace, Tokyo, 1992

Takashi Oka

"This island country off the Asian coast has maintained a solid security relationship with the United States. The alliance has been more than a free Japanese ride at American expense. During the years when the Soviet threat was still active, US bases in Japan projected American power to the other side of the Pacific, maintaining stability in a region important both to the United States and Japan. Japan not only pays more for the upkeep of US bases than any NATO country, it has also been an active security partner of the United States, providing economic aid for strategic military, rather than strictly commercial, reasons to countries like the Philippines, Pakistan, and Turkey."

Takashi Oka, excerpt from "Japan's New Focus" reprinted by permission from World Monitor The Christian Science Monitor Monthly. © *1991 The Christian Science Publishing Society. All rights reserved.*

William Chapman

"There had been unrelenting pressure on Japan to strengthen her armed forces to join in the anti-Communist resistance. Until the early 1980s, Japan largely resisted that pressure and kept her military budget at modest levels. This greatly irritated the United States....

In little more than a decade, the American attitude had been reversed. The arms buildup promoted by Prime Minister Nakasone gave Japan one of the strongest sea and air forces in Asia... Indeed, it appeared that by 1990 the United States had become concerned not with the weakness of Japan's military but with its potential strength.... This was a remarkable turnabout, and it produced one of the finer ironies of the postwar relationship. Instead of issuing warnings about Soviet threats and urging bigger arms budgets, the United States, by 1990, was recording a diminished threat and implying that Japan should curb its military spending...."

William Chapman, Inventing Japan, *Toronto: Prentice-Hall, 1991, p. 280.*

sent a contingent of 1800 troops to that country for noncombat duties.

Calls for increased military and political involvement present serious difficulties for Japan. **Pacifism** is now deeply entrenched, a result of the nation's rejection of its militarist past and the horrors of atomic war. Many Asian nations that were once occupied by Japan also fear a renewed Japanese military presence. In particular, China, a traditional rival, opposes a stronger, rearmed Japan. The re-emergence of Japan as a major military power will continue to create controversy.

JAPAN IN THE FUTURE

Japan seems destined to play a strong role in the next century. Japanese leaders are hoping for a permanent seat on the UN Security Council in recognition of the nation's increasingly important role in the world community. But friction with neighbours such as China, North Korea, and Russia persists. There are also ongoing tensions in the close relationship between Japan and the United States. The future for Japan and its role in the rest of the world promises to be full of change and controversy.

IN REVIEW

1. What conditions did the United States impose on Japan after the Second World War?

2. How did Japan launch its economic reconstruction after the war?

3. List the reasons for Japan's economic success since 1945.

4. a) What impact did the energy crisis have on Japan's economy?
   b) How did Japan deal with the energy crisis?

5. a) What criticisms have been levelled against Japan's role in world affairs? Why?
   b) How has Japan responded to these criticisms?

6. List the arguments for and against the rearmament of Japan.

CHINA

During the Second World War, Japanese forces controlled most of the coastal areas and the major cities of eastern China. They were opposed by a fragile coalition of China's two most important military-political forces—the Chinese Communists, led by Mao Zedong, and the **Kuomintang**, led by Jiang Jie Shi. When Japanese forces withdrew from China following their defeat in 1945, the Communists and the Kuomintang turned on each other in a bloody and brutal civil war. When the war ended in 1949, China, the world's most populous nation, was a bastion of communism.

THE KUOMINTANG AND THE COMMUNISTS

In 1912, after years of rebellion and bloodshed, China ceased to be an empire and became a republic. The National People's Party, or Kuomintang (also referred to as the Nationalists), was organized that year as a political party under the leadership of Dr. Sun Yat-sen. The goals of the new party were to defeat the warlords who controlled China, to unite China under a democratic government, to help the peasants obtain land, and to eliminate foreign control in China.

When Dr. Sun died in 1925, Jiang Jie Shi assumed the leadership of the Kuomintang. Jiang did not share Sun's commitment to democracy and socialism, and unlike Sun he was opposed to the Communist Party, which had emerged in 1921. The Soviet Communists had been supporting the Kuomintang, which by 1924 included many Chinese Communists who were helping to organize the workers. Jiang wanted to eliminate the Communist influence in the Kuomintang and in China.

In 1927, Jiang launched a campaign to destroy the Communists. In Shanghai, Communists, trade unionists, workers, and anyone suspected of being a Communist sympathizer were attacked by supporters of Jiang. An estimated 330 000 people were killed in battles and extermination campaigns waged by the Kuomintang during the 1930s. The Communists came close to being annihilated. Hundreds of thousands of peasants starved to death or were killed as a result of the Kuomintang's actions. The Communists under Mao had the support of China's peasants; they treated the peasants fairly and redistributed land wherever they gained power. Jiang's corrupt military bureaucracy, on the other hand, operated for its own enrichment and served the interests of business rather than the people.

In 1937, the Kuomintang was unable to defend China from Japanese invasion and was forced to retreat to a remote province of China. During the Second World War, both sides fought the Japanese, but the Communist forces, who employed guerrilla tactics and adhered to a strict code of behaviour, were the superior fighting force. While the Kuomintang was backed by the United States and the Soviet Union,

> "The civilization of Europe and America is completely materialistic. There is nothing more vulgar, more brutal, more evil. We Chinese call that barbarism."
>
> *Sun Yat-sen, Chinese revolutionary leader, 1925*

the Communists had to resort to capturing their arms and supplies from the enemy.

As the war drew to a close, Jiang expected to assume the leadership of China once the Communists were defeated. Stalin and Truman also expected that Jiang would defeat Mao, but no one had anticipated the strength, discipline, organization, and popular support of the Communists. Jiang's Kuomintang army numbered more than 3 million soldiers. It was supported by the United States, which

A Canadian doctor, Norman Bethune, travelled to China in 1938 to provide medical care for wounded Communist soldiers and injured civilians. Appalled at the primitive conditions, Bethune established a modern mobile medical unit to treat the wounded. Operating under extremely adverse conditions, he performed medical emergencies close to the front lines. In 1939, Bethune's life was cut short by an infection that set in from a minor wound. At a memorial service, Mao told those assembled, "We mourn more than the passing of a man. All of us should emulate his unselfish spirit." Bethune's story is well known throughout China where he is lionized as a hero and a model of self-sacrifice.

Civilians in Shanghai fled the advancing communist forces in April 1949.

The peace that came with the end of the Second World War was extremely short-lived in China. Civil war erupted almost immediately as the Kuomintang and the Communists fought for control. By 1949, the remnants of the Kuomintang had taken refuge on the island of Taiwan, driven from mainland China by Mao's forces. The victorious Communists proclaimed the establishment of the People's Republic of China in 1949. From his base in Taiwan Jiang Jie Shi continued to claim sovereignty over all of China. The Nationalist government of the Republic of China in Taiwan was recognized by the West as the official government of China, a situation that continued until 1971.

instructed the Japanese to surrender to the Kuomintang and not to the Communists. The US even airlifted Kuomintang troops to Japanese-held areas in northern China to try to prevent the Communists from liberating those regions. In spite of these advantages, Jiang quickly lost ground to the Communists, who rushed to liberate Japanese-held territory. While Mao's People's Liberation Army was smaller, it was supported by the peasants. In addition, many Kuomintang troops, disillusioned with the corruption of Jiang's army, defected to the Communist side.

The United States backed the Kuomintang out of a philosophical opposition to communism. The Soviet Union supported the Kuomintang because of rivalries and suspicions between the Soviet Communist Party and the Chinese Communist Party.

CHINA UNDER MAO

In 1950, the Korean War began when North Korea decided to unite North and South Korea by force. The United Nations condemned the action and sent American-led troops to defend South Korea. The UN troops pushed the North Koreans back to the Chinese border; in response, Mao warned that China would attack if the UN did not pull back. When his warning was ignored, Mao sent an army to North Korea. By the time the war ended in 1953, China had lost more than 1 million soldiers and China and the United States had become confirmed enemies.

Following the Korean War, Mao set out to strengthen China from within and make it impervious to outside

PROFILE

MAO ZEDONG (1893-1976)

Politician, poet, philosopher, and soldier, Mao Zedong was one of the twentieth century's most radical and successful revolutionaries. Through years of battle he led 25 per cent of the world's people in a revolutionary war and was the first chairperson and chief architect of the People's Republic of China. Why do you think Mao is considered one of the most important figures of the twentieth century?

"Every Communist must grasp the truth. 'Political power grows out of the barrel of a gun.'"
Mao Zedong, 6 November 1938

"Letting a hundred flowers blossom and a hundred schools of thought contend is the policy for promoting progress in the arts and the sciences and a flourishing socialist culture in our land."
Mao Zedong, 27 February 1957

Born in Hunan province to a peasant family in 1893, Mao became a revolutionary early in life. In 1911, he joined the revolutionary army during the first rebellion against the Manchu dynasty. He already supported nationalist movements when he enrolled in Beijing University in 1919. There Mao became a Marxist and in 1921 he co-founded the Chinese Communist Party.

Mao publicly supported a united front with the nationalist Kuomintang. When Jiang Jie Shi assumed the leadership of the Kuomintang in 1925, however, he wanted to sever any connection with the Communists. Jiang's bloody campaign against the Communists forced Mao's army to retreat to the countryside. From there Mao trained his supporters in the tactics of guerrilla warfare.

Mao disagreed with the Marxist-Leninist view that revolution must be based on the class struggle of industrial workers. He believed that since China was an agricultural society, it was the power of the peasants that would bring about revolution. In 1929, he established the Chinese Soviet Republic in southern Kiangsi province, winning the support of the peasants by redistributing land, reducing taxes, and establishing schools.

In 1934, the Communists were forced to evacuate Kiangsi. Enduring cold, hunger, and attacks from warlord troops and bandits, the Communist army marched for more than a year. The epic Long March, as it came to be known, covered nearly 10 000 km, crossed eighteen mountain ranges and twenty-four rivers, and ended at the mountain fortress of Yenan in the northern province of Shensi. Almost 90 000 people set off on the march but only 8000 survived. Those who made it to Shensi were a hardened and dedicated military force.

In 1937, the Japanese began a full-scale war in China. They overran the north and by 1938 had taken several cities, including Shanghai, Guangzhou, and Hangzhou. From his stronghold in Yenan, Mao launched daring guerrilla attacks against the Japanese. He agreed to an alliance with the Kuomintang during the Second World War in order to combat Japanese forces. But with the collapse of Japan in 1945, Mao and Jiang squared off in battle over China once again. In the next four years, the Kuomintang was crushed, Jiang fled to Taiwan, and Mao proclaimed the People's Republic of China in 1949. He would continue to be the dominant force in Chinese politics until his death in 1976.

Red Guards marched throughout China spreading the word of the Cultural Revolution.

Battle Song of the Red Guards

We are Chairman Mao's Red
  Guards,
We steel our hearts in great winds
  and waves.
We arm ourselves with Mao
  Zedong's Thought
To keep away all pests...
Dare to struggle,
Never stop making revolutionary
  rebellion.
We will smash the old world
And keep our revolutionary state
  for ten thousand generations.

forces. A Ministry of Public Security was established to find and punish "enemies of the people." Denunciations, arrests, confessions, and punishments allowed Mao to rule with an iron grip. But it was the propaganda campaigns that were Mao's most effective method of control. The media were subjected to intense censorship. Children were taught to love Mao and to study his writings. They were also taught to spy on their parents and inform on them if they failed to embrace Mao's teachings.

In 1958, Mao launched the Great Leap Forward to expand and modernize industries. Iron and steel plants were constructed and citizens were directed to boost steel production by building backyard smelters. These initiatives created short-term increases in steel output, but the long-term consequences proved to be less desirable. Agriculture suffered as crops were left to rot in the fields while workers laboured to produce inferior steel in inefficient smelters. The Great Leap Forward ended in widespread famine and economic chaos. Estimates of deaths from starvation between 1959 and 1961 ran as high as 30 million people, although officially the famine was attributed to natural disasters. In 1959, in the face of mounting criticism, Mao retired as leader of the People's Republic. But he continued to strongly influence policy as chairperson of the Chinese Communist Party.

The Cultural Revolution

By the mid-1960s, Mao believed his revolution was being threatened by capitalist forces. In 1966, he called upon China's youth to lead a great proletarian **Cultural Revolution** to rid China of the "Four Olds"—old ideas, old culture, old customs, and old habits—and purge the Communist Party of elitists and **revisionists**. It was a desperate act to regain control of his revolution and pass on the revolutionary zeal that had fuelled his own career.

Millions of young people, known as the **Red Guards**, were released from schools and factories to criticize, beat, exile, and murder political leaders, government officials, scientists, musicians, writers, teachers, and other **bourgeois** elements. One of Mao's prime targets was his revisionist successor as head of the People's Republic, Liu Shao-chi. He was removed from office and imprisoned until his death from pneumonia in 1969.

The Red Guards destroyed priceless antiquities, libraries containing precious books and scrolls, monasteries, statues, foreign-made goods—anything that offended their revolutionary sensibilities. They were allowed to travel freely carrying the Cultural Revolution throughout China. A collection of Mao's writings, known as the *Little Red Book*, was carried by every Red Guard and came to symbolize the Cultural Revolution.

Eventually the Cultural Revolution took on the semblance of civil war as workers, farmers, and soldiers armed themselves in opposition to the Red Guard. In July 1968, Mao called upon Red Guard leaders to curtail their chaotic activities. In only a few months, the political, educational, and economic systems of the country had been shattered and the lives of thousands of people had been destroyed. But the forces of the Cultural Revolution that Mao unleashed did not completely disappear until Mao's death in 1976.

China, the Soviet Union, and the United States

China and Russia had been traditional rivals for centuries. But after both countries adopted communism, it was expected they would establish closer ties. Instead they vied with one another for leadership of the world communist revolution.

During the Second World War, the United States believed that if China fell to Mao's Communists the country would become a puppet of the Soviet Union. What they failed to realize was that Mao and Soviet leader Joseph Stalin distrusted each other. Stalin resented Mao's independence and Mao was wary of Stalin's ambitions in China. Not wishing to see a strong, united China, Stalin withheld Soviet support for the Chinese Communists in their struggle against the Kuomintang and later the Japanese. Instead, he supported the Nationalists, and in 1949 he urged Mao to settle for control of northern China and leave the rest to Jiang Jie Shi.

Mao, of course, disregarded Stalin's advice. When he achieved victory over the Kuomintang in 1949, Mao asked Stalin for help in rebuilding China. But their talks in Moscow ended in argument, and Chinese-Soviet relations declined rapidly thereafter.

In the 1950s, the Soviet Union refused to share its nuclear weapons technology with China. In response, China conducted its own nuclear research and in 1964 exploded its first atomic bomb. Three years later China tested its first hydrogen bomb.

Tensions between China and the Soviet Union continued. Mao was critical of the Soviets for straying from what he considered to be the pure form of communism—that practised by the Chinese. The Soviet invasion of Czechoslovakia in August 1968 further heightened Chinese suspicions. When Soviet premier Leonid Brezhnev announced the Brezhnev Doctrine, which asserted the Soviet Union's right to invade rebellious communist countries, Chinese officials were convinced they had much to fear from their neighbour.

China followed a policy of peaceful co-existence and established friendly relations with non-communist states. By 1971, China was no longer internationally isolated and the People's Republic of China was admitted to the UN, replacing the Nationalist Chinese republic in Taiwan.

An outright confrontation between China and the Soviet Union was ignited in the spring of 1969 over an island in the Ussuri River, which forms part of the long boundary between the two countries. Violent skirmishes continued until September when both sides agreed to negotiate a peaceful settlement of the dispute. But the issue remained unresolved and by the early 1970s there were over 1 million troops amassed on each side of the border.

The hostilities between China and the Soviet Union prompted Mao to make overtures of friendship to the United States. The first move came in 1971 when China invited an American table tennis team to China for a tournament. Official political visits began shortly thereafter, including the historic visit by US president Richard Nixon in February 1972.

The American government was eager to develop stronger ties with China to create a counterbalance to Soviet influence in Asia. In 1979, the United States and China entered into formal diplomatic relations and the US terminated its recognition of the Republic of China in Taiwan as the legal government of China. With their political disagreements set aside, the way was cleared for economic co-operation between the two nations.

China After Mao

When Mao died on 9 September 1976, his legacy was considerable. He had built a communist revolution based on poor peasants rather than urban workers. China had emerged as one of the world's great military powers. The Communist Party was firmly in control of China's destiny. How long Mao's revolution would survive the challenges of economic growth and political reform now rested in the hands of his successors and with the Chinese people themselves.

Immediately following Mao's death, two factions sought to fill the power vacuum his death created. One was the radical group known as the Gang of Four, which included Mao's widow, Jiang Qing. The other was a group of political moderates headed by Deng Xiaoping, a former premier. Less than a month after Mao's death, Jiang Qing and the remaining Gang of Four were arrested for plotting to seize power. In 1980, they were blamed for the excesses of the Cultural Revolution and were found guilty of crimes against the state.

Deng Xiaoping emerged as the most powerful figure in the country. He earned a reputation as a pragmatic leader, willing to bend communist ideology to achieve results. The China that Deng inherited was in a state of disarray. The agricultural sector was inefficient and much of the food supply had to be imported. Industrial productivity was hopelessly low. Lawlessness born of a frustration with poverty and hunger was sweeping the land. To turn the country around, Deng pursued the Four Modernizations, a program to achieve real development in agriculture, industry, science and technology, and defence.

Farming communes were broken up and the land distributed to the workers. Increased production was encouraged through incentives and decentralized control. Private enterprise was permitted in certain areas and local managers were given greater

decision-making authority. Food and housing subsidies were reduced to allow prices to better reflect market conditions. To improve industries, foreign investment was encouraged, as was the transfer of technologies from other countries. Small- and medium-sized industries were emphasized instead of heavy, capital-intensive projects. Thousands of students were sent abroad to study to help achieve these goals.

The reforms opened the country to the international community and loosened its ties to socialist doctrine. The changes were welcomed by some but resented by others. Deng had to balance the need for economic reforms with resistance to political change on the part of the Communist establishment. Some pro-democracy forces began to advocate a Fifth Modernization —greater political freedom.

THE TIANANMEN SQUARE MASSACRE

As political change swept across the Soviet Union and Eastern Europe, many Chinese citizens were eager for similar reforms in their country. Student demonstrations for democracy culminated in a massive protest in Tiananmen Square in Beijing in April 1989. When the government failed to meet the protestors' demands, many students began a hunger strike. This launched a vast popular movement that united the students with intellectuals, professionals, workers, and peasants against the communist

Pro-democracy demonstrations in Beijing's Tiananmen Square were quashed by the Red Army.

regime. On May 20th **martial law** was declared. Within the government, a power struggle was developing between Communist hardliners and a more conciliatory wing of the party. Ultimately the hardliners gained the upper hand and on June 3rd the army moved into Tiananmen Square. Over 100 000 citizens tried to block the troops and tanks. When tear gas failed to move the human barricade, the killing began. Students and other demonstrators were shot down or crushed by army tanks. Thousands were killed and even more were injured.

Following the massacre 300 000 troops occupied Beijing. There were mass arrests throughout China as the government initiated a crackdown. Official statements branded the students as counter-revolutionaries trying to overthrow the government. But the massacre at Tiananmen Square had been witnessed around the world via television. The international community reacted with horror at the brutal tactics used to put down a peaceful demonstration. Some countries, including Canada, withdrew their ambassadors from China and adopted economic sanctions. But most of these actions were short-lived and had little impact on China.

China, Hong Kong, and Economic Prosperity

In 1842, China was forced to cede part of Hong Kong to Britain and in 1898 to lease additional lands on a ninety-nine-year lease. With its excellent port facilities, convenient access to the rest of Asia, and efficient labour force, the British colony flourished economically to become the world's third largest financial centre. In 1997, Britain's lease on this bastion of capitalism expires and Hong Kong reverts to the People's Republic of China.

In the 1980s, China began negotiating for the return of Hong Kong. The Chinese government has agreed that the existing economic and social systems, based on capitalist principles, will be left intact for fifty years. In spite of China's assurances that it will respect the rights of individuals, many Hong Kong entrepreneurs have chosen to emigrate rather than live under communist rule. Throughout the 1980s and 1990s, a steady flow of people and capital left Hong Kong.

Faced with slow economic growth, the Chinese government hopes to utilize the wealth and expertise of Hong Kong to improve the economy of the whole nation. Cities close to Hong Kong have been granted status as Special Economic Zones with greater economic freedoms and tax incentives to encourage foreign investment. Cities such as Shenzen, Zhuhai, and Shantou have been experiencing economic booms as a result of their SEZ status. In 1992, Deng Xiaoping called for the country to build "several Hong Kongs." Chinese officials seem willing to bend communist ideas of state ownership and central planning to achieve economic progress.

They are not willing, however, to relax their authoritarian control. New democratic reforms introduced in Hong Kong in 1992 by the British governor caused renewed tensions between Britain and China. The Chinese government viewed the reforms as a means of undermining its ability to establish political authority in 1997. Further

"Hong Kong constantly lives on the brink of extinction. That's why it always behaves as if there is no tomorrow."

Charles Kao, Chinese University Vice-Chancellor, 1993

negotiations between British and Chinese officials on democratic and economic reforms under Chinese rule ended in 1993 without resolution. China's leaders are aware that more liberal attitudes in Hong Kong could rekindle democracy movements across the country.

Thus the transition of authority in Hong Kong raises many questions: Can a communist giant successfully absorb a spectacularly prosperous capitalist haven? Can China's aging regime contain the democracy and freedom experienced by the people of Hong Kong? Will the transfer of Hong Kong be peaceful and orderly, or will the world witness a new flashpoint for international conflict?

Hong Kong exports more manufactured goods annually than all of eastern Europe.

IN REVIEW

1. Outline the struggle between the Kuomintang and the Communists up until 1949.

2. Explain the Great Leap Forward.

3. a) What was the purpose of Mao's Cultural Revolution?
    b) What was the result of the Cultural Revolution?

4. a) What was the relationship between China and the Soviet Union?
    b) How did this relationship influence China's foreign policy towards the United States?

5. What reforms were introduced by Deng Xiaoping following Mao's death?

6. What led to the massacre in Tiananmen Square?

7. What problems might be encountered after Hong Kong reverts to China?

SUMMARY

At the end of the twentieth century, the focus in the Asian Pacific basin has shifted from political and military concerns to economic issues. Led by Japan, a few newly industrialized nations have emerged as key players on the world economic stage. Yet this prosperity overshadows the poverty and lack of development opportunities that still exist throughout much of Asia. Improving the quality of life in these countries remains one of the challenges of the twenty-first century.

Other issues also loom in Asia, however. Japanese-American relations, Chinese-Hong Kong relations, North and South Korea, and religious and ethnic conflicts in Central Asia may all command attention in the new world order.

MAKING CONNECTIONS

1. In your opinion, what are the most significant forces affecting events in Asia?

2. Widespread instability occurred in Asia after the Second World War and again in the late 1980s and the 1990s with the rapid rise in economic importance of a handful of Asian countries. Compare these two periods in chart form under the following headings: Major Forces, Key Countries, Important Issues.

3. Compare the case studies of Japan and China. Record your points in a comparison chart under the following headings: Economic Conditions, Political Conditions, Important Problems, Possible Future Developments.

DEVELOPING YOUR VOICE

4. a) In a small group, brainstorm the problems facing the countries of Asia. After you have prepared your list, select the three most important problems.
    b) If you were a leader in one of these countries, what policies would you propose to try to solve these problems?

5. Compare and contrast the ideas of Mao Zedong and Mahatma Gandhi. Which leader's philosophy do you think is more appropriate in today's world? Why?

6. In small groups, discuss this statement: "As the twentieth century ends, the era of North America is on the wane while that of Asia is on the rise."

RESEARCHING THE ISSUES

7. Research the economic relationships between China and Canada, and Japan and Canada. In chart form, record your findings, including total value of imports and exports, types of imports and exports, foreign investment, joint ventures, etc.

8. Maintain a media watch of press clippings and magazine articles on the current situation in Hong Kong.

9. Select one country in Asia and prepare a case study outlining the major issues this country has faced since 1945. Discuss the present situation and the prospects for the future.

VIEWPOINTS

ISSUE: WILL JAPAN BECOME THE WORLD'S LEADING ECONOMIC POWER?

As the twentieth century draws to a close, considerable economic power and prestige has shifted from the West to the Pacific Rim. Japan has emerged as an economic superpower rivalling the United States. Some observers believe that Japan is poised to challenge the United States for economic supremacy in the world. Others feel that Japan has reached its peak of economic power and that it cannot replace the United States as the world's leading economic nation.

In the first viewpoint, Jacques Attali, president of the European Bank for Reconstruction and Development, argues that Japan has already surpassed the United States as an economic power. He states that the US is unable to compete in the new global economy and has fallen behind Japan. He believes that it will not be long before this shift in economic power is widely recognized in the international community. Karl Zinsmeister of the American Enterprise Institute argues that Japan will not surpass the United States as an economic power. He believes that weaknesses in the Japanese economy limit the country's influence on the world stage and that emerging social trends will hinder Japanese expansion.

Read each of these viewpoints carefully, then complete an Argument Analysis and Evaluation Summary for each reading.

Jacques Attali

"In the Pacific Basin, we are witnessing the formation of an integrated economic core. This immense region—which by my definition excludes China but includes Japan, Korea, Malaysia, Indonesia, Singapore, Taiwan, the Philippines, Hong Kong and the West Coasts of both Americas—is partaking of one extensive economic boom. Population and production are growing strongly; transportation and communication networks are rapidly expanding; internal commerce is growing faster than the rest of the world.

"Inside this Pacific region, the internal balance is shifting as overall power increases: the dominant locale of power is about to jump from its East Coast—the US—to its West Coast—Japan.

"The signs of America's relative decline are converging and unquestionable. Japanese productivity is increasing at three times the US rate.... Traditional consumer items once associated with American industrial strength, like television sets or cars, are no longer produced competitively for export. Periodic bouts of devaluation to compensate for a weakening competitive position change nothing fundamentally.

"With the exception of two areas in which the US has had a long-standing position of quasi-monopoly—computers and aerospace—the trade deficit in high-technology exports has increased sixfold in the last decade.

"The growing US commercial deficit accompanies the shrinkage of the American role in the global economy. Over the past 15 years, the US share of global production fell six per cent while Japan's rose by 15 per cent....

"The imbalance of trans-Pacific trade cruelly reveals the relative decline of the US, for merchandise moves across the Pacific mainly in one direction. The American trade deficit with Asia will soon comprise two-thirds of its total deficit. Japan alone will be owed $100 billion....

"While Japanese protectionism aggravates American decline, it is not the primary cause. The cause is slackening competitiveness....

"Japan...possesses the key attribute necessary

for it to become the core of the Pacific—control of investment capital that will structure the industries of the future.

"At present, the 10 largest banks in the world are Japanese. While the US share of the global value of equities has diminished from 40 per cent to 20 per cent during the 1980s, the value of Japanese stock assets has risen from 10 per cent of the global share to 55 per cent. Japan is wisely using its surplus to further establish a hegemonic position in world markets.

"Japanese companies define very far in advance the consumer goods for which they believe there is a market, and derive the necessary technologies therefrom. Through a banking system intertwined with industry, the Japanese can offer low-priced products that enable them to conquer markets through undercutting competitors....

"Much of Japan's success, like America's demise, finds its explanation in cultural factors. The scarcity of inhabitable land on an insular island has favored the mentalities of frugality and miniaturization; the fear of isolation has fostered development of communication technologies; a long and violent history has produced a method of consensus-based change that provides for a steady, steam-roller momentum once the direction is set....

"More than any other nation, Japan's cultural characteristics propel it toward the future. It saves more than it consumes; it exports more than it imports; it has a long-term vision of its interests; it possesses the capacity to work and maintain quality; it has the aptitude to conceive and produce new consumer products *en masse*; it is aggressively expanding its external commercial networks....

"Despite this enormous dynamism, Japan's capacity to organize the Pacific Rim as a rival to Europe depends on its ability to conquer that blue distance across the Pacific.

"Telephone, fax, cables and satellites now permit transmissions of plans, calculations, software and money at the speed of light. It is no accident that Japan ranks first in information transmitting technologies.

"Plans for a Mach 3.5 and Mach 5 jet, which would bring any point in the Pacific to within two hours travel time from Tokyo, are already on the drawing board. To accommodate hypersonic transport, Japan is building an artificial island off its east coast replete with all the communication and meeting facilities necessary for rapidly expanding commerce.

"Within 15 years, scientific progress in materials research and propulsion will put all Asian ports at less than a day at sea from Japan, also reducing the trans-Pacific journey by three days.

"Japan is also working on a revolutionary hydrogen-powered motor that promises, within the next 15 years, to place all cities in Japan within one hour of Tokyo. This development will transform the Japanese archipelago into a unified metropole of a scope that can anchor the vast Pacific prosperity."

An abridged version of "Lines on the Horizon: A New Order in the Making," *by Jacques Attali,* New Perspectives Quarterly, *Spring 1990. Reprinted by permission.*

Karl Zinsmeister

"Japan...is not an unerringly successful nation. The Japanese, too, have their societal weaknesses, their inefficient sectors, their economic failures....

"The first thing to be said about Japanese productive prowess is that an inventory of the consumer products in your house and garage is a misleading way to gauge it. Japanese successes are concentrated in manufacturing...and further focused within a narrow band of export durables like home electronics and cars.

"A broad comparison of productivity in Japan and the United States...found that Japanese output lagged behind US standards in 16 of 29 major industries (and that the United States was actually widening the gap in 12 of these). Japan had an edge in ten.

"Using GNP [gross national product] per person—the broadest possible measure—overall Japanese productivity is still only about three-quarters of the American level. US transportation and communications workers, for instance, are about twice as productive as those in Japan. In retailing and service industries, Americans are about half again as fruitful, and US farmers are more than four times as efficient as their Japanese counter-parts. Japan's poor performance in such areas is often masked by measures that shelter her weak industries from competition. These protective measures are a source of friction with her trading partners, and they also exact a stiff penalty on the Japanese standard of living....

"Now that Japanese are beginning to travel abroad and otherwise becoming more open to the world, they are at last recognizing the weakness of many of their public services and demanding improvements in everything from parks to sewers. This will require vast expenditures—the government expects to commit trillions of dollars in the 1990s to infrastructure spending. While improvements in the quality of Japanese life will certainly result, there will also undoubtedly be some damping effect on private investment as a result of so much cash being soaked up for other purposes.

"This is particularly important in light of recent political and demographic trends. For all the hullabaloo over US budget deficits, the truth is that Japan has been the deficit and debt champ among major countries since the mid-1970s. Japan's budget went deeply into the red after 1975, with government borrowing covering more than a quarter of all spending in some years during the 1980s....

"Japan's rising infrastructure bills and high debt are particularly relevant in light of its coming retirement (and social security and health expenditure) boom. Japan is rapidly on its way to becoming the world's oldest nation. The percentage of elderly in the population will pass US levels in 1990, and between now and 2010, the ratio of working-age to above-working-age citizens will tumble rapidly.

"As a result, demand on the national income stream for old-age support will increase sharply—from 12 per cent of average pre-tax wages now to around 23 per cent 20 years hence. Having had the advantage of a very light public-sector load for more than a generation, Japan's private producers are going to find their burden increasing dramatically from now on.

"Its rising costs is only one of the problems of the Japanese government. A deeper one is weak political leadership. Japan is hardly democratic in the American sense of that word. While a political meritocracy sprang from the ashes of World War II, political leadership today is rarely rejuvenated by fresh talent. One-third of ruling politicians have inherited their seats from their fathers or business groups, and the office-holding clique is solidifying itself through intermarriage and nepotism....

"Private industry, too, has its laggards in Japan. Telecommunications, for instance, are not particularly efficient. A domestic long-distance call costs more than three times as much in Japan as in the United States, and calling abroad from Japan is much more expensive than the reverse. Though the Japanese are significant exporters of telecom equipment, it is mostly low-end technology not in heavy demand in the United States and other competitive markets. Much the same situation applies to Japanese computers. Japanese attempts to build a leading biotechnology industry have also fizzled, as have efforts to manufacture civilian airliners.

"Energy is a critical sector in which Japan is particularly frail. The country is dependent upon imports for every bit of its petroleum; worse, the Ministry of International Trade and Industry [MITI] has badly damaged the nation's oil industry over recent decades with what has been called the worst national energy policy on the globe....

"Tighter oil supplies and higher prices in the years ahead will pinch the Japanese disproportionately, not only because of their complete reliance upon imports, but also because 35 per cent of Japanese gross domestic product comes from manufacturing—the most oil-hungry of productive sectors. (By comparison, only 19 per cent of US output comes from manufacturing.)...

"Japan is in the midst of an explosion of consumerism. Traditionally, the Japanese frowned on borrowing. Today, however, home equity loans have caught on, and the number of credit cards in Japan jumped from 40 million in 1983 to 110 million by 1987. A boom in expensive overseas travel is underway, with 10 million Japanese going abroad in 1989. Japan's saving rate...has fallen....

"Another factor that is moderating some growth is the fact that Japan has lost its wage advantage. The country is in the midst of a serious worker shortage, and pay levels are rising sharply.

In manufacturing, Japanese wage costs per worker are now higher than in the United States and about five times prevailing standards in South Korea and Singapore. In labor-intensive industries like textiles, the 'Four Dragons' (Taiwan, Hong Kong, Singapore, and South Korea) had overtaken Japan in competitiveness by the early 1970s. For durable consumer goods, they passed the Japanese in the mid-1980s....

"Even in famously successful Japanese industries like steelmaking and shipbuilding, offshore cost advantages have sometimes idled domestic production. In areas of current Japanese superiority like silicon chip production, competitive pressure from newly industrialized countries will also increasingly be felt....

"Competition from the United States is also increasing. The fall in the value of the dollar from its artificial heights in the late 1980s returned a considerable number of American exports to comparative advantage. Some longer-term structural changes favor American competitiveness as well. For one, tax conditions in America and Japan have to a considerable extent reversed....

"The United States is beginning to solve other problems that have hampered it in matching Japanese performance. The ratio of engineers and scientists to the total labor force, for instance, has recently been rising faster here than in Japan. Many American corporations slimmed down and toughened up their operations during the 1980s. The federal budget deficit has been reduced.... Immigration continues to bring new talent and inspiration to the American labor force. And our defense burden is shrinking. Unsurpassed wealth, the world's most-educated populace, and nonpareil science give the United States three very strong cards for the long haul.

"To say that the confluence of factors that produced Japan's remarkable successes in the 1980s will be difficult to sustain indefinitely is not to say Japan is going to crash.... Japan will almost certainly be a fast-growing, impressively prosperous nation for many years to come. Its people's attitudes and the soundness of its social institutions guarantee that.

"The point here is simply that the Japanese are not exempt from the laws of gravity or economics. Their present-day triumphs are aberrant in many ways, even by their own high standards, and by the end of the 1990s it is quite likely that Japan's Superman mantle will have disappeared. Japan will then have to content itself with being 'merely' one of the world's most productive societies, the second-leading economic power for the foreseeable future.

"It is a good wager that these times will someday be viewed as the peak of Japan's contemporary bloom, an abnormal era that whisked Japan into a rightful position among the top rank of nations, where she then settled in for a long period of shining, but not overwhelming, success."

An abridged version of "Shadows on the Rising Sun," *by Karl Zinsmeister*, The American Enterprise, *May/June 1990. Reprinted with permission of the American Enterprise Institute for Public Policy Research, Washington, DC.*

ANALYSIS AND EVALUATION

Refer to the Argument Analysis and Evaluation Guide on page viii.

1. Using the Argument Analysis and Evaluation Guide, compare the readings by Attali and Zinsmeister. On what do they agree? On what do they disagree?

2. Decide which of the viewpoints you tend to support and explain why. Be sure to use specific information from this textbook, the readings, and other sources to support your position.

3. State and support your position on the issue: "Will Japan become the world's leading economic power?

CHAPTER ELEVEN

Latin America: The Challenge of Poverty

"All people in this hemisphere are entitled to a decent way of life. Those who make peaceful revolution impossible will make violent revolution inevitable."

US president John F. Kennedy, 1961

"What is to become of Latin America...? Are we to become the shanty towns of the world, while Japan, the United States, and the industrialized nations thrive?"

Arturo O'Connell, former director of Argentina's central bank, 1990

Left: Cuban refugees flee their homeland

❖ OVERVIEW

Today, over 40 per cent of the people of Latin America live in poverty. Some of the hardship is the result of corrupt governments with self-serving policies. Yet the heart of the problem can be traced to Latin America's colonial past. While nationalist movements swept across the region in the early 1800s, independence did little to eliminate the social stratification that colonialism had created. The result has been a continuous cycle of poverty for many Latin Americans.

Latin America is a large and diverse region that encompasses Mexico, Central America, South America, and some of the Caribbean islands. The case studies explored here show two countries that have followed markedly different paths. Cuba embraced a communist revolution led by the charismatic leader Fidel Castro. Argentina, on the other hand, has experienced democracy, military rule, and a return to democracy. These two case studies provide a sample of the diversity of Latin America.

and Central America had developed a wide range of societies, from nomadic hunters and gatherers to the empires of the Incas and the Aztecs. After Columbus arrived in 1492, the European settlers quickly transformed much of the continent. They established farms, mines, and towns to exploit the rich natural resources of the region. Their activities laid the foundations for the economic, political, and social conditions that exist in Latin America today.

The Spanish were the dominant colonial power in Central and South America. They brought with them many of their European traditions, including the values of the Roman Catholic Church and the feudal system of land distribution. Thus the role of the Church in the affairs of state in Latin America had a deep-rooted tradition. Likewise, the introduction of the feudal system had a lasting impact on the economy of the region and the prosperity of its people.

Those who owned the land and mines—the elite of society—required a substantial supply of labour for their huge operations. Local peoples were contracted to work in the fields and mines. They were often enticed to accept these contracts by what appeared to be attractive loans from the landowners. But their wages were never enough to repay the loans and so they became indebted for life. These debts were passed on from generation to generation, creating a class of *peons*—landless agricultural and mine workers who were destined to spend their lives in poverty.

FOCUS QUESTIONS

1. What economic circumstances helped to shape modern Latin America?

2. In what ways does the class structure of Latin American society restrict social change?

3. Why did democracy fail to take deep root in Latin America?

4. What are the key features of the Cuban Revolution?

5. What challenges faced Argentina in the twentieth century?

THE SEARCH FOR STABILITY

Long before the arrival of European settlers, the native peoples of South

THE QUEST FOR INDEPENDENCE

In this atmosphere of a distinct and structured social hierarchy, the seeds of independence began to take root. Each element of society had its own reasons for wanting to sever ties with the home country. The poor simply hoped independence would give them freedom and ultimately a better way of life. The middle and elite classes opposed the trade restrictions and heavy tax burdens that imperial countries imposed on their colonies. The rich landowners and merchants saw independence as an opportunity to expand their own power and control while retaining their privileged positions.

The opportunity to break away from Spain was presented when French emperor Napoleon Bonaparte invaded Portugal and Spain in 1808. In the political and military upheaval that ensued, the Latin American colonies were able to gain control from Spain.

AFTER INDEPENDENCE

The liberation of Latin America was a revolution in the political sense only; in a social context, things remained unchanged. Latin America continued to be divided by race and social status. Whites retained their position of power and privilege. People of mixed

One of the leaders of the independence movement was Simon Bolívar. Born to a wealthy merchant family in Venezuela in 1783, Bolívar was educated in Spain and travelled in Europe during the French Revolution. Inspired by that revolt, he returned to Venezuela to lead nationalist revolutionary armies against Spain. He battled colonial forces in several uprisings and succeeded in liberating Venezuela (1821), Colombia and Ecuador (1822), Peru (1824), and Bolivia (1825).

Figure 11.1:
Independence in Latin America. The year of independence is indicated in brackets.

Figure 11.2: Racial Composition of Spanish-speaking Countries in Latin America, 1825

Race	Spanish America (%)
White	18
Mixed race	28
Black	12
Native	42

The population of Latin America developed into distinct classes. Initially there was a small elite of European origin who controlled the farms and mines. Eventually, a small merchant middle-class developed, most of whom were of mixed European and native descent. The rest of society comprised the poor masses, descended from native peoples or Africans, or of mixed race.

European and native descent formed the middle class. The majority of the population, however, was either native Indian or black. Most Indians lived in isolated communities, desperately trying to earn a subsistence living from the poor soils. Most blacks remained in slavery; those who were freed became the poorest of the poor. Independence looked remarkably like colonialism.

Not everyone accepted the status quo, however. There were political clashes between conservative and liberal elements. The conservative faction favoured retaining the status quo, including the power and influence of the Roman Catholic Church. Under conservative rule, the power of the military increased substantially as a means of ensuring control over the masses. The conservatives were challenged by

Under Mexican dictator Porfirio Diaz the concentration of land ownership among the elite increased. By 1911, 95 per cent of all people who earned their living in farming owned no land whatsoever, while less than 3000 families owned almost 50 per cent of all of Mexico.

liberal reformers who favoured greater democracy, basic social reforms, and a loosening of the ties between Church and state. The conflict sometimes led to violent confrontations. Yet when the liberal factions gained control, few lasting reforms were ever implemented.

ECONOMIC IMPERIALISM

In the late nineteenth century, the governments of Latin America sought to modernize their countries. Lacking the financial resources to do so on their own, they encouraged foreign investment from the industrialized nations of Europe. Foreign companies gained control of large segments of the Latin American economy. Their economic clout enabled them to dictate development policies and projects that benefited their interests rather than those of the host country or its people. In the early twentieth century, political imperialism in Latin America had been replaced by **economic imperialism**.

There were further obstacles to economic development, however. Geographically, Latin America was isolated from the vast and wealthy markets of Europe. Much of the population was uneducated and illiterate. Domestic **infrastructures**, such as roads and communications networks, were inadequate. The uneven distribution of land and wealth meant that economic progress benefited the foreign investors and the elite of Latin American society, but did little for the middle and lower classes.

The Emergence of Military Dictatorships

The great inequities between the wealthy elite and the underprivileged majority led to the emergence of left-wing opposition groups throughout Latin America. The elite had a vested interest in maintaining the status quo; they supported the rise of military dictatorships, which also benefited from a wealthy, elitist ruling class. These repressive regimes suppressed opposition from all sides and succeeded in presenting a façade of political stability in the region—a necessary prerequisite for continued foreign investment.

ECONOMIC CHANGE

The First World War resulted in a major change in the economic situation in Latin America. Ravaged by years of war on the home front, European nations were no longer able to make large investments abroad. While American investors, who were enjoying prosperity in their own market, were eager to take advantage of the opportunities this situation created, they could not completely fill the void. In response, Latin American nations attempted to establish their own manufacturing industries to produce basic goods for domestic use. While these industries enjoyed modest success, Latin America remained essentially an agricultural region.

The Great Depression of the 1930s caused foreign investment in Latin America to come to a screeching halt. Economies were devastated as the value of natural resource exports plummeted by 65 per cent. Across Latin America, one nation after another defaulted on its foreign debt payments.

In response to the economic crisis, governments moved quickly to introduce economic reforms. In Mexico, the government took control of all foreign oil companies in the face of a labour dispute between Mexican workers and their American employers. The Mexican government's action caused panic among American investors; many called for military intervention. US president Franklin Roosevelt, however, responded to the situation with the "Good Neighbour" policy. He offered

Mexico long-term loans that would enable the government to compensate the American companies for their oil fields. The Good Neighbour policy was extended to other Latin American countries eager for American economic aid to help combat the depression.

POLITICAL INSTABILITY

The Allied victory in the Second World War unleashed a wave of democratic movements in Latin America. By 1959, the military dictatorships that had dominated in recent decades had been replaced by democratically elected governments in all but four countries. The middle class spearheaded the postwar drive for democracy, but like their predecessors they were primarily concerned with their own interests. The landless poor were locked out of the election process through regulations requiring land ownership or literacy in order to vote. Maintaining the status quo resulted in a slowdown in industrial development. Unemployment rose as a result and civil unrest grew. By the 1960s, authoritarian regimes were regaining control in Latin America. Between 1962 and 1964, eight countries experienced military takeovers. By 1970, military governments controlled most of Latin America.

The military governments did not condone opposition. They crushed political parties, arguing that they needed authoritarian control to fight the economic challenges of spiralling

Costa Rica was an exception in Latin America. Its democratic traditions were well established before the Second World War. Its army was disbanded in 1948, enabling the government to channel funds into social services and economic development.

Land reform policies were one source of civil unrest in Latin America in the 1960s. In this incident in Peru in 1964, a protest by plantation workers was put down by a police assault force.

to bring about change, new rebel guerrilla movements emerged throughout Latin America in the 1960s. The rebels demanded sweeping reforms, including the **nationalization** of natural resources and land redistribution. In the context of the Cold War, many of the rebel groups were Marxist organizations, backed militarily and/or financially by the Soviet Union. The United States viewed Soviet intervention in the region as a threat to American security and interests. In response, the American government initiated the Alliance for Progress, a multi-billion-dollar program aimed at fostering democracy and promoting economic development in Latin America. Initially the program showed modest progress in building schools and hospitals. But the economic development side of the plan gradually lost its momentum. Instead, the program concentrated on American military aid to help governments fight guerrilla insurgents.

American military aid continued throughout the 1970s and 1980s. Generous supplies of arms were shipped to countries like Honduras, El Salvador, and Nicaragua. The United States also engaged in many direct interventions in Latin America, including the invasion of Grenada in 1983 to depose the Marxist government there and the arrest of Panama's dictator Manuel Noriega in 1989.

inflation and growing foreign debt. Since the military in most countries maintained strong ties to the elite, their policies generally benefited the wealthy.

GUERRILLA ACTIVITIES

Frustrated by the failure of both democratic governments and military **juntas**

The Organization of American States (OAS) was founded in 1948 as a regional alliance designed to achieve "peace and justice and to promote American solidarity." The original membership has expanded from nineteen to thirty-five, including Canada, which joined in 1990.

A RETURN TO DEMOCRACY

The 1980s witnessed the re-emergence of democracy in Latin America. While the various military governments had promised economic progress in the 1970s, by the 1980s their economies were in steady decline. Born out of frustration with the growing economic crises, civil unrest and strikes spread throughout the region. Demands for democratic elections eventually forced the military regimes to relinquish control. By 1990, most countries of Latin America had some degree of democracy.

Yet the political future remains uncertain. The fragile democracies are continuously challenged by political and criminal violence, military and civilian conflicts, economic instability, and social inequality. The failure to resolve these problems means that democratic governments may once again fall prey to military rule or repressive dictatorships.

ECONOMIC CHALLENGES

Following the Second World War, the economic future of Latin America seemed encouraging. During the boom years of the 1950s and 1960s, there was worldwide demand for resource products like coffee, beef, timber, and minerals, which Latin American countries could supply in abundance. In addition, there was an increase in foreign investment capital. As a result, most countries enjoyed steady annual growth rates, reaching as high as 3.4 per cent by 1975.

But the Latin American economies collapsed with the worldwide recession of the mid-1970s. At first the economic problems the recession created were considered short term, but the economic decline in Latin America continued long after other nations had weathered the crisis and entered the prosperous 1980s. In fact, in Latin America the opposite had happened; in most countries, with a few exceptions, the growth rate had actually reversed itself. By the end of the 1980s, the Gross Domestic Product of

In the interest of containing communism, the United States routinely supported corrupt and repressive military regimes. In the aftermath of the Cold War, however, American intervention shifted from containing communism in Central America to fighting a drug war in the Andean region of South America.

American military intervention in Latin American countries like Grenada has been a source of controversy.

VOICES

ON MISUNDERSTANDING GOOD NEIGHBOURS

Ana Figueroa was a leading figure in education and diplomacy in Chile. In 1947, she toured several high schools in the United States. She was surprised to discover that American students had little factual knowledge of South America; instead they held stereotyped images generated by the media which, in reality, did not exist. Read Figueroa's reflections on her observations and consider in what ways we form our perceptions of people in other countries.

Ana Figueroa

"At the beginning of my visits, I was somewhat surprised when pupils in the last year of high school asked me about the geographical location of Chile. Full of curiosity, they asked me to give them a description of the typical costume used in that country, inquired whether Chilean women also wear the large Mexican sombrero, and whether I had dressed in European fashion for the first time when I came to the United States. Later, when teachers of Spanish asked me whether the language spoken in Chile was Portuguese or French, I found that I need not have wondered at the questions put to me by the children.

"The means of communication and transportation between countries have been advanced so rapidly by technology that it is urgent that the peoples of a world, which is becoming geographically smaller, understand and respect each other. [However] in the majority of secondary schools that I visited, especially in the West, the rooms in which Spanish is taught are profusely decorated with posters printed to attract tourists to Mexico showing the Indian man dressed in multicolored costumes and the Indian woman with a large hencoop lifting a big basket of fruit to her head. A picture that I saw hundreds of times shows a Mexican Indian sleeping cuddled up close to an enormous cactus and practically lost under a large sombrero. I was not surprised, then, when teachers asked me how I could get used to doing without my siesta.

"On the basis of some 35 [movies] that I have seen about Latin America produced in the United States, I have reached the following conclusions: All of them show the typical and picturesque, which actually does not exist in our countries: the Indian stretched on the ground asleep; great gun fights in bars; and children dragging themselves along on the floor surrounded by a swarm of flies.

"And now we might ask ourselves just what do South Americans know about the English-speaking peoples and the North Americans: We are no better informed. Of the culture and civilization of the United States we believe what the movies tell us: it is the country of chewing gum and divorce, of Chicago gangsters, and of cowboys in Texas."

Abridged from Ana Figueroa, "On Misunderstanding Good Neighbors," School and Society, 66:90-92 (August 2, 1947).

many countries was less than at the beginning of the decade.

Causes of the Decline

What caused the economic crisis? The countries of Latin America still depended on imported manufactured goods while their prime exports were raw materials. The cost of manufactured imports continued to climb, but prices for natural resource exports were generally low and tended to fluctuate wildly. Therefore most countries usually paid out more in imports than they earned from exports. Governments also continued to borrow heavily to finance ambitious modernization programs, and foreign bankers continued to provide the loans. By the mid-1980s, many countries were borrowing money simply to pay the interest on previous loans. These factors, combined with poor government fiscal policies, resulted in runaway inflation. In turn, the currencies of Latin American countries became worthless on the international market.

As a result of the economic crisis, many governments began to default on their loans. In response, lending institutions began demanding austerity programs in the debtor nations. Governments were forced to freeze wages, end food and gas subsidies, and terminate public works projects. As a result, unemployment escalated and higher prices reduced the real income of workers. In addition, investment capital dried up, just when it was needed most to aid in economic recovery.

Debt and Hunger

The austerity measures introduced to repay foreign debts had a devastating effect on the standard of living. This was most keenly felt among the poor. To improve the quality of life (and to appease demands for political change), governments routinely subsidized food prices on basic items like corn, rice, and beans. Burdened with the debt crisis, however, they were forced to drop these subsidies. As a result, food prices escalated with the skyrocketing inflation. The poor could no longer afford to buy even basic food items, and hunger became widespread.

Economic Prospects

While the 1980s in Latin America have been called the "lost decade," there is cautious optimism about the region's economic future. New democratic

Poverty is one of the greatest challenges in Latin America.

In 1989, the annual rate of inflation was 3700 per cent in Argentina, 3400 per cent in Nicaragua, and 3000 per cent in Peru.

Figure 11.3: Leading Debtor Nations, 1988

Country	External Debt	Per Capita	Value of Exports
Brazil	US$120 billion	US$813	US$23 billion
Mexico	107 billion	1185	21 billion
Argentina	60 billion	1885	9 billion
Venezuela	35 billion	1809	10 billion
Nigeria	31 billion	269	7 billion
Philippines	30 billion	513	7 billion
Yugoslavia	22 billion	1005	13 billion
Morocco	22 billion	833	4 billion
Chile	21 billion	1355	8 billion
Peru	19 billion	917	3 billion
Colombia	17 billion	561	5 billion
Cote d'Ivoire	14 billion	1221	6 billion

Source: World Bank

governments are trying to eliminate the economic excesses of past military regimes. Long-term economic reforms are being formulated and **debt-recycling** programs are being negotiated with foreign lenders. Governments have turned to **privatization** of state-owned businesses, selling these operations to foreign buyers and using the foreign capital from these sales to pay down their debts.

As a result of these reforms, currencies and inflation rates have stabilized. Economic growth has resumed in many countries, including Chile, Argentina, and Venezuela. With the improved economic environment, investment funds are returning to Latin America.

Mexico's economic recovery suffered a serious setback in 1994-95 as the value of the peso plummeted. The crisis prompted a multi-billion-dollar aid package from the United States and Canada.

OTHER CHALLENGES

Urbanization

Latin America's economic problems have contributed to the rapid urbanization of the region. Unable to break out of the cycle of poverty first established by the feudal system, peasant farmers move to the cities in search of jobs. But there are not enough jobs for all who arrive. Those who do find work are willing to accept extremely low wages. But they cannot afford to live in the city and governments cannot afford to provide low-cost housing. As a result, **squatter settlements** ring the cities of Latin America. People claim any unused plot of land to build makeshift shacks of cardboard, plastic, and tin. The squatter settlements have no sewers, no running water, and no electricity. The people are hungry and malnourished. Today almost 50 per cent of people in the capitals of Latin America live in squatter settlements.

Drug Trafficking

Some of the most lucrative export crops in Latin America are illegal drugs. The income generated by the production of cocaine has encouraged some governments to tolerate, and even encourage, drug trafficking. The huge drug profits have resulted in government corruption at the highest levels. Yet even when governments are determined to put drug traffickers out of business, the drug barons and their operations are hard to control.

Destroying the coca plantations is one method, but this is only a temporary measure as the crops are simply replanted elsewhere and ready for harvest within six months. The same applies to the jungle laboratories that refine the coca leaves.

At its core, drug trafficking is a result of Latin America's social and economic problems. Without economic development alternatives, the incentive for growing illicit drugs remains for both farmers and governments alike.

Squatter settlements are becoming home to a growing number of people in Latin America.

PROSPECTS FOR THE FUTURE

While the challenges facing Latin America are many, some positive steps are being taken towards the future. Throughout the region nationalist sentiments are being replaced by economic realities. Free-trade alliances are being forged to strengthen local economies by bringing down trade barriers. There is a growing recognition that economic co-operation benefits all of the participants.

On 1 January 1995, the **Mercorsor Agreement** formally eliminated tariff barriers among the signatories— Argentina, Brazil, Paraguay, and Uruguay. This trade alliance created South America's richest market, comprising 190 million people with a regional trade value of $4.9 billion. Talks with Canada, Mexico, and the United States about joining the **North American Free Trade Agreement** (NAFTA) have also been initiated, with Chile slated as the first South American nation to join the alliance. Through

greater international co-operation, Latin America is seeking to find its place in the new world order.

The birth rate in squatter settlements is extremely high and many of the children are forced to live on the streets. Children as young as six and seven resort to crime just to survive. In some cities, right-wing death squads hunt down street children, killing them on sight.

When the Colombian government attempted to end the drug trade, anarchy erupted as private armies, government troops, guerrillas, and death squads battled for control. By 1990, the death toll was 11 000, including presidential candidates, cabinet ministers, judges, and journalists. Colombia's drug profits in 1993 were estimated at US$20 billion.

IN REVIEW

1. How did colonialism lay the foundations for the social and economic structure of Latin America?

2. What factors contributed to the military takeovers in the countries of Latin America in the 1960s?

3. a) What prompted the guerrilla movements of the 1960s?
   b) What action did the United States take?

4. What are the challenges the new democracies of Latin America face?

5. a) What caused the economic crisis in Latin America after 1975?
   b) What actions were governments forced to take to address the debt crisis?
   c) What impact have these actions had?

6. Why is urbanization a serious problem in Latin America?

7. Describe the challenges of the drug war. How do you think this problem can be solved?

CUBA

At the beginning of the twentieth century Cuba was much like many other Latin American countries. Its economy was based on supplying sugar and cigars to the United States and Europe. When full independence from Spain was granted in 1802, a weak government was elected that was controlled by the United States. The US routinely intervened in Cuba's domestic affairs to ensure American interests were served.

The United States dominated Cuba's economy. Most of the sugar plantations and mills were owned by US interests and over 75 per cent of the sugar output was destined for the American market. While the economy flourished, the prosperity was enjoyed by only a few—the foreign owners living in the island's capital of Havana. Aside from a small middle class, the majority of Cubans lived in poverty.

In 1934, civil unrest and a general strike paved the way for an ambitious army sergeant to gain control of the government. With the support of the army, the civil service, and the trade unions, Fulgencio Batista instigated a military coup against the government. For the next six years Batista ruled Cuba through a succession of presidential figureheads. In 1940, he himself was elected president.

While Batista's first regime was not a particularly violent one, his government was corrupt. In 1944, Batista lost the election, and he spent the next five years in the United States. He returned in 1949 and won a seat in the senate. In 1952, he gained control of the country in a second coup. This regime was corrupt, brutal, and repressive, and it sparked an attempted revolution by the Cuban People's Party in 1953. One of the rebels arrested for the coup attempt was a young lawyer named Fidel Castro. In 1959, Castro led a successful revolution against Batista and assumed control over Cuba.

CUBA UNDER CASTRO

When Castro took power in 1959, he promised free elections, but none were ever held. Instead he set out to contain all opposition to his regime through government control of the media, the trade unions, and the University of Havana. Those who opposed Castro's government had three alternatives: silence, imprisonment, or exile.

The government took control of the economy as well. Economic policy was directed by a central planning authority controlled by Castro. Private enterprises were nationalized and foreign-owned businesses and properties were confiscated, including nearly US$1 billion in property owned by American interests. All large estates were expropriated and divided into plots for small landowners. Extensive public housing projects were undertaken, and education and health care were made available to all Cubans at government expense. In time, Castro's regime succeeded in creating a first-class health care system and an education system unequalled in Latin America.

AMERICAN REACTIONS

The confiscation of American property angered the United States. In retaliation, President Dwight Eisenhower imposed a trade embargo on Cuba. American goods could not be exported to Cuba, nor could Cuban goods be imported to the United States. In need of political and economic support, Castro found a willing ally in the Soviet Union. The USSR bought huge quantities of sugar from

Cuba and gave large sums of money for the purchase of equipment. The Soviets also began to ship military weapons and personnel to the Caribbean island. To the United States, there was no question that Castro was a communist.

Worried over a build-up of hostile arms so close to the continental US, in April 1961 the Americans backed the Bay of Pigs invasion by CIA-trained Cuban exiles. (See page 138.) But the invasion was easily repelled and as the invaders were quickly rounded up by the Cuban army.

The Bay of Pigs incident led the Soviet Union to believe that the Americans would take other actions to regain control of Cuba. The Soviet government began to install intermediate-range nuclear missiles on the island. When the United States discovered the missiles in October 1962, it demanded

Batista's government troops and Castro's rebel forces battled for control of Havana in 1958.

The capital city of Havana in prerevolutionary Cuba was characterized by gambling, crime, nightclubs and prostitution.

PROFILE

FIDEL CASTRO (1926-)

Fidel Castro remains one of the most famous and long serving revolutionary leaders of the second half of the twentieth century. He is one of only a handful of revolutionary leaders to maintain power successfully for more than thirty years. To many Cubans and foreign observers alike, Castro embodies the Cuban Revolution. But Castro is an aging man. Do you think the Cuban Revolution can be sustained in a post-Castro era?

"History will absolve me."
Fidel Castro, 1953

"Men do not shape destiny. Destiny produces the man for the hour."
Fidel Castro, 1962

Fidel Castro was born and raised in the town of Biran, the son of a sugar planter. He was educated at a Jesuit school before enrolling at the University of Havana to study law.

In 1947, Castro joined the Cuban People's Party. There he began to forge a relationship with the Cuban peasants that would last throughout the second half of the century.

In 1953, Castro led an unsuccessful revolt against Batista's corrupt regime. He was arrested and imprisoned, but was released in 1955 under a general amnesty. Castro went into exile in Mexico where he organized further guerrilla campaigns. In 1956, he was once again in Cuba to launch a second unsuccessful rebellion against Batista. This time Castro and the twelve survivors of the revolt were forced to seek refuge in the Sierra Maestra mountains. From there they began a series of successful guerrilla raids. In December 1958, Castro led a march into Havana, forcing Batista to flee the island. On 1 January 1959, Castro proclaimed the Cuban Revolution.

As the self-proclaimed prime minister of Cuba, Castro moved quickly to rid the country of foreign interests and regain control of Cuba's economy. His socialist policies pitted the island nation against the United States. Castro turned to the other superpower, negotiating credit, arms, and food supplies with the Soviet Union. His alignment with the Soviets encouraged Castro to increasingly embrace Marxist doctrine.

Castro enjoyed great support in Cuba as his reforms achieved significant improvements in health, education, and housing. His popularity increased with his determination to stand up to American power and intimidation. Castro was also admired by revolutionary organizations throughout Latin America and Africa. In Angola and Ethiopia, Castro supplied Cuban forces to actively participate in revolutionary movements there. Within the developing world, Castro played a leading role in the nonaligned movement.

As political change swept across Eastern Europe and the Soviet Union in the 1980s, Castro lost the military and economic alliance that was the foundation of his revolution's success. Without the financial backing of the Soviet bloc, the Cuban economy went into a tailspin. While popular support among Cubans for Castro and his revolution remained strong in the 1990s, the future of Castro's Cuba is uncertain.

their immediate removal. The Cuban Missile Crisis brought the world to the brink of nuclear war. (See pages 138-39.) Finally a compromise was reached: the Soviets withdrew their missiles; in return, the United States promised not to invade Cuba.

ECONOMIC RELATIONS WITH THE SOVIET BLOC

The American embargo forced Cuba to rely on the Soviet bloc as its primary trading partner; 85 per cent of all Cuba's trade was with the Soviet Union and Eastern Europe. Cuba was also almost completely dependent on the USSR for its oil supply, with 90 per cent being imported from the superpower. Cuba supplied the Soviet bloc with sugar, tobacco, and citrus fruits; in return, it relied on the bloc to supply much needed foodstuffs, including wheat, dried milk powder, and meat.

By the 1980s, the Soviet Union provided over US$6 billion annually in aid to Cuba. The funds were used to maintain Cuba's successful social programs and to build a more diverse economic base. In effect, however, Cuba had exchanged economic dependence on the United States for economic dependence on the Soviet Union. The USSR's inability to solve its own economic woes in the late 1980s, however, meant that it was increasingly less generous with its aid.

Food shortages became part of everyday life in Cuba following the collapse of communism in the former Soviet Union and Eastern Europe.

Figure 11.4: Cuban Health and Education, 1958 and 1989

	1958	1989
Life Expectancy	58 years	73 years
Infant Mortality	70/1000 births	17/1000 births
Persons per Doctor	1040	417
Literacy	24%	96%
Students per Primary Teacher	50	13

Under more lenient emigration rules, many Cubans fled the island in any vessels that would float.

Cuba After the Cold War

With the fall of communism in Eastern Europe and the disintegration of the Soviet Union, Cuba found itself isolated in the world community. The loss of trade with the Soviet bloc created shortages of every conceivable item. Between 1989 and 1992, Cuba's imports plummeted by 60 per cent.

The economy was in a shambles. Cuba, once the only Latin American country to have eliminated hunger, was now faced with extreme food shortages. Its world-acclaimed health care system was threatened by a lack of medicines and supplies. Paper shortages meant that the education system suffered as there were no textbooks. Housing projects were put on hold as there were no materials to complete

the jobs. The oil shortage decimated Cuba's transportation network, forcing a massive reduction in bus services. Cuba's standard of living plunged at a dizzying rate.

In response to the crisis, Cuba launched an emergency plan that included food rationing and energy conservation. Agricultural production shifted from export crops to domestic staples. Cuba looked to other exports, in particular medical products that resulted from the country's advanced research in biotechnology.

The tourist industry offered Cuba its greatest hope for foreign capital. In an effort to expand tourism, the government opened the economy to foreign investment, most notably in resort properties. Canada, Latin America, and Europe have provided an increasingly steady supply of tourists each year. But the biggest tourist market is the United States, and US law prevents American tourists from travelling to Cuba.

Political Reforms

Castro's government had been reluctant to introduce political reforms. In 1991, however, some concessions were made, including allowing direct elections to the National Assembly. Although the one-party system is still in effect, Cubans now have a choice of Communist Party candidates.

Anti-government demonstrations in August 1994 prompted Castro to loosen emigration restrictions. Many Cubans fled the country, piled on board any vessels that might float. To stem the tide of boat refugees, the US announced that all Cuban refugees would be detained. In September, Cuba and the United States reached a rare agreement over Cuba's emigration policy.

While most Cubans agree that they are in a state of economic crisis, there seems to be little support for the alternatives. They have witnessed the collapse of communism in Eastern Europe

To conserve energy and ease the transportation crisis, Cuba imported 1 million bicycles from China to replace motorized vehicles. In some areas, tractors have been replaced by oxen and horse-drawn carts have taken the place of trucks.

VOICES

US SANCTIONS AGAINST CUBA

The United States has maintained a trade embargo against Cuba since 1961. The Americans hoped that an embargo would force Cuba's communist regime to its knees, but in over three decades that has not been the case. With the fall of the Soviet Union, the US government has tightened its economic restrictions in the belief that Cuba is on the verge of collapse. Opponents argue, however, that sanctions against Cuba serve little purpose now that the Cold War is over. As you read these opinions, consider whether or not it is time for the United States to drop its sanctions against Cuba.

Gillian Gunn

"The only important foreign actor not rethinking its approach in Cuba is, ironically, the United States. Parts of the American academic community, moderate Cuban-American organizations, and some human rights activists in Cuba have argued that a less confrontational posture would undermine Castro's political base more effectively than confrontation, because it would limit the Cuban leader's ability to appeal to Cuban nationalism and divert blame for the island's economic predicament.

"Official United States policy remains largely unresponsive to these ideas. In mid-1991 the embargo was tightened....

"...In short, the cold war continues in the Caribbean even as it melts virtually everywhere else."

Gillian Gunn, excerpt from "Cuba's Search for Alternatives," is reprinted with permission

from Current History *magazine (February 1992). © 1992 Current History, Inc.*

Linda Robinson

"America's relations with Cuba have been frozen for more than 30 years, since Fidel Castro took power in Havana and declared himself a Communist. A well-organized and well-financed Cuban-American lobby has helped to ensure that neither Democrats nor Republicans, in the White House or in Congress, ever went soft on communist Cuba. But now, with Castro's Soviet backers gone and Cuba's revolution faltering, what is good for the exile lobby may no longer be good for America."

Linda Robinson, "After Castro Moves Out," U.S. News and World Report, *4 May 1992.*

Fidel Castro

"Cuba loses with the blockade, but the United States also loses; we, as...a small country, lose in a higher proportion. The United States loses... morally and politically before the world, because there is no political or moral justification to sustain the blockade against a small country....It constitutes a giant hypocrisy to speak of human rights while they deprive a population of 11 million of the possibility of acquiring medicine and food from the United States. This did not have...nor will it ever have, justification, much less now when one cannot speak of the cold war or tensions between the west and the east."

Fidel Castro, 1991

and the Soviet Union and the economic chaos that has ensued in those countries. They have only to look to the extreme poverty in Haiti and the Dominican Republic to see what capitalism has done for their island neighbours. Still, the future for Cuba and its socialist revolution remains uncertain in the new world order.

IN REVIEW

1. What factors led to Castro's rise to power?

2. What reforms did Castro introduce in postrevolutionary Cuba?

3. What was the American reaction to Castro's revolution?

4. What was Cuba's economic relationship with the Soviet bloc?

5. a) Describe the effects of the collapse of communism in the Soviet bloc on the economy of Cuba.

   b) What measures has Cuba taken to survive the economic crisis?

ARGENTINA

Argentina is distinct from other Latin American countries in a number of ways. Between 1850 and 1930, it was the destination of a large number of European immigrants, primarily from Italy and Spain, but also from Russia, Poland, France, and Germany. By 1914, 30 per cent of the population was foreign-born, compared with 13 per cent in the United States the same year. Immigrants stimulated the economy. Workers found jobs in manufacturing and service activities in the cities as well as on the farms of the pampas. Argentina had only a small native population. As a result, it did not develop a two-tiered feudal society with an agrarian peasant class as other Latin American countries did. Instead, a large urban working-class society emerged.

JUAN PERÓN COMES TO POWER

Democratic roots were planted in Argentina in 1853 when the country adopted a constitution and elected its first president. This democratic tradition continued until 1930, when a military coup ousted the elected president in the face of government corruption and dissatisfaction with foreign policy. A series of military governments followed. In 1943, a group of military officers, inspired by the fascists in Europe, seized the reins of power. They dissolved Congress and abolished all political parties.

Within the new military government, one member quickly emerged as the real power in Argentina. As labour secretary, General Juan Perón set out to win the support of the labour unions and the working class. He introduced legislation establishing social benefits and better working conditions. He intervened in strikes, settling them in favour of the workers, and cultivated the support of labour leaders. When general elections were held in 1946, Perón was elected president.

Between 1946 and 1950, workers' wages jumped sharply and standards of living improved. Most of Perón's reforms were at the expense of the wealthy merchants and landowners. Perón tried to keep a clamp on dissent by suppressing the freedoms of both speech and the press. Eventually, however, Perón's reforms conspired against him. In the early 1950s, inflation soared. Severe drought devastated agricultural production. Exports to Europe

"If I had not been born Perón, I would have liked to be Perón."

Juan Perón, 21 February 1960

PROFILE

EVA PERÓN (1919-52)

Juan Perón's greatest political asset was perhaps his second wife, Eva. The former actress turned politician, known as "Evita" (little Eva), was a champion of the rights of the poor. She was idolized by millions of Argentinians. During her short time at the political forefront, she became a legend whose story is heralded even today. What special qualities do you think enable a single individual to inspire a nation?

"What we are fighting for is to destroy the inequalities between you and the wives of your bosses."
     Eva Perón, 1946

"Some day [poor women] will be able to sit next to rich women, on the basis of complete equality."
     Eva Perón, 1948

"I am nothing—my work is everything. Time is my enemy."
     Eva Perón, 1951

Maria Eva Duarte was born to a poor family in Los Toldos in 1919. As a teenaged girl she set out for Buenos Aires to pursue a career in theatre. She established a singing career in nightclubs and radio and eventually became a minor film actress.

Duarte became politically active as a member of the radio workers' union in 1944. It was through union activities that she met Juan Perón, who was then the minister of labour. They were married in 1945, and together they hit the campaign trail, a first in Argentine politics.

After Perón's election as president of Argentina in 1946, Eva devoted her time, energy, and influence to alleviating poverty and enacting social reforms. She became, in effect, the minister of health and labour. In the first year of Perón's administration, Eva channelled over $4 million in food, clothing, textbooks, and other necessities to the poor of Argentina.

Eva championed women's rights and played an instrumental role in the passing of legislation giving women the vote in 1947. Her political life blossomed after that. In July 1948, she established the Eva Perón Foundation, a social assistance program funded by the government, labour unions, and the private sector. The foundation sponsored the construction of hospitals, schools, and housing projects.

As a public speaker, Eva Perón captured the hearts of the Argentinian people with her sincerity and concern for the underprivileged. Her tireless campaigning was a significant factor in her husband's re-election in 1951. Eva herself made a bid for the vice-presidency in that campaign, but her efforts were blocked by the military, which viewed her as a socialist threat.

In 1952, the brief but remarkable career of Eva Perón came to a tragic end. Her death from cancer at the age of thirty-three stunned her supporters and sent the nation into mourning.

General Juan Perón returned to Argentina as president after eighteen years in exile.

slumped as industries there recovered from the Second World War. Argentina was mired in a growing public debt. Perón responded with a tough stabilization program that included wage controls, cutbacks in government spending, and tight credit. But it was not enough to quell the growing discontent. In 1955, another military coup forced Perón to flee to Paraguay.

PERÓN'S RETURN TO POWER

Between 1955 and 1972, a succession of military governments held power in Argentina. Economic and social conditions steadily deteriorated. In desperation, the military legalized political parties in 1971. In 1973, the Péronista Party won a large majority in national elections. In September of that year, Juan Perón returned from exile in Spain to assume the party leadership. After almost twenty years, Perón was once again elected the president of Argentina. His vice-president was his third wife, Isabel, a former cabaret dancer whom he had met and married while in exile.

Perón was unable to reverse Argentina's escalating economic crisis, nor could he heal the deep social and

political rifts that divided the country. Even as he called for "peace and conciliation," bloody street fighting was taking place among factions of his own party. Ten months after regaining office, Perón died of heart failure in July 1974, leaving Isabel Perón as president. But she was ill prepared for the role and found herself unable to control Argentina's escalating problems, including spiralling inflation and violent leftist opposition to the government. On 24 March 1976, Isabel Perón was ousted by a military coup.

ARGENTINA'S "DIRTY WAR"

The military junta that gained control in Argentina in 1976 quickly launched a program of economic reform. Wages were frozen, taxes were increased, and price subsidies were cancelled. To stifle criticism, the junta launched a campaign of terror against all opposition. Over a period of five years, 15 000 to 20 000 people disappeared after being arrested by government death squads in the "dirty war" of political terrorism. Still, the civil unrest could not be quelled. The economy deteriorated. In an effort to distract Argentinians from the country's economic woes and their loss of civil liberties, in 1982 the military government made a momentous decision—to go to war with Britain over the Falkland Islands.

THE FALKLAND ISLANDS WAR

Known as *Las Malvinas* in Latin America, the Falklands are a group of 200 windswept Atlantic islands 400 km off the southern tip of Argentina. Inhabited by 1800 British subjects and 600 000 sheep, the British have occupied the islands since 1833.

In 1982, a minor dispute between the two countries touched off a seventy-four-day war. It was a lopsided event as the better trained and equipped British troops won a decisive victory. By the time it was over, 650 Argentinian soldiers were dead or missing and over 1000 were wounded; 11 000 Argentinians had been taken prisoner. The devastating defeat shattered Argentina's national pride. But even more damaging was the fact that the war consumed scarce financial resources and pushed the country to the brink of economic collapse. Completely discredited, the military junta relinquished power and democracy returned to Argentinian politics once again.

DEMOCRACY RETURNS

In democratic elections in October 1983, a civilian moderate named Raúl Alfonsín won the presidency of Argentina. The economic challenges of the new government were stunning in magnitude. The annual inflation rate exceeded 3700 per cent. Argentina's currency was so worthless that angry demonstrators hurled money at police. Hungry mobs looted grocery stores for food as the average take-home pay of 1 million pesos a week—roughly US$19 —was not enough to feed their families. By 1988, the foreign debt was US$60 billion, one of the highest in the world.

Unable to resolve the country's economic crisis or to calm the masses, Alfonsín declined to seek re-election. In 1990, Carlos Saúl Menem was elected on the promise of new solutions to old problems. The stringent reforms he introduced shocked the nation and sharply lowered the standard of living. In despair, thousands of Argentinians applied to emigrate to Spain and Italy, which their grandparents and great grandparents had left for a better life more than a century ago.

Gradually, however, Menem's measures began to produce positive results. Wage and price controls brought inflation down to acceptable levels. The sale of government-owned industries reduced the foreign debt. Industrial and agricultural policies increased export sales. Between 1990 and 1994, the Gross National Product and annual per

Mothers and human rights activists (wearing masks to represent the disappeared) demonstrated in Buenos Aires and other cities to demand information about those people who went missing during the "dirty war."

"You can save democracy only when you can show that democracy matters and that democracy works....Democracy for us has been nothing."

Argentinian political scientist Atilio Boron, 1990

Angry Argentinians protested against the amnesty granted in 1990 to the junta leaders of the "dirty war."

THE FUTURE FOR DEMOCRACY

As in much of Latin America, economic instability in Argentina has shaken the country's fragile democracy. In response, some people have renewed their support for right-wing military parties. Others have looked to a new generation of leaders who draw on the people's frustration and disaffection with the government. But Argentinians are also learning to use the democratic process to launch grass roots movements intended to persuade politicians through the popular will. As in much of Latin America, the key question is, can democracy survive without economic prosperity?

capita income doubled. With a more positive economic climate, capital is now being invested in Argentina's future.

IN REVIEW

1. In what ways is Argentina not typical of Latin American countries?
2. How did Juan Perón first gain popular support in the election of 1946?
3. What economic problems contributed to Perón's downfall in 1955?
4. How did the Falklands War contribute to the fall of the military junta in 1983?
5. Why is democracy fragile in Latin America?

SUMMARY

As the twentieth century comes to a close, Latin America is seeking its place in the new world order. After decades of political and economic instability, democratic governments have emerged and new economic alliances have been formed. Yet the new democracies are fragile and economies can be volatile. While there is hope for economic renewal in Latin America, the future remains uncertain.

MAKING CONNECTIONS

1. Create a flow diagram to show how social inequalities and political change in Latin America have been shaped by economic conditions.

2. One method of comparing the quality of life for people in different countries is to compare the amount of energy consumed per capita. The table shown below gives electricity consumption per capita for selected countries.
   a) What conclusions can you draw from this table?
   b) What might explain the differences in electricity consumption?

Country	Electricity Consumed Per Capita in kWh, 1991
Haiti	74
Bolivia	251
Nicaragua	376
Mexico	1 270
Argentina	1 450
Chile	1 616
Canada	17 872

3. Mexico and Canada both share a border with the United States. What benefits might both countries share in common as a result of their location next door to a superpower? What problems might they share?

DEVELOPING YOUR VOICE

4. True or false: Economic inequalities have created the social inequalities in Latin America. Explain your answer.

5. Heberto Padilla is a Cuban-born poet who was influential during the early years of Castro's revolution. By the late 1960s, however, he had become sceptical of socialism and critical of Castro. He wrote "In Trying Times":

> They asked him for his legs
> hard and knotted
> (his wandering legs),
> because in trying times
> is there anything better than a pair
> of legs
> for building or digging ditches?
> They asked him for the grove that
> fed him as a child,
> with its obedient tree.
> They asked him for his breast,
> heart, his shoulders.
> They told him

that that was absolutely necessary.
They explained to him later
that all this gift would be useless
unless he turned his tongue over to
  them,
because in trying times
nothing is so useful in checking hatred and lies.

    a)   What message is Padilla communicating in the poem?

    b)   Many Cubans did not resent the conformity required by Castro's regime, as Padilla did. Why do you suppose some people were satisfied with Castro's leadership?

6.   At some point the governments of both Cuba and Argentina have tried to control or prohibit opposing viewpoints.

    a)   What actions did these governments take to stop dissent?

    b)   To what extent are opposing viewpoints permitted or encouraged in Canada?

    c)   What is the value of encouraging opposing viewpoints in a society?

RESEARCHING THE ISSUES

7.   Research a Latin American country of your choice to determine the major themes or topics of its history since the Second World War. Prepare a comparison organizer to relate your country to either Cuba or Argentina.

8.   Use library and classroom resources to prepare a three-page report on one of these research topics:

- the impact of new technologies on the quality of life in Latin America
- women and politics in Latin America
- environmental issues in South and Central America
- the future of the Caribbean tourist industry
- the benefits and disadvantages of the North American Free Trade Agreement for Mexico
- the difficulties of introducing social reforms in Latin America
- the role of Canada in assisting Latin American countries.

9.   In the 1980s, the Americans took military action in Latin America on several occasions, including Grenada (1983) and Panama (1989). Research one of these incidents to discover:

- the causes
- the people involved
- the issues
- the outcomes.

Present your findings in a two-page written report.

VIEWPOINTS

ISSUE: WAS THE US INVASION OF PANAMA JUSTIFIED?

There is a long history of American intervention in Latin America. American interest in Panama was particularly strong with the completion of the Panama Canal in 1914. The 81 km long Panama Canal is a vital transportation link, providing a shortcut for ships passing from the Atlantic to the Pacific oceans. In 1903, the US negotiated a treaty for perpetual control of a 16 km wide Canal Zone. However, in 1973, after constant Panamanian pressure, the US agreed to return the Canal Zone to Panama by the year 2000.

The Republican administrations under presidents Reagan and Bush in the 1980s were opposed to any American withdrawal from the Canal Zone. In 1983, they supported General Manuel Noriega's rise to power in spite of his association with arms and drug dealing. Noriega was pro-American for many years but his regime was clearly repressive and his drug connections were an embarrassment to the US. As US pressure to fight the "war on drugs" mounted, Noriega became alienated. In order to maintain his political power base in Panama he became strongly anti-American. In December 1989, Bush authorized an invasion of Panama. Massive US forces quickly overpowered the Panamanian troops, although many civilians died in the fighting. Noriega was captured and brought to the US, where he was put on trial on a variety of drug charges.

The Panama invasion immediately raised questions about the role of the US as the world's police force. Was the US justified in sending troops to a sovereign country and arresting its leader on drug charges? Was this just a smoke screen for the real purpose of making sure the Panama Canal remains under American control? How could the US justify this invasion? Robert Kagan argues that the US has a responsibility to itself and to the people of Latin America to enforce a strong leadership role. US Democratic Senator Edward Kennedy argues that the US was not justified in this or other invasions in Latin America.

Read each of these viewpoints carefully, then complete an Argument Analysis and Evaluation Summary for each reading.

Robert Kagan

"In the United States today, two opposite brands of escapism are forming a tacit alliance to shape US policy in Latin America. The left-liberal view gained strength at the time of President Johnson's intervention in the Dominican Republic, but its origins date back at least to the beginning of the century. This view sees Latin America as a kind of Eden and the United States as destroying innocence and leaving sin in its trail. Mesmerized by Latin Americans shaking their fists at Yankee imperialism, eager from Vietnam days to find the United States guilty of transgressions abroad, the left-liberals see the solution and the salvation in disengagement. They would have the United States withdraw from the region, except for providing economic aid without imposing obligations on the recipients.

"The conservative view...is that Latin America is a pit of hell. American efforts to 'civilize' the Latins are not only futile but unappreciated. Equally influenced by shaking fists, these conservatives see no allies in Latin America...."

"The common ground between these viewpoints is that the United States no longer has real interests in Latin America....

The Exercise of Will

"With the invasion of Panama, the United States has now sent its troops into combat in Latin

American and Caribbean lands more than a dozen times in less than a hundred years, at least eight times in significant invasions and occupations. Americans risk blood and treasure in the region, on average, at least once every ten years, twice in the last seven. In addition to the troops, we have spent billions of dollars, sent thousands of advisers, authorized extensive meddling by the CIA, and dispatched countless proconsuls to manage the internal affairs of Latin nations....

"While the reasons for this constant American involvement have changed over time, fear of foreign intervention has usually been the stated rationale. The Monroe Doctrine and the 'Roosevelt Corollary' of 1904 proposed to prevent European colonial powers from exploiting endemic instability in Latin America to gain a foothold. Another Roosevelt worried about the Nazis; his successors, about international communism backed by the Soviet Union. In theory, the strategic issue has never been Latin America itself, therefore, only the possibility that some hostile or competitive power—the Spanish, French, British, Germans, or Soviets—could gain strategic advantage in America's backyard....

"The historical weakness of Latin American states has created and perpetuated a vacuum of power in the region. As the closest great power, the United States has ventured or been drawn in to fill that vacuum from a variety of motives.

"When American power grew unchallenged in the hemisphere, so did ambitions and expectations. Because their country was strong, the American people could satisfy imperial ambitions, but in the end they did not seek empire or colonies. Instead successive American leaders sought to ensure that this hemisphere would be one place where Americans could travel and do business free from arbitrary power, economic warfare, or threat of violence....

"Americans, therefore, have historically been intolerant of both indigenous and foreign threats to the safe and lucrative order they desired in Latin America. What they might need to tolerate in Asia, Africa, and the Middle East, they would not tolerate in Latin America. The history of mankind offers few examples of a great power that takes no interest in the weak states on its borders, either as a place to exercise its own will, or to prevent others from exercising theirs. It would be a peculiar form of American exceptionalism to assert that the United States alone could ignore a power vacuum in its part of the world, and history has shown that the United States is not exceptional in this respect. The invasion of Panama, for example, suggests that we have not yet entered the millennium....

"It is natural for the United States to be deeply involved in this hemisphere, and as part of that involvement to seek to build and protect an order where democratic principles—which most Americans believe are universal if not universally respected—can be upheld.... The United States has rarely intervened in a Latin American nation without trying to leave a stable democracy behind when it withdrew, no matter what the original cause for involvement....

"The United States cannot disengage from Latin America, and it cannot engage successfully except on the side of democracy. This would be true if there had never been a Soviet Union and will remain true in the decades ahead. The question is not whether American interests in Latin America are as great as in Europe or Japan. What matters is that we recognize the interests we do have, and that we are prepared to protect them. The long history of American involvement in Latin America, the strong emotional ties to the region, the influence of ideology, and simple proximity all make Latin America an interest of the United States that cannot be wished away, and that we ignore to our detriment.

The Most Recent Lesson
"Panama alone should teach us our lesson. The invasion of that country was a successful and proper use of American power. But American *policy* in Panama over the past four years was a failure.... Fortunately for the United States, overwhelming power in the region makes up for many errors.

"For four years, the United States ignored, even denied, its interests in Panama. The prevailing opinion in both the Reagan and Bush administrations, particularly in the Pentagon, was that

American interests were not harmed if the leader of Panama was a military dictator; nor did it affect our interests if he...played with drug dealers. After all, the American mission in Panama was to defend the canal....

"The American people, however, leading or being led by their elected representatives, perceived interests in Panama unrelated to the canal. Angered by the dictator's involvement in drugs and appalled by the beatings his thugs inflicted on opposition political candidates, people led, or were led by, their politicians into an increasingly open and vocal confrontation with Noriega. Responding to the growing clamor, two consecutive American presidents publicly called for General Noriega's ouster....

"It is reasonable to assume that Noriega decided over time that the United States was a blowhard and a paper tiger. He began probing the limits of American tolerance....

"Noriega, like Hitler, miscalculated. He declared the United States and Panama to be in a state of war. His troops felt emboldened first to beat up one soldier, threaten an American woman with sexual abuse, then kill another soldier. It hardly mattered whether Noriega ordered these actions personally. He made them possible....

There to Stay

" 'There are certain geographical considerations which impose upon us a very special interest as to how...these nations fulfill the responsibilities which go with sovereignty and independence,' Henry Stimson said of Central America in 1927. The United States may now take a less paternalistic attitude toward Latin America than in those days. But if our actions are any indication, whatever our rhetoric, we have not drifted far from Stimson's perception of our interests. As we look to the future, whether the Cold War has ended or not, we have to expect that the same problems that have preoccupied us over the past hundred years in Latin America will persist. Poverty, instability, lawlessness, violence, and tyranny will continue to threaten our interests at some level and draw us into the region, whether we like it or not....' "

From Robert Kagan, "There to Stay: The U.S. and Latin America," The National Interest (Spring 1990). Copyright © 1990 by The National Interest, Washington, D.C. Reprinted by permission.

Edward M. Kennedy

"[N]ow that United States troops are coming home from Panama, it is time for Congress to begin to reflect on the implications of the United States invasion of that country....

"I have serious reservations about the justification for the invasion itself. The administration has offered four rationales for its action. It claims that the invasion was necessary to:

Save American lives;
Protect the Panama Canal;
Restore democracy to Panama; and
Bring General Noriega to justice.

"Nothing on the public record makes any of these justifications persuasive. Certainly, the United States does not have the right under international law or any other law that I know of to roam the hemisphere, bringing dictators to justice or installing new governments by force on other nations. Surely, it is a contradition in terms and a violation of America's best ideals to impose democracy by the barrel of a gun on Panama or any other nation.

"There was no imminent threat to the Panama Canal. In fact, for the first time in its history, the canal was shut down—because of the US invasion.

"Was the invasion necessary to save American lives? We will never know the true answer to that question, because we will never know what would have happened had there been no invasion. But we know certain facts.

"In October [1989], President Bush had been embarrassed and criticized for failing to do enough to ensure the success of a coup against General Noriega. The coup failed, perhaps because of US blunders.

"On the Friday before the invasion, the Noriega-created Panama Assembly passed a resolution saying that a 'State of War Exists' in Panama, and listing a series of what it considered acts of aggression by the United States against Panama, including United States economic sanctions. It is difficult to call this resolution a declaration of war by Panama against the United States.

"On the Saturday before President Bush acted, four unarmed United States servicemen were stopped in their car at a roadblock in front of the headquarters of the Panama defense forces. When they attempted to drive off, one of the servicemen was shot and killed, and another was wounded. A Navy lieutenant and his wife who witnessed the incident were taken into custody by the PDF and beaten, and the lieutenant's wife was sexually threatened. Two nights later, the invasion began.

"These incidents followed 2 years of PDF harassment of American servicemen and their wives. Over 750 such incidents passed without significant US protest, including cases involving serious assaults and even shootings.

"According to the Army Times of March 20, 1989, 'US servicemen in Panama have been abducted, beaten, kicked and had handguns held against their heads.' Either our Government underreacted to these incidents, or overreacted to the incidents of last December.

"As a result of the invasion, 23 American servicemen are dead; 3 American civilians are dead; 300 other Americans are wounded; 500 Panamanians are dead; thousands of Panamanians are wounded, and vast physical destruction has been wreaked on Panama City. On this record, it is difficult to deny that the invasion cost more lives than it saved.

"Contrary to the administration's threadbare and legalistic claims, the invasion violated our fundamental commitments under the United Nations Charter and the Charter of the Organization of American States. The administration's claim that the invasion was somehow justified as an act of self defense is not credible. It is no surprise that the United States was overwhelmingly rebuked for the invasion—by a vote of 20 to 1 in the Organization of American States, and by a vote of 75 to 20 in the United Nations General Assembly.

"In the Declaration of Independence, the Founders of our Nation proclaimed their liberty and spoke of 'a decent respect to the opinions of mankind.' Two centuries later, we have still not learned to pay that respect....

"As we enter a new decade, perhaps it is time for the United States also to make a profound decision, look at our own mindset, and change our own thinking on the way we deal with Latin America.

"The United States invasion of Panama reflects the long-standing predisposition of this country to bail out flawed policies through United States unilateral military interventions that ride roughshod over the sovereignty of other nations in the hemisphere. For years, we have viewed Panama as something just short of the 51st state. No other nation depends so heavily on the dollar for its economy. The original Panama Canal Treaty was negotiated without a Panamanian present. And throughout the century, we have built up a military structure in Panama that would do our bidding and restrain any overly independent political figures.

"Over the last decade, the administration lent legitimacy and support to one election farce after another in Panama. We continued to support the military and cultivate individuals who would be loyal and do our bidding. Manuel Noriega fit that mold. He was a bright, ruthless officer, and it was only logical that we would bring him into our camp.

"Our support for individuals such as Noriega and our repeated unilateral military interventions are natural and predictable outcomes of our misplaced, ill-advised and paternalistic approach toward the region. Unless we learn from our past history, we will be condemned to repeat it.

"Throughout Central America, as in Panama, we have supported coups, recognized blatantly fraudulent elections, and ignored corruption and flagrant human rights abuses—all in the name of US interests and regional stability.

"Over the last two centuries, we have invaded Nicaragua 10 times, Panama 10 times, Honduras 7 times, and El Salvador once.

"In Nicaragua, we supported the Dictator Somoza while driving many true democrats into the Soviet, Cuban, and Sandinista camps.

"In El Salvador, Honduras, and Guatemala, we

have enthusiastically built up large military forces and structures which have become uncontrollable bastions of corruption, death squads, and brutal human rights abuses.

"Our emphasis on military solutions in Central America has polarized those societies and impeded economic growth and social progress.

"It is no mere coincidence of history that the only country in the region that has shed its military force—Costa Rica—boasts four decades of peace, prosperity and some of the highest living standards in the region.

"In sharp contrast, Costa Rica's five neighbors —Honduras, Guatemala, Nicaragua, El Salvador, and Panama—continue to suffer war, poverty, so-cial and political conflict, plummeting living standards, and atrocious human rights violations.

"It is time for the United States, once and for all, to abandon this failed policy of easy resort to military intervention in our hemisphere.

"If we heed these lessons, then perhaps the invasion of Panama in 1989 will come to be seen as the last example of 'old thinking' by the United States in Latin America, and that 1990 will mark the dawn of a new era of respect by the United States to our neighbors and a new alliance for progress in the region."

From Edward M. Kennedy, "The Panama Invasion," Congressional Record *(23 January 1990), pp. S12-S14.*

ANALYSIS AND EVALUATION

Refer to the Argument Analysis and Evaluation Guide on page viii.

1. Using the Argument Analysis and Evaluation Guide, compare the readings by Kagan and Kennedy. On what do they agree? On what do they disagree?

2. Decide which of the viewpoints you tend to support and explain why. Be sure to use specific information from this textbook, the readings, and other sources to support your position.

3. State and support your position on the issue: "Was the US invasion of Panama justified?"

CHAPTER TWELVE

The Middle East: Conflict or Co-operation?

"We have to try to build a new Middle East.... Resolving the Palestinian-Israeli conflict and building economic hope for the future is the only solution."

Shimon Peres, World Press Review, *September 1991*

"Let no one mistake the magnitude of this challenge. The struggle we seek to end has a long and violent history. Every life lost—every outrage, every act of violence—is etched deep in the hearts and history of the people of this region. Theirs is a history that weighs heavily against hope. And yet history need not be man's master.... Peace in the Middle East need not be a dream."

US president George Bush, Madrid, Spain, 31 October 1991

Left: Yasser Arafat rides through Jericho on his historic return to Palestinian land, July 1994

❖ OVERVIEW

The Middle East gave birth to three of the world's great religions: Islam, Judaism, and Christianity. Culturally, most of the region is Arabic, with the exception of Israel, which is Jewish, and Iran, which is Farsi. Politically, the hereditary monarchies in the Gulf states are surrounded by authoritarian regimes. Economically, there is a stark contrast between wealthy oil countries like Saudi Arabia and poor countries like Egypt. This diversity has led to intense political and religious conflicts between and within states.

At the centre of Middle Eastern politics is the Jewish state of Israel. The distrust felt by Arab states towards Israel has been the focus of many conflicts in the region. Until the Israelis and the Arabs can reach a lasting compromise, peace in the Middle East will remain elusive.

This traditional balance shifted in Europe's favour in the nineteenth century. The Ottoman Empire, which had ruled much of the Islamic world since the 1500s, began to lose its power and influence to Europe. As European imperialism reached its peak, Western interests surpassed those of the Ottoman Empire in much of the Middle East. By 1914, only Turkey, Palestine, Syria, and part of the Arab Peninsula remained under Ottoman control.

Britain, Russia, France, and Italy attempted to expand their interests in the Middle East. Their imperialist ambitions did not meet with the same success as in other parts of the world, however. The long history of interaction between the two civilizations, along with the unity of the Islamic culture, combined to offer strong resistance to Western influences. By the early 1900s, nationalist movements began to emerge in the Middle East.

In the aftermath of the First World War, a new political order emerged in the Middle East. What remained of the Ottoman Empire collapsed. Its territories were divided between Britain and France as **mandates**. These were former colonial holdings that the League of Nations considered unprepared for self-rule. The mandates were placed under the administrative control of a league member, although they were not owned by that country.

FOCUS QUESTIONS

1. What factors have made the Middle East such a volatile region?
2. What factors led to the creation of the state of Israel?
3. How has the Arab-Israeli conflict affected the region and the world?
4. What hopes are there for a lasting Middle East peace settlement?
5. What is the role of Saudi Arabia in the region and the world?

REGION OF CONFLICT

Historically, the Middle East had long maintained contact with the countries of Europe. The region's technological capabilities had equalled, and at times exceeded, those of Europe. While both European and Middle Eastern cultures had occupied each other's territories at various times, their civilizations had remained separate and distinct.

INDEPENDENCE AND REVOLUTION

Britain and France established political boundaries in the Middle East with little regard for ethnicity. Instead,

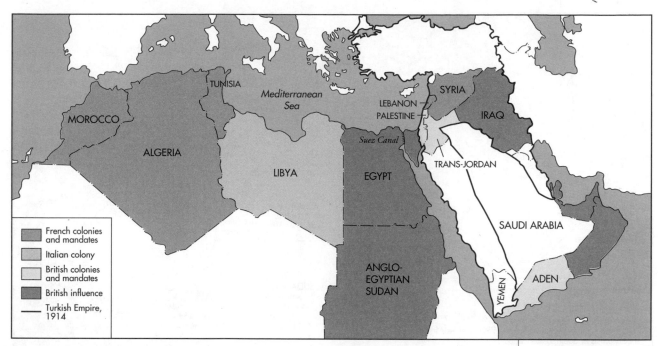

Figure 12.1:
European Control in the Middle East, 1914

artificial borders were created by agreements and treaties between European powers. The establishment of foreign boundaries restricted the nomadic lifestyles of many peoples, which altered cultural and economic traditions and created extreme hardship. The political systems established by the colonial powers proved incapable of effectively governing the diverse jurisdictions they had created.

Between the First and Second World Wars, discontent with European rule was widespread. Nationalist movements gained momentum, and by the end of the war they were prepared to challenge British and French authority. In the 1950s, independent states began to emerge in the Middle East.

Many of the countries that gained independence became monarchies still largely influenced by Western interests. Revolutionary movements in some countries overthrew these monarchies in favour of republican forms of government.

In 1952, the Free Officers Revolution, led by Colonel Gamal Abdel Nasser, ousted Egypt's unpopu-

lar ruler, King Farouk. The new government launched a program of reform aimed at ending foreign control and interests and improving the quality of life in the desperately poor country.

In neighbouring Libya, King Idris was deposed by a military coup in 1969. The new ruler, Colonel Muammar Qadhafi, was an **Islamic fundamentalist** (see page 346) who steadfastly opposed both capitalism and communism. He used his country's wealth from oil to improve social services and raise the standard of living.

When independence was achieved, the artificial boundaries remained, sometimes uniting diverse peoples in a single country, as in Lebanon and Syria. At other times, a single culture was divided by international boundaries, as with the Kurds who were split among Iran, Iraq, and Turkey. These political divisions have been responsible for many conflicts in the region.

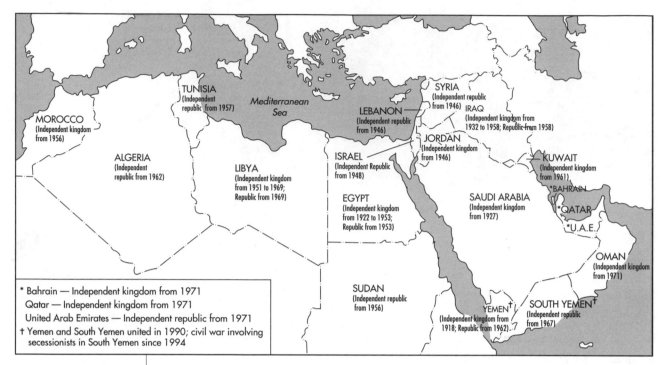

Figure 12.2:
Independence in the Middle East

In Iran, Shah Pahlavi had forged an alliance with the United States and had introduced a number of Western-style reforms to the Muslim nation. The shah was ousted in 1979 by an Islamic fundamentalist revolution led by Ayatollah Khomeini, who sought to banish Western influences and restore traditional Islamic values.

FLASHPOINTS

The Iran-Iraq War

Following the fundamentalist revolution in Iran, Ayatollah Khomeini sought to export the revolution to neighbouring Iraq. In response, Iraq's leader, Saddam Hussein, ordered an attack against Iraq, thereby launching the

> Ayatollah Khomeini proclaimed the conflict with Iraq a Holy War, or *jihad*. In addition to the regular army, hundreds of thousands of civilians were conscripted to fight for the cause.

bloodiest war in the region in modern times. Iraq was supported by moderate Arab nations as well as Western countries, including the United States, and the Soviet Union, all of which were eager to suppress a rise in fundamentalism. They supplied Iraq with the latest weaponry, including the technology for chemical and nuclear weapons. Iran, on the other hand, became even more economically and diplomatically isolated.

Battles continued intermittently between Iraq and Iran throughout most of the 1980s. With help from the West, Iraq gained air superiority in 1985. In 1987, Iran heightened the hostilities by attacking commercial shipping in the Persian Gulf. The United States and other nations provided naval escorts, but confrontations continued. Meanwhile, bombs and missiles bombarded cities on both sides. Both Iran and Iraq also resorted to chemical warfare, which claimed the lives of countless innocent civilians.

In 1987, the UN Security Council called for a cease-fire. Iraq agreed, but

Iran refused. Ongoing negotiations orchestrated by the United Nations Secretary General Javier Pérez de Cuéllar finally led to Iran's agreement to a peace settlement in August 1988. The long and bloody conflict had cost at least 1.5 million lives.

Conflict in Lebanon

The population of Lebanon is composed of Muslims and Christians, with distinct factions within the two groups. When Lebanon gained independence in 1944, a balance of power was created in the government, with the Christian majority wielding greater leverage.

This delicate balance collapsed with the influx of Muslim Palestinian refugees to the country following the creation of Israel in 1948. As the flood of refugees continued, tensions increased until civil war finally erupted in 1958. American troops restored political order, but the religious conflicts continued to simmer, causing two decades of unrest.

In 1975, war erupted in Lebanon once again. Palestinian guerrillas operating out of southern Lebanon launched raids against Israel. The Israelis retaliated with attacks against Lebanon. The presence of the Palestinian guerrillas further widened the rift between Muslims and Christians. The Muslims supported the Palestinians, while the Christians objected to their presence and their activities in Lebanon. Civil war erupted once again until Syrian intervention restored some semblance of order.

In June 1982, Israel invaded Lebanon and occupied the capital of Beirut. Israeli occupation only added to the chaos, however. American, British, French, and Italian troops were deployed to restrain the hostilities. But the Western forces were the targets of numerous terrorist attacks. In October 1983, 241 American and 31 French

troops were killed in a bombing. Shortly thereafter, the remaining troops were withdrawn and Lebanon returned to the chaos of the 1970s.

By 1987, the worst violence was focused in southern Lebanon. Confrontations between Christians and Muslims continued, occasionally interrupted by brief cease-fires. In 1989, Saudi Arabia and the Arab League pressured the Lebanese government to hammer out a new constitution. In the 1990s, some semblance of peace

The Islamic fundamentalist revolution led by Ayatollah Khomeini was enthusiastically supported by many Iranians.

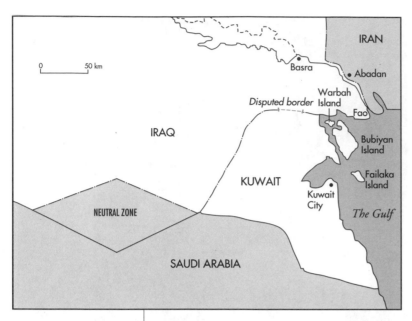

Figure 12.3:
Iraq and Kuwait

Saddam Hussein visited Iraqi troops following Iraq's invasion of Kuwait.

own access to the Persian Gulf and the Indian Ocean, however, Britain had created the separate state of Kuwait as a British protectorate. (Kuwait gained independence in 1961.) Kuwait's presence limited Iraq's access to the Persian Gulf to a 10 km stretch of coastline. Iraq disputed the boundary between the two countries. On 1 August 1990, negotiations between Iraq and Kuwait over boundaries, payments for oil shipments, and oil quotas broke down and Iraq invaded Kuwait.

The United Nations condemned the invasion and demanded withdrawal of Iraqi forces. Within days, an economic boycott was imposed on Iraq and a massive US-led international military coalition was established. But Iraq's leader, Saddam Hussein, adamantly refused to withdraw from Kuwait.

The day after the deadline for the withdrawal of Iraq passed, the coalition forces attacked. For thirty-eight days, air units from the United States, Britain, France, Saudi Arabia, Canada, and other countries pounded Iraqi targets. The ground war lasted only 100 hours before US president George Bush ordered a cease-fire. By this time, an estimated 120 000 Iraqi soldiers were dead, while only 200 coalition personnel had been killed.

The UN forces drove the Iraqi troops out of Kuwait but stopped short of a full-scale invasion of Iraq. Still, Hussein faced domestic problems of staggering proportions. The country's economy was shattered and its infrastructure lay in ruins. Iraq was forced to pay war

was restored to the war-torn region, although clashes along the border with Israel continued. By 1995, however, there were hints that progress towards peace with Israel was possible.

The Persian Gulf War
Before Iraq gained independence from Britain in 1921, Kuwait had been part of its southern territory. To ensure its

reparations to Kuwait. International sanctions crippled Iraq's economy and impoverished its citizens. Sporadic bombing of Iraqi military targets by the UN continued in retaliation for Iraq's violations of the peace agreement. While the war had officially ended, conflict with Iraq was anything but over.

OIL AND ECONOMIC DEVELOPMENT

Following the Second World War, oil became the Middle East's most valuable commodity. As Western nations set about the task of postwar reconstruction, the demand for oil steadily increased.

Prior to the war, most of the oil fields were operated and controlled by British and American oil companies, which held **concession rights** on the land. But as independence movements swept across the region, there were demands to nationalize foreign oil operations. Fearing the outright takeover of their operations, the Western oil companies conceded more control over oil resources and distributed greater oil profits to Middle Eastern governments.

With the wealth that the industry created, oil-rich nations channelled their profits into industrial development and social programs. Agricultural reforms were also introduced, including land redistribution and irrigation projects. By the 1970s, the standard of living in the oil-producing nations had increased substantially.

Development brought with it new schools, hospitals, and transportation and communications networks. The number of educated people, both men and women, has doubled in some countries and increased ten times in others. New opportunities in industry have lured rural workers away from the farms into the cities. Literacy rates have skyrocketed from an average below 10 per cent to between 50 and 70 per cent in some countries. Improved health care is enhancing the quality of life and increasing life expectancy.

Yet modernization has created problems as well. In many countries, only the elite and the middle class have reaped the benefits of industrial development. Rapid urbanization has overwhelmed many cities, which are unable to keep pace with the demands of their growing populations. Many people who have come to the cities seeking a better life find themselves mired in poverty.

Modernization has also created challenges to traditional values. The process of **Westernization** that has accompanied economic development has disrupted some social customs. Many younger Arabs, for example, admire Western ideas, entertainment, and clothing, which often puts them in conflict with the traditional values of their parents. Many Arabs believe that Western innovations should be carefully scrutinized. Those aspects that benefit society, such as science and

The majority of Middle East countries have vast oil resources, while some, like Jordan, have little or no oil. Politically stable countries like Kuwait, Saudi Arabia, and the United Arab Emirates enjoy some of the world's highest incomes. Other countries like Iran, Iraq, and Libya have missed opportunities to improve the lives of their people through military ambitions or economic isolation. The income disparities that oil, or the lack of it, have created are a source of instability in the region and make the prosperous sheikdoms of the Gulf tempting targets for invasion.

At a UN population conference in Cairo in 1994, Muslim women prayed for world peace.

Islamic Fundamentalism

The rise of Western influence in the Middle East has led to a revival of religious values in some Arab societies. Islamic fundamentalism embraces this religious consciousness. Fundamentalists participate in traditional activities that reconfirm Islamic values. They emphasize Islamic unity in the Arab world and reject any and all Western influences. Increasingly, the actions of some fundamentalists are directed against Western governments and symbols.

PROSPECTS FOR THE FUTURE

While the economies of the oil-rich countries of the Middle East have flourished, other countries remained trapped in the cycle of poverty. In these poor countries, the populations are growing rapidly, placing an additional burden on the development process. It is estimated that the total population of the region will double in less than twenty-five years, creating increased pressure for food, water, and land.

Politically, the Middle East remains one of the world's most volatile regions. While progress has been made towards peace in recent years, religious, ethnic, and political rivalries continue to threaten to ignite a variety of Middle East powder kegs.

technology, should be adopted while those that challenge traditional values, such as family roles and entertainment, should be rejected. The challenge for many countries of the Middle East is to blend modern concepts with traditional values.

> The Egyptian population of 55 million is increasing by 1 million every eight months. In Cairo, where the population exceeds 13 million, many people live in shantytowns, cemeteries, alleyways, and doorways.

IN REVIEW

1. What was the fundamental reason behind the revolutionary movements in the Middle East?

2. How did oil transform the economies of the oil-rich nations?

3. What problems did development create?

4. a) Why did Iraq invade Kuwait?
   b) What was the outcome of the Persian Gulf War?

ISRAEL

The Middle Eastern territory of Palestine has been a land of hope and despair, miracles and massacres. Over thousands of years, it has endured a succession of invasions in which its people have been uprooted and dispossessed. In the twentieth century, Jews and Arabs have fought tenaciously to possess this holy land. The bitter struggle over Palestine has inflamed all of the Middle East and at times has threatened the security of the world at large.

PALESTINE: A RELIGIOUS BATTLEFIELD

Palestine, and its holy city of Jerusalem, is the home of three world religions: Judaism, Christianity, and Islam. Throughout history this strip of the Mediterranean coastline has been fought over by Jews, Egyptians, Persians, Syrians, Greeks, Romans, Muslims, and Christian Crusaders. The Ottoman Turks controlled the region from 1517 to 1918.

The Zionist Movement

The Jews were expelled from Palestine by the Romans in 135 AD. This began the **diaspora**—the dispersal of Jewish people around the world. For centuries, Jews nurtured the dream of returning to Palestine, their "Promised Land." This hope assumed a political character under the name **Zionism** in the late nineteenth century.

The Balfour Declaration of 1917, which offered British support for the establishment of a Jewish homeland in Palestine, and the granting of Palestine as a British mandate in 1920, gave great impetus to the Zionist movement. Jews, confident that their dream of a Jewish state was now a real possibility, began to migrate to Palestine.

Figure 12.4: Growth of the Jewish Population in Palestine

Year	Jews	%	Total Population
1882	24 000	na	na
1922	83 790	11.1	753 048
1928	151 656	16.9	935 951
1937	395 836	28.2	1 401 794
1945	554 329	30.6	1 810 037

(Note: Illegal immigrants not included.)
Adapted from S. Hadawi, *Bitter Harvest* (New York: Olive Branch Press, 1991).

As the number of Jewish immigrants swelled, they faced increasing hostility from the Arabs, who feared that they would be overrun in the land they had lived in for centuries.

The creation of a Jewish state conflicted with Britain's earlier promises of Arab independence in 1916. Riots broke out in Jaffa in 1920 and in Jerusalem in 1921 and again in 1929. Increased Jewish immigration to Palestine fanned the fires of Arab nationalism. In 1936, severe riots erupted. Roads were blocked and trains were sabotaged. Britain imposed martial law and sent in 20 000 troops to restore order.

In 1939, a Palestinian Conference was held in London, but it failed to produce a resolution to the dispute. During the Second World War, both Jews and Arabs supported Britain, although extremist activities on both sides kept the conflict boiling.

THE PARTITIONING OF PALESTINE

At the end of the war in 1945, Britain again focused its attention on Palestine.

Theodore Herzl shaped the early Zionist movement in his book *The Jewish State* (1896). The establishment of the World Zionist Organization quickly followed in 1897.

Anti-Semitism in Germany and Poland in the early 1930s increased immigration to Palestine. In 1935, over 60 000 Jews from these countries sought safe haven in Palestine.

Figure 12.5: *Ethnic Breakdown of Palestine, 1948.*

In the eyes of the Western allies, the horrors of the Holocaust made a true Jewish homeland a necessity. To the dismay of Arabs living in Palestine, the West seemed prepared to give Holocaust survivors Arab land. In response, the **League of Arab States** was formed in 1945 to promote the interests of Arab peoples. Specifically, this meant organized opposition to the creation of an independent state of Israel in Palestine. As the number of Jewish refugees arriving in Palestine increased, violent clashes escalated between the two sides. Frustrated by the ongoing conflict, Britain agreed to a United Nations Commission in 1947.

Pressured by the United States, the United Nations established a plan to partition Palestine into a Jewish and an Arab state. (See Figure 12.6.) The Zionists accepted the plan, albeit reluctantly. But the Palestinian Arabs rejected it, claiming that all of Palestine belonged to them. As the deadline for British withdrawal on 15 May 1948 neared, the Jewish-Arab conflict escalated as both sides moved to establish their territories. It was clear that the UN scheme would be decided on the battlefield.

FLASHPOINTS

The First Arab-Israeli War, 1948-49
The Israeli forces soon extended the boundaries of their new nation. Neighbouring Arab states provided military support for the Palestinians in an effort to drive the Israelis back. War raged in the region for more than a year. Hundreds of thousands of Palestinians were forced to flee their homes. The United Nations responded to the refugee crisis by establishing camps near the Israeli borders. Most of Palestine was now under Israeli control. Arab nations were pledged to the

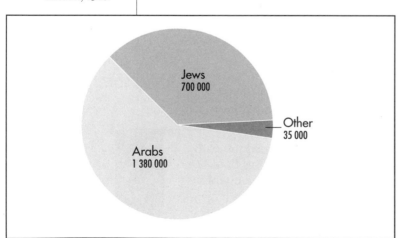

Jews
700 000

Other
35 000

Arabs
1 380 000

destruction of Israel. The stage was set for decades of conflict.

The Suez Crisis, 1956

The next major flashpoint was the Suez Crisis. Riding a wave of Arab nationalism, Gamal Abdel Nasser wrested control of Egypt in a military coup in 1954. In July 1956, he nationalized the Suez Canal.

In response, in October Israel invaded Egypt under a secret agreement with Britain and France to regain control of the canal. While their actions failed, the crisis heightened Arab suspicions of Israel's intentions in the region. (See pages 173-76 for details on the Suez Crisis.)

The Six-Day War, 1967

In May 1967, Egypt was mounting increasing pressure on UN forces in the Sinai to withdraw from the Israeli frontier. At the same time, Egyptian troops were amassing in the Sinai, and Egypt was blockading the Israeli port of Elat. In swift response to the Egyptian action, Israel launched a surprise attack on 5 June 1967. Within two days, Israel had amassed troops at the Suez Canal. They crossed the canal and advanced south into Egypt. At the same time the Egyptian army in the Sinai was encircled. Israeli forces seized Old Jerusalem and the West Bank. On June 9th and 10th, Israeli tanks occupied the Golan Heights and advanced into Syria. Air strikes destroyed the Egyptian air force on the ground; airfields in Syria, Iraq, and Jordan were also bombed. On June 7th, Jordan accepted a UN cease-fire, followed by Egypt on June 8th, and Syria on June 9th. Israel agreed to a cease-fire on June 10th, ending its most remarkable victory over its Arab neighbours.

Israel was now in a better defensive position than ever before. Israeli forces occupied Egypt's Sinai Peninsula, the Gaza Strip, all of Jerusalem,

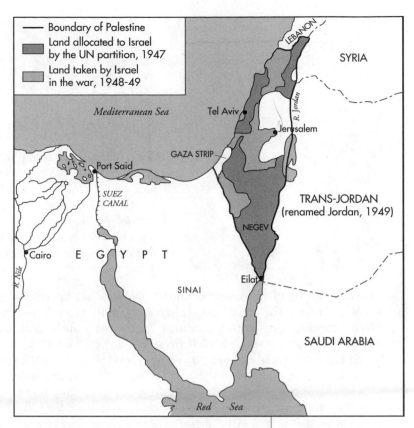

Syria's Golan Heights, and the West Bank of the Jordan River. In six days, Israel had gained control of an area three times larger than it had in 1949.

The Yom Kippur War, 1973

While Israelis observed Yom Kippur on 6 October 1973, Egyptian and Syrian forces launched a surprise attack. Following the 1967 war, both nations had rearmed with modern, sophisticated weaponry provided by the Soviet Union. They captured Israeli positions in the Sinai and the Golan Heights. Caught off guard, Israeli forces initially suffered serious losses, but then launched a successful counter-attack. By the time a cease-fire was reached three weeks later, Israel was threatening to overrun the Egyptian capital of Cairo.

The war almost ignited a global conflict. The Soviets had aided the Arab nations once they had been

Figure 12.6:
Israel, 1947-49

PROFILE

GOLDA MEIR (1898-1978)

Golda Meir spent fifty years of her life in the turbulent world of Zionist, and later Israeli, politics. She was a significant part of the Zionist dream of a Jewish homeland in Palestine. In 1969, she became prime minister of Israel. Golda Meir was a guiding force for peace in the Middle East, but she did not hesitate to commit Israeli troops to battle when necessary. Do you believe a politician can maintain both positions?

"There is a type of woman who cannot remain at home. In spite of the place her children and family fill in her life, her nature demands something more; she cannot divorce herself from the larger social life.... For such a woman, there is no rest."

Golda Meir, 1928

"We only want that which is given naturally to all peoples of the world, to be masters of our own fate, only of our fate, not of others, and in co-operation and friendship with others."

Golda Meir, 1957

"A leader who doesn't hesitate before he sends his nation into battle is not fit to be a leader."

Golda Meir, 1970

"Our generation reclaimed the land, our children fought the war, and our grandchildren should enjoy the peace."

Golda Meir, 1977

Born in Kiev, Ukraine, Goldie Mabovitch emigrated with her family to the United States in 1907. Married in 1917, she and her husband emigrated to Palestine in 1921 to live on a **kibbutz,** or communal farm. Meir was active in the Women's Labour Council and served as head of the Political Department of the Jewish Agency. She worked effectively to free Jewish activists detained by British authorities in the troubled days before the foundation of the state of Israel.

In 1948, Meir was one of the signatories to the Israeli independence declaration. She served as ambassador to the Soviet Union, home of millions of Jews eager to claim Israeli citizenship. Later she became minister of labour and minister for foreign affairs, roles which gave her a visible profile in the world political community.

Meir held a seat in the Israeli parliament, the Knesset, from 1949 to 1974. She helped mould one of Israel's strongest political organizations, the Labour Party. In 1969, she became prime minister of Israel in a coalition government. Meir defended Israel and attacked its enemies with determination. She was particularly skilled at building support for Israel against the attacks of Palestinian terrorists.

During the 1973 Yom Kippur War, Israel fared badly at the outset of the struggle, although Israeli forces later recovered in stunning fashion. Meir was held responsible for the high number of casualties and the early losses. In 1974, she resigned her office. A year later, she published her autobiography, *My Life*. Golda Meir died in 1978 after a twelve-year battle with leukemia.

pushed back beyond the 1967 cease-fire lines by the Israelis. The United States had ordered its nuclear forces put on full alert as a counter move to direct Soviet intervention. Intense negotiations succeeded in diffusing the powder keg. But the war clearly demonstrated that the Middle East was a potential threat to global security.

THE PALESTINE LIBERATION ORGANIZATION

Arab resistance groups flourished in the Palestinian refugee camps around Israel. But a lack of organization and supplies meant that these groups had little success against Israel. In 1964, the Arab states created the **Palestine Liberation Organization** (PLO) to provide a voice for the Palestinian people. For the most part, the Arab countries saw this as a way of controlling the Palestinians and preventing them from drawing the Arab world into a war with Israel. The PLO received most of its financing from the Arab states.

The PLO assumed a degree of sovereignty over some of the refugee camps. Militant guerrilla groups used the camps as their bases for launching raids into Israel. Their actions brought retaliation from Israel, however, and

increased the tensions between the Palestinians and their hosts, especially Lebanon and Jordan.

In 1969, Yasser Arafat was elected to lead the PLO. He was the head of the Al Fatah guerrilla group, which had been waging military operations against the Israelis.

Air strikes were an integral part of Israel's victory during the Six-Day War.

Figure 12.7: *Israeli Expansion After the Six-Day War*

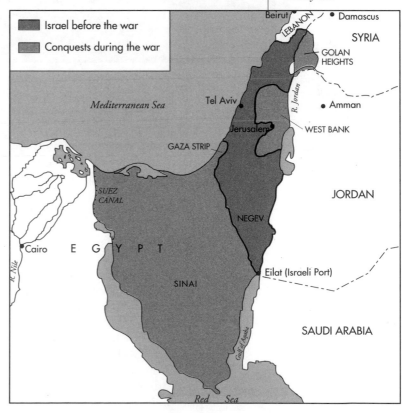

Israel before the war

Conquests during the war

Beirut • LEBANON • Damascus

SYRIA

GOLAN HEIGHTS

Mediterranean Sea   Tel Aviv •

R. Jordan

• Amman

Jerusalem •   WEST BANK

GAZA STRIP

SUEZ CANAL

JORDAN

NEGEV

Cairo •   E G Y P T

R. Nile

Eilat (Israeli Port)

SINAI

Gulf of Aqaba

SAUDI ARABIA

Red   Sea

During the 1972 Olympic Games in Munich, Arab guerrillas (shown here on the balcony with an Olympic official) raided the Israeli quarters, killing two men and holding nine others hostage. In the rescue attempt, all of the hostages were killed, as well as five of their captors. The remaining guerrillas were flown to Libya.

TERRORISM

The unresolved issue of the Palestinian refugees and the creation of organizations like the PLO meant continued violence and unrest in the Middle East. Arab nations supported various organizations whose goal was to liberate Palestine from Israeli occupation and destroy the state of Israel.

Israel and much of the West viewed Arab terrorism as horrific acts of violence. Palestinians and their Arab supporters, however, viewed terrorists as freedom fighters courageously battling for the rights of a dispossessed people. Terrorists or freedom fighters, the battles in the Middle East often flowed over borders to involve nations and citizens around the globe.

Terrorism, however, failed to gain

concessions from Israel or its supporters and was unsuccessful in liberating a single metre of Palestinian soil. The terrorists did succeed in drawing world attention to the volatile Middle East and the plight of the Palestinians. But by the late 1980s, there was a growing realization that terrorism only hardened the resolve of the Israelis and damaged the image of Palestinians abroad. In the 1990s, terrorist activities were in decline.

THE OCCUPIED TERRITORIES

In March 1978, Israeli forces invaded southern Lebanon, destroying PLO bases there. In June 1982, they launched a full-scale military operation against Palestinian bases in the Lebanese capital of Beirut. After several months, the Palestinian guerrillas abandoned Beirut. With the PLO rendered relatively ineffective, the Israelis undertook a new venture, the establishment of Jewish settlements in the **Occupied Territories**.

The Territories the Israelis had captured during the 1967 war were ruled by military law. Palestinians living there were given no rights as citizens of Israel; many were restricted to living in refugee camps. On the other hand, Jews who chose to establish settlements in the Occupied Territories were given the full benefits of Israeli citizenship. The number of Jewish settlements grew from 36 in 1977, with 5000 people, to over 120 in 1987, with 70 000 settlers. By 1987, half of the West Bank was occupied by Israelis.

Through the mid-1980s, Palestinians demonstrated against Israeli domination of the Occupied Territories. In December 1987, a series of incidents between Israelis and Palestinians led to the protest uprisings known as the **Intifadah**. Violent demonstrations tore apart the Gaza Strip and the West Bank in early 1988. Israeli troops retaliated by shooting the demonstrators. Mass arrests were made and many people suspected of complicity in the demonstrations were deported. The unrest continued for months. By July, 300 Palestinians had been killed. Israel's heavy-handed response to the *Intifadah* provoked harsh international criticism, even from its staunchest supporter, the United States.

In an effort to ease the tensions, in December 1988 Arafat recognized Israel's right to exist, provided that a Palestinian state existed as well. In response to Arafat's overture, Israeli defence minister Itzhak Rabin offered a tentative peace proposal to the PLO in the form of elections in the Occupied Territories, provided the *Intifadah* ceased. But the uprising continued unabated, in part because the *Intifadah* drew its energy from the Palestinians and not the PLO.

Clearly the *Intifadah* signalled a change in Palestinian attitudes. Gone was the willingness to simply allow the PLO to speak for them. Instead there was a new attitude of nationalism and confrontation. The PLO was not instrumental in either igniting the unrest or maintaining it. The *Intifadah* got its strength from the people of the Occupied Territories.

By 1993, 950 Palestinians had been killed and over 100 000 had been injured in confrontations with Israelis; over 15 000 people were being held in detention camps. In the meantime, the

Figure 12.8:
The Occupied Territories, 1967-82

peace talks dragged on with little movement on either side.

Towards Peace

The series of Arab-Israeli wars from 1948 created only increased bitterness on all sides. The Israelis, while victorious on the battlefield, faced revenge

---

Intifadah

With petrol bomb and stone
I will build my state,
I will bear my revolution.
May my strength increase.
My land, my people.
Strike with the stone.
Burn, burn the tyre,
Put up barriers.
Revolution, revolution, do not fade.

*Lyrics from a best-selling
Palestinian song*

PROFILE

YASSER ARAFAT (1929-)

Yasser Arafat is one of the most beloved and reviled figures in the world today. As leader of the Palestine Liberation Organization, his goal is singularly clear: the creation of an independent Palestinian state out of land occupied by Israeli forces. To many Palestinians, he is a proud symbol of hope. To many Israelis, he is a terrorist. Arafat presents a complex image: on the one hand, a defiant freedom fighter, armed and dangerous; on the other hand, a reasonable diplomat searching for peace. How would you classify Arafat?

"...I call upon Jews, one by one, to turn away from the illusory promises made to them by Zionist ideology and Israeli leadership. Those offer the Jews perpetual bloodshed, endless war and continuous thraldom.

"We invite them to emerge from their moral isolation into a more open realm of free choice.... We offer them the most generous solution that we might live together in a framework of just peace in our democratic Palestine.... I announce here that we do not wish the shedding of one drop of either Arab or Jewish blood: neither do we delight in the continuation of killing, which would end once a just peace, based on our people's rights, hopes, and aspirations, is finally established."

Yasser Arafat in a speech to the UN General Assembly, 13 November 1974

Born in Jerusalem to a middle-class family opposed to Zionist expansion, Yasser Arafat required little persuasion to be drawn into the bitter, brutal world of politics in Palestine. He studied civil engineering at Cairo University in the early 1950s. He became leader of the League of Palestinian Students, which was extremely vocal in its calls for the destruction of Israel. During the Suez Crisis in 1956, Arafat served briefly in the Egyptian army.

In 1963, Arafat helped to found Al Fatah, an Arab guerrilla group pledged to war against Israel.

Al Fatah became part of the PLO in 1964 and within five years was its major force, with Arafat as the PLO's leader. A wave of guerrilla raids brought the PLO global recognition and recrimination. In 1974, the PLO was given observer status at the UN and Arafat was invited to address the General Assembly.

In spite of its political initiatives, the PLO remained a military force responsible for a wave of attacks against Israel. When PLO activity in Lebanon appeared to pose a serious threat to Israeli security in 1982, Israel invaded Lebanon and decisively defeated Arafat's forces. Arafat's leadership was openly challenged the following year.

In the face of Arab division and Israeli military success in the 1980s, Arafat's leadership continued to decline. In the 1991 Gulf War, he allied the PLO with Iraq's leader Saddam Hussein, which further weakened him in both Arab and Western eyes. However, in 1993 Arafat returned to centre stage. Working behind the scenes, he negotiated an agreement with Israel which paved the way for his triumphant return to Palestinian soil in July 1994 after a twenty-seven-year absence.

by their Arab neigh-bours and unremitting attacks by Palestinian terrorists. The Israeli economy was heavily burdened by the cost of maintaining a large, well-equipped military. The Occupied Territories, with their hundreds of thousands of Palestinian refugees, posed a continuous threat to Israel's security.

In the late 1970s, the United States took the lead in attempting to find peace in the Middle East. Dr. Henry Kissinger, the US secretary of state, met separately with Arab and Israeli leaders to encourage them to soften their positions. This so-called **shuttle diplomacy** gradually resulted in the return of small amounts of land in the Sinai to Egypt.

Further negotiations continued under the administration of US president Jimmy Carter. In March 1979, Egyptian president Anwar Sadat and Israeli prime minister Menachem Begin signed the Camp David Accord. Thirty years of conflict between the two nations ended with Israel's agreement to withdraw in stages from the Sinai and with the establishment of formal relations between the two countries. Israeli zealots opposed the accord, as did the PLO, and the Arab League expelled Egypt from the organization.

Aside from the Egyptian-Israeli peace accord, however, the combatants in the Middle East remained polarized. In spite of the efforts of moderate politicians and diplomats on all sides,

little was achieved in peace talks other than vague promises and temporary cease-fires.

In the early 1990s, however, the situation began to change. Moderate Israelis and Palestinians appeared to be gaining the upper hand. The United States, freed from the Cold War, pursued its peace initiatives in the Middle East with renewed vigour. Terrorism seemed to be on the wane and a new generation of Palestinian leaders presented their case to the international community. World opinion had also changed as the notion of Israel as the courageous underdog had been destroyed by its response to the *Intifadah*.

In October 1991, delegates representing Israel, the Palestinians, Egypt, Lebanon, Syria, and Jordan met in Madrid. This marked the first time that

Palestinians faced off against Israeli troops during the Intifadah.

VOICES

THE CREATION OF A PALESTINIAN STATE

At the centre of the Palestinian-Israeli conflict is the issue of an independent Palestinian state carved out of Israeli-occupied territory. Salah Khalaf, a key member of the Palestine Liberation Organization, argues that the time has come for the Arab world to recognize the legitimacy of the state of Israel and for Israel to allow a homeland for the displaced Palestinian people. But David Bar-Illan, an Israeli who heads an anti-terrorist foundation, argues that an independent Palestine would present an even greater threat to Israel. As you read their opinions, consider ways in which this complex issue could be resolved.

Salah Khalaf

"Strange as it may seem at first glance, Israel and the Palestinian people have similar and compatible goals. Israel wants to be master of its own fate—an independent state, secure, and at peace with its neighbors. We ask for nothing more than the same rights for ourselves. The Israeli government believes the two nations' objectives are mutually exclusive. Its view is that the independence, security, and peace of Israel are attainable only if the Palestinians' right to those same privileges is denied or at least severely restricted. The Palestinians now believe that the two peoples' separate quests for independence, security and peace will either fail together or succeed together. The Palestinian peace plan is built on that conviction. The plan itself is simple. The state of Israel would live in peace with the state of Palestine, which would be established in the West Bank and Gaza Strip, with East Jerusalem as its capital. This final settlement would be part of a comprehensive Arab-Israeli agreement that would establish peace between the Jewish and Arab states, thus allaying Israel's security concerns."

> *Reprinted with permission from* Foreign Policy 78 *(Spring 1990). Copyright 1990 by the Carnegie Endowment for International Peace.*

David Bar-Illan

"Israel is in a bad situation. Not because it won the 1967 war and, as a result, added a million hostile Arabs to the population under its control; not because it suffers universal calumny for allegedly mistreating them; not because the higher Arab birth rate poses a demographic threat; and not even because the territory of the land of Israel is also claimed by [Arabs]. Difficult as these problems are, they can all yield to rational resolution. What defies resolution and what makes Israel's situation truly bad is that 170 million Arabs consider the very existence of Israel an offense to their sense of history and destiny....A Palestinian state in Judea-Samaria [the West Bank] and Gaza would cut through Jerusalem and flank the city on three sides, touch on Tel Aviv's suburbs, and have a long border, nine to fifteen miles [15 to 24 km] from the sea, with Israel's most thickly populated areas. Palestinian militias...would have Israeli pedestrians within rifle range.... Israel would be reduced to responding with retaliatory ground raids, the way it did against Jordanian-held territories in the 50s and 60s—or with air raids.... Real peace can only come in the event...that a very large number of Jews from the Soviet Union, South and North America, and Europe immigrate to Israel. A massive settling of Judea and Samaria would then make Israel's presence there irreversible...and finally convince the Arab states to resign themselves to the existence and indestructibility of Israel and give up the war they have been waging against it since the day of its birth. Failing such eventualities, the world will have to get used to the idea that the Israel-Arab conflict, like the conflicts in Northern Ireland, the Basque region, Cyprus, Sri Lanka, the Punjab, and others is insoluble for the foreseeable future. Bad as this is, the only real alternative is worse."

> *David Bar-Illan, "Can Israel Withdraw? No!"* Commentary, *1988.*

Israel had met face to face with its Arab neighbours (with the exception of Egypt). While these initial talks resolved nothing, they laid the foundations for future negotiations.

In September 1993, Palestinian and Israeli leaders finally reached an accord. Israel agreed to withdraw from the Occupied Territories of Gaza and the West Bank town of Jericho and accepted limited self-rule for the 1.8 million Palestinians living in the Occupied Territories. Israel accepted the PLO as the legitimate representative of the Palestinians. In return, the PLO renounced terrorism and its threats to destroy Israel.

While most of the world community welcomed news of the accord, not all were in favour. Both Arafat and Israeli prime minister Itzhak Rabin encountered severe opposition from their respective communities, including threats of assassination.

Still, the peace process continued. In May 1994, an agreement formally initiating self-rule was signed. On July 1st, Arafat crossed Egypt into the Gaza Strip, stepping onto Palestinian soil for the first time in twenty-seven years. On July 5th, he became the head of the new Palestinian National Authority (PNA). In August, Israel agreed to shift administrative functions in the West Bank to the PNA, giving it control over health, welfare, education, tourism, and taxation.

The agreements between Israel and the Palestine Liberation Organization marked a significant achievement in the Middle East peace process. But extremist opposition continues on both sides. A complete and lasting peace in the region is still uncertain.

Egyptian president Anwar Sadat and Israeli prime minister Menachem Begin ended thirty years of conflict between their two nations in 1979.

"What we seek is a Middle East where vast resources are no longer devoted to armaments;...a Middle East no longer victimized by fear and terror; a Middle East where normal men and women lead normal lives."

US president George Bush, Madrid, 30 October 1991

In July 1994, Israel and Jordan formally ended their forty-six-year state of war. In October 1994, the two countries signed a peace treaty.

IN REVIEW

1. a) What was the immediate impact of the creation of the state of Israel on the Palestinians?
   b) What were the long-term consequences?

2. What did the PLO hope to accomplish? Was it successful?

3. What were the chief consequences of the Arab-Israeli wars from 1948 to 1973?

4. How did the Camp David Accord split the Arab world?

5. a) What prompted the *Intifadah* in the Occupied Territories?
   b) What was Israel's response?

6. Outline the steps taken towards resolving the Israeli-Palestinian issue since 1988.

SAUDI ARABIA

Saudi Arabia stands in marked contrast to other nations of the Middle East. A stable monarchy based on fundamental Islamic principles has enabled it to grow and develop into one of the wealthiest countries in the world.

In 1902, Abd al-Aziz Al-Saud launched a successful campaign to drive the Ottoman Turks from Arab lands. In 1932, he proclaimed the Kingdom of Saudi Arabia. The country's political system was based on Islamic law, with a single monarch and no political parties. Abd al-Aziz ruled the country until his death in 1953. He was succeeded by his eldest son, Saud, but he proved to be ill-suited to the task. A Council of Ministers was formed as an advisory group, although all of the important posts were held by members of the royal family. In 1958, King Saud was persuaded to let his brother, Prince Faisal, take charge of the government. Faisal introduced a new financial system, which included government budgets and allowances for the royal family.

Faisal became king in 1964. He was assassinated in 1975 and was succeeded by his brother Khalid. Upon his death in 1982, another brother and Khalid's principal advisor, Fahd, became king of Saudi Arabia.

AN OIL ECONOMY

Before the discovery of oil, Saudi Arabia was an agrarian society. Most people herded flocks or grew dates and a few other crops. Commercial quantities of oil were first discovered in 1938, but the Second World War postponed any possibility of reaping the benefits of the find. Following the war, however, there was an explosion of activity in Saudi Arabia's oil industry.

In 1960, Saudi Arabia became a founding member of the **Organization of Petroleum Exporting Countries** (OPEC), along with Iran, Iraq, Kuwait, and Venezuela. (OPEC later expanded to include thirteen countries.) The purpose of OPEC was to assert greater control over the oil industry, which was dominated by Western oil companies.

During the 1960s, an abundance of oil kept prices relatively low. But rapid economic growth in the oil-hungry

West in the late 1960s and early 1970s increased the demand. The 1973 oil embargo initiated by Saudi Arabia in the wake of the Arab-Israeli War created a further oil shortage. The price of crude oil skyrocketed from $2.50 a barrel in 1970 to $32 a barrel in 1980. But the high prices resulted in overproduction, creating a glut on the oil market. Prices plummeted to $9 a barrel in 1986, but rebounded to $20 a barrel by 1990.

Despite such fluctuations, Saudi Arabia's oil prosperity seems destined to continue. Major new oil discoveries outside the country's traditional oil fields promise a secure future.

ECONOMIC DEVELOPMENT

Oil wealth enabled Saudi Arabia to transform itself from an agrarian society to a modern nation. Vast sums of money were invested in improving education and health care. Advanced transportation and communications networks were expanded around the country. Public works such as sewers and desalinization plants were constructed. The high salaries enjoyed by oil industry workers enabled them to buy cars, appliances, cameras, and other consumer goods from the West. Saudi Arabia had achieved one of the highest standards of living in the world.

Figure 12.9: Oil Reserves, January 1994

	Reserves (million barrels)	Years of Production at 1994 Levels
Middle East OPEC		
Saudi Arabia	261 200	133
Iraq	100 000	97
United Arab Emirates	98 100	150
Kuwait	96 500	162
Iran	89 300	89
Qatar	3 700	32
Other OPEC		
Venezuela	64 500	85
Nigeria	17 900	28
Indonesia	5 800	17
Ecuador	2 000	15
Gabon	1 300	9
Rest of World		
Mexico	50 800	56
United States	30 200	10
China	24 000	23
Norway	9 400	20
Canada	7 300	13
Other	147 300	—
World Total	1 009 300	44

From the *BP Statistical Review of World Energy*, June 1995

Saudi Arabia's rapid development led to an influx of foreign workers. Most had specialized skills or training that were in short supply among the Saudi population. Foreign workers included over 100 000 Westerners, most of whom lived in separate compounds near the oil fields.

In 1950, Saudi Arabia's oil revenue was US$57 million. By 1988, oil revenue had soared to US$23 *billion.*

Jeddah in Saudi Arabia is a prosperous city with one of the highest standards of living in the world.

during the Gulf War in 1991, and it was Saudi leadership that enlisted the support of Arab countries, the United States, and other nations in confronting Iraq and its leader, Saddam Hussein.

SAUDI ARABIA AND ISRAEL

As a member of the Arab League, Saudi Arabia opposed the creation of the state of Israel in 1948. But the Saudis avoided direct involvement in the conflict until the Arab-Israeli War of 1973. Although not involved militarily, Saudi Arabia supported Egypt and Syria by placing an oil embargo on Israel's closest ally, the United States. The embargo was lifted in 1974 after a number of countries, including Japan, agreed to condemn Israel for its actions in the war.

The Arab-Israeli conflict placed Saudi Arabia in a tenuous position. Antagonism towards Israel jeopardized Saudi Arabia's relationship with the United States, which supplied the country with arms and bought considerable quantities of oil. On the other hand, its failure to act aggressively against Israel brought criticism from other Arab nations.

The Saudis' balancing act was again tested in 1978 with the Camp David Accord. The United States pressured Saudi Arabia to support the Egyptian-Israeli peace treaty. But the Saudis believed that Egypt had abandoned the Arab cause. Ultimately they joined other Arab nations in denouncing the agreement and banning Egypt from the Arab League.

Modernization also created a new middle class of civil servants, teachers, and entrepreneurs. Most had been educated in the expanded universities in Saudi Arabia or at universities overseas. In the 1990s, some members of this new elite were challenging the existing political order of the Saudi monarchy.

LEADERSHIP ROLE

Following the oil embargo of 1973, Saudi Arabia emerged as the major Arab oil producer as well as a world financial power. Oil wealth became a key factor in Saudi diplomacy. Saudi Arabia was generous in its financial support of the Palestine Liberation Organization, yet it also used its petrodollars to purchase sophisticated military equipment from the United States. By 1985, Saudi Arabia had the best-equipped armed forces in the Gulf region, ready to defend a peninsula that contained almost half of the world's oil reserves. The Saudis' military preparedness proved invaluable

CULTURE AND CONFLICT

Saudi Arabia lies at the centre of Islam. Two of Islam's holy sites, Mecca and Medina, lie within its borders. Saudis practise a fundamentalist form of the religion. The extended family is the most important element in society. Loyalty to one's family and moral discipline are highly valued. Like other Arab nations, Saudi Arabia faces conflict between the need to adopt modern and more democratic social, educational, and political institutions, and the religious traditions of Islam.

Family honour is one of the greatest values in Saudi Arabian society. To ensure that dishonour does not fall on any member of the family, strict codes of behaviour are followed. Men and women do not have open contact with one another. Women are prohibited from having contact with any men outside of their own family. They cannot go out alone and are often excluded from social gatherings. Few women work outside the home; those who do work in an all-female environment, such as schools and banks for women. While women's public role may be restrictive by Western standards, in the family women wield considerable power. Theirs is the decisive voice in most domestic matters, and their status and power is enhanced with age.

Most Saudis view their customs not as repressive but as complimentary to the status of women. Women themselves generally feel satisfied that their traditions provide them with security, respect, and protection. But as global interactions become more commonplace at the end of the twentieth century, some women have begun to view their situation quite differently and are demanding greater social, legal, and personal freedom.

In accordance with Islamic law, alcohol is banned in Saudi Arabia;

Saudi women are highly respected in family and domestic matters.

public entertainment, such as theatres and nightclubs, is also prohibited. As more Saudis travel to the West, however, their exposure to more liberal Western attitudes has led to increasing

Formal education of girls began in Saudi Arabia in 1956. By 1974, the number of female students had risen from virtually none to 300 000. By 1980, almost all girls attended school.

pressure to ease some of the conservative restrictions. Perhaps Saudi Arabia's greatest challenge lies in maintaining fundamentalist values in a society increasingly exposed to Western social trends.

IN REVIEW

1. In what ways is Saudi Arabia different from other Arab countries?
2. In what ways has oil transformed the Saudi Arabian economy?
3. Why does Saudi Arabia have a difficult balancing act in terms of Middle East politics?
4. Why might Islamic fundamentalism and economic development not co-exist in relative harmony?

SUMMARY

As the twentieth century ends, there is cautious hope for a peaceful resolution to the conflicts that trouble the Middle East. Delegates from all sides continue to meet face to face to discuss their points of view. Will these talks be a major turning point in the path towards peace? Or is peace ultimately a mirage on the desert sands of the Middle East?

MAKING CONNECTIONS

1. In what way do you think opposition to Western power and influence fuelled Islamic fundamentalism in some countries of the Middle East?

2. The Arab-Israeli struggle has often been described as a case of "right against right." Explain this statement with reference to the rights and aspirations of both the Israelis and the Palestinians.

3. In what ways might Islamic restrictions on the role of women hamper economic development?

DEVELOPING YOUR VOICE

4. Imagine you are a spokesperson for the Palestine Liberation Organization. Write a brief speech in which you present your case for a Palestinian homeland to a Canadian audience.

5. Canada joined the UN coalition in the Gulf War in 1991 and participated in several jet fighter offensives against Iraqi targets. Do you think Canada should have become involved in this conflict? Give reasons for your answer.

6. Do you think the United States should continue to support Israel? Give reasons for your answer.

RESEARCHING THE ISSUES

7. Maintain an ongoing file on peace initiatives in the Middle East since 1994.

8. Syria and Jordan have suffered greatly because of the creation of Israel and the hostilities between Arabs and Israelis. Research to find out the political, economic, and social impact on *one* of these countries.

9. How has the way of life for Muslim women in the Arab world changed over the past several decades? Collect three to five articles on this topic using magazine and newspaper indexes. Prepare a written, visual, or oral report to summarize your conclusions.

VIEWPOINTS

ISSUE: WHICH SIDE HAS THE GREATER RESPONSIBILITY FOR THE ARAB-ISRAELI CONFLICT IN THE MIDDLE EAST?

The Middle East has been a focus of conflict for most of the twentieth century. One of the most persistent disputes is between Israel and the Arab states. Although some progress has been made towards peace in the region, the conflicts between nations have deep roots in both politics and culture.

The underlying causes of the Arab-Israeli conflict are the source of considerable debate. Sami Hadawi, a Palestinian scholar and author of numerous publications on the Middle East, argues that the conflict is the result of the Zionists' unjust occupation of Palestinian land. Daniel Pipes, director of the Foreign Policy Institute in Philadelphia, argues that the conflict is not between Israel and its Arab neighbours but among opposing Arab nations and groups vying for control of Palestine.

Read each of these viewpoints carefully, then complete an Argument Analysis and Evaluation Summary for each reading.

Sami Hadawi

"It is not the first time in history that partition has been resorted to as a solution to a problem. In ancient times, King Solomon ruled: If you cannot give one child to each of the two who claim to be the mother, then split the child into two and give half to one and the second half to the other.

The Division of Palestine

"An analogous scene was re-enacted in Palestine three thousand years later, except that the wisdom of Solomon in the judgment was lacking in this case. Like the false mother who welcomed the bisection of the child who was not hers, the Zionists accepted partition of the Holy Land because it gave them something they did not own and to which they were not entitled in justice or in equity.

"Partition of countries against the will of the people is not only wrong in principle; it has been proved to be inhuman too. Wherever applied, partition has brought tragedy, destruction and suffering to millions of human beings. War came to Korea only because of the partition of the land into North and South; and the fierce battles that raged for ten years in South Vietnam with the loss of hundreds and thousands of lives and considerable destruction, came to an end only after the North and South were reunited....

"The powers that resist the will of the people of these three countries to unity and impose upon them a partition that can only be maintained by force of arms, are the same powers that have inflicted the tragedy of partition on Palestine, with one additional iniquity—they first gave equal validity to the *claim* of the Zionists to Palestine and the *right* of the Arabs to their homeland in order to justify their plan of partition, then went to a step further by encouraging the dislodgement of the Arabs from their homes and property.

"After thirty years of tribulation and suffering, the world has come to recognize the error of its judgment in partitioning the Holy Land in 1947; but there is nothing that can be done to remove the evil that has been unleashed upon a peaceful people and a land held sacred by the adherents of the three great faiths. The least that can now be done is to undo the injustice by recognizing that a wrong has been committed against an innocent people and to redress it in a just manner.

"There is probably no subject fraught with so

many distortions and misrepresentations as the Palestine problem. It has been widely discussed, debated, lectured upon and written about in the past six decades, but still it is far from being correctly understood.

"World opinion has been led to believe that the Palestine problem is a conflict between Israel and the Arab States over the sovereignty of territory that the Arab States regard as part of the Arab homeland. The Israelis, on the other hand, claim Palestine as theirs by reason of the Balfour Declaration of 1917, the United Nations Partition Resolution of 1947, subsequent military conquests and what is commonly referred to as the "Biblical Promises." In other words, it is presumed to be a territorial dispute between nations, similar in some respects to the dispute between India and Pakistan over Kashmir.

"This Zionist approach is not without a motive. It is intended to confuse the issue and to obliterate the memories of the crimes committed against the Palestine Arabs—crimes which have been described by British historian Arnold Toynbee as no less heinous than the Nazi crimes against the Jews. Its purpose is also to by-pass standing United Nations resolutions calling upon the Israelis to surrender the extra territory they occupied by force of arms beyond the area assigned to the 'Jewish State' under the Partition Plan of 1947; to give the refugees the choice between repatriation and compensation; and to permit the internationalization of Jerusalem. To label the conflict as a dispute between nations divests it of its human and just elements and puts it in the same category as other world territorial issues where the parties proffer claims and counter-claims perhaps of equal strength.

"The truth of the matter is that the Palestine problem must be called first and foremost a dispute between the Palestine Arabs and the Jews before it can be labelled as an Arab States-Israeli conflict. The issue is fundamentally one of individual rights and principles, as well as of territory, and must be treated as a moral and political issue.

"No matter what language diplomacy uses in defining the rights of the Palestine Arabs, the fact remains that the major portion of the territory now called 'Israel' is legitimately owned by individual Arabs. Their rights derive from the universally accepted principle that a country belongs to its indigenous inhabitants. The fact that the Arabs fled in terror, because of real fear of a repetition of the 1948 Zionist massacres, is no reason for denying them their homes, fields and livelihoods. Civilians caught in an area of military activity generally panic. But they have always been able to return to their homes when the danger subsides. Military conquest does not abolish private rights to property; nor does it entitle the victor to confiscate the homes, property and personal belongings of the non-combatant civilian population. The seizure of Arab property by the Israelis was an outrage. It was described by many distinguished writers as 'robbery.'

"The position of the Arab States fully supports the Palestine Arabs' demand for rights to homes and country. Any solution agreed to by the Palestine Arabs would be acceptable to the Arab States. Conversely, the Arab States cannot conclude a settlement that is unacceptable to the Palestine Arabs...."

Excerpted, with permission, from Bitter Harvest *by Sami Hadawi. Brooklyn: Olive Branch Press, 1990. Copyright © 1990 Sami Hadawi.*

Daniel Pipes

"In Arab eyes, who should inherit Palestine? The leaders most directly concerned with this issue disagree, sometimes violently, among themselves as to who should rule Palestine and even where its rightful boundaries lie....

"These competing ambitions are not momentary breaches in an otherwise unified Arab position, but deep and abiding divisions that, more than the Arab confrontation with Israel itself, constitute the center of gravity in the Arab-Israeli conflict. The fact that so many Arab parties lay claim to Israel's territory renders accommodation unlikely and prolongs a conflict that otherwise might be settled. Indeed, relations between the Arab states determine the future course of that conflict far more than actions by Israel, the United States, or the Soviet Union.

"Four Arab groups have had the longest and most important historical roles in the Arab struggle for Palestine: Palestinian separatists, Arab nationalists, the Jordanian government, and the Syrian government. Actors of secondary importance include fundamentalist Muslims and West Bank notables....

Palestinian Separatists

"The PLO has carried the standard of this group, often known as Palestinian nationalists, since 1964. Palestinian separatists envisage an independent state in the area that Israel now controls; this state of Palestine should possess all the conventional signs of sovereignty—borders, customs, embassies, a flag, an army, and membership in the United Nations. The Palestinian separatist claim dominated Arab efforts to control Palestine during two periods: from late 1920 to the declaration of Israeli statehood in 1948, and from the Six Day War of 1967 to the Battle for Beirut in 1982....

Arab Nationalists

"Palestinian separatism is often confused with Arab nationalism, though their goals are incompatible. The former aspires to make Palestine a fully independent country; the latter would integrate it into a much larger entity, the Arab nation. Arab nationalists (also called Pan-Arab nationalists or Pan-Arabists) hope to build a state that will eventually comprise all Arabic speakers between the Atlantic ocean and the Persian Gulf, from Morocco to Oman. Palestinian separatists see Palestine as an independent state; Arab nationalists envision it as a province of a much larger unit....

Jordan

"Jordan has had two major kings, 'Abdallah, who ruled from 1921 to 1951, and his grandson Husayn, who has ruled since 1953. Both of them aspired to Palestine....

"An opportunity to seize Palestinian territory came in 1948 when Great Britain gave up its mandate. With British cooperation, the Transjordanian army already occupied parts of Palestine by the time imperial troops evacuated in May 1948. It subsequently attacked the fledgling state of Israel and captured the territory that came to be known as the West Bank. Transjordan was renamed Jordan in June 1949 and the West Bank became part of Jordan in April 1950. Only Great Britain recognized this incorporation of the West Bank; the Arab states, unwilling to accept the Jordanian claim to Palestine, refused to sanction Abdallah's land grab....

"Certain characteristics have distinguished the Jordanian position over nearly seven decades: enmity toward the Palestinian separatists, friendship with the West, pragmatism, disagreement with the Arab consensus, and stable working relations with the Jews....

Syria

"As the years passed, Syria's leaders continued not to reconcile themselves to their borders. Its own president in 1953 referred to Syria as 'the current official name for that country which lies within the artificial borders drawn up by imperialism'— an extraordinary remark by a head of state. Syria's delegate to the UN Security Council observed in 1967 that it was Syria 'from which Palestine was severed and from the territory of which Israel was created.'

"These assertions acquired additional force in 1974, when the Asad regime made Greater Syria a central foreign policy objective. Since then, Syrian officials repeatedly argued that Palestine is Southern Syria....

The Causes of Conflict

"Finally, inter-Arab relations—and not Arab-Israeli relations—are the cause of political volatility in the Middle East. The center of gravity lies in meetings of the Arab League, subsidies given to the PLO, press denunciations of Arab leaders who negotiate with Israel, terrorism against Arab diplomats, and the like. These drive the conflict far more than such factors as Israeli policy on the West Bank or US willingness to sell arms to Saudi Arabia."

ANALYSIS AND EVALUATION

Refer to the Argument Analysis and Evaluation Guide on page viii.

1. Using the Argument Analysis and Evaluation Guide, compare the readings by Hadawi and Pipes. On what do they agree? On what do they disagree?

2. Decide which of the viewpoints you tend to support and explain why. Be sure to use specific information from this textbook, the readings, and other sources to support your position.

3. State and support your position on the issue: "Which side has the greater responsibility for the Arab-Israeli conflict in the Middle East?"

CHAPTER THIRTEEN

The New World Order

"We live in an era in the history of nations when there is greater need than ever for co-ordinated political action and responsibility."

Gro Harlem Brundtland, Our Common Future, *1987*

"It is important that the nations of the world become sufficiently unified to face the problems which attack us as a unit. These problems...do not distinguish among us. How then can we distinguish among ourselves?

Isaac Asimov, "For Mutual Survival We Must Bring Our World Together," The Humanist, *September/October 1989*

Left: Earth Day Celebrations in New York

❖ OVERVIEW

At the end of the twentieth century, a new world order is emerging. Military alliances are diminishing while economic alliances are assuming centre stage. The world powers are no longer those with the greatest military strength but those with the greatest economic clout.

Within this new world order, however, there remain pressing global problems. Poverty, overpopulation, and pollution threaten the future of the planet. Human rights issues threaten the security and prosperity of millions of people. Peace and security are threatened by military regimes and terrorist groups. How will the world respond to the challenges?

FOCUS QUESTIONS

1. What are the prospects for global co-operation and conflict in the near future?

2. What is the significance of the new global marketplace?

3. What is the interrelationship among poverty, population, and the environment?

4. What are some key trends and issues before us as we prepare to enter the twenty-first century?

INTERNATIONAL CO-OPERATION

In the new world order, international co-operation is emerging as the key to peace and prosperity. Since its inception after the Second World War, the United Nations has fostered co-operation among nations through its many agencies and services. (See chapter 6.) Yet there are over 3000 other associations that promote international co-operation and interdependence.

NON-GOVERNMENTAL ORGANIZATIONS

Non-governmental organizations (NGOs) are, as the name implies, organizations that operate independently of any government. In most cases, NGOs draw their financial and human resources from the developed world and distribute them for use in economic and social development in developing countries. Although NGOs may receive some of their operating revenues from governments, they raise most of their funds through private sources. This arms-length relationship allows NGOs to set aside political issues in favour of developmental concerns.

Most NGOs are staffed by dedicated workers with a genuine desire to improve the quality of life in poor countries. NGO workers voluntarily give up the comforts of the developed world to live and work in places where human survival is a challenge. At their best, non-governmental organizations serve to showcase the possibilities and rewards of international co-operation.

Not all NGOs are working only to foster economic and social development, however. Some organizations have been criticized as little more than thinly veiled attempts to impose Western views on vulnerable societies. A high percentage of the revenues of some NGOs are used simply to pay for fund-raising activities, while only a small percentage actually reaches the developing countries. In other situations, well meaning but poorly conceived and implemented programs have in fact been detrimental rather than beneficial.

In spite of such criticisms, however, billions of dollars annually are invested in developing countries through the efforts of NGOs. In an era of greater international co-operation, the important role these organizations play will continue.

THE GLOBAL ECONOMY

The disintegration of the Soviet Union and a relative waning of the economic prominence of the United States has created a new world order based on economic power rather than military strength. Today power rests with those countries or regions that meet the demands of the global marketplace with competitively priced goods and services. Those countries that fail to adapt to the new global marketplace, or that lack the physical and human resources to do so, will face a bleak political and economic future.

Trading Blocs and Free Trade

In the new world order, trade alliances are the growing trend. Trading blocs provide an international structure in which groups of countries work together to further their own interests in the global marketplace. Individual countries within blocs must set aside some of their own aspirations and make certain concessions, such as the elimination of protective trade barriers against their trading partners. Marginal industries that were protected by tariffs and trade restrictions are left to survive or collapse on their own. The lifting of protective tariffs usually creates a period of adjustment in some sectors of the economy. Workers and capital shift from unproductive sectors to more productive industries, creating a certain amount of **structural unemployment** in the process. Proponents of trading blocs argue that the end result—highly competitive activities specializing in areas of greatest profit—is

NGOs like OXFAM–Canada support small-scale production facilities such as this woodworking co-operative in Namibia.

worth any economic and political upheaval during the adjustment period.

NAFTA

The **North American Free Trade Agreement** (NAFTA) among Canada, the United States, and Mexico officially took effect on 1 January 1994. This created a vast market of over 370 million people. All sides stressed the advantages for them in the agreement. Mexico gambled that its wage rates, at approximately 10 per cent of American

It is unlikely that global trading alliances will eliminate poverty in small countries like Trinidad and Tobago in the Caribbean.

wanted access to Mexico's oil reserves. Canada, of course, expected great opportunities in the huge American market.

These high expectations may or may not be met. Along with expanded markets comes the problem of job loss and economic dislocation. The sudden drop in the Mexican peso in 1995 forced Canada and the United States to spend billions of dollars in aid and loans. Thus there are benefits and costs to economic integration.

Poverty in the Global Marketplace

In a new world order of trading alliances, what will become of those countries that are not part of a trading bloc? Some analysts suggest that the world will soon consist of three trade groups—the European Union (see pages 218-21), the Pacific Rim (see pages 284-85), and North America. Countries in Africa and South Asia will be excluded; Caribbean and small Latin American countries have only an outside chance of being invited into the North American trading group. China, the most populous nation on earth, stands apart from any bloc. These countries will face trade protection measures designed to limit their access to the richest markets in the world. Their goods and services will be more expensive due to the improved economies of scale in the trading blocs. They will also have limited access to the new technologies of bloc nations. Thus the poorer countries seem destined to remain poor, forever on the fringe of the world's economy.

MILITARISM

The new world order created an atmosphere of optimism that the military threat to world peace and security had been eliminated. Indeed, many people believe there is no place for militarism in the world of the twenty-first century.

and Canadian rates, would attract new businesses and industries. Even before the agreement was signed, American firms had opened 1500 assembly plants in northern Mexico manufacturing everything from toys to auto parts. The American and Canadian governments wanted unrestricted access to the expanding Mexican market of almost 100 million people. The United States also

In 1994, Chile applied for membership in NAFTA.

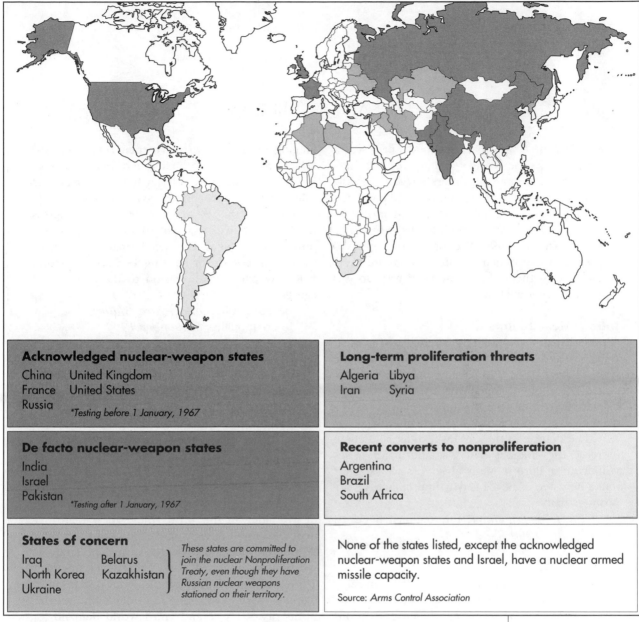

Acknowledged nuclear-weapon states

China   United Kingdom
France   United States
Russia
*Testing before 1 January, 1967

Long-term proliferation threats

Algeria   Libya
Iran   Syria

De facto nuclear-weapon states

India
Israel
Pakistan   *Testing after 1 January, 1967

Recent converts to nonproliferation

Argentina
Brazil
South Africa

States of concern

Iraq   Belarus
North Korea   Kazakhstan
Ukraine

These states are committed to join the nuclear Nonproliferation Treaty, even though they have Russian nuclear weapons stationed on their territory.

None of the states listed, except the acknowledged nuclear-weapon states and Israel, have a nuclear armed missile capacity.

Source: *Arms Control Association*

Figure 13.1:
Global Nuclear Proliferation

This new world order, however, will require mutual co-operation among states. In theory, they will be rewarded with a **peace dividend**—that is, increased prosperity through reduced defence spending. Global interrelationships will mean that all countries will be mutually vulnerable; political and economic pressures will prevent any one state from taking action that will have harmful effects on the rest of the world. Over time, international organizations such as the United Nations might take on more

The idea of deterring war through the accumulation of nuclear weapons to absurd levels was labelled "mutually assured destruction"—or MAD.

VOICES

THE THREAT OF MILITARY CONFRONTATION

The end of the Cold War established a new world order in which the world's military rules are less clearly defined. Some observers suggest that developing countries will use the reduced emphasis on global military strength to achieve their own local military objectives, as Iraq intended when it invaded Kuwait in 1990. The opinions expressed here suggest that military confrontations are likely to increase in the wake of the Cold War. Do you agree with their analysis?

John J. Mearsheimer

"Bipolarity, an equal military balance, and nuclear weapons have fostered peace in Europe over the past 45 years. The Cold War confrontation produced these phenomena; thus the Cold War was principally responsible for transforming a historically violent region into a very peaceful place....

"The demise of the Cold War order is likely to increase the chances that war and major crises will occur in Europe. Many observers now suggest that a new age of peace is dawning; in fact the opposite is true."

John J. Mearsheimer, International Security, *Summer 1990.*

Michael Nacht

"With respect to regional conflicts, the centrality of military strength continues unabated. The proliferation of nuclear weapons, chemical weapons and ballistic missiles is simultaneously placing enormous military capabilities at the disposal of national leaders, some of whom have not shown a great capacity for moderation."

© *1990 The Washington Post. Reprinted with permission.*

Behrouz Afagh

"The superpowers have often been blamed for meddling in Third World trouble spots and pro-longing wars there to serve their own interests. Will there now be more chance of peace? Maybe. But there has been a tendency to overestimate the role played by superpower rivalry in Third World conflicts. Of the 23 major conflicts in progress in 1989 only five or six of them had any superpower involvement. The fact is that people have their own reasons for fighting. Perhaps the world will now pay more attention to these real local causes...."

Behrouz Afagh, "*Backyard Bullies,*" The New Internationalist, *September 1990*

David M. Markowitz

"Instruments of Armageddon have moved from the arsenals of the superpowers to the armories of those Third World countries willing to pay. Nuclear and chemical weapons are emerging around the globe.... Since the end of World War II, the intensity of wars between Third World nations has increased. The anti-colonial rebellions of the late 1940s and 1950s, the fully mechanized Arab-Israeli wars of the late 1960s and early 1970s and the 'war of the cities' in the 1980s Iran-Iraq War are evidence of how the destructive power of the Third World has been rising. The influx of strategic weapons is an integral part of this development.... Third World powers are acquiring for [use in] local disputes what were once considered the mechanisms of total war, and Third World demand for apocalyptic instruments is bound to only increase over time. Weapons of mass destruction have become the armaments of choice; the Third World will not give them up."

David M. Markowitz, "Strategic Weapons in the Third World," Harvard International Review, *Fall 1989.*

peacekeeping roles designed to prevent conflict between nations, perhaps through the establishment of an international police or military force.

Not everyone agrees with this perspective, however. There are those who believe that the new world order will lead to greater militarism rather than less. They argue that the Cold War acted as a deterrent to military conflict. The bipolar world was balanced militarily because neither superpower could dominate the other and their vast nuclear stockpiles ensured that they would not risk a large-scale confrontation. Even most smaller nations were discouraged from military confrontations because of the threat that the superpowers might become involved through their alliances. Without the Cold War, therefore, there is less deterrent to military confrontation.

The issue of nuclear weapons was not solved with the end of the Cold War, however. Individual republics of the former Soviet Union tussled over control of the nuclear weapons that had been stockpiled in their territories. With the breakup of the USSR, Ukraine suddenly became the third largest nuclear superpower. In addition, some developing countries (notably Iraq and North Korea) began shopping around to buy the technology and expertise to establish their own nuclear capabilities. Thus in some ways security from the threat of nuclear war became even more elusive. The tight control over nuclear weapons by the two former Cold War enemies was lost.

THE ENVIRONMENT

The 1960s saw a marked increase in concern for the environment, led by writers such as Rachel Carson, who pointed out the dangers of abusing the earth's natural ecological systems in *Silent Spring* (1962). But the movement was eclipsed by what many considered to be more urgent problems in the 1970s—the war in Vietnam, the energy crisis, and the global recession. The environmental movement experienced a revival in the 1980s, however, with the growing realization that we faced several serious environmental problems, including holes in the ozone layer, global warming, toxic chemical pollution, and tropical rainforest destruction.

These threats to the environment signalled the need for immediate changes in the ways in which people interacted with the environment. The report issued by the UN Commission on Environment and Development in 1987 spawned a number of environmental initiatives. Among them was the 1988 **Montreal Protocol**, a treaty signed by forty-seven countries, including Canada, to control the use of chemicals that destroy atmospheric ozone. The environmental movement of the 1980s took a realistic view of the world, recognizing that development must continue but in environmentally responsible ways.

> Canadians consume more energy and produce more garbage per capita than any other people on earth.

POVERTY, POPULATION, AND THE ENVIRONMENT

Absolute poverty affects one in five people in the world today. While eliminating poverty is a moral responsibility, it is also essential for the preservation of the world environment.

Recent rapid population growth in Africa, Asia, and Latin America has placed incredible pressure on the environment through increased demand for land, food, and water. The problems of

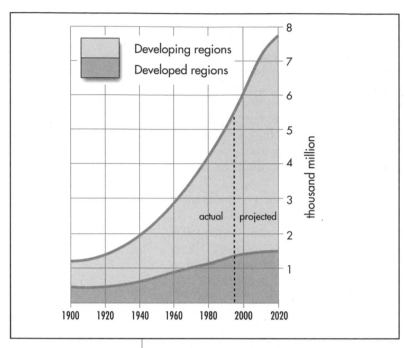

Figure 13.2:
Population Growth,
Actual and Projected to
2020

Simple water purification
projects help to improve
sanitation in developing
countries.

which in turn disrupts existing economic and social systems.

As the twenty-first century dawns, the world must re-evaluate its development policies. Recent experiences have indicated that small grassroots projects that respond to local needs and conditions and that involve both men and women have greater success than large-scale projects implemented through national and international aid programs. Many experts believe that this revised approach will yield the greatest benefits in reducing poverty while preserving local environments.

Industrialization and the Environment

Increased population is one of many of the world's problems. Consider the impact of people on the life-support systems of the planet. People in the developed world use far more of the earth's resources than the people of Africa, Asia, or Latin America. Our lifestyles have an environmental impact 300 times as destructive as the lifestyles of people living in sub-Saharan Africa or Bangladesh, for example. From this perspective, the population problem is not that there are too many poor people but that there are too many *rich* people. If there were fewer people in the developed world or, more realistically, if we changed our lifestyle and consumed fewer of the world's resources, we would eliminate much of the stress placed on the global environment.

Few people, of course, are prepared to sacrifice their quality of life. What is needed is a willingness to work towards a better

poverty and environmental destruction go hand in hand.

Economic development has traditionally been considered the most effective means of eliminating poverty. But in many cases, development has failed to have any beneficial impact on poverty. Instead, large-scale development projects can make poverty worse by increasing environmental damage,

PROFILE

GRO BRUNDTLAND (1939-)

Gro Harlem Brundtland is a leading figure in the environmental movement as well as the prime minister of Norway. Since entering politics in 1974, Brundtland has promoted the protection of delicate, life-sustaining ecosystems from the Arctic to the Amazon. Her report on the environment, entitled Our Common Future *(1987), is one of the guiding forces in the international environmental movement. Do you think environmental protection should be a priority of the Canadian government?*

"The environment and resources of developing countries...have become the victims in a troubled world economy."
Gro Brundtland, 1988

"The Earth is one, even if the world of man is still divided. The atmosphere knows no boundaries."
Gro Brundtland, 1988

"Our generation is the first one to have seen planet earth from a distance. And from that perspective it is all too apparent that our species is dependent on a single, tiny, fragile globe floating in space, a closed and vulnerable system."
Gro Brundtland, "How To Secure Our Common Future," Scientific American, *September 1989*

Gro Brundtland was born in Oslo, Norway, the daughter of a Labour Party politician. After graduating from medical school, she became a medical officer of health in Oslo.

In 1974, Brundtland entered politics and became the minister of the environment in a Labour government. In 1981, she served briefly as prime minister, during which time her government introduced policies for the protection and preservation of the environment.

In 1983, Brundtland was appointed chair of the UN World Commission on Environment and Development. The commission was charged with investigating environmental problems and the ways and means of protecting the environment globally. *Our Common Future*, the commission's report published in 1987, exposed the extent of the global environmental problem. The report suggested that a marriage of economic and ecological priorities, in which both governments and citizens create policies to promote development and protect the environment, was the only way to save humankind from destruction. The concept of **sustainable development**—development for the long term using natural resources wisely—was central to the recommendations of the Brundtland report.

Following her work with the United Nations, Brundtland was elected prime minister of Norway, first in 1986 and again in 1990. Her government continued to be a world leader on environmental issues.

Oil tanker disasters like this one in Britain's Shetland Islands wreak havoc on the environment.

quality of life around the globe using techniques that do not damage the planet's life-support system. The basic solution to the world's environment problems is to reduce consumption. This could be achieved by using less and/or finding alternative technologies that are environmentally friendly. Using less, however, will require a fundamental change in our attitudes towards economic growth and mass consumption, and technological solutions to environmental problems will take time.

WOMEN'S RIGHTS

Discrimination against women is deeply entrenched in cultural beliefs and traditional values. Throughout the world women are relegated to inferior social and political positions. While women make up over 50 per cent of the world's population, their representation in the highest echelons of government is less than 10 per cent.

Women have been seeking to gain a greater voice in political affairs through grassroots organizations and

political campaigning. These frequently serve as springboards to elected office. Yet even when women are appointed to high-level government positions, they are often assigned to education, health, and social welfare portfolios. Few women are given responsibility for finance, industry, or defence. Even when women head governments, there is not automatically a "trickle down" effect in which a large number of women receive influential positions. In Britain, for example, former prime minister Margaret Thatcher's cabinet following the 1987 election did not include a single woman.

There is no correlation between economic development and greater political representation for women. In Bangladesh, one of the world's poorest nations, 10 per cent of the legislative members are women; in the highly industrialized country of France, the figure is less than 6 per cent. In 1959, Sirimavo Bandaranaike was elected prime minister of Sri Lanka, at a time when women in Switzerland still did not have the right to vote.

The Nordic countries of Finland, Norway, and Sweden stand out among the nations of the world for their successful integration of women into the political system. The education of women is given top priority and women's organizations play an influential role in these societies. In Finland, 38.5 per cent of elected representatives are women, as are seven of the seventeen cabinet members. In Norway, 34 per cent of parliamentary representatives are women, along with half of the cabinet members. In Sweden, 50 per cent of ministers and 41 per cent of representatives are women.

At the end of the twentieth century, some progress has been made towards the greater integration of women into political systems. But greater efforts are still needed to ensure political equality. These include specific policies designed to increase the proportion of women involved in the political process, securing women's right to vote and hold office in all countries, and encouraging women to exercise their right to vote. The new world order offers a new opportunity to restructure societies to eliminate discrimination and foster equality for women in all spheres of life.

Figure 13.3: Women's Representation in Government by Region, 1990

	Upper House (%)	Lower House (%)
Europe	13.4	18.7
North and Central America	12.7	9.2
Africa	8.3	8.4
Asia	6.8	7.2
South America	3.2	4.4

The Feminization of Poverty

In all societies, women dominate the lowest rungs of the socioeconomic ladder. As the twentieth century ends, there is a growing trend towards the **feminization of poverty**.

Everywhere in the world, women are found in jobs that are low in pay and social status. This **pink ghetto** exists in all countries, regardless of levels of economic development or political equality. Women fill a large proportion of clerical, sales, and service positions, but are significantly underrepresented in manufacturing, transportation, and management. Typically, women earn less than men for performing work of equal value. Women are also more likely to become single heads of households faced with the responsibility of raising a family, often without financial support from their former partners.

In developing societies, women typically work twice as many hours as men but earn only 10 per cent of the total income. Women may be prohibited from owning property and their access to credit and technology is usually limited. Women must often bear family burdens alone as their husbands migrate to the cities in search of work.

Sometimes women themselves abandon rural areas to seek a better life in urban centres. But without education, skills, or political clout, women are often destined to work in sweatshops where both the working conditions and the wages are deplorable.

When Britain's former foreign secretary, Sir Geoffrey Howe, visited Pakistan during Benazir Bhutto's term as prime minister, his wife asked a little boy what he would like to be when he grew up. "A truck driver," mused the child. Surprised at this modest ambition, Lady Howe persisted: "But surely you would like to go into politics, even become prime minister?" Back came the answer, "No, that's women's work."

Anecdote quoted by Dr. Nafis Sadik, executive director of the United Nations Population Fund

Women cast their ballots in a democracy referendum in Malawi in June 1993.

In many developing countries, the debt crisis of the 1980s has contributed to the desperate plight of women. Governments burdened with huge foreign debts have been forced by lending agencies to make drastic cuts to social programs, including education, health services, and food subsidies. Typically these cutbacks have disproportionately hurt women and children. While national governments and international organizations have recently recognized the adverse effects these measures have had and have taken steps to alleviate them, critics argue that their response has been too little, too late. Women's rights groups maintain that only with the creative participation of women in social and economic planning and policies will the feminization of poverty be arrested.

"All democratic experiments, all revolutions, all demands for equality have so far, in every instance, stopped short of sexual equality."

Rosalind Miles, The Women's History of the World, *(London: Palladin, 1990), p. 287.*

HUMAN RIGHTS

Human rights violations exist in many countries around the world. Human rights include all civil, social, and political rights. They also include the abuses of torture, disappearance, and state terrorism. The protection of human rights was first formally documented in 1948 by the United Nations in the Universal Declaration of Human Rights. They have since been reinforced by several specific documents.

In the new world order, there is increasing demand that all nations respect human rights. Monitoring organizations like **Amnesty International** work to expose violations of human rights and to pressure authorities to change their practices. The biggest weapon monitoring groups has is public opinion. By heightening public awareness of torture and inhumane practices, pressure can be exerted on repressive governments through trade sanctions, the suspension of foreign aid, and other forms of political protest. Thousands of prisoners have been released as a result of pressure from monitoring groups. Countless thousands more have received more

VOICES

CHILD LABOUR

Between 100 million and 200 million children under the age of sixteen work for wages. In a few South Asian countries, the number of working children is as high as 60 per cent. Some are in the workforce as young as six years old. The children do not have a choice. They must either work or starve.

Child labour is the result of poverty. Parents cannot afford to feed and house their children, so the children are forced to work to support themselves and the family. Child labour is usually exploited by unscrupulous businesses. Wages paid to children are several times less than those paid to adults. Hours are usually long and working conditions can be hazardous. Working children get trapped in the cycle of poverty because they lack the opportunity to receive an education or any skilled training.

The story of Shadab is typical of children forced to work in developing countries. As you read this account, consider what steps the United Nations should take to eliminate child labour.

"Shadab is 9. Since he was 6, he has spent 12 hours a day, six days a week, squatting in semidarkness on damp ground, polishing little pieces of metal on a high-speed grinding wheel. In the lock factory near New Delhi where he works, the gloom is broken only by a few narrow shafts of light entering through holes in the brick walls, and by a single light bulb. The air is visibly, palpably thick with metal dust, the temperature about 120°F [50°C]. The bare floor is damp with acid that sloshes from big vats onto the ground. Shadab is a bright-eyed child with an eager smile and a quick intelligence. He is small and alarmingly thin. Though his skin is normally brown, by noon every inch of him has turned a metallic grey-black, coated with metal dust. His hair is stiff with it. His voice is hoarse with it. All around the child, the unprotected belts that drive the grinding wheels whir. Metal pieces rasp and clang. When Shadab bends over to work, his face a few inches from his wheel, splinters of metal occasionally fly up into his eyes. He has never seen a pair of safety goggles. Shadab says he likes his job. He likes making money—about 17 cents a day. His father is dead, and he is proud that his mother, two brothers, and sister depend on his contribution for survival."

Kristin Helmore, excerpt from "Children in Darkness," reprinted by permission from the Christian Science Monitor. © *1987 The Christian Science Publishing Society. All rights reserved.*

humane treatment while in prison as the harsh glare of the world spotlight is focused on the actions of repressive governments.

Human rights activists advocate that foreign aid, weapons sales, and trading status should be linked to a country's human rights record. Increasingly, more countries are embracing this philosophy. In 1990, both Canada and Britain declared their intention to restrict economic assistance to those countries that respect democracy and human rights. In 1991, the European Union established the link between foreign aid and human rights

Many countries detain prisoners of conscience. These are people who are jailed because of their beliefs, colour, gender, ethnic origin, language, or religion, and who have not resorted to or advocated violence in support of their cause.

Protests by members of Amnesty International focus attention on human rights abuses around the world.

NORTH-SOUTH RELATIONS

While the Cold War dominated the world stage, the emphasis was on relations between East and West. Much of the developing world maintained a policy of nonalignment. However, the end of the Cold War has created a new opportunity to redefine global relationships. The focus of the new world order has shifted to North-South relations.

in its charter. Many critics charge, however, that while the democratic countries pay lip service to linking human rights and financial aid, in practice they continue to support corrupt and repressive regimes.

Many states that receive aid challenge the right of foreign governments and institutions to establish human rights criteria in their countries. They consider such intervention to be a violation of their sovereignty. Thus the debate over human rights will continue in the new world order.

"We could always tell when international protests were taking place.... The food rations increased and the beatings were fewer. Letters from abroad were translated and passed around from cell to cell."

A former prisoner in Vietnam, in The Amnesty International Handbook

Over 3.5 billion people—75 per cent of all humanity—live in the developing world. While individual nations are diverse in size, political structure, and levels of economic development, they share some fundamental traits: most of their people are poor, their economies are weak, and they wield relatively little power in the global arena.

A conference of 128 nations was convened in Jakarta, Indonesia, in September 1992. Recognizing that the term *nonalignment* had lost its relevance in a post-Cold War world, the conference adopted a new name for the developing world, the **Global South**, and declared that the next era would be one of re-evaluating and restructuring North-South relations.

The conference underlined the political and economic grievances the nations of the South had against the North, including ineffective and often insensitive aid and development policies. The conference declaration advocated seeking a greater voice in world affairs through a strengthened United Nations in which more power is awarded to the General Assembly while the power of the Security Council is reduced.

As the twentieth century reaches an end, the Global South is seeking to set its own agenda and priorities. The South recognizes it needs the resources, markets, and technology of the North to realize its economic potential. Yet in the new world order this should be achieved without fostering economic dependence on the North. This will mean discarding old ideas, policies, and practices. In their place a new set of principles should be established in which a genuinely interdependent world is realized.

UNDERSTANDING OUR PAST: THE INTERPRETIVE APPROACH

The present generation is fortunate to be living in an historic time. We are at the end of an era in which a Cold War dominated international relations for forty-five years. The end of any era creates a period of change and uncertainty. What will the future bring? Have we finally reached the age of peace and security in which the world order is one of co-operation, democracy, and freedom? Or are we headed for anarchy in a world made up of warring nations?

The trends for the future are based on the ashes of the past. We can now look more objectively at the global forces that led to the beginning and end of the Cold War. Was the Cold War essentially a struggle between communism and capitalism? Was it a struggle between democracy and totalitarianism? Or was it simply a selfish struggle for world domination between two superpowers?

For many people in the West, the end of the Cold War is seen as a victory for freedom and democracy. This viewpoint is presented in an article by Francis Fukuyama entitled "The End of History," published just as the Cold War ended. In this remarkable thesis, Fukuyama states:

> "What we may be witnessing is not just the end of the Cold War, or the passing of a particular period of postwar history, but the end of history as such: that is, the end point of mankind's ideological evolution and the universalization of Western democracy as the final form of human government."
>
> *From Francis Fukuyama, "The End of History",* The National Interest *(Spring, 1990).*

Fukuyama argues that not only has the West won a decisive victory at the end of the twentieth century, but that this is a permanent victory. Western liberal democracy and capitalism will rule forever and thus history will end. Yet Fukuyama's interpretation is only one of many. Others, such as historian John Gaddis, see the Cold War quite differently, in Gaddis's case as a period of peace and stability.

> "Who is to say...how the historians a century from now...will look back on us? Is it not at least plausible that they will see our era, not as 'the Cold War' at all, but rather, like those ages of Metternich and

> "The dominance of a few countries, which has become prominent, could result in further inequities, uncertainties, and instabilities. The failure to redress the widening gap between the affluent North and the impoverished South is looming as the central issue that could threaten international security and stability."
>
> *The Jakarta Declaration, 6 September 1992*

Bismarck, as a rare and fondly remembered 'Long Peace'?"

From John Gaddis, The Long Peace: Inquiries into the History of the Cold War *(New York: Oxford University Press, 1989).*

Do the lessons of the Cold War, or any other historic event, teach us anything about the future? In this book you have engaged in argument analysis and evaluation of many key issues in the twentieth century. These exercises were designed to improve your abilities as a critical thinker. Your experience with the interpretive approach to the study of history should assist you in dealing with issues in the future. In confronting other issues it is hoped that you will appreciate and understand that there are different viewpoints to consider.

Thus Fukuyama's interpretation of the Cold War is based on his belief that the Cold War was an ideological struggle between totalitarian communism and Western liberal democracy. If this view is correct, then we could predict a long period of stability, security, and prosperity as all nations strive to become liberal democracies. On the other hand, if we accept Gaddis's interpretation that the Cold War was actually a "long peace," our view of the future could be quite different. Instead of security and stability we might predict uncertainty and conflict as nations seek new alliances and fight for their own self-interests. Gaddis's view helps to explain the rise of bitter conflicts in many former Soviet bloc nations. However, Fukuyama could also be correct because many former communist nations are striving to achieve democracy. Which argument is most compelling? That, of course, is what you must decide. We must ensure that we are open to the analysis and evaluation of many interpretations and remain cautious as we reach our own decisions on an issue.

In Review

1. a) Describe the purpose of non-governmental organizations.
   b) Why are some NGOs criticized?

2. a) What are the perceived benefits of free trade alliances?
   b) What impact might these alliances have on countries not in any alliance?

3. Explain the nuclear threat in the aftermath of the Cold War.

4. Why do some analysts believe that militarism will increase in the post-Cold War world?

5. a) Outline the relationship between poverty, overpopulation, and the environment.
   b) In what way does the industrialized world threaten the environment?

6. What obstacles do women in developing countries face?

7. How can the international community curb human rights abuses?

8. What are the important issues to be addressed in North-South relations?

SUMMARY

Heading into the twenty-first century, the world must prepare for many challenges. A new economic order will redefine the world's power structure. Yet while power in the new world order may be measured by economic clout rather than military strength, it will be imperative to maintain peace and stability in a heavily armed world. Working together co-operatively, the developed and developing countries must also find solutions to the problems of poverty, overpopulation, and environmental destruction.

Whether the new world order will be one of co-operation or conflict is yet to be revealed in the twenty-first century.

MAKING CONNECTIONS

1. What are the greatest barriers to co-operation between countries? How can these barriers be reduced?

2. Is the new world order likely to make it easier or harder for developing countries to achieve prosperity? Explain your answer.

3. Outline the circumstances that will make the following global problems difficult to solve: militarism; poverty; human rights abuses.

DEVELOPING YOUR VOICE

4. There has been a disturbing trend in recent years for toxic waste to be "exported" from developed countries to developing countries for disposal. This has been termed **garbage imperialism**.
   a) Why would developed countries ship toxic waste to other countries? Why would other countries accept toxic waste?
   b) What does trade in toxic waste indicate about the relationship between developed and developing countries?

5. Suggest ways in which the new world order will influence Canada. Consider political relationships, economic potential, and international reputation.

6. Prepare a written plan of action for one of the issues discussed in this chapter. Your plan must include:
   a) a goal statement that is specific and measurable
   b) a list of resources that will enable you to reach your goal
   c) a list of problems that may prevent you from reaching your goal
   d) strategies to overcome these problems.

RESEARCHING THE ISSUES

7. Research Canada's links with other countries. Identify five groups under each of the following categories: International Organizations, Non-governmental Organizations, International Movements. What conclusions can you draw from your lists?

8. Research the impact of the North American Free Trade Agreement on Canada. Consider the unemployment rate; Gross National Product; degree of foreign ownership; per capita income; and growth rates among Canadian-owned versus foreign-owned enterprises. Express your findings in a mock interview between a journalist and a government trade official.

9. Compare the economic progress of a developed nation and a developing nation since 1990. Select countries that appear to be typical of their region. Record your information in a comparison chart and write a summary statement.

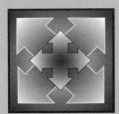

VIEWPOINTS

ISSUE: WILL THE NEW WORLD ORDER BE ONE OF CONFLICT OR CO-OPERATION?

With the end of the Cold War there is hope for a more peaceful world. Is this hope grounded in reality, or is it an illusion? The fear of a nuclear world war has diminished significantly with the collapse of the former Soviet Union. This has created the opportunity to reduce military spending and refocus our attention on other problems facing the world. However, wars and conflicts continue to exist. The Gulf War and the conflict in the former Yugoslavia are only two reminders that our hopes for a peaceful world may be premature.

Bruce Russett, a professor of international relations at Yale University, argues that the end of the Cold War could usher in a new era of peace. He bases his argument on the belief that the spread of democracy in the world will promote peace. John Mearsheimer, a political scientist from the University of Chicago, argues that the end of the Cold War will not lessen conflicts. He claims that there is no historic reason to believe that democratic nations will be more peaceful.

Read these viewpoints carefully, then complete an Argument Analysis and Evaluation Summary for each reading.

Bruce Russett

"Two apparent facts about contemporary international patterns of war and peace stare us in the face. The first is that some States expect, prepare for, and fight wars against other States. The second is that some States do not expect, prepare for, or fight wars at least against each other. The first is obvious to everyone. The second is widely ignored, yet it is now true on an historically unprecedented scale, encompassing wide areas of the earth. In a real if still partial sense, peace is already among us. We need only recognize it, and try to learn from it....

Peace Among Democracies

"I am referring to the peace among the industrialized and democratically governed States, primarily in the northern hemisphere. These States—members of the Organization for Economic Cooperation and Development (OECD: Western Europe, North America, Japan, Australia, and New Zealand), plus a few scattered less industrialized democratic States—constitute a vast zone of peace, with more than three quarters of a billion people. Not only has there been no war among them for almost 45 years,...there has been little expectation of, or preparation for, war among them either. By war, I mean large-scale organized international violence with at least 1000 battle deaths (by a conventional social science definition). In fact, even much smaller-scale violence between these countries has been virtually absent. The nearest exception is Greece and Turkey, especially with their brief and limited violent clashes over Cyprus. They are, however, among the poorest countries of this group and only sporadically democratic.

"In the years before 1945, many of them fought often and bitterly, but always when at least one of the States in any warring pair was ruled by an authoritarian or totalitarian regime. Despite that past, war among them is now virtually unthinkable.... By the standards of world history this is an extraordinary achievement.

Explanations for Peace

"It is not easy to explain just why this peace has occurred. Partly it is due to the network of international law and institutions deliberately put into place to make a repetition of the previous world wars both unthinkable and impossible....

"In part it is due to favorable economic conditions associated with advanced capitalism. Fairly steady economic growth, a high absolute level of prosperity, relative equality of incomes within and across the industrial States, and a dense network of trade and investment across national borders all make resort to violence dubious on cost-benefit grounds; a potential aggressor who already is wealthy risks much by resorting to violence for only moderate gain....

"These explanations, [however] are at best only partial ones, and we are driven back to observing that the period of peace among the highly industrialized States essentially coincides with the period when they all have been under democratic rule....

"With only the most marginal exceptions, democratic States have not fought each other in the modern era....

"There are powerful norms against the use of lethal force both within democratic States and between them. Within them is of course the basic norm of liberal democratic theory—that disputes can be resolved without force through democratic political processes, which in some balance are to ensure both majority rule and minority rights. A norm of equality operates both as voting equality and as certain egalitarian rights to human dignity. Democratic government rests on the consent of the governed, but justice demands that consent not be abused. Resort to organized lethal violence, or the threat of it, is considered illegitimate and unnecessary to secure one's legitimate rights. Dissent within broad limits by a loyal opposition is expected and even needed for enlightened policymaking, and the opposition's basic loyalty to the system is to be assumed in the absence of evidence to the contrary.

"All participants in the political process are expected to share these norms. In practice, the norms do sometimes break down, but the normative restraints on violent behaviour—by State and citizens—are fully as important as the State's monopoly on the legitimate use of force in keeping incidents of the organized use of force rare....

"Democratic peoples...sense that somehow they and other peoples ought to be able to satisfy common interests and work out compromise solutions to their problems, without recourse to violence or threat of it. After all, that is the norm for behavior to which they aspire within democratic systems. Because other people living in democratic States are presumed to share those norms of live and let live, they can be presumed to share their moderate behavior in international affairs as well. That is, they can be respected as self-governing peoples and expected to offer the same respect to other democratic countries in turn....

"Realism has no explanation for the fact that certain kinds of States—namely, democratic ones—do not fight or prepare to fight one another. One must look instead to the liberal idealist vision of Immanuel Kant's Perpetual Peace, embodied also in Woodrow Wilson's vision of a peaceful world of democratic States. This same vision inspired US determination to root out fascism and establish the basis for democratic governments in West Germany and Japan after World War II (and partly also explains, and was used to justify, interventions in Vietnam, Grenada, Nicaragua, and so on)....

A Shift Toward Democracy

"The end of World War II brought in its wake the demise of colonial empires; it brought a degree of self-determination to the formally colonized peoples. Unfortunately, that self-determination was often highly restricted, limited in part by ties of economic and military neo-colonialism. Self-determination also was often limited to the elites of the new States, as the governments installed were frequently authoritarian and repressive—anything but democratic. Yet there has been, since the mid-1970s, some evolution toward greater democracy in large parts of what is called the Third World. In 1973 only two Spanish- or Portuguese-speaking States in South America were governed by democratic regimes (Colombia and Venezuela); [in 1990] only two are ruled by military dictatorships (Paraguay and, in transition, Chile). Democracy remains fragile and imperfect in many of them, but the relative shift away from authoritarian rule is palpable.

"This shift shows up statistically on a worldwide basis. A long-term observer of political rights and civil liberties, Raymond Gastil, has carried out, over this period, a project of rating countries according to their degree of 'political freedom.' His rating is not meant to reflect a broad definition of human rights that includes, for example, the so-called second generation economic rights to employment or the satisfaction of basic physical needs. Rather, it addresses first generation rights: electoral practices, the accountability of the executive and legislature, judicial procedures, and freedom of expression and association—in short, dimensions of the traditional political definition of democracy. For some of his purposes, Gastil uses two scales of seven points each; for others he collapses these complex judgments into three categories of States: free, partly free, and not free. The distribution of States in these three categories has varied over time.

"By this evaluation, there has been a substantial decline in the number of strongly authoritarian (not free) States and a similarly substantial increase in the number of partly free States, especially if 1973 is used as the base year. These trends can be seen in many parts of the world: the demise of dictatorships in Greece, Portugal, and Spain in Europe; Gastil's recent characterization of Hungary, Poland, and even the Soviet Union with scores in the 'partly free' range; improvements he noted in China (as of 1988, and still overall 'not free'); and shifts in several large, important countries elsewhere. Does this analysis imply something more, that if the shift toward democracy does continue, we would then move into an era of international peace? If all States were democratic, could we all live in perpetual peace? Does a solution lie in creating a world where all countries are governed by democratic practices?...

"A serious reservation, however, must concern interpretation of the word 'creating.' The argument here does not imply that the route to ultimate perpetual peace is through wars, or threats of war, to make other countries democratic....

"A second temptation, related to the first, may be to define 'democracy' too narrowly and ethnocentrically, equating it too readily with all the particular norms and institutions of the Western parliamentary tradition....

"Whatever the faults of Western liberal (bourgeois) democracy, a world of spreading democratic ideology and practice offers some significant possibilities for spreading peace. Those possibilities can be enhanced by attention to implementing a broad definition of human rights and institutionalizing greater information flows. Human rights and information constitute elements both of greater global democratization and of direct and indirect contributions to international peace. In a world of imperfect democratization, such measures can help reduce those imperfections and compensate for some of them in the avoidance of war."

Bruce Russett, "Politics and Alternative Security: Toward a More Democratic, Therefore More Peaceful, World," in Alternative Security: Living Without Nuclear Deterrence, *Burns H. Weston, editor. Boulder CO: Westview Press, 1990. Reprinted with permission.*

John J. Mearsheimer

"Peace: it's wonderful. I like it as much as the next man, and have no wish to be willfully gloomy at a moment when optimism about the future shape of the world abounds. Nevertheless, my thesis in this essay is that we are likely soon to regret the passing of the Cold War.

"To be sure, no one will miss such by-products of the Cold War as the Korean and Vietnam conflicts. No one will want to replay the U-2 affair, the Cuban missile crisis, or the building of the Berlin Wall....

"We may, however, wake up one day lamenting the loss of the order that the Cold War gave to the anarchy of international relations. For untamed anarchy is what Europe knew in the forty-five years of this century before the Cold War, and untamed anarchy—Hobbes's war of all against all—is a prime cause of armed conflict. Those who think that armed conflicts among the European states are now out of the question, that the two world wars burned all the war out of Europe, are projecting unwarranted optimism onto the future. The theories of peace that implicitly undergird this optimism are notably shallow constructs. They stand up to neither logical nor historical analysis. You would not want to bet the farm on their prophetic accuracy.

Testing the Theories of War

"The world is about to conduct a vast test of the theories of war and peace put forward by social scientists, who never dreamed that their ideas would be tested by the world-historic events announced almost daily in newspaper headlines. This social scientist is willing to put his theoretical cards on the table as he ventures predictions about the future of Europe. In the process, I hope to put alternative theories of war and peace under as much intellectual pressure as I can muster. My argument is that the prospect of major crises, even wars, in Europe is likely to increase dramatically now that the Cold War is receding into history. The next forty-five years in Europe are not likely to be so violent as the forty-five years before the Cold War, but they are likely to be substantially more violent than the past forty-five years, the era that we may someday look back upon not as the Cold War but as the Long Peace, in John Lewis Gaddis's phrase.

"This pessimistic conclusion rests on the general argument that the distribution and character of military power among states are the root causes of war and peace. Specifically, the peace in Europe since 1945—precarious at first, but increasingly robust over time—has flowed from three factors: the bipolar distribution of military power on the Continent; the rough military equality between the polar powers, the United States and the Soviet Union; and the ritualistically deplored fact that each of these superpowers is armed with a large nuclear arsenal....

"Europe is reverting to a state system that created powerful incentives for aggression in the past. If you believe (as the Realist school of international relations theory, to which I belong, believes) that the prospects for international peace are not markedly influenced by the domestic political character of states—that it is the character of the state system, not the character of the individual units composing it, that drives states toward

war—then it is difficult to share in the widespread elation of the moment about the future of Europe. The year 1989 was repeatedly compared to 1789, the year the French Revolution began, as the Year of Freedom, and so it was. Forgotten in the general exaltation was that the hope-filled events of 1789 signaled the start of an era of war and conquest....

Is War Obsolete?

"Many students of European politics will reject my pessimistic analysis of post-Cold War Europe. They will say that a multipolar Europe, with or without nuclear weapons, will be no less peaceful than the present order. Three specific scenarios for a peaceful future have been advanced, each of which rests on a well-known theory of international relations. However, each of these 'soft' theories of peace is flawed.

"Under the first optimistic scenario, a non-nuclear Europe would remain peaceful because Europeans recognize that even a conventional war would be horrific. Sobered by history, national leaders will take care to avoid war. This scenario rests on the 'obsolescence of war' theory, which posits that modern conventional war had become so deadly by 1945 as to be unthinkable as an instrument of statecraft. War is yesterday's nightmare.

"The fact that the Second World War occurred casts doubt on this theory: if any war could have persuaded Europeans to forswear conventional war, it should have been the First World War, with its vast casualties. The key flaw in this theory is the assumption that all conventional wars will be long and bloody wars of attrition. Proponents ignore the evidence of several wars since 1945, as well as several campaign-ending battles of the Second World War, that it is still possible to gain a quick and decisive victory on the conventional battlefield and avoid the devastation of a protracted conflict. Conventional wars can be won rather cheaply; nuclear war cannot be, because neither side can escape devastation by the other, regardless of what happens on the battlefield. Thus the incentives to avoid war are of another order of intensity in a nuclear world than they are in a conventional world....

Is Prosperity the Path to Peace?

"Proponents of the second optimistic scenario base their optimism about the future of Europe on the unified European market...the realization of the dream of the European Community. A strong EC, they argue, ensures that the European economy will remain open and prosperous, which will keep the European states cooperating with one another. Prosperity will make for peace. The threat of an aggressive Germany will be removed by enclosing the newly unified German state in the benign embrace of the EC. Even Eastern Europe and the Soviet Union can eventually be brought into the EC. Peace and prosperity will then extend their sway from the Atlantic to the Urals.

"This scenario is based on the theory of economic liberalism, which assumes that states are primarily motivated by the desire to achieve prosperity and that leaders place the material welfare of their publics above all other considerations, including security. Stability flows not from military power but from the creation of a liberal economic order....

"This theory has one grave flaw: the main assumption underpinning it is wrong. States are not primarily motivated by the desire to achieve prosperity. Although economic calculations are hardly trivial to them, states operate in both an international political and an international economic environment, and the former dominates the latter when the two systems come into conflict. Survival in an anarchic international political system is the highest goal a state can have....

"Take away the Soviet threat to Western Europe, send the American forces home, and relations among the EC states will be fundamentally altered. Without a common Soviet threat or an American night watchman, Western European states will do what they did for centuries before the onset of the Cold War—look upon one another with abiding suspicion. Consequently, they will worry about imbalances in gains and about the loss of autonomy that results from cooperation. Cooperation in this new order will be more difficult than it was during the Cold War. Conflict will be more likely.

"In sum, there are good reasons for being skeptical about the claim that a more powerful EC can provide the basis for peace in a multipolar Europe.

"Under the third scenario war is avoided because many European states have become democratic since the early twentieth century, and liberal democracies simply do not fight one another. At a minimum, the presence of liberal democracies in Western Europe renders that half of Europe free from armed conflict. At a maximum, democracy spreads to Eastern Europe and the Soviet Union, bolstering peace....

"This scenario rests on the 'peace-loving democracies' theory. Two arguments are made for it.

"First, some claim that authoritarian leaders are more likely to go to war than leaders of democracies, because authoritarian leaders are not accountable to their publics, which carry the main burdens of war. In a democracy the citizenry, which pays the price of war, has a greater say in what the government does.

"The second argument rests on the claim that the citizens of liberal democracies respect popular democratic rights—those of their countrymen, and those of people in other states....

"The first of these arguments is flawed because it is not possible to sustain the claim that the people in a democracy are especially sensitive to the costs of war and therefore less willing than authoritarian leaders to fight wars. In fact the historical record shows that democracies are every bit as likely to fight wars as are authoritarian states, though admittedly, thus far, not with other democracies.

"Furthermore, mass publics, whether in a democracy or not, can become deeply imbued with nationalistic or religious fervor, making them prone to support aggression and quite indifferent to costs....

"At first glance the historical record seems to offer strong support for the theory of peace-loving democracies. It appears that no liberal democracies have ever fought against each other. Evidentiary problems, however, leave the issue in doubt.

"First, democracies have been few in number over the past two centuries, and thus there have not been many cases in which two democracies were in a position to fight with each other. Three prominent cases are usually cited: Britain and the United States (1832 to the present); Britain and France (1832-1849; 1871-1940); and the Western democracies since 1945.

"Second, there are other persuasive explanations for why war did not occur in those three cases, and these competing explanations must be ruled out before the theory of peace-loving democracies can be accepted. Whereas relations between the British and the Americans during the nineteenth century were hardly blissful, in the twentieth century they have been quite harmonious, and thus fit closely with the theory's expectations. That harmony, however, can easily be explained by common threats that forced Britain and the United States to work together—a serious German threat in the first part of the century, and later a Soviet threat....

No Guarantee of Peace

"While the spread of democracy across Europe has great potential benefits for human rights, it will not guarantee peaceful relations among the states of post-Cold War Europe. Most Americans will find this argument counterintuitive. They see the United States as fundamentally peace-loving, and they ascribe this peacefulness to its democratic character. From this they generalize that democracies are more peaceful than authoritarian states, which leads them to conclude that the complete democratization of Europe would largely eliminate the threat of war. This view of international politics is likely to be repudiated by the events of coming years."

John J. Mearsheimer, "Why We Will Soon Miss the Cold War," *The Atlantic, August 1990. Reprinted with permission.*

ANALYSIS AND EVALUATION

Refer to the Argument Analysis and Evaluation Guide on page viii.

1. Using the Argument Analysis and Evaluation Guide, compare the readings by Russett and Mearsheimer. On what do they agree? On what do they disagree?

2. Decide which of the viewpoints you tend to support and explain why. Be sure to use specific information from this textbook, the readings, and other sources to support your position.

3. State and support your position on the issue: "Will the new world order be one of conflict or co-operation?"

SELECTED BIBLIOGRAPHY

Chapter 1

Kennedy, Paul. *The Rise and Fall of the Great Powers*. New York: Random House, 1987.

Keylor, William R. *The Twentieth Century World: An International History*. Oxford: Oxford University Press, 1984.

Trevor, Lloyd. *Suffragettes International: The Worldwide Campaign for Women's Rights*. London: Library of the Twentieth Century, 1971.

Tuchman, Barbara. *The Proud Tower*. New York: Bantam Books, 1989.

Chapter 2

Herwig, Holger H. *The Outbreak of World War 1: Problems in European Civilization*. 5th ed. Toronto: D.C. Heath and Co, 1991.

Eksteins, Modris. *Rites of Spring: The Great War and the Birth of the Modern Age*. Toronto: Lester & Orpen Dennys, 1989.

Winter, J.M. *The Experience of World War I*. Oxford: Southside Ltd., 1988.

Chapter 3

Bullock, Allan. *Hitler: A Study in Tyranny*. New York: Pelican Books, 1962.

Lefeber, Walter. *The American Century*. New York: Alfred Knopf, 1986.

Mee, Charles L. Jr. *The End of Order: Versailles 1919*. New York: E.P. Dutton, 1980.

Chapter 4

Parker, R.A.C. *Struggle for Survival: The History of the Second World War*. Oxford: University Press, 1989.

Robertson, Esmonde M. (ed) *The Origins of the Second World War*. London: Macmillan Education Ltd., 1988.

John Toland (1976). *Adolf Hitler*. (Vols. 1 and 2). New York: Doubleday, 1976.

Chapter 5

Caputo, Philip. *A Rumor of War*. New York: Ballantine Books, 1987.

Halle, Louis J. *The Cold War as History*. New York: Harper Torch Books, 1991.

Hierring, George C. *America's Longest War: The United States and Vietnam, 1950-1975*. Toronto: McGraw-Hill Ryerson, 1986.

Chapter 6

Gibbons, S.R. and P. Morican. *The League of Nations and the UNO*. London: Longman Group Ltd., 1990.

Granatstein, L.J. and David Jay Bercuson. *War and Peacekeeping: From the Boer War to the Gulf War—Canada's Limited Wars*. Toronto: Key Porter, 1991.

Schell, Jonathan. *The Fate of the Earth*. New York: Avon Books, 1982.

Chapter 7

d'Encausse, H.C. *The End of the Soviet Empire*. New York: New Republic Books, 1993.

Hyland, W.G. *The Cold War Is Over*. New York: Times Books, 1990.

Sixsmith, M. *Moscow Coup: The Death of the Soviet System*. London: Simon and Schuster, 1991.

Chapter 8

Bergner, J.T. *The New Superpowers*. New York: St. Martin's Press, 1991.

Cipkowski, P. *Revolution in Eastern Europe*. New York: John Wiley and Sons, 1992.

Thurow, L. *Head to Head: The Coming Economic Battle Among Japan, Europe, and America*. New York: William Morrow and Co., 1992.

Chapter 9

Harding, J. *The Fate of Africa: Trial by Fire*. New York: Simon and Schuster, 1993.

Mallaby, S. *After Apartheid: The Future of South Africa*. New York: Time Books, 1992.

Rohr, J. (ed). *Problems of Africa: Opposing Viewpoints*. St. Paul, MN: Greenhaven Press, 1986.

Chapter 10

Collinwood, D. *Global Studies: Japan and the Pacific Rim*. Guilford, CT: Dushkin Publishing Group, 1991.

Craddock, P. *Experiences of China*. London: John Murray Publishers, 1994.

Terrill, R. *China in Our Time*. New York: Simon and Schuster, 1992.

Chapter 11

Barry, T. *Central America Inside Out*. New York: Grove Weidenfeld, 1991.

Krauss, C. *Inside Latin America*. New York: Touchstone, 1991.

Skidmore, T.E. and P.H. Smith. *Modern Latin America*. New York: Oxford University Press, 1984.

Chapter 12

Shipler, D.K. *Arab and Jew: Wounded Spirits in a Promised Land*. New York: Penguin Books, 1987.

Sluglett, P. and M. Farouk-Sluglett. (eds) *The Times Guide to the Middle East*. London: Times Books, 1993.

Spencer, W. *Global Studies: The Middle East*. Guilford, CT: Dushkin Publishing Group, 1992.

Chapter 13

Kennedy, P. *Preparing for the Twenty-first Century*. Toronto: HarperCollins Publishers, 1993.

Polesetsky, M. (ed) *The New World Order: Opposing Viewpoints*. San Diego: Greenhaven Press, Inc., 1991.

Wright, R. and D. McManus. *Flashpoints: Promise and Peril in a New World*. New York: Alfred A. Knopf, 1991.

GLOSSARY

alliance system: The division of Europe into two rival camps, the Triple Alliance and the Triple Entente, which resulted in the escalation of the international tensions that led to the First World War.

alliances: A formal treaty or agreement of co-operation between nations.

Amnesty International: An organization that monitors human rights violations around the world and exerts pressure on repressive governments through public awareness.

anarchist: A person who rebels against any authority, established order, or ruling power.

apartheid: A racial policy introduced in South Africa in 1948 classifying residents into two separate and distinct classes: white and non-white. The policy resulted in racial segregation and restrictions on marriages, residences, and education.

appeasement: The policy of making concessions to satisfy the demands of Nazi Germany prior to the Second World War.

armistice: A temporary truce between two opposing parties.

arms race: The competition between rival states to gain superior military weapons and technologies.

Aryans: A term used by Nazi Germany to describe non-Jewish people, especially of Nordic heritage.

Association of South East Asian Nations (ASEAN): An organization established in 1967 to promote peace, economic and cultural growth, and free trade within its membership.

authoritarian: Relating to a leader or government that holds absolute power and is not constitutionally responsible to the people.

Benelux countries: Belgium, the Netherlands, and Luxembourg, which established a customs union in 1948 creating the first free-trade market in Europe.

biculturalism: Relating to or including two distinct cultures.

bilingualism: The ability to speak two languages.

bipolar: A state of two diametrically opposed forces.

Black Hand: The name of a Serbian secret society formed in 1911 which sought the union of Serb minorities in Austria-Hungary and Turkey with Serbs living in independent Serbia.

Blackshirts: An organization of the unofficial Italian militia created by Mussolini in 1921 to intimidate opponents.

blitz: The intensive German bombing of Britain during the Second World War, specifically during the Battle of Britain in which an estimated 30 000 civilians died.

Bolsheviks: An extremist wing of the Russian Democratic Party that opposed participation in the First World War. Led by Lenin, the party seized power during the Russian Revolution in 1917 and later became the Russian Communist Party.

bourgeoisie (bourgeois): The middle class (or relating to the middle class) of a capitalist society.

buzz bombs: Unguided jet-propelled missiles used by Germany against Britain during the Second World War.

capitalism: An economic system characterized by private or corporate ownership of capital goods, production, and distribution. A free-enterprise system with relative absence of economic control by the government.

Central Treaty Organization (CENTO): A mutual defence policy between Turkey, Iraq, Iran, Pakistan, Britain and the US against the USSR in 1958.

Cold War: The period after the Second World War until 1990 when increasing diplomatic and political tension between the United States and the Soviet Union created a constant threat of war.

collectivization: The Soviet plan to create an agricultural co-operative through consolidation of peasant villages into state-controlled collective farms.

Cominform: The Communist Information Bureau established in 1947 to co-ordinate Communist Party activities and strengthen the position of the Soviet Union in Europe.

Comintern: An organization founded by Lenin and the Soviet Communist Party in 1919 to encourage worldwide communism.

command economy: An economy in which production and distribution of goods are controlled by a central power.

Common Market: See European Economic Community.

Commonwealth: An association of nations that were once subject to the imperial government of the United Kingdom.

communism: A system based on the principle of communal ownership of all property.

concentration camps: A prison system established by the Nazis in the Second World War for the confinement, slave labour, and mass execution of political prisoners. More than 6 million Jews were killed in these camps.

concession rights: A lease of land granted by the state for purposes of profit.

conscription: A law requiring mandatory military service.

containment: The defensive American foreign policy in 1947 to contain the spread of communism through economic and technical assistance to threatened countries. The policy later included military force.

constitutional monarchy: A king, queen, or emperor whose powers are limited by the constitution.

contras: A guerrilla group opposed to the Sandinista government in Nicaragua.

co-operative federalism: A policy in which provinces are consulted on a wide range of federal matters.

counterculture: A culture with values in conflict with those of established society.

coup: The sudden and often violent overthrow of a government by a group, such as the military.

Cubism: An art style of abstract structure that displayed several aspects of the same object simultaneously in fragmented form.

Cultural Revolution: The political upheaval in China between 1965 and 1968 that called for a return to Mao's revolutionary ideals and the abandonment of liberal practices.

debt recycling: A program in which a developing nation pays off a portion of its debt to a foreign bank with the agreement that the bank will reinvest the money into the local economy.

demilitarized zone: An area that is prohibited from military use.

desertification: The process of land being transformed into desert as a result of mismanagement of natural resources.

détente: The relaxation of international tensions, specifically between the Soviets and Americans in the 1970s.

diaspora: The dispersal of Jews around the world.

Diet: The Japanese parliament.

draft: Compulsory enrolment of eligible citizens for military service.

draft dodgers: Individuals who avoid compulsory military service by fleeing the country.

dreadnought: A battleship introduced by Britain in 1906 that represented a revolution in naval shipbuilding.

economic imperialism: Control of a nation through foreign investment in which the foreign government dictates development policies and projects that benefit its interests rather than those of the host country or its people.

economic rivalry: Competition between nations to produce the greatest economic growth.

enfranchisement: The right to vote in elections and to be recognized as a citizen of society.

ethnic cleansing: The displacement or murder of one ethnic group by another.

ethnic federalism: A governing structure in which a central government shares power with a variety of political and ethnic parties.

European Community (EC): The term for three European Communities that merged in July 1967: the European Economic Community, the European Coal and Steel Community, and the European Atomic Energy Community. The EC's objective is to create a free and unified market. In 1994, the EC became the European Union (EU).

European Economic Community, or Common Market (EEC): An economic association of nations formed in 1958 to promote free trade among members, joint social and financial policies, and free movement of capital and labour.

fascism: A movement emphasizing national and racial superiority and a centralized, autocratic government headed by a dictator.

feminization of poverty: The condition in which women are disproportionately represented among the poor. Discrimination against women in education and job opportunities pushes them into the lower classes.

final solution: Hitler's plan for the systematic murder of all European Jews between 1941 and 1945. More than 6 million Jews were killed during this period.

flashpoints: A moment or event that triggers sudden action that may result in conflict.

Fourteen Points: US president Wilson's statement of principles that he believed should be the basis of the peace settlement at the end of the First World War.

garbage imperialism: The exporting of toxic waste from developed countries to developing countries for disposal.

General Assembly: The body of the United Nations in which each member country has one vote and all nations are given the opportunity to express their views.

genocide: The extermination of a race by deliberate and systematic means.

Gestapo: The secret state police of Nazi Germany that was notorious for its brutality.

ghettos: Sections of a city where Jews are forced to live in Nazi Germany.

glasnost: A policy of openness and increased freedom in social and cultural matters in the Soviet Union, introduced by Gorbachev in 1986.

Global South: The name given to the developing countries of the world.

guerrilla warfare: Military activity that relies on surprise raids and unconventional military tactics.

hotline: A direct telephone line between the heads of state in Washington and Moscow for immediate emergency communication and to prevent nuclear war.

human rights: The freedom granted to all people protecting them from unlawful arrest, torture, or execution.

imperialism: The policy of extending the authority of a nation over foreign countries through the acquisition of colonies.

infrastructures: The system of roads and communication networks of a country, state, or region.

intercontinental ballistic missile (ICBM): A missile capable of travelling between continents.

Intifadah: Violent demonstrations by Palestinians against Israeli rule in the Gaza Strip and on the West Bank of Jordan that began in 1987.

Islamic fundamentalist: A strict follower of Islam who rejects Western influences and any deviation from the sacred laws of Islam.

juntas: A group of persons controlling a government after a revolutionary seizure of power.

kamikaze: The suicide missions of Japanese air force pilots who crashed their aircraft into enemy targets during the Second World War.

kibbutz: A communal farm or settlement in Israel.

Kristallnacht (9 November 1938): The attack by German Nazis on Jewish communities across Germany; also known as "The Night of Broken Glass," the violence marked an escalation in the Nazi plan of Jewish persecution.

kulaks: Russian peasants who became prosperous farmers of mid-size farms as a result of agrarian reforms in 1906 and who were eliminated in 1929 by Stalin because of their opposition to collectivization.

Kuomintang (the Chinese Revolutionary National Party): A political party that ruled all or part of mainland China from 1928 to 1949 and subsequently ruled Taiwan.

League of Arab States: An organization formed to promote Arab unity and co-operation that opposes the creation of an independent state of Israel in Palestine.

left: A political view advocating reform in the established order to better represent the people.

mandates: Former colonial territories of the Ottoman Empire that were consigned by the League of Nations to other nations to administer.

Manhattan Project: The code name of the US research project charged with developing the atomic bomb.

Marshall Plan: A proposal by US secretary of state George Marshall in 1947 to offer American financial aid to countries devastated by the Second World War. It resulted in the growth of industrial Western Europe and the stimulation of the US economy through exports.

martial law: Enforced military law, introduced by government, to maintain public order and safety.

McCarthyism: A campaign led by US senator Joseph McCarthy and the House Un-American Activities Committee to search for communist infiltrators in American society.

Mensheviks: A wing of the Russian Social Democratic Party during the Russian Revolution that believed that socialism should be gradually achieved through parliamentary methods rather than revolution.

Mercorsor Agreement: A 1995 trade alliance between Argentina, Brazil, Paraguay, and Uruguay to eliminate tariff barriers among the signatories.

military-industrial complex: A state's armed forces, including technology and product suppliers.

mixed economy: An economy that contains elements of both private and state enterprise.

Molotov Plan: The Soviet plan to create a bilateral trade agreement within the Soviet bloc in 1947 in response to the US Marshal Plan.

monarchist: A person who believes in a constitutional king or queen as hereditary head of state.

national self-determination: The free choice of a nation to establish its own political affairs.

national sovereignty: The power and authority of a nation over its own affairs.

nationalism: A sense of national consciousness that fosters loyalty to the country.

nationalization (nationalize): The transfer of private ownership and control to the state.

New Deal: The policy of social and economic reforms introduced by US president Roosevelt to relieve the Great Depression.

New Economic Policy: A policy introduced by Lenin in 1921 following food shortages and peasant riots in which communist economic practices were relaxed to allow limited private commerce and internal trade.

noble destiny: The belief that a course of events is pre-determined by superior status and ideals.

Non-governmental organizations (NGOs): Organizations that operate independently of any government and draw resources from the developed world to assist in the economic and social development of developing countries.

North American Aerospace Defence Command (NAADC): See North American Air Defence Command.

North American Air Defence Command (NORAD): A joint American-Canadian organization established in 1957 to monitor nuclear tracking, warning, and control stations across the northern Arctic. In 1981 the name was changed to North American Aerospace Defence Command.

North American Free Trade Agreement (NAFTA): The treaty creating a North American trading bloc and a common market among Canada, the United States, and Mexico. The agreement may be expanded to include other countries in Latin America, such as Chile which was applied for membership.

North Atlantic Treaty Organization (NATO): A mutual defence pact, established in 1949 to counter the threat of the Soviet bloc. Members include the United States, Canada, Britain, France, Belgium, the Netherlands, Denmark, Norway, Iceland, Italy, Portugal, Greece, Turkey, and Spain.

nuclear age: The era following the Second World War that produced the threat of nuclear war.

nuclear arms race: The competition between nations for the superior build up of nuclear weapons.

Nuremburg Laws: Nazi legislation in 1935 that reduced all Jews in Germany to second-class citizens.

Occupied Territories: The West Bank and the Gaza Strip (taken over by Israel after the 1967 Six-Day War), the Golan Heights (annexed by Israel in 1981), and East Jerusalem (annexed by Israel in 1967). The Sinai Peninsula was also taken in the Six-Day War but it was returned to Egypt in 1979 as terms of a peace treaty.

Organization for African Unity (OAU): An agency established in 1963 to promote African unity and solidarity, to co-ordinate political, economic, defence, and social policies of all members, and to eliminate colonialism.

Organization of American States (OAS): An agency founded in 1948 to promote co-operation and security among American nations and to discourage European intervention in the Americas.

pacifism: A policy of opposition to war and violence.

Palestine Liberation Organization (PLO): An umbrella political organization formed in 1964 to centralize Palestinian leadership and create a democratic Palestinian state.

Pan-Slavism: The movement by Russian nationalists to gain influence and power over Serbia by calling on the Slavic people in the Balkans to unite under their leadership against Austria-Hungary.

pass laws: Legislation in the apartheid state of South Africa that required non-whites to carry identification passbooks for presentation on demand to authorities.

pax Britannia: A period of general international peace under the military power of Britain.

peace dividend: The benefits of redirecting funds once designated for military expenditures into domestic spending.

peacekeeping: The activities, mediation, and deployment of UN forces in civil or international wars to help maintain peace between two conflicting parties.

peacemaking: The activities, mediation, and deployment of UN forces in civil or international wars to establish peace or provide a settlement between two conflicting parties.

perestroika: Gorbachev's policy of restructuring economics and government in the Soviet Union in the 1980s.

pink ghetto: A situation in which women have inferior status in society and limited opportunities. Typically, women fill a large proportion of clerical, sales, and service positions but are under-represented in management and manufacturing and earn less than men for work of equal value.

plebiscite: A vote by the entire voting community on a major issue.

privatization: The change of businesses from public to private control or ownership.

purges: The removal of suspected enemies from the Communist Party and the Soviet Union by Stalin. Between 1935 and 1938, an estimated 11 million people were sent to labour camps or were executed in the purge known as the Great Terror.

racial superiority: Discrimination based on the belief in the relative superiority of one race over other races.

radar: A technology used to detect the nature, position, and movement of an object using electromagnetic waves.

Red Guards: A youth organization in China created to help Mao combat revisionists.

Reichstag: Germany's parliament.

reparations: Compensation in money or materials paid to the victorious country by the defeated country for the damage inflicted by war.

revisionists: Communists who favour evolutionary reform rather than revolutionary change.

right: A conservative political view that opposes change to the established government and advocates traditional attitudes and practices.

scapegoating: Shifting the blame for a problem to some other person or group.

Schlieffen Plan: Germany's military strategy in 1914 for attacking France through its unprotected Belgian border.

Secretary General: The principal administrator of the United Nations.

Security Council: The UN council charged with the duty of maintaining international peace and security.

Selective Service Act: A conscription act passed by US president Harry Truman in response to the Soviet-backed communist takeover of Czechoslovakia.

self-determination: The free choice of a people of a nation for their own political future.

shuttle diplomacy: A diplomatic arrangement in which a third party intermediary shuttles back and forth between negotiating nations.

skinheads: Youth gangs, usually white male, with shaved heads who are violent in their promotion of white-supremacist beliefs.

South East Asia Treaty Organization (SEATO): An alliance established in 1954 among the United States, Australia, New Zealand, the Philippines, Thailand, Pakistan, Britain, and France providing for collective action in the event of an attack or internal subversion.

sphere of influence: A major power's domination over a geographic area.

squatter settlements: Regions in which people have claimed unused plots of land to create makeshift lodgings and villages.

state socialism: A system of government in which the state controls most of the means of the production and distribution of goods.

structural unemployment: A state that is created when significant changes in demand or technology occur, creating long-term unemployment because workers' skills cannot be easily transferred to the new technologies.

sustained development: The development of natural resources for long-term use that aims to conserve it as a renewable resource.

Treaty of Versailles: The peace settlement negotiated at the Paris Peace Conference that ended the First World War. Its terms included reparation payments, limitations on Germany's military force, the surrender of German colonies, and the establishment of the League of Nations.

Triple Alliance: The alliance in 1882 of Germany, Austria-Hungary, and Italy in an attempt to isolate France.

Triple Entente: The 1907 alliance of Britain, France, and Russia in response to the rising powers of Germany, Austria-Hungary, and Italy (the Triple Alliance).

Truman Doctrine: US president Harry Truman's policy to fight the spread of communism around the world through US military and economic aid.

U-boat (*Unterseeboot*): A German submarine introduced during the First World War.

ultimatum: A final proposal of terms which, when rejected, may end negotiations and result in war.

Uniting for Peace resolution: A United Nations resolution passed in 1950 that gave the General Assembly power to deal with issues of international aggression if the Security Council is deadlocked.

universal suffrage: The right to vote extended to all citizens of a society despite social class.

war communism: The period following the Russian Revolution in 1917 in which the Bolsheviks attempted to establish communist rule in the face of foreign military intervention in the civil war.

Warsaw Pact: A mutual defense pact signed by the Soviet Union, Albania, Bulgaria, Czechoslovakia, East Germany, Hungary, Poland, and Romania, as a communist counterpart to the North Atlantic Treaty Organization.

welfare state: A social system based on government-sponsored social welfare programs, including health plans, unemployment insurance, and social security programs.

Westernization: The influence of Western ideas and customs on a country and its culture.

zaibatsu: Large family-owned businesses in Japan prior to the Second World War.

Zionism: An international movement for the establishment of a Jewish state in Palestine.

INDEX

PHOTO CREDITS

t=top; b=bottom

Bettmann: The Bettmann Archive
CWM: Canadian War Museum/Photography by William Kent
Granger: The Granger Collection, New York
Hulton: Hulton Deutsch Collection
NAC: National Archives of Canada
Ponopresse: Ponopresse Internationale

4 The Mansell Collection; 7 Toronto Transit Commission; 9 Hulton; 10 Museum of London/S2 Cat and Mouse, WSPU poster; 11 British Columbia Archives and Records Service/39854/B6791; 12 The Mansell Collection; 15 Courtesy National Child Labor Committee/Photo by Lewis Hine; 18 Granger; 21 Bettmann; 30 Over the Top by A. Bastien/CN#8058: Copyright CWM; 34 Hulton; 43 NAC/PA2162; 44 Provincial Archives of Newfoundland and Labrador/B5-192; 47 Granger; 48 Bettmann; 51 Women Making Shells by M. May/CN#8409: Copyright CWM; 52 The Taking of Vimy Ridge by R. Jack/CN#8178: Copyright CWM; 56 Kandinsky/Granger; 61 Hulton; 66 UPI/Bettmann; 68 Hulton; 70 Granger; 71 Granger; 73 UPI/Bettmann; 76 Bettmann; 77 UPI/Bettmann; 84 Infantry near Numegan by Alex Colville/#12172: Copyright CWM; 87 Hulton; 89 Hulton; 90 David Low/Solo Syndication Ltd.; 94 (t, b) UPI/Bettmann; 95 (t) UPI/Bettmann, (b) Bettmann; 97 Hulton; 100 Bettmann; 101 (t, b) UPI/Bettmann; 102 (t) Bettmann, (b) Popperfoto; 107 UPI/Bettmann; 120 UPI/Bettmann; 124 Bettmann; 125 Bettmann; 127 UPI/Bettmann; 132 UPI/Bettmann; 135 UPI/Bettmann; 137 UPI/Bettmann; 139 UPI/Bettmann; 140 UPI/Bettmann; 141 UPI/Bettmann; 143 Camera Press/Ponopresse; 145 UPI/Bettmann; 147 UPI/Bettmann; 149 UPI/Bettmann; 160 United Nations photo; 163 David Low/Solo Syndication Ltd.; 164 United Nations photo; 166 Gysembergh/Gamma/Ponopresse; 168 Bettmann; 175 United Nations photo; 177 NAC/PA117597; 183 Serge/Gamma/Ponopresse; 190 Rex/Ponopresse; 193 Reuters/Bettmann; 195 Reuters/Bettmann; 196 Blanche/Gamma/Ponopress; 199 Alfred/Sipa/Ponopresse; 200 Reuters/Bettmann; 203 Shone/Gamma/Ponopresse; 204 USSR Gamma/Ponopresse; 207 Reuters/Bettmann; 216 Charles/Sygma/Publiphoto; 222 Bergman/Gamma/Ponopresse; 224 Hulton; 225 Hulton; 227 Niviere/Sipa/Ponpresse; 222 Bergman/Gamma/Ponopresse; 224 Hulton; 225 Bergman/Gamma/Ponopresse; 224 Hulton; 225 Hulton; 227 Niviere/Sipa/Ponpresse; 228 Reuters/Bettmann; 231 UPI/Bettmann; 236 Reuters/Bettmann; 237 Cipelli/Sipa/Ponopresse; 244 Kuus/Sipa/Ponopresse; 250 UPI/Bettmann; 253 Yamashita/Woodfin Camp & Associates; 255 Bernheim/Woodfin Camp & Associates; 259 Reuters/Bettmann; 260 Reuters/Bettmann; 261 Fernandez/Gamma/Ponopresse; 263 UPI/Bettmann; 266 Reuters/Bettmann; 268 Reuters/Bettmann; 274 Deville/Gamma/Ponopresse; 280 UPI/Bettmann; 283 Reuters/Bettmann; 285 Baldev/Sygma/Publiphoto; 286 UPI/Bettmann; 287 Zylberman/Sygma/Publiphoto; 290 Reuters/Bettmann; 294 UPI/Bettmann; 295 UPI/Bettmann; 296 UPI/Bettmann; 299 Reuters/Bettmann; 301 Alistair/Spooner/Gamma/Ponopresse; 308 Antonio/Gamma/Ponopresse; 314 (t, b) UPI/Bettmann; 315 UPI/Bettman; 317 Taylor/Sygma/Publiphoto; 319 Atlan/Sygma/Publiphoto; 321 UPI/Bettmann; 322 Reuters/Bettmann; 323 Caron/Sygma/Publiphoto; 324 Antonio/Gamma/Ponopresse; 327 Wollman/Gamma/Ponopresse; 328 La Penna/Gamma/Ponopresse; 329 Reuters/Bettmann; 330 Wollman/Gamma/Ponopresse; 338 Reuters/Bettmann; 343 Abbas/Gamma/Ponopresse; 344 Demulder/Sipa/Ponopresse; 346 Reuters/Bettmann; 348 UPI/Bettmann; 350 UPI/Bettmann; 351 UPI/Bettmann; 352 (t, b)UPI/Bettmann; 354 UPI/Bettmann; 355 Reuters/Bettmann; 357 UPI/Bettmann; 360 Minosa-Scorpio/Sygma/Publiphoto; 361 Mauger/Explorer/Publiphoto; 368 Halebian/Gamma/Ponopresse; 371 Courtesy of OXFAM-Canada/Photographer: J. Liebenberg; 372 Woolfitt//Woodfin Camp & Associates; 376 Courtesy CARE Canada; 377 UPI/Bettmann; 378 Paul/Gamma/Ponopresse; 380 Bettmann; 382 Courtesy of Amnesty International, Canadian Section (English-speaking).